THE PALESTINIAN ECONOMY

Studies in Development under
Prolonged Occupation

Edited by
GEORGE T. ABED

ROUTLEDGE
London and New York

First published in 1988 by
Routledge
a division of Routledge, Chapman and Hall
11 New Fetter Lane, London EC4P 4EE

Published in the USA by
Routledge
a division of Routledge, Chapman and Hall, Inc.
29 West 35th Street, New York NY 10001

Printed in Great Britain by
Billing & Sons Ltd, Worcester

British Library Cataloguing in Publication Data

The Palestinian economy: studies in
 development under prolonged occupation.
 1. Palestine. Economic development,
 1918–1985
 I. Abed, George T.
 330.95694'04
 ISBN 0-415-00471-3

Library of Congress Cataloging-in-Publication Data

ISBN 0-415-00471-3

Contents

Foreword

This volume brings together the principal results of a symposium on 'Economic Development under Prolonged Occupation' held at St Catherine's College, Oxford University, England during the period 3 to 5 January 1986. The symposium was sponsored by the Welfare Association, a private, non-profit, development assistance foundation in Geneva, Switzerland. The basic aim of the symposium was to stimulate research and discussion on issues of economic development in the Palestinian occupied territories, especially in light of the enormous complexities introduced into the process of economic development by a prolonged and repressive occupation. The symposium brought together a number of development economists, representatives from development assistance organisations and other individuals engaged in one facet or another of social and economic development in the occupied areas. They presented papers, exchanged experiences and generally struggled with the difficult issues raised by the search for concepts and methodologies suitable for the situation at hand.

In all, eighteen research papers were prepared, of which fifteen were discussed at the symposium. The present volume contains thirteen of these papers, together with an introduction and a summary chapter prepared by the editor. The selection of papers for publication was made with a view to preserving the thematic unity of the various contributions, while keeping in mind limitations of space. In this regard, important and highly stimulating contributions to the symposium were made on relevant development experiences in other areas of the developing world, notably in South Africa (by Stanley Greenberg and Harold Wolpe) in the Basque Country of Spain (by Jose Ramon Elorza) and in Sri Lanka (by A.T. Ariyaratne), as well as on other issues related to the main theme of the symposium by Bassam Saket and Abbas Abdul-Haq. Some of this valuable work is referred to in the concluding chapter but, regrettably, not all of it could be included in the volume.

This work, as can be expected, reflects both the strengths and the weaknesses of a book of essays. It comprehends numerous contributions and a variety of viewpoints, yet it contains the inevitable, and hopefully less than irksome, degree of duplication. Some subjects have been treated more fully than others, while others still may have been left out altogether. Other limitations relate to the passage of time and the inevitable intrusion of events since the material was prepared (for the most part during 1986). This is especially relevant in the ever-changing and unpredictable conditions surrounding the question of Palestine in general and the occupied territories in particular. Some of the intervening developments would have merited inclusion and many would have provided useful updates, but probably none would have required fundamental changes in the central themes of this book. In any event, it is hoped that the omissions would prove minor in relation to the wealth of material presented.

A more serious limitation, and a very specific one in this context, is the heavy reliance of researchers on data generated by Israeli sources, official and otherwise. The absence of sovereign Palestinian national institutions in the occupied areas and Israeli restrictions on the conduct of comprehensive and regular surveys to generate original data have forced Palestinian researchers into the troubling position of having to view their own society and economy largely through the eyes of their oppressors. Most of the researchers who work in this area are of course aware of this fact and some have tried to ameliorate its implications, but very few can, in the present circumstances, escape its effects on their analyses and conclusions. It is hoped that this state of affairs will stimulate further research into the statistical sources and methods of Israeli-generated statistics on the occupied areas thereby shedding light on their inherent limitations and paving the road for the eventual development of an authentic Palestinian data base.

Numerous individuals participated in organising the symposium and in the subsequent preparation of the material for publication. Their counsel and assistance are gratefully acknowledged. I would like to express my great appreciation for the work of the Symposium Steering Committee, and particularly that of the host members at Oxford, Roger Owen and Robert Mabro. A debt of gratitude is owed especially to the late Professor Bakir Abu Kishk whose death, in June 1986, deprived us all of a valued colleague, a dedicated patriot and a respected scholar. Special thanks are due Mr Lakhdar Ibrahimi who, as a keynote speaker at the symposium and as a constant friend of the Association, provided keen insights and challenging thoughts on development in an emancipatory context. Camillia Fawzi el-Solh, as symposium manager and in the numerous other essential roles she so capably executed, also deserves special thanks. Mohammed Shadid, John Richardson and Margaret Owen provided valuable assistance in various phases of preparing the material for publication and I am grateful to them. Other friends and colleagues graciously agreed to read some of the material and their observations and comments are greatly appreciated. Needless to say, none of these persons should be held in any way responsible for remaining errors or deficiencies.

The views expressed in this volume, including those of the editor, are strictly those of the individual contributors and should not be ascribed in any way to the institutions with whom they are associated nor to the institutions or individuals whose assistance is acknowledged here or in other parts of the book. More specifically, the Welfare Association, as a non-political, humanitarian and development assistance foundation, does not necessarily endorse any of the statements or views expressed in this volume.

G.T.A.
Geneva, Switzerland

Contributors

George T. Abed is the Director General of the Palestine Welfare Association, a non-profit development assistance foundation in Geneva, Switzerland. He holds a doctorate in economics from the University of California, Berkeley. Before assuming his present post he was a senior staff member of the International Monetary Fund, Washington, D.C. He has published numerous articles in professional journals on the economics of energy, manpower planning, international economics and economic development in the Arab countries.

Ziad Abu-Amr is Assistant Professor of Political Science at Birzeit University in the West Bank. He holds a doctorate in comparative politics from Georgetown University, Washington, D.C. His current research concerns social and political developments in the occupied areas on which he has published a number of papers.

Bakir Abu Kishk was at the time of his death, 20 June 1986, an Associate Professor in the Department of Economics, Iowa State University, Ames, Iowa. He had previously taught at Birzeit University where he was Dean of the Faculty of Commerce and Economics. His writings include a number of publications on economic development issues in Palestine.

Hisham Awartani is an Assistant Professor of Economics at Al-Najah National University, Nablus, in the West Bank. He holds a doctorate from the University of Bradford, UK. His main interests are resource and agricultural economics with special reference to the occupied territories. He has published a number of works in these fields.

Ibrahim Dakkak is Chairman of Al-Multaqa (Arab Thought Forum), a public policy research organisation in the West Bank. He studied at the American University in Cairo and Roberts College in Istanbul. He is an engineer by profession and is also involved in development issues in the occupied territories on which he has written and published extensively.

Harold Dick was, until the summer of 1987, the Director of the Mennonite Central Committee Programme in Jerusalem, a development assistance programme concerned with rural development in the West Bank and Gaza. He holds a BA in history and theology from Winnipeg University, Canada. Before taking up his present post he worked in marketing and product development for Rank Xerox in Canada.

Laurence Harris is Professor of Economics at the Open University, Milton Keynes, UK. He holds a doctorate from the London School of Economics. His fields of research include monetary economics and development theory and he has published widely in these fields.

Raja Khalidi is Economic Affairs Officer at UNCTAD, Geneva. He holds a postgraduate degree from London University. His research interests are agricultural development, regional economics and Palestinian development planning.

Atif A. Kubursi is Professor of Economics at McMaster University, Hamilton, Ontario, Canada. His current research interests include macro-economic theory, energy economics, manpower development and quantitative economics on which he has published books and numerous articles in professional journals.

Antoine Mansour is Industrial Development Officer at UNESCWA, Baghdad, Iraq. He holds a doctorate from the University of Grenoble in France. His research and publications include works on development in the Arab countries, the Israeli economy and the economic development of the occupied territories.

Roger Owen is a lecturer and fellow of St. Antony's College, Oxford. He holds a doctorate from the University of Oxford and his academic interests include Middle East history, contemporary politics and economic history in general. He is the author of a number of books and articles in professional journals.

Alex Pollock is a doctoral candidate at the University of Strathclyde, Scotland, UK. He was until 1987 a researcher at Al-Multaqa (Arab Thought Forum) in Jerusalem. He supervised research and wrote a number of papers on development issues related to the occupied territories.

Yusif A. Sayigh is Emeritus Professor of Economics at the American University in Beirut. He holds a doctorate from Johns Hopkins University in the USA. He has served in senior advisory posts with many Arab regional organisations and has published widely in the fields of energy economics, regional planning and economic development with special reference to the Arab countries.

Mohammed K. Shadid holds a doctorate from George Washington University in the USA. He taught for a number of years in the USA before joining the faculty of Al-Najah National University in Nablus in 1980 where he is an Associate Professor of Political Science. He has published widely on the Palestine issue and on social and political developments in the occupied territories. He is currently on research leave from the University.

1

The Palestinian Economy under Occupation: Introduction and Overview

George T. Abed

The modern history of Palestine has evolved in the shadow of seemingly endless political turbulence and human tragedy. After centuries of Ottoman rule, Palestine awakened, along with the neighbouring Arab regions, to high expectations of unity and independence. Instead, under the administration of a mandate sanctioned by the League of Nations, the Palestinian Arab people saw their historic homeland being progressively settled by the vanguards of a stirring Zionist movement. Horror and tragedy in Europe swelled the number of Jewish immigrants thus sparking Arab fears and rebellion. The British administration of Palestine, vacillating and even duplicitous at times, remained true to its commitments to the Zionist movement[1] as it presided over a decisive shift in demography and economic power. For in less than three decades from the start of the Mandate, the Palestinian Arabs found themselves dispossessed of more than three-quarters of their land, and a majority of them dispersed as refugees across the landscape of the remaining part of Palestine and the contiguous Arab states.

Less than one generation later, the Jewish state extended its control to all of Palestine, the Syrian Golan Heights and the vast Sinai Peninsula (since then relinquished). Today, the land of Palestine is inhabited by 3.5 million Jews and 2.1 million Palestinian Arabs.[2] Nearly 3 million more Palestinians[3] live in a diaspora of their own, maintaining a precarious existence in neighbouring Arab states and in lands farther afield.

The dramatic events of the last few decades have left deep scars on the physical, social and economic landscape of Palestine. The economy of Palestine had made notable advances during the later part of the nineteenth and early part of the twentieth centuries. It consolidated these gains and made further progress towards modernisation and

1

industrial development during the British mandate. As Roger Owen notes in his contribution to this volume, although the British viewed the Palestinian economy in the context of their own colonial mission and concerned themselves primarily with administration and security, several factors combined to spur economic growth and raise per capita incomes considerably during the period. Among these were the substantial inflows of capital and technology, the steady urbanisation and rising educational levels, the expansion of trade in both goods and services and, above all, the rapid industrialisation induced by the requirements of the Allied campaign in the region during World War II.

The establishment of the State of Israel on the largest and most highly developed part of Palestine left the Palestinian Arab economy battered, dismembered, and severely handicapped. The ensuing merger of the West Bank with Transjordan and the institution of Egyptian administration over the Gaza Strip, while providing life-saving links to the larger Arab world, also confirmed the divisions wrought by the turbulent events of 1948/9. About 320,000 of the original inhabitants of the land conquered by the Jewish forces were displaced to the West Bank and about 180,000 to the Gaza Strip, while 160,000 more were isolated within the newly established Jewish state. Another 300,000 found themselves in exile, mainly in Transjordan, in Lebanon and in Syria.[4]

The Palestinians who suddenly found themselves an 'Arab minority' in Israel had to contend with the usurpation of most of their land, the dislocation and disruption of economic activity, and most important of all, the institution of emergency regulations governing virtually every aspect of their daily lives. More than two generations later, the national aspirations of this section of the Palestinian community remain unfulfilled. They are not fully integrated into the state of which they are citizens, yet they carry the burdens of estrangement from the larger Palestinian community. Despite notable advancements in levels of education and some hard-won improvements (and occasional breakthroughs) in certain economic sectors, the Palestinian Arabs in Israel continue to suffer from the inherently discriminatory policies of the Zionist state.

It was, however, in the West Bank where the largest number of Palestinians lived. The links with the East Bank of Jordan had had a long, if variable, history even before 1948, but the fusion of the two banks in 1950, as Antoine Mansour notes in his paper, expedited the eastward flow of labour, capital and technology, which were attracted by greater economic rewards and the magnetic pull of political authority. West Bank public infrastructure and industry, and to a lesser extent agriculture, improved although somewhat more slowly than in the East Bank. Investment in housing, small-scale industries and tourism helped to promote growth in these sectors, with the necessary funds having come primarily from remittances of Palestinians in Jordan and other Arab countries. Mansour observes that in 1966, the West Bank realised a JD 9 million balance of payments surplus despite a trade deficit of more than twice that amount.

The Gaza Strip has often been called the 'forgotten corner of Palestine' and, in a more contemporary context, 'the poorer sister of the West Bank'. A flat, sandy strip of coastal terrain, 360 square kilometres in area, the Gaza Strip was shaped in the aftermath of the Zionist forces' sweep of the southern region of Palestine. By the time the Armistice Agreements were signed in 1949, the Strip had become home for more than 180,000 refugees from other parts of Palestine who, in sheer numbers at least, overwhelmed the indigenous population of about 80,000. Under Egyptian administration, the Gaza Strip population grew to about 400,000.[5] Little economic development took place during the period, although trade, especially with Egypt, prospered and remittances from workers abroad helped finance higher levels of consumption. The arable land that was available was more intensively developed with citrus and vegetables; fishing provided another avenue for economic activity. But as Ziad Abu-Amr notes in his paper, overpopulation and the severity of the resource constraints rendered the task of economic development exceedingly difficult.

The 1967 war and the conquest by Israel of the remaining areas of Palestine created about 250,000 more refugees[6] and brought under Israeli control over a million more Palestinian Arabs in the West Bank and Gaza. As Mohammed Shadid documents in his contribution to this volume, the occupation authorities immediately moved to seal their control over the areas' resources, most critically land and water, and to institute a myriad of regulations, via military orders, governing every significant aspect of the social, economic and political life of the newly disenfranchised Arab population. Military orders set up security zones over vast areas of land which could no longer be used by Palestinians. Quantities of water drawn from existing agricultural wells were virtually frozen at their 1967 levels, causing severe constraints on agriculture and, ultimately, choking off growth in output of certain key crops. Arab banks were closed and replaced by branches of Israeli banks, while restrictions on the expansion of economic activity froze local employment opportunities.

The adverse economic effects of the occupation were mitigated to a

3

degree by the oil-induced economic boom in the Arab countries during the middle and late 1970s, which attracted increasing numbers of Palestinian workers from the occupied territories. The remittances which these expatriates transferred to their families, always an important source of income for residents of the West Bank and Gaza, increased considerably. They helped finance not only rising consumption levels, but also some investment in more intensive agriculture, in services and, most notably, in private housing.

The development promoting impact of these transfers, however, remained limited. By the time the oil boom subsided in the early 1980s, the economies of the West Bank and Gaza had made little progress in achieving the structural changes needed for balanced development. Public physical infrastructure deteriorated for lack of investment and public institutions withered because of lack of resources, deliberate neglect and outright hostility from the occupation authorities. In both regions, the agricultural sectors weakened as large areas were taken out of cultivation and agricultural employment declined steadily. The industrial sector stagnated and, in several key respects, deteriorated. The combined effects of the emigration of the more skilled and entrepreneurial groups, together with the unfavourably skewed skill structure of demand for labour in the Jewish economy, discouraged education and skill formation. Raja Khalidi refers to the 'de-skilling' of Palestinian manpower while Atif Kubursi notes the strangely negative relationship between education and employment. With trade flows between the occupied territories and the Arab markets restricted to a trickle, the territories' economy was forced to re-orient itself toward the dominant Israeli economy, creating an unequal and highly disadvantageous relationship. By the mid-1980s, the combined GDP of the occupied territories amounted to no more than 4 per cent of that of Israel.

In the meantime expropriation of land by Israel in the West Bank and Gaza continued. By the mid-1980s more than half of the area of the former and about 30 per cent of the latter had been placed under Israeli control.[7] The number of Jewish settlements exceeded 118 with a total population of about 65,000.[8] Between 1967 and 1986, total expenditures on establishing and maintaining these settlements approached US$ 2 billion.[9] This is in addition to the intensive colonisation of the East Jerusalem area where more than 30 settlements have been established, accommodating a Jewish population of more than 100,000.[10]

In order to integrate the Jewish settlements more fully into the State of Israel, a new transportation and communication infrastructure was constructed to serve the settlements, generally by-passing Arab towns and villages and redefining the shape of the historic Palestinian land-scape. To complete the cycle of alienation and dispossession (and in a manner akin to that previously employed in the Arab areas conquered in 1948), the occupation authorities proposed in 1982 a 'land use plan' which would restrict Arab development in the West Bank and Gaza to certain zones within, and immediately around, Palestinian towns and villages.[11] This would leave the remaining, vast areas 'open' for exploitation by Jewish settlements, or merely 'in reserve'. The important fact is that for the Palestinian Arab population, these areas would finally and permanently be kept out of reach. The plan itself has not been formally instituted, but given the history of Israel's actions since 1948, the plan, if unchecked, could materialise as yet another *fait accompli*. The minority Jewish population would thus ultimately dominate the broad landscape, leaving the majority Arab population confined to a restricted and progressively deteriorating constellation of under-developed towns and villages. The parallels with South Africa's Bantustan policy are striking.

Grim as these conditions might be, the Palestinian communities in Palestine have persisted in their daily struggle to ameliorate the impact on their lives of the policies and practices of dispossession and occupation, while concomitantly fighting against the social and economic ills they had inherited from a colonial past.

The Arab community in Israel quadrupled in number between 1948 and 1986 and, despite enormous handicaps, was able steadily to improve its own economic and social conditions. In 1954 only a handful of Arabs graduated from university; by 1984 the cumulative number of university graduates had approached 9,000.[12] Dispossessed of the bulk of their land and allocated only a fraction of their share of the country's agricultural water supplies, the Palestinian Arabs in Israel have succeeded in overcoming these discriminatory policies in small but significant ways. Raja Khalidi notes, in his contribution to this volume, that 'the value productivity of a unit of water in Arab agriculture was double that in the Jewish sector in 1981/2'. This was achieved despite the fact that Arab agriculture possessed only a fraction of the capital enjoyed by its Jewish counterpart.

In the West Bank, emigration had slowed the overall rate of population growth, but by 1986 more than 960,000 inhabitants were living there.[13] The Palestinians' irrepressible pursuit of educational opportunities, even in adversity, made for the establishment of five universities enrolling 10,400 students,[14] all funded from Palestinian and other Arab sources. Although educational facilities and academic standards in the public school system (under the responsibility of the occupation authorities) broadly deteriorated, the Palestinians' own efforts helped redress the decline through increased support to non-government schools.

Similarly, lack of investment in health facilities caused the number of hospital beds per 10,000 population to decline from 26 in 1974 to 18 in 1985.[15] With the help of voluntary work and largely their own financial resources, Palestinian communities were able to establish scores of clinics serving broad sectors of the urban as well as rural population and to fund improvements in hospital facilities as well.

In the economic domain, the improvement in incomes was largely due to the rise in Palestinian expatriate remittances, assistance from Arab governments and international organisations, and the West Bankers' own grudging toil in the occupier's economy. Agriculture shrank and industry stagnated. As Harold Dick points out in his paper on entrepreneurship, however, the industrial sector displayed surprising resilience nonetheless. In agriculture, Palestinian farmers, showing remarkable ingenuity under severe constraints, refocused their efforts on intensive, carefully irrigated agriculture, achieving remarkable gains in productivity. However, restrictions on water use and on marketing ultimately halted further growth in productivity and depressed output.

Creative and ingenious solutions to ostensibly intractable problems were being continuously devised in other sectors as well. As Laurence Harris explains in his paper, the closure of the banks made for the development and expansion of a rather sophisticated system of money changers that took on many of the tasks normally undertaken by banks. Official prohibitions on marketing of Palestinian agricultural products within Israel did not stop Palestinian farmers from finding means to sell a considerable share of their products there. A handful of industries were able to compete successfully with their Israeli counterparts, some even in the Israeli market. Restrictions on the planting of olive trees, always a symbol of the continuity and endurance of Palestinian agriculture, did not prevent an increase in the number of such trees since the occupation.

In the Gaza Strip, social and economic conditions have always been more harsh and the prospects more bleak. The expropriation of land for Jewish settlements, the burgeoning population on an already crowded strip of land and the paucity of natural resources challenged the ingenuity and endurance of the more than half a million inhabitants. Lacking a port facility and suffering severe restrictions on its activity, the fishing industry in the Gaza Strip nonetheless showed remarkable resilience. Prohibitions on the establishment of agro-industries based on the Strip's traditional citrus agriculture and crippling constraints on the marketing of citrus fruits have diminished this once-prosperous sector. But Gazans continued to market their citrus, even if in reduced quantities, and other forms of intensive agriculture have defiantly sprung up and survived.

Health facilities in the Gaza Strip, traditionally weak and inadequate, slowly but decidedly deteriorated under occupation. The number of hospital beds per 10,000 of population declined from 25 in 1974 to 17 in 1985.[16] To help ameliorate the consequences of this decline a number of more modest facilities have been established by Palestinian voluntary institutions, some with the help of international development agencies. One local Palestinian health institution, prevented by military orders from receiving aid from the outside, prohibited from raising funds within the community and sanctioned against any expansion of services, somehow continues to operate and, in some instances, expand. The pursuit of educational opportunities also continued apace. The school population more than doubled and a university was opened with the help of Palestinian and other Arab funding.

Thus, prevented from constituting a representative national authority of their own, and governed by a surrogate power whose stewardship ranges between benign neglect and systematic repression, the Palestinian people in the occupied areas have had to rediscover within themselves the strength to survive and to overcome. Voluntary organisations have been created to deal with the myriad of social and economic tasks that, under normal circumstances, would be performed by some organ of a state authority. Scores of such organisations now operate throughout Palestine in various areas of education, health, culture and social services and engaging the energies of innumerable publicly spirited individuals. Particularly noteworthy is the prominent role of Palestinian women in these organisations. This form of self-reliant development appears to be transforming the mundane process of material improvement into an act of liberation and self-renewal.

To the development economist, the situation of the occupied areas represents a daunting challenge indeed. In a third-world context, where most governments provide the minimal guarantees of sovereignty and the resources that can be mobilised by virtue of it, the task of social and economic development has been portrayed generally in the narrow terms of the allocation of resources towards desired ends. With the aid of international development agencies and their own state machinery, the less developed countries have formulated development programmes and actively sought the resources to implement them.

Although the achievements of the developing countries in the social and economic domains remain limited, their progress is at least unencumbered by one crucial constraint. The typical less developed country is not occupied by a force that is bent on dispossessing the indigenous population. In such a country, development projects are commonly promoted, often subsidised and generally nurtured to maturity; they are not obstructed or deliberately starved for funds. Resources, above all land and water, are protected and developed, at least nominally, for the welfare of the community; they are not expropriated and denied. The productive sectors, especially agriculture and industry, receive preferred treatment in the form of publicly funded infrastructure, subsidised credit and protected markets; they are not repressed or dismembered. The educational system is often generously funded and is oriented to the developmental needs of society; it is not deliberately distorted and made irrelevant. Community-based, voluntary effort aimed at tackling local problems is generally welcomed and encouraged, not thwarted and harassed.

The process of economic development takes on a distorted look when viewed through the dense prism of occupation, especially one that has endured for a generation. Almost half of the population living in the West Bank and Gaza has been born since the occupation began. More than three-quarters have grown to know no other condition.[17] The economic consequences of a prolonged occupation, as distinct from a short-lived emergency measure, are grave and fundamental. A prolonged occupation threatens the core structure of the social and economic system, and not merely its surface manifestations. Most economies can withstand brief periods of war-related restrictions and disruptions to their productive machinery. But not many could do so for a generation or more.

More importantly, Israel's occupation of the West Bank and Gaza, if the fundamental tenets of Zionist doctrine are to be believed, represents not a prolonged foray into alien territory, but the extension of Jewish control over the remainder of the 'land of Israel'. This has the effect of redefining the nature of the condition that governs the lives of the Palestinian people in Palestine as it clearly goes beyond the notion of occupation. It is uprootedness and dispossession. Furthermore, the concept of dispossession in this context needs to be understood not only in the narrow sense of rendering the population landless, in itself a grave enough form of dispossession, but in the broader meaning of robbing the affected population of the material basis to live and prosper as a community and further to deny this population the right and means to redress the grievances that arise as a result of this usurpation. Given that Israel's occupation has also sought to deny, restrict or expropriate the Palestinian people's own culture and symbols of national identification, the concept of dispossession takes on an even larger meaning in the circumstances.

How then does the specialist approach the question of economic development under conditions of dispossession and prolonged occupation? To begin with the omnipresent political context conditions and colours every activity undertaken within the framework of a development programme. Economic activity is no longer neutral (if it ever was). Under these conditions, every development programme, every project, every economic act is to be judged as to whether or not it reinforces the occupation or weakens it, whether or not it promotes dependency or self-reliance. Moreover, some of the basic concepts of development that may be central in more normal circumstances somehow lose their poignancy, while others, not even relevant, take on decisive weight. This has the effect of redefining priorities, strategies and even instruments of development.

The goal of full employment, for instance, a constant feature of almost all development plans promulgated by the less developed countries, needs to be heavily qualified in the case of the occupied territories. Should employment be promoted even when virtually all new entrants into the labour force end up as marginal day workers in low-skill occupations in the Israeli economy? What does it mean to have 'full employment' in the context of such a grossly distorted economic structure? Similarly, the goal of maximising production and income (subject to resource and other constraints of course) needs to be re-examined in the circumstances. Would the mere fact that the higher income generated by say, an Israeli sub-contracting activity in the West Bank or in Gaza, justify this activity's economic superiority to a smaller cottage industry relying on indigenous raw materials, labour and markets?

What is the impact on the drive to achieve higher growth in an agricultural or industrial operation when, beyond a certain limit defined by the requirements of the local market, virtually all the extra output has to be marketed through channels over which the Palestinian producer has no control and where the probability that such channels will be blocked is overwhelmingly high? The severe constraints on the use of land and water also have similarly adverse effects on the development effort. All of this does not of course take account of the 'security-related' risks that arise out of the conditions of military occupation (e.g. outright confiscation of land, area-wide curfews and large-scale detentions, destructive attacks on property by Jewish settlers).

The development specialists represented in this volume all struggle, to varying degrees, with the issues raised here. Others who may be, in one way or another, associated with the development effort in the occupied areas and whose views may not be reflected in the selection of essays in this volume must also confront the difficult questions concerning 'development under prolonged occupation'. The answers that emerge vary from the one extreme which negates the possibility of any meaningful development under conditions of occupation, to the other extreme which advocates that any improvement in the living conditions of the people under occupation, no matter what the context may be, is a gain for development. These two views, and innumerable shades of opinion in between, may be gleaned from the papers in this volume, but also from the discussions among and within the agencies and individuals concerned with social and economic change in the occupied areas.

The papers in this volume reflect a shared recognition of the severity of the constraints impinging on any programme for social and economic development, but arrive somehow at varying conclusions. Yusif Sayigh deals with the question at the conceptual level and finds that 'meaningful and far-reaching development cannot be achieved, or even sought, under the conditions of dependence-cum-dispossession. Given present constraints, the economies of the West Bank and the Gaza Strip can only be maintained at a low level of economic performance'. In such circumstances, Sayigh continues, 'it is unrealistic to set out to design broad plans and programmes for development'. Ibrahim Dakkak, however, dealing with the question also at a conceptual level but sensing the urgency of the matter from his vantage point, states that 'social and economic development in the occupied territories is not a choice but a necessity. Israel's planned destruction of Palestinian infrastructure and denial of their right to develop must be countered by a strategy of resistance and development'. Concerning the articulation of a development plan or programme, this, Dakkak states, must be viewed as 'interim and transitional'.

Other authors, while not denying the validity of the Sayigh thesis, nevertheless see windows of opportunity in the present situation that must be used to resist the tendency to stagnation and decline that pervade the economies of the occupied areas. Awartani, Abu Kishk, Abu-Amr and Dick offer a number of suggestions in this respect. On a grander scale, Dakkak follows through on his theme concerning the necessity of development and advances the thesis of *sumud muqawim* - resistive or dynamic steadfastness - as a strategy to confront the challenge of occupation and dispossession in the domain of social and economic development.

Perhaps a useful way of approaching the issue is to go back to a more basic interpretation of the mission of social and economic development. Before one proceeds to discuss agriculture, industry, trade and finance (even before one begins to outline the basic functions of the economic system in the case of the occupied areas) one needs to address more fundamental questions still. How is cohesion maintained in a weak and vulnerable society under conditions of occupation, impoverishment and dispossession? How is the social infrastructure to be sustained so as to carry the burdens of implementing development programmes and activities? How is the prolonged isolation of the Palestinian community to be prevented from degenerating into self-destructive divisiveness and alienation?

Transposing these concerns into the social and economic sphere might serve to imbue them with somewhat more specific content and thereby make the approach more amenable to the formulation of a strategy of development. But first one must confront the inescapable conclusion stated by Sayigh, and not disputed in its fundamentals by any of the other authors, that genuine and far-reaching social and economic transformation of the occupied territories can only come about under conditions of full national sovereignty. This may not be a sufficient condition (much more would be needed as evidenced by the large number of fully sovereign states that have not achieved genuine development), but it is an absolutely necessary one.

Pending the achievement of full sovereignty, what sort of development is possible, and would such development be consistent with even a minimalist interpretation of the national aspirations of the Palestinian people? Clearly the question gives rise to fundamental issues at both the methodological as well as practical levels. The following essays help define and elaborate some of these issues and the reader is invited to explore the material at hand. One only hopes that those who do so will find the experience instructive not only for the situation in the occupied areas of Palestine, but also in the more generalised context of social and economic development under severely repressive conditions.

NOTES

1. Britain's promise to help establish a national home for the Jews in Palestine as expressed in the Balfour Declaration of November 2, 1917 was later incorporated into the Mandate document of July 22, 1922. For text of the Mandate document see: Palestine Government, *A Survey of Palestine* (3 vols.,

Jerusalem, 1946), vol. 1, pp. 2-10.

2. Calculated from, Central Bureau of Statistics, *Statistical Abstract of Israel,* no. 37, 1986 (Central Bureau of Statistics, Jerusalem, 1986), pp.26, 683.

3. There are various estimates of the Palestinian population outside Palestine but they vary within a moderately narrow range. This figure is calculated from inter alia, Central Bureau of Statistics, *Palestinian Statistical Abstract,* no. 4 (Economic Department, Palestine Liberation Organisation, Damascus, 1982), p.32.

4. Calculated from, Janet Abu-Lughod, 'Demographic characteristics of the Palestinian population: relevance for planning Palestine Open University', unpublished study, UNESCO, Paris, 1980, p.18; Central Bureau of Statistics, *Statistical Abstract of Israel,* no.37, 1986, p.26; and Rosemary Sayigh, *Palestinians: From Peasants to Revolutionaries* (Zed Books, London, 1979), pp. 99-100.

5. Janet Abu-Lughod, 'Demographic characteristics of the Palestinian population', p. 18; and Janet Abu-Lughod, 'The demographic transformation of Palestine' in Ibrahim Abu-Lughod (ed.) *The Transformation of Palestine* (Northwestern University Press, Evanston, Illinois, 1971), pp. 159-62.

6. Janet Abu-Lughod, 'Demographic characteristics of the Palestinian population', p.24.

7. Meron Benvenisti, *The West Bank Data Project: A Survey of Israeli Policies* (American Enterprise Institute, Washington, D.C., 1984) pp. 20-1; and Meron Benvenisti, *The West Bank Data Base Project: 1986 Report* (The West Bank Data Base Project/The Jerusalem Post, Jerusalem, 1986), p.25.

8. Meron Benvenisti, *The West Bank Data Base Project: 1987 Report* (The West Bank Data Base Project/The Jerusalem Post, Jerusalem, 1987), pp. 52,54.

9. Meron Benvenisti, *The West Bank Data Base Project: 1986 Report,* p.51.

10. Arab Labour Organisation, *Israeli Settlements and Their Destructive Implications* (Arab Labour Organisation, Baghdad, 1987), pp. 21-2.

11. Raja Shehadeh, *Occupier's Law: Israel and the West Bank* (Institute for Palestine Studies, Washington, D.C., 1985), pp.51-7.

12. Calculated from *Statistical Abstract of Israel,* No.37, pp.608-9.

13. Ibid., 1986, pp. 42, 683. The figure of 960,000 includes the Arab population of the Jerusalem area.

14. Council for Higher Education, *al-dalil al-ihsa'i li-al-jami'at al-filastiniyya* (Statistical guide for Palestinian universities) (Council for Higher Education, Jerusalem, 1986), p. 32.

15. Calculated from, Ihsan Atiya et al., *manatiq 'arabiyya muhtalla: haqa'iq wa-arqam* (Occupied Arab areas: facts and figures) (Arab Studies Society, Jerusalem, 1985) pp. 175-8.

16. Ibid., pp.187-9.

17. This includes all of the population under the age of 30 years, 58% of whom were born since the occupation began in 1967. In addition, 18% of the population was then nine years of age or younger. Calculated from *Statistical Abstract of Israel,* no. 37, p. 685.

2

Economic Development in Mandatory Palestine: 1918-1948

Roger Owen

I. INTRODUCTION

The examination of the economic history of Palestine under the British Mandate presents a number of special problems. One is the absence of data about a great many important aspects of economic life and the highly political character of much of what does exist. A good example of the former is that the land survey was left incomplete, so that there is no proper record of the state of land holdings throughout the country. As for the latter, there were a whole series of highly charged political interventions by Arabs and Jews with respect to almost every important subject, from the very general - for example the size of what was known as 'the economic absorptive capacity' of Palestine in terms of its cultivable area, its water resources, etc. - to the particular, for example, the number of Arab peasants displaced by Jewish land purchase or the volume of Arab or Jewish unemployment.

Another problem is the fact that there has been very little academic work on the subject and that, for the most part, what there is deals only with the two decades up to 1939, ignoring the extremely important process of economic transformation which took place during World War II and just after.

A third and final problem concerns the very difficult question of just what type of economy there was. To oversimplify greatly, those who have written on the subject tend to look at the problem through one of three different perspectives: Palestine as a colony (the preferred Arab view), Palestine as containing two quite separate economies with minimal interaction between them (the conventional Jewish view) and Palestine as a colony containing a capitalist and a pre-capitalist sector (the view favoured by writers influenced by Marxism or some

13

version of dependency theory).

To put forward my own view at this stage I think that all these three perspectives contain some important aspects of the truth. However, I also think that it is vital to begin the analysis from the position that, after the establishment of Palestine's modern borders in the early 1920s, we are dealing with a single economy which was created and run by the British as though it was an ordinary colony with a Currency Board in London (rather than a Central Bank in Palestine itself), membership in the Sterling Area and a colonial pattern of revenue and expenditure with particular emphasis on administration and security and very little on government-sponsored development or on welfare services. However, it was a colony with some very special features, most obviously the commitment, written into the terms of the Mandate itself, to facilitate the establishment of a Jewish National Home. This at once obliged the British to concern themselves with questions of Jewish immigration and land purchase as well as, given Palestine's general lack of resources, with ways of stimulating economic development, for example by giving monopoly concessions to Jewish companies like those formed by Rutenberg to generate hydroelectricity on the Jordan River (1921) or the Palestine Potash Co. which exploited the mineral resources of the Dead Sea.

Two more points are necessary in order to complete the introductory analysis. The first is that, although the Jewish immigrants created structures which had many similarities with those in the capitalist sectors dominated by the white settler colonialists in other parts of the British Empire, they also had a number of atypical features, notably the fact that their major economic links were not with Britain itself but with the wider world and that they were usually willing to forego short-term profits in the interests of the larger political project of establishing a National Home. This last was especially obvious in their drive to employ Jewish rather than Arab labour even when it was much more expensive and, more generally, to ensure that the Jewish community was able to enjoy a near European standard of living in order to attract, and then to keep, new immigrants. Second, while it is true that the various separate enclaves of Jewish activity did tend to coalesce into something, which, by 1936, could reasonably be called a 'Jewish economy', this entity had many more points of contact with the different sectors of the wider Palestinian economy than some writers generally allow, whether directly through land purchase or competition (for example in industry or in the huge investment in rival citrus groves in the 1930s) or indirectly through the differential effect of taxes, tariffs, wages, etc., many of them mediated by the Mandatory government itself and the result of pressures put on it. I will now attempt to demonstrate these special features of the Palestinian economy in their historical context, beginning with an examination of the salient features of the first two decades, 1918-1939, then focusing on the neglected period of World War II and finishing up with a brief conclusion outlining some of its more obvious political consequences for the tragic events of 1948 and after.

II. THE ECONOMY, 1918-1939

There are only a few continuous series of figures on which to base an analysis of the performance of the Palestinian economy before 1939. Of these the most important are those for population (based on the censuses of 1922 and 1931 together with later government estimates) (Table 2.1), foreign trade from 1922 onwards (Table 2.2) and the production of the principal agricultural crops from 1927 (Table 2.3). The one and only official attempt to calculate national income was made in 1944, although there are some unofficial estimates for the late 1930s. I will use these data to look at the growth of population and at the different economic and social characteristics of the Arab and Jewish communities, and then at trade, agriculture and industry, before making a few general comments about the overall performance of the economy during the whole period.

1. Growth in Arab and Jewish population

The population of Palestine doubled between 1922 and 1939, from 750,000 to 1,500,000. This was largely the result of natural increase among the Arabs but it was also affected by increasing waves of Jewish migration: 35,000 immigrants between 1919 and 1923, 82,000 (1924-31) and 217,000 (1932-38).[1] The arrival of so many newcomers, most of them with European education and consumption patterns and many of them with European capital and skills, clearly had an important effect on the economy. One way of looking at this is in terms of the degree of urbanisation of the two communities and their quite different patterns of employment. Whereas the Arab population was still largely rural in the mid-1930s with only a quarter of it living in towns, the Jewish population was just the opposite with three-quarters in towns and just a quarter on the land.[2] Examination of the

15

occupational structure tells more or less the same story. While in 1936 some 21 per cent of Jewish wage earners worked in agriculture and 20 per cent in manufacturing with almost 50 per cent in services (roughly the same proportions as would have been found in contemporary Eastern Europe), the comparative Arab figures were 62 per cent agriculture, 8 per cent manufacturing and 14 per cent services.[3]

Table 2.1: The population of Palestine in selected years: 1922 - 1947

	Arabs[a]	Jews	Total
1922 (Census)	668,258	83,790	752,048
1931 (Census)	858,708	174,606	1,033,314
1939 (Estimate)	1,056,241	445,457	1,501,698
1944 (Estimate)	1,185,922	553,702	1,739,624
1946 (Estimate)	1,200,000	600,000	1,800,000

Note: a. includes 'Muslims', 'Christians' and 'others'.
Sources: Palestine Government, *A Survey of Palestine* (3 vols., Jerusalem, 1946), vol. 1, p. 41 and Cunningham Papers (St. Antony's College Oxford, Middle East Centre), Box 1, File 2, tg 1775 of 23 September 1946.

Certain other features are also important to an understanding of the significant differences between the two populations. While the Arabs, with perhaps half their numbers under 15 and few women in the labour force, had the same low labour participation ratio characteristic of most of the rest of the Middle East, some 50 per cent of all Jewish migrants from 1929 to 1948 were aged between 15 and 29, producing an employment structure which meant that almost as many Jews were at work as Arabs in spite of the great disparity in overall numbers.[4] If we add that according to the 1931 Census well over 90 per cent of Jewish males over seven were literate compared with around 30 per cent of Arab males in the same age group, and that Jewish wage rates were anything up to three times as high as those of the Arabs, it is no wonder that the first attempts to calculate National Income showed that the Jewish community as a whole had a per capita income of some £P 44 compared with an Arab one of only £P 17.[5]

The analysis of the economic relationship between the Jewish community and the rest of the population of Palestine is perhaps the most difficult to undertake, not only because of the fierce political passions which it aroused but also because the facts and figures on which it has to be based come largely from Jewish sources and tend to represent only the situation as it existed in the late 1930s. As is the case with any foreign settler community of European origin, the Jews tended to obtain more of the goods they required from abroad or from their own growing industry than from the local economy. But, unlike most other such communities, their purchase of local services was also constrained, for political and ideological reasons, by the drive towards self-sufficiency. Thus in 1936, according to Szereszewski's estimate, Jewish purchase of goods and services from abroad (£P 9.5 million) were nearly three times those from the Arab sectors while Jewish exports (£P 3 million) were also about three times the value of sales to non-Jewish sectors.[6] However, even if these figures are substantially correct, it has to be noted that this was the year of the general strike at the beginning of the Arab rebellion and thus a time when both communities were doing their best to limit purchases from each other.

An equally important point concerns the fact that Jewish purchases, even if only a fraction of their own total outlay, still had a significant effect on the Arab community with its very much lower level of capital resources. As must always be the case when a capitalist sector interacts with a fundamentally pre-capitalist one, the effect was both to create certain new opportunities while destroying or distorting old structures. Far and away the most significant example of this is the vexed question of Jewish land purchases which, because of their once-and-for-all nature, permanently denied Arab agriculturalists access to an increasing area of land at a time when the country's own population was advancing at a rapid rate. While there is no great disagreement about the amount of land involved (some 850,000 dunums between 1920 and 1939) it is unlikely that the complete effect of Jewish purchase will ever be evaluated satisfactorily.[7] On the one hand, if Smith, Stein and others are correct, at least one-third of this amount was purchased from persons resident in Palestine, thus injecting several millions of pounds at least into the local economy.[8] On the other, as Stein also demonstrates very clearly, British efforts to assess the numbers of agriculturalists who suffered from this process were immediately undermined by political and bureaucratic disputes about the types of persons who should, correctly, be placed on the Landless Labour register. The final number, 664, bore little relation to the magnitude of the original injury.[9] For the rest, Jewish purchase of other local goods and services must have had the same complex bundle of effects, raising prices, increasing income, creating shortages and so on. Finally, a complete picture of Arab/Jewish economic relations would also require proper consideration of the effects of government policies on communities with widely divergent structures, whether these involved the direct consequences of such things as tariffs, taxes and public sector wage rates or such negative ones as governmental failure to enforce its own legislation, for example that forbidding certain types of Jewish land purchase in the 1930s.[10]

2. Foreign trade

Table 2.2: The foreign trade of Palestine: 1922-1947 (annual averages)[a]

	Imports £P million	Exports £P million	Citrus Exports £P million
1922-4	5.36	1.34	
1925-9	6.85	1.52	0.65
1930-4	9.39	2.33	2.13
1935-9	14.75	4.76	3.31
1940-4	22.14	8.87	0.25
1945-7	58.80	14.07	n.a.

Note: a. Excludes transit trade.
Sources: *Survey of Palestine*, 1, p. 462 and Cunningham Papers, Box 1, File 4, tg 43 of 6 March 1947 and 160 of 15 April 1947; Box 2, File 2, tg 147 of 20 March 1948.

The figures in Table 2.2 show that the foreign trade of Palestine rose rapidly in the inter-war period and much faster than the average for world trade in general, particularly during the great depression of the early 1930s. Apart from this, its main features were as follows:

(a) Although the value of the Palestinian exports increased at a faster rate than that of imports, the country experienced a growing trade deficit until the mid-1930s. Even in the late nineteenth century there had been a tendency to import more than was exported due to the fact that in most years it could not achieve self-sufficiency in cereals and that it produced few agricultural or manufactured goods for export other than citrus fruits and soap. After 1918 the situation worsened as population increased much faster than agricultural output, as the growth of local industry became heavily reliant on imported raw materials, and, most important of all, as the Jewish community required an increasing volume of imports to sustain itself. As Halevy's figures show, total imports exceeded exports by a cumulative sum of some £P 111 million between 1922 and 1939.[11] But, as he also points out, this shortfall was almost exactly covered by transfers of Jewish funds, three-quarters of them consisting of money brought to Palestine by the individual immigrants themselves.[12]

18

(b) The effect of Jewish immigration can also be seen in the structure of imports. As the figures in Table 2.3 show, manufactured goods made up well over half of all purchases from abroad in the 1930s, with goods in the category 'food, drink and tobacco' generally making up another quarter. The latter were dominated by wheat and flour for bread making and barley for animal feed. As for exports, in spite of the steady growth in manufacturing industry, almost all its output was consumed locally, with only a small quantity for export - just under 5 per cent in 1935.[13] In these circumstances Palestine came to rely more and more on citrus exports (oranges and some grapefruit), the contribution of which increased from 43 per cent of total value in 1927 to over 70 per cent in the late 1930s.

Table 2.3: Composition of Palestine's imports by value in selected years: 1931-1944 (percentage)

	1931	1935	1939	1944
Food, drink and tobacco	24	20	26	40
Raw materials and articles mainly unmanufactured	7	7	10	38
Articles wholly or mainly manufactured	55	60	64	22
Miscellaneous including live animals	12	12	-	-

Sources: *Survey of Palestine*, 1, p. 467 and Palestine Government, *Statistical Abstract of Palestine 1943* (Jerusalem, 1943), p. 94. Percentages do not add up to 100 due to rounding.

(c) A third feature of the inter-war period was a marked change in the direction of trade, notably a large reduction in the proportion of exports sent to the other countries of the Middle East, which declined from 60 per cent of total value in 1924 to 46 per cent in 1928 and only 10 per cent in 1939. Here the main causes were the redirection of citrus sales towards Europe combined with growing protectionism in Egypt and elsewhere which severely reduced the regional market for Palestinian goods. Reliance on imports from the Middle East also tended to drop but not by anything like as much, as the country continued to require significant quantities of cereals from Syria and elsewhere to feed itself in most years.

(d) A last, and very unusual, feature of Palestine's foreign trade was its enormous size relative to the local National Product. According to Himadeh's calculations the total value of imports and exports in

1935 was equal to 1.35 times that of both industry and agriculture combined.[14] One implication of this is that movements in the terms of trade must have played an exceptionally important role in Palestinian economic life. But, unfortunately, there has been no attempt to examine this question in detail so far. A second implication concerns government policy which also exercised an important influence over the pattern of imports and exports. In spite of the fact that there were quite considerable constraints on the freedom of the local authorities to set local tariffs - notably the provision in the Mandate forbidding them to discriminate against members of the League of Nations and the British government's unwillingness to cancel the Anglo-Japanese trade agreement of 1911 which continued to prevent efforts to limit competition in textiles even after Japan left the League in 1935 - there were significant efforts to protect and encourage local industry, beginning in the 1920s, and to do the same for Palestinian agriculture in the 1930s.[15] Once again this is a subject which has not been examined in enough detail to allow any hard and fast conclusions about the effect of colonial policy on Palestinian trade.

3. Agriculture and industry

It goes without saying that at the start of the mandatory period Palestine was a predominantly agricultural country. Figures for the exact amount of land available for cultivation were hotly disputed in the 1930s but according to the government's calculations they came to some 2.3 million dunums on the coastal plain and another 5 million dunums up in the hills, with further amounts of mostly marginal land in the Beer Sheba sub-district in the south.[16] By far the greatest part of the cultivated area was used to grow winter cereals - mainly wheat and barley - while most of the rest was devoted to other cereals (notably dura), fruits and vegetables. Irrigated agriculture was generally confined to the coastal plain where it was used to produce citrus fruits and some vegetables.

The size of the cereal crop relied heavily on the amount and timing of the winter rains and, as in southern Syria, there was a tendency for good and bad harvest to run in three or four yearly cycles. Partly because of the marked fluctuation from good times to bad it is difficult to establish any trend for overall output. But the averages given in Table 2.4 would suggest that, while there was no obvious increase in the wheat crop between the wars, barley output nearly doubled. Much of the cereal harvest was grown for the cultivator's own use and Brown calculates that only about one-third of the wheat was available for marketing.[17]

Table 2.4: Estimated production of principal crops: 1920-1945 (annual average in metric tons)

	1920-4	1925-9	1930-4	1935-9	1940-2	1945[a]
Wheat	84,670	90,534	69,073	88,291	110,280	58,355
Barley	38,852	49,514	45,642	70,491	95,301	74,906
Olives	n.a.	12,895	11,101	36,380	40,649	79,469
Vegetables	n.a.	16,122	22,015	99,405	194,098	244,834

Note: a. Figures for 1945 are believed to be an underestimate due to the institution of compulsory distribution.
Sources: M. Brown, 'Agriculture' in Sa'id B. Himadeh, (ed.), *The Economic Organisation of Palestine* (Beirut, 1938), pp. 128-9.

Cereal production was very much at the centre of the great crisis which afflicted most of Arab agriculture in the early 1930s. The big fall in price at the beginning of the world depression was followed immediately by a series of bad harvests due to poor rains, from 1931/2 to 1933/4. According to one set of figures, the price of wheat dropped from £P 10.81 a ton in 1929 to £P 6.97 in 1931, while the price of barley went down from £P 7.66 to £P 3.03 during the same period.[18] To make matters worse, 1928 had also seen the introduction of a new system of land tax based on the commutation of the old Ottoman tithe valued in terms of the much higher crop prices reigning during the years 1924 to 1927, thus squeezing the agriculturalists between what were now crippling tax rates, and a tremendous fall in income. In these circumstances, the government was forced to remit taxes on a large scale and provide loans for the purchase of seeds and other vital inputs.

The crisis also prompted the government to try to get to the root of some of the underlying problems affecting peasant farming, particularly in the hills and a series of commissions pointed to such basic features as population pressure, the fragmentation of plots, the effects of Jewish land purchase and growing indebtedness. To take only one example, the Johnson-Crosbie survey of 104 villages (containing just over one-quarter of the agricultural population) in 1930 revealed that the average level of indebtedness was £P 27 per family, compared with an average income of only £P25-30 in 1929 - even before the collapse of cereal prices.[19] Given the fact that interest was usually charged at some 30 per cent, the authorities rightly concluded that there was little chance of poor farmers escaping from the grip of the money lenders in any foreseeable future. However, efforts to protect peasants from the effect of their reliance on local usurers ran into all the usual problems which face any government trying to reach the bottom stratum of a rural hierarchy dominated by large land owners and merchants, and it seems likely that much more was achieved by the lowering of tax rates in the new Rural Poverty Tax introduced in 1935.

Jewish agriculture must also have been seriously affected by falling incomes during this period. But here the effects were very much cushioned by the fact that Jewish farmers were already highly subsidised by such organisations as the Keren Kayemeth (Jewish National Fund), the Keren Hayesod (Jewish Foundation Fund for Settlement, Education and Capital Works) and the PICA (Palestine Jewish Colonial Association), all with quite considerable funds at their disposal.

The two main growth areas in Palestinian agriculture at this time were fruit and vegetable production, both of which involved considerable Arab as well as Jewish effort. The amount of land devoted to citrus trees of all kinds (oranges, lemons and grapefruit) rose from 30,000 dunums in 1922 to almost 300,000 dunums in 1939, with ownership divided almost equally between Jews and Arabs. The main period of expansion came in the 1930s, allowing exports to rise from 2.4 million cases in 1930/1 to a peak of 13 million cases in 1938/9. This gave Palestine a significant share in the international market (some 23 per cent in 1939), but only at the cost of making a major contribution to world overproduction so that, according to one estimate, the average profit per case was almost halved between 1932/3 and 1938/9, triggering off quite a considerable crisis even before the outbreak of World War II took away almost all of Palestine's European export markets.[20] Arab-owned groves tended to be smaller than those of the Jews and they were very much less well provided with institutional support for either credit or marketing. But they made up for this to some extent by having cheaper labour costs. As for vegetable production, there was a steady increase in output during the 1930s with major attention being devoted to tomatoes followed by onions, cucumbers and potatoes.[21]

Turning now to manufacturing industry, here too there was considerable growth during the inter-war years. Bearing in mind all the problems involved in defining what is or what is not an industrial plant, the number of enterprises would seem to have grown from around 1,240 in 1913 to 3,505 in 1927 (with 17,955 workers) and about 6,000 (with 40,000 workers) in 1936 (Table 2.5). The vast majority were very small and more correctly described (with Himadeh) as handicrafts workshops. Of the rest only 317 employed more than six workers in 1927 while a mere 583 possessed some form of motor power.[22] Even after the great spurt of industrialisation in

Table 2.5: Indicators of the growth of Palestinian industry: 1913-1947[a]

(a) Estimates of total employment in industry

	Arabs	Jews	Total
1921-2		4,750	
1927 (Census)			17,955
1930			15,000
1933		19,595	
1936		30,040	
1939	3,728		48,000
1942			64,000
1944			60,000
1944/5	13,000	65,000	
1947		46,000	

(b) Estimates of number of manufacturing enterprises

	Arabs	Jews	Total
before 1914	925	300	1,236
1927 (Census)			3,505
1933		3,388	
1935		4,615	
1936		5,606	6,000
1939	350		
1943		6,116	

(c) Estimates of value of industrial output (£P million)

	Jewish	Total
1921/2	0.5	
1927	2.3	3.89
1929	2.5	
1933	5.4	6.0
1935		7.0-10.0
1936	8.6	9.1
1943		36.0

Note: a. Definitions of what constituted industry or industrial employment vary widely.

Sources: S.B. Himadeh, 'Industry' in Himadeh, (ed.), *Economic Organisation*; E. Broido, 'Jewish Palestine: The social fabric' in J.B. Hobman, (ed.), *Palestine's Economic Future* (London, 1946); R.A. Nathan, D. Gass and D. Creamer, *Palestine: Problem and Promise* (Washington, D.C., 1946); R. Szereszewski, *Essays on the Structure of the Jewish Economy in Palestine and Israel* (Jerusalem, 1968); U.K. Department of Overseas Trade, *Palestine: A Review of Commercial Conditions* (February 1945) and *The Palestine Economist Annual 1948*.

the mid-1930s the number of factories with over 100 workers in 1937 was no more than 16.[23]

Not surprisingly, a major impetus to industrialisation came from Jewish immigration. Not only did Palestine attract a number of Jewish entrepreneurs, particularly in the mid-1920s and early 1930s, but many of them also brought considerable quantities of money and machinery with them as well as their own talents and skills.[24] Again, the Jewish community itself provided a growing market for local manufacturers, particularly the building sector which experienced a major boom between 1925 and 1935 (with a total investment of £P 36.5 million) and stimulated a rising demand for cement and metal and wood products such as pipes, doors, window frames, baths and other fittings.[25] Figures in Table 2.5 provide some evidence for this. They show, for example, that the number of Jewish enterprises rose from 3,388 in 1933 (with a capital of £P 5.37 million) to 5,600 enterprises in 1937 (with a capital of £P 11.64 million).

Far less is known about the development of Arab manufacturing industry during this same period. To judge from Himadeh's figures, there was more activity in the first decade of the Mandate than the second, with 1,373 new enterprises being established between 1918 and 1927 (with a capital of £P 13,000) and only 529 between 1931 and 1937.[26] But it may well be that the size of plant and the average amount of capital was much greater in the 1930s. What is not clear is the degree to which Jewish economic activity both provided opportunities for Arab industrialists while, at the same time, creating considerable barriers. Examples of the former would be the availability of electricity from the Rutenberg concession (the Palestine Electric Corporation) and the additional market provided by the Jews for certain Arab-produced products such as cigarettes and flour. On the other side of the equation, the existence of a well-organised Jewish competition with considerably larger capital resources at its disposal must have either blocked off important avenues for Arab entrepreneurs or, as in the case of soap, kept them fixed firmly in only a tiny corner of their traditional market.

A final comment concerns the way in which Palestinian industry, both Arab and Jewish, sought to develop. This was very obviously along the well-known lines of import substitution, with only a minor emphasis on production for export. There were, however, a number of significant differences: whereas Arab industrialists seem to have followed the familiar pathway from processed foodstuffs and simple textiles to cigarettes, matches and leather products, Jewish entrepreneurs paid less initial attention to textiles (perhaps because of the unsolved problem of Japanese competition) and proceeded very quickly to chemicals, electrical goods and metalwork of types far more varied and technically advanced than anything elsewhere in the Middle East. However, in the case of both Arabs and Jews it would seem reasonable to assume that their products were relatively costly by contemporary international standards, as is usually the case with import substitution, but with the Arabs receiving some local advantage from the fact that their labour was very much cheaper than that of the Jews.

4. The performance of the economy, 1918-1939

There is no doubt that the Palestine economy enjoyed a high rate of growth during the inter-war period, whether measured in terms of foreign trade, government revenue or industrial output (Tables 2.5 and 2.7). Thus the total value of trade increased by nearly three times between 1922 and 1929 and total revenue by six times during the same period. However, it is also clear that this advance was due largely to the peculiar feature of Jewish immigration and large Jewish capital transfers, most of which went to create special enclaves where the inhabitants were able to develop a very much higher standard of living than the rest of the population. In what are admittedly very rough estimates by Gross and Metzer, Jewish income per capita increased from around £P 20 in 1923/4 to perhaps £P 50 in 1935.[27] It will be remembered that a first estimate for Arab income per capita gives this as £P 17 in 1936.[28]

A second feature of Palestine's economic performance is that it tended to grow more rapidly at periods when the world economy was slowing down, as in the mid-1920s and early 1930s. There is no secret about the reason for this: these were also moments when persecution in Europe encouraged a greater flow of Jewish refugees, some with substantial capital assets, and bigger contributions to Jewish voluntary funds. By the same token, the late 1920s and late 1930s were much less good times in Palestine with relatively high unemployment and a contraction of business activity and rapid investment which had marked the previous boom. On the whole, Arab economic activity seems to have followed the same cycles, sharing in the booms of the mid-1920s and mid-1930s but then being hurt, not only by the general downturn, but also by the political reaction which always followed periods of rapid Jewish migration, most notably during the rebellion of 1936-9. The one exception to this phenomenon, when the economy in general, and the Arab sectors in particular, moved in association with (and not against) world economic trends was during the very first years of the 1930s when, as already noted, agriculture was hard hit by a combination of factors including the great slump in world commodity prices.

Table 2.6: Estimates of Palestine's national income and its sectoral composition

(a) National income (£P million)

	Arab	Jewish	Total
1922		1.6	
1936	16.0	17.8	33.8
		23.4 (GDP)	
1939		17.2	30.2
1940		20.6	
1945		88.2	

(b) National income per capita (£P)

	Arab	Jewish
1923/4		20
1935		50
1936	17	44
1944	165	

(c) Sectoral contribution
(1) Output value in agriculture and manufacturing in Palestine economy (£P million)

	Agriculture	Manufacturing
1927		3.89
1936	5.6	5.4
1939	5.59	
1943	19.0	
1944/5	21.8	

(2) Sectoral distribution of output in the Arab and Jewish economies: 1936 (%)[a]

	Agriculture	Manufacturing	Construction	Services
Arab	25.0	13.0	2.0	60.0
Jewish	9.5	22.0	8.6	59.9

Note: a. Jewish income measured as NDP.
Sources: N.T. Gross and J. Metzer, *Public Finance in the Jewish Economy in Interwar Palestine* (Jerusalem, 1977); N. Halevi and R. Klinov-Malul, *The Economic Development of Israel* (New York, 1968); Nathan, Gass and Creamer, *Palestine*; Szereszewski, *Essays; Survey of Palestine* (Jerusalem, 1946). J. Metzer, 'Fiscal incidence and resource transfer between Jews and Arabs in mandatory Palestine', *Research in Economic History*, vol.7 (Jerusalem, 1982).

Support for this general analysis comes not only from the figures for trade or government revenues but also from the first attempts to estimate Jewish economic performance in the 1930s (Table 2.6) which show that income and output grew rapidly up to 1936 and then remained almost level until the outbreak of World War II.

A final comment refers not so much to improvements in the standard of living as to changes in the quality of life enjoyed by different communities in Palestine. As many commentators have noted, the mandatory government pursued a typical colonial pattern of finance, with nearly 60 per cent of its expenditures going to administration, defence and security in the 1920s and 1930s and only about 12 per cent each to public works and welfare.[29] One result was the very low level of spending on such essential matters as education so that, for example, the government only built five Arab elementary schools between 1918 and 1945.[30] Once again this produced a major difference between the Jewish and Arab communities, with the Jews using a significant proportion of the Zionist budget, about 40 per cent for most of the period, to provide themselves with the educational, medical and other welfare facilities which the government could not provide.[31]

III. THE WARTIME ECONOMY, 1939-1945

The outbreak of the war in September 1939 rescued the Palestinian economy from recession and catapulted it into a major role in the British Middle Eastern military effort. Not only was it developed into a large British base with all the attendant barracks and fortifications but its people were also mobilised behind a programme designed to reduce dependence on outside sources of supply and to expand Palestine's industrial base so as to enable it to make an important contribution to supplying British military needs as well as to providing a whole array of consumer and other goods for a regional market starved of European and American imports. The result was a major boost for both the Arab and Jewish sectors of the economy, a considerable rise in income and a great acceleration in the process of social change.

Table 2.7: Some indices of economic growth

a. Sales of electric power to industry (KwH million)

	Palestine Electric Corporation Ltd	Jerusalem Electric and Public Services Corp. Ltd
1926	1.43	
1930	2.19	
1935	17.17	
1939	25.1	0.48
1941	32.87	0.71

b. Apparent consumption of cement and cotton piece goods (kg)

	Cement	Cotton piece goods
1928	61,909	2,070,387
1930	71,201	2,518,209
1935	355,553	4,048,669
1939	143,888	3,326,748
1942	218,869	5,250,492[a]

Note: a. Includes consumption by armed forces

Source: *Statistical Abstract of Palestine* 1943, pp. 179-81.

1. Foreign trade

The war years saw a great increase in the nominal value of
Palestine's foreign trade, from some £P 20 million in 1939 to around
£P 50 million in 1944. Once again there was a growing balance of
payments deficit financed this time by a combination of well over £P
100 million of British military purchase and a further transfer of
perhaps as much as £P 38 million of Jewish funds.[32] However, as the
war was also a time of considerable price inflation, these figures hide
the fact that imports fell by nearly one-half by volume between 1939
and the first three quarters of 1945, with a particularly large decrease
in manufactured goods (over two-thirds, from 1939 to 1945) and a
smaller one in the category 'food, drink and tobacco' (29 per cent from
1939 to the period of the worst shortages in 1943 - but only 3 per cent
to 1945).[33]

The war also produced a major shift in the composition of exports
and in the general direction of trade, notably a switch back to the
Middle East as the country's major market and source of supply. In
proportional terms, the percentage of total exports by value going to the
Middle East went up from 10 per cent in 1939 to a high of 75 per cent

in 1942. Imports from the region climbed from 18 per cent in 1939 to 60 per cent in 1943.[34] On the export side, far and away the most important factor was the sale of manufactured goods which, in value terms, rose from a mere £P 750,000 at the start of the war to over £P 7 million at the end.

2. Agriculture and industry

Once the war was under way, both the British authorities in the Middle East and the mandatory government in Jerusalem made every effort to increase Palestine's productive resources using such newly created institutions as the Middle East Supply Centre in Cairo and the War Supplies Board (1941) and the Directorate of War Production (1942) in Palestine itself. In the case of agriculture, however, the figures in Table 2.4 would suggest that there was no great success in increasing the size of the cereal harvest, perhaps because of a growing shortage of labour, and the major improvements came in the field of vegetable production (which nearly doubled between 1939 and 1945), olives and poultry and dairy products. There were also considerable problems to do with the citrus industry which almost entirely ceased to export. It had to make do with sales in the local market and to the military - some of it in the form of juice. Arab growers found it slightly easier to keep going on account of their lower costs. Nevertheless, taking the industry as a whole, two-thirds of all producers needed some form of government financial assistance to survive.

It was in the industrial sector that the major expansion took place with an enormous increase in capacity and output required to meet demand in three large markets: the British military, Palestine itself and the rest of the Middle East, including Turkey. Unfortunately, the government was unable to obtain precise figures to illustrate this process, but according to one estimate, output in Jewish-owned factories increased by 200 per cent between 1939 and 1942 and that in Arab-owned enterprises by 77 per cent.[35] Other figures to be found in Tables 2.5 and 2.7 show that the amount of electric power consumed by industry went up three-fold during the war years while the numbers employed increased from some 40,000-50,000 to perhaps 70,000-80,000.

Military-related activity was controlled and monitored by the Directorate of War Production and was at its peak during the North African campaign of 1943. Between 1942 and 1944 the factories it supervised produced over 3.6 million anti-tank mines, nearly 8 million steel containers and a whole host of other goods including accumulators, petrol storage tanks, hydraulic jacks and special bodies for certain types of military vehicles.[36] In 1944 some of these factories were redirected to producing consumer goods which were in short supply for the home market. For the rest, the list of new products introduced during the war for the civilian sector, mostly from Jewish factories, was extraordinarily extensive, ranging from industrial machinery and tools, spare parts for cars and medical and electrical implements to kitchen utensils, false teeth and pharmaceuticals. In all of this, both the British military and the Jewish factory owners received important support from Jewish scientific institutions at the Hebrew University and elsewhere, whether in the development of better products or the more efficient use of local raw materials. Finally, the war saw a great expansion in the diamond cutting and polishing industry started by Jewish refugees just before 1939. By 1945 it consisted of over 30 factories employing some 3,000 workers.[37]

3. Income and welfare

Government figures show that there was a considerable growth in incomes during the war years. Thus while the official cost of living index rose by 154 per cent between 1939 and 1945, average industrial earnings are estimated to have grown by 200 per cent for Arabs and 258 per cent for Jews during the same period, while those of unskilled construction workers climbed by 405 per cent and 329 per cent respectively.[38] Conditions in the rural areas may have been even better. Prices of locally grown agricultural products are said to have gone up seven-fold during the war and agricultural wages by the same amount by mid-1943.[39] In these circumstances it is not surprising to find that the official government figures show that total agricultural income quadrupled between 1939 and 1944/5 (in money terms) providing the Arab peasant with 'a large measure of prosperity' and leading to a dramatic decline in the need to borrow from money lenders in many districts.[40] As for the Jewish community, Szereszewski calculates that its Net National Product nearly doubled in real terms during the war, from £P 16.7 million (valued at constant 1936 prices) to £P 29.9 million.[41]

A last note concerns the interpretation of the aggregate figures. In spite of the general rise in incomes, it also has to be remembered that the war period was a time of shortages and rationing, with consumption of many goods severely reduced. It also took the government some time to organise machinery for subsidising a whole variety of necessities in the interest of keeping inflation under control. This last was the work of the War Economic Advisory Council which was only created in July 1943 after a general period of considerable labour unrest including the threat of a general strike. All in all, it would seem that conditions were probably at their worst in early 1943 and that the main improvements came in the last two years.

4. The two communities

The events of the war years brought important changes in the structure of the Arab and Jewish communities. It may also have increased the density of economic interaction between them after the boycotts of the late 1930s, as Horowitz has argued, but this remains to be proved.[42] There must certainly have been a greater exchange of goods between them once the volume of imports began to fall. Against this, there is no evidence that more Arabs were employed in Jewish factories in spite of what must have been a considerable shortage of Jewish labour.[43]

As far as the Arab side was concerned, probably the most important developments in the period were the huge mobilisation of labour which took many hundreds of thousands away from their villages on either a daily or a more permanent basis and the stimulus given to Arab industry. According to Taqqu's estimate, about one-third of the male Arab work force was employed in wage labour by 1945, most of them by the government and military but with some 13,000 in some aspect of manufacturing.[44] Data about industrialisation are, if anything, even more scarce. Information in the *Survey of Palestine* suggests that Arab factories provided about half of Palestine's cigarettes and flour during the war and 20 per cent of its woven cloth, with quite considerable capacity in boot and shoe making as well. The Arabs also had a small toehold in the metalwork industry making iron doors and windows.[45] If these suggestions are correct, it would seem reasonable to suppose that all, or almost all, of the major military contracts went to the more technically developed Jewish firms. It does not follow, however, that Arab firms were any less competitive than Jewish ones when it came to producing the same line of goods. According to a government examination of 12 industries making similar commodities in 1942, greater Jewish productivity was usually more than offset by lower Arab labour costs.[46]

To turn now to the Jewish community, official policy was to concentrate on the twin tasks of assisting the Allied war effort while continuing to build up Zionist institutions. Palestine government statistics indicate that the ceiling of 75,000 new immigrants laid down in the 1939 White Paper had been reached by the end of 1945, to which should be added a considerable number of illegal immigrants as well. Jewish funds increased, land purchase continued (although at a slightly lower rate) and 31 new settlements were established. Just as important, the growth of war-related industry and the fact that there were 27,000 Jews serving with the British armed forces gave the community a military potential far in excess of anything it had possessed before. It also hastened the development of a socio-economic structure with a profile (in terms of the relative contribution of industry and agriculture) remarkably similar to those to be found in some of the more advanced countries of Europe.

IV. THE LAST THREE YEARS

During the last three years of the Mandate, economic activities in Palestine were clearly overshadowed by political events both inside and outside the country. Nevertheless, there were still a number of important developments which played a significant role in the fortunes of the two communities. As in many other parts of the world, the economy remained subject to a considerable degree of rationing and control maintained by authorities trying to ensure a smooth transition from wartime mobilisation back to peace. As elsewhere, too, there was a sudden release of spending by consumers and investors once foreign goods began to be available again. Finally, the fact that Palestine remained an important British military base and a member of the Sterling Area until February 1948 also had important consequences for economic life.

To begin with foreign trade, even though many imports still required a licence there was usually a postwar boom with the volume of purchases from abroad doubling between 1945 and 1946, to exceed their pre-war level for the first time since 1939.[47] Not surprisingly, it was foreign manufactured goods which led the way with a 250 per cent increase over the two years and there was another big jump in 1947. Exports remained more quiet. To set against the recovery of the European market for citrus there was the Arab boycott of Jewish goods which more or less barred them to all the Middle East customers they had been able to reach during the war.[48] As it was, diamonds made up nearly 60 per cent of the value of exports in 1946, with citrus contributing most of the rest.[49]

Stored up wartime demand was also an important factor in providing a further stimulus to local industry, particularly anything involved with materials for construction. Many firms expanded their capacity, a few of them bringing in the latest equipment from Europe to help them do it.[50] There were also a number of new factories, some producing bricks, marble and cement, others textiles (including at least one Arab-owned plant near Acre), metal and glassware and canned orange juice.[51]

In these circumstances there were few signs of the growth of unemployment which the government feared and by 1947 it felt able to release men whom it had kept on in official or military employment against just such a possibility. There was, however, a number of bitter labour disputes in 1946, a year in which there was a 13 per cent rise in the official cost of living index and when, as Taqqu speculates, there may also have been some downward pressure on real wages.[52] But, as she also argues, this was not enough to push many of the Arab peasants who had got used to wage employment during the war back to their villages. On the basis of the few statistics which the government was able to collect from the rural areas after the war, it would seem that, anyway, agriculture was in a somewhat depressed condition at this time with a very small olive crop in 1946/7 and poor rains in 1947, particularly in the south.

To conclude with a few words on a more political note. It would seem from contemporary sources that, while the Jewish community used the last years of the Mandate to maintain its wartime economic momentum - aided by its access to foreign currency for the purchase of capital equipment and its greater control of its labour force - these same years found the Arabs in a process of rapid socio-economic change and caught between two leaderships: the traditional notables of the hills and the new groups with new claims to modern expertise in the growth areas down on the coast.[53] In this context it is surely significant that, once public meetings were allowed again after the war, an increasing number of Arab organisations began to hold them in Haifa, Jaffa and the other centres where entrepreneurs, contractors, technicians and skilled workers were now concentrated. By the same token this new situation provides further proof of the enormity of the losses which the Palestinian Arabs suffered in 1948, for it was just these same areas, with their valuable plant and other assets, which fell so easily into the hands of the new Jewish state.

NOTES

1. M. Halevi and R. Klinov-Malul, *The Economic Development of Israel* (New York, 1968), p. 16.

2. L.G. Hopkins, 'Population' in Sa'id B. Himadeh (ed.), *The Economic Organization of Palestine* (Beirut, 1938), pp. 31-6.

3. R. Szereszewski, *Essays on the Structure of the Jewish Economy in Palestine and Israel* (Jerusalem, 1968), Table 5; Halevi and Klinov-Malul, *Economic Development*, p. 16.

4. Halevi and Klinov-Malul, *Economic Development*, p. 19.

5. R.A. Nathan, O. Gass and D. Creamer, *Palestine: Problem and Promise* (Washington D.C., 1946) p. 150.

6. Szereszewski, *Essays*, p. 9.

7. Palestine Government, *A Survey of Palestine* (3 vols., Jerusalem, 1946), Vol. 1, p. 243; K.W. Stein, *The Land Question in Palestine, 1917-1939* (Chapel Hill and London, 1984), Appendix 2. One dunum is approximately 0.25 acres (1,000 square metres).

8. B.J. Smith, 'British economic policy towards the development of the Jewish National Home, 1920-1929' (unpublished D. Phil. thesis, Oxford University, 1978), p. 179; Stein, *Land Question*, p. 178.

9. Stein, *Land Question*, pp. 146-58; *Survey of Palestine*, 1, pp. 295-7

10. T. Asad, 'Class transformation under the Mandate', *MERIP Reports*, 53, p.5; Stein, *Land Question*, chapters 4 and 6.

11. Halevi and Klinov-Malul, *Economic Development*, p. 19.

12. Ibid.

13. B. Veicmans, 'Internal trade' in Himadeh (ed.), *Economic Organization*, p. 348.

14. S.B. Himadeh, 'Industry', in Himadeh (ed.), *Economic Organization*, pp. 296-8.

15. H. Sawwaf, 'Foreign trade' in Himadeh (ed.), *Economic Organization*, pp. 432-9; *Survey of Palestine*, 1, pp. 452-9; Smith, 'British economic policy', pp. 320-50.

16. S.B. Himadeh, 'Natural resources', in Himadeh (ed.), *Economic Organization*, pp. 44-5.

17. M. Brown, 'Agriculture', in Himadeh (ed.), *Economic Organization*, pp.128-9.

18. Stein, *Land Question*, p. 143.

19. Quoted in *Survey of Palestine*, 1, p. 368.

20. J. Ziman, *The Revival of Palestine* (New York, 1946), p. 135; Nathan, Gass and Creamer, *Palestine*, pp. 210-11.

21. Brown 'Agriculture' in Himadeh (ed.), *Economic Organization*, pp. 159-62; Palestine Government, *Statistical Abstract of Palestine 1943* (Jerusalem, 1943), pp. 70, 72.

22. Himadeh, 'Industry', in Himadeh (ed.), *Economic Organization*, pp. 230-9.

23. Nathan, Gass and Creamer, *Palestine*, p. 223.

24. Himadeh, 'Industry' in Himadeh (ed.), *Economic Organization*, pp. 228-9.

25. Ibid., p. 263.

26. Ibid., pp. 230, 245.

27. N.T. Gross and J. Metzer, *Public Finance in the Jewish Economy in Interwar Palestine* (Jerusalem, 1977), Table A-5.

28. See note 5.

29. Gross and Metzer, *Public Finance*, p. 80.

30. Y.N. Miller, *Government and Society in Rural Palestine, 1920-1948* (Austin, 1985), pp.152-3.

31. Gross and Metzer, *Public Finance,* Table 9.

32. *Survey of Palestine,* 1, pp. 464-5.

33. Ibid., p. 467.

34. Ibid., p. 481.

35. Nathan, Gass and Creamer, *Palestine,* p. 162.

36. 'Wartime economic management' in *Survey of Palestine,* 2, pp. 1011-12.

37. Cunningham Papers (St. Antony's College Oxford, Middle East Centre), Box 1, File 4, tg 160 of 15 April 1947.

38. *Survey of Palestine,* 3, p. 1309.

39. D. Horowitz, 'The Arab economy in Palestine' in J.B. Hobman (ed.), *Palestine's Economic Future* (London, 1946), p. 55; Middle East Supply Centre, *Middle East Economic and Statistical Bulletin,* no. 3 (Cairo, June 1943), p. 10.

40. *Survey of Palestine,* 1, pp. 365-7.

41. Szereszewski, *Essays,* p. 56.

42. Horowitz, 'Arab economy' in Hobman (ed.), *Palestine,* p. 55.

43. R. Taqqu, 'Peasants into workmen: internal labor migration and the Arab village community under the Mandate' in J.S. Migdal (ed.), *Palestinian Society and Politics* (Princeton, 1980), p. 274; Musa al-Budayri, *tatawwur al-haraka al-'arabiyya fi filastin* (Development of the Arab movement in Palestine) (Beirut, 1981).

44. Taqqu, 'Peasants into workmen' in Migdal (ed.), *Palestinian Society,* p. 267.

45. *Survey of Palestine,* 1, p. 516.

46. Ibid., 3, pp. 1277-8.

47. Cunningham Papers, Box 1, File 4, tg 160 of 15 April 1945.

48. Ibid., Box 1, File 1, tg 518 of 29 March 1946 and tg 920 of 4 June 1946; Box 1, File 2, tg 1393 of 2 October 1946.

49. *Palestine Economist Annual 1948* (Jerusalem, 1948), pp. 94-5.

50. For example, Cunningham Papers, Box 1, File 4, tg 160 of 15 April 1947.

51. *Palestine Economist Annual 1948,* pp. 88, 94-7, 107 etc.; Cunningham Papers, Box 2, File 1, tg 200 of 12 May 1947 and tg 169 of 9 July 1947.

52. Taqqu, 'Peasants into workmen' in Migdal (ed.), *Palestinian Society,* p. 281.

53. For example, Y. Porath, 'Social aspects of the emergence of the Palestinian Arab national movement' in M. Milson (ed.), *Society and Political Structure in the Arab World* (New York, 1973) and Salim Tamari, 'Factionalism and class formation in recent Palestinian history', in R. Owen (ed.), *Studies on the Economic and Social History of Palestine in the Nineteenth and Twentieth Centuries* (Basingstoke and London, 1986), pp. 177-202.

3

The Economy of the Palestinian Arabs in Israel

Raja Khalidi

Since the establishment of the State of Israel in 1948 the fate of those Palestinian Arabs[1] isolated within Israel's borders from their compatriots in the West Bank, the Gaza Strip and exile has acquired a growing significance and attention. This has been manifested politically in that this community's role in the Israeli-Palestinian conflict has grown appreciably. In addition, its unique position within the state has been the subject of an abundance of sociological, anthropological, political, geographic and economic studies since the 1970s.

In certain fields, such as education and political status, this attention has produced clear and definitive results. However, in other subjects, extensive research has been largely inconclusive, notably that having to do with social and economic change and status. Different ideological and methodological studies have provided the basis for often contradictory hypotheses and research conclusions, with the result that no lasting or comprehensive understanding of these issues has been arrived at.

On the whole, discussion of the Arab economy of Israel has only taken place in the context of other issues. This is particularly due to the fact that it has been sociologists, anthropologists and political scientists who have taken the lead in analysing the economic position of Arabs in Israel from their respective disciplinary standpoints. I do not wish to argue for a narrow 'economistic' approach to what is clearly not a clear-cut 'economic' issue, but I would contend that study of economic issues within the terms of the discipline itself is the most fruitful starting point for any overall understanding of the Arabs in Israel which also integrates analysis of economic status. This becomes all the more necessary when it is realised that the existing theoretical (and terminological) characteristics of the Arabs in Israel all reflect definite political and ideological viewpoints. Though this is unavoidable in most socio-economic research, it becomes academically unacceptable when studies become more concerned with justifying or proving ideological positions, than with accurately or honestly depicting and explaining issues.[2]

I shall attempt to view this issue in a different and more comprehensive economic framework by bringing together the different data sources and analyses into one synthesis which explicitly examines the economy of the Arabs in Israel and by offering a more precise and thorough treatment of the issues than has thus far been available.

I. THE PLACE OF THE PALESTINIANS IN ISRAEL

The pattern of economic development of the Palestinians in Israel is significant for three reasons: their relevance to other Palestinian communities, particularly those under occupation; their role and position in Israel; and the third-world development context of their experience.

The Palestinian experience in Israel since 1948 bears certain striking similarities to that of Palestinians under occupation in the West Bank and the Gaza Strip. Though legally and politically this is not strictly a case of 'prolonged occupation', but rather the processes and effects of domination by Israeli Jewish society, the economic and political regimes of the Palestinian Arabs correspond in these two cases too closely to be disregarded.

The 601,500 Arabs in Israel (excluding the populations of annexed East Jerusalem and Golan Heights) constitute over 30 per cent of the Palestinians living under Israeli rule.[3] If we include the 126,500 inhabitants of Arab Jerusalem, the figure rises to 728,000 or some 36.5 per cent of the Palestinians inside mandatory Palestine.

There are a number of obvious themes in the Palestinian experience in Israel which have characterised the situation in the 1967 occupied territories:[4]

(a) land expropriation, especially in the 1950s, but continuing intermittently in the Galilee until today;

(b) the associated problems of access to natural resources, notably cultivable land and water, faced by the Arabs in Israel;

(c) the difficulties undeveloped Arab industrial potential faces in competition with the highly capitalised and aggressive Israeli

Jewish industrial sector;

(d) the intervention in, and acquisition of, external trade channels and markets of the Arab economy by Israeli Jewish public and private sector institutions and simultaneous exclusion of Arabs from participation in that process and enjoyment of the accruing benefits;

(e) the utilisation of a large and relatively unskilled, mobile and manual labour force in specific tasks in construction, agriculture and industry;

(f) the experience of military rule which, though lifted inside Israel by 1966, left its specific imprint on the mass conception of the state's interests and methods towards the Arab population.

In terms of its size and experience the Arab population inside Israel occupies a position of special relevance to other Palestinian communities. It is estimated that in 1983, Palestinians totalled some 4.5 million (extrapolated, at assumed 3.2 per cent annual growth, from figures for 1980 Palestinian population in UNECWA, 1985).[5] Palestinians in Israel constituted some 15 per cent of that total. Their experience has much to offer not only in terms of important political and 'developmental' lessons acquired through three decades of regular contact with the Israeli regime and economy. It is equally significant in Palestinian terms in light of the recent crystallisation of national sentiment and identity among this section of the Palestinian people, which until the mid-1960s had been given up by most of their compatriots as a lost cause - the so-called 'Arabs of Israel'.[6]

There are of course a number of significant differences between the situation of Palestinians in Israel and that of other Palestinians which have a bearing on their developmental experiences. Most obvious is that Palestinians in Israel are citizens of that state, entitled in principle to the benefits, rights and obligations which derive from that condition. Palestinians in Israel have recourse (again, in principle) to institutions and legal channels, contacts and work opportunities and certain overall benefits (social security, services and relatively unhampered trade union activity) not afforded to the population of the occupied territories. In certain aspects of economic activity, this can provide both relative and absolute advantages that other Palestinians cannot enjoy. Palestinians' legal status in Israel and the policies pursued by the regime and Zionist institutions have over the years produced a much greater degree of co-operation/collaboration between certain sections of Arab society in Israel and the state than is the case in the occupied territories. This can result in a very different conception of individual and community self-interest, desired paths of economic development and the political and legal prerequisites of social and economic change and prosperity.

On the other hand, the period from 1948 to 1967 allowed the West Bank to develop economic sectors and various institutions within the Jordanian and Arab environment which are still operative and relevant (for example, export over the Jordan River bridges is still a vital aspect of West Bank economic relations). This and other factors often advantageous to the 1967 occupied territories, and related to differential historical determinants, resource endowments and regional and social links, combine to distinguish the two experiences while at the same time maintaining their mutual relevance. Though study of the Arab experience in Israel demands its own outlook, approach and methods, its relation to the wider Palestinian context should always be borne in mind, for both methodological and policy purposes.

Palestinian Arabs have a significant position and role within Israeli society and economy. In 1984, over 14 per cent (excluding Jerusalem, or 17 per cent including the city) of the Israeli population was Arab.[7] This has been the cause of a growing dilemma for Israeli policy makers, for demographic, political and economic reasons. Certain productive sectors in the national economy, primarily construction, but also some agricultural and industrial branches, utilise a relatively high proportion of Arab labour. While this was initially provided from within Israel, it now comes increasingly from the occupied territories. The Arab areas which supply this mobile labour force also constitute an important market for consumption of a portion of national product, much of which is produced outside the area.

The gradual but steady growth in the relative size of the Arab population as a whole - from 11 per cent in 1951[8] to the 1984 figure of 14 or 17 per cent depending on whether or not Jerusalem is included - is seen as a serious ideological, political and security problem by the Israelis. There are regular pronouncements of academic or official concern for the 'Jewishness' of the state, of labour, of land, of the Galilee, etc. Indeed, while state policy has oscillated over the years between the view of the need to accommodate and exploit the Arab 'contribution' to Israeli economic growth, and the requirement to maintain the 'Jewishness' of the state, relations between it and the Arab community have yet to stabilise into any defined, institutionalised and consistent pattern.

The position of Arabs in Israel can also be seen to have a certain relevance to the international development debate. This has been reflected in the attempts to apply various methodologies derived from the third-world experience to this particular case: such methodologies include dualism and unbalanced development; internal colonialism; pluralist democratic models; control system theories and analyses of modernisation. However, it does not seem to me to be especially important to establish whether one or another theory fits the situation, but whether the position of Arabs in Israel rightly deserves consideration as an issue of third-world development, especially since Israel cannot itself be considered to be part of the third world, either politically or economically.

II. THE ARAB ECONOMY IN ISRAEL: THE EXOGENOUS DETERMINANTS

1. The physical and demographic framework[9]

Arabs in Israel live in 157 exclusively Arab localities, plus 8 mixed towns: this total includes East Jerusalem, 5 annexed villages surrounding it, 28 recognised and spontaneous Beduin localities in the Galilee and central districts and 31 Beduin settlements in the Negev.[10] Excluding the Negev, of the total of 126 Arab localities, only 3 have municipality status,[11] 51 are local councils and the remaining 72 are grouped in regional councils with Jewish localities or have no local authority status at all.

Of the total Arab population, including Jerusalem, some 25 per cent live in the eight mixed cities and localities (Jerusalem, Haifa, Jaffa, Acre, Lydda, Ramleh, Maalot-Tarshiha, Upper Nazareth). If Jerusalem is excluded from the calculation, the mixed localities' Arab population constitutes only 9 per cent of the total Arab population. This means that a total of 547,000 Arabs live in exclusively Arab localities, and 55,000 live in almost exclusively Arab quarters of predominately Jewish cities.

In the 1972-82 period, Arab population growth averaged 3.7 per cent per annum compared with the Jewish rate of 2.1 per cent and by 1983 exhibited a significantly younger age structure than the Jewish population. The average Arab household in 1983 numbered 6.14 persons, compared to a Jewish level of 3.34 persons. Housing density was greater among Arabs than Jews: an average density of 2.2 persons per room compared with 1.1. Some 29 per cent of Arab households live three-plus to a room compared to only 1 per cent of Jewish households.

More than three decades of residential segregation,[12] differential local and regional planning and resources and the consolidation of a particular Arab demographic structure (more in common with that of the West Bank than with the Jewish settlements of the Galilee) have created 'facts' of a distinctly Arab existence in Israel.

2. Legal status and state development policy

From the earliest days of Israeli rule, the legal position of Arabs in Israel was that 'at best their legal rights as citizens of the state of Israel would be protected'.[13] Effective state policies rest on the series of laws and regulations which explicitly and implicitly constrain Arab development. These are applied in the spheres of land ownership and use, occupational advancement and allocation of natural resources and public utilities. They are enforced through a system which has as one of its precepts the maintenance of the 'Jewishness' of the state and the supremacy of its interests at all levels of political and economic power. It is not necessary here to document this issue which has been extensively researched and written on elsewhere, but I shall briefly summarise those characteristics relevant to our discussion.

Some 34 laws legitimised the process of expropriation of private land, a practice which continues until today.[14] Between 1948 and 1962, some 72 per cent of the pre-1948 holdings of still existing villages had been confiscated, totalling well over 2 million dunums.[15] The two main effects of this process were to deny the Arab population their main productive base while also constricting the area available for expansion of towns and villages. The shortage of land for housing is furthered by the limitations placed by the state on building zones in Arab villages and long delays in authorising town plans without which legal construction cannot start. Only a handful of Arab localities have obtained authorised town plans and the housing problem is continually growing.[16] Confiscated land is either held directly by Zionist bodies, such as the Jewish National Fund, or in association with them. Legally, therefore, it becomes the 'inalienable property of the Jewish people' and Arabs are precluded from leasing or using it.[17]

The explicit exclusion of 'non-Jews' from employment in parts of the military-related industrial sector, the larger public enterprises and the higher echelons of the state and civil service, is another element in the system of legal barriers.[18] Other measures, especially under military rule in the 1960s, restricted and regulated movement, usually according to economic and labour demand requirements.[19] Similarly, political constraints and discrimination restrict Arab residence in Jewish population centres. This part of the system has a dual role of effectively limiting employment and advancement opportunities while perpetuating the dependency of the lower-skilled commuting Arab worker on Jewish employers.

State resource distribution policy, while not always embodied in specific laws, also affects the scope for industrial and agricultural growth. These institutionalised arrangements include: the selective expropriation of the better, more irrigable land; [20] the discretionary powers of the water authority in allocation of quotas;[21] the exclusion of Arab farmers from the important co-operative systems which manage a significant part of the agricultural production and marketing processes;[22] the slow provision of electricity, water and road networks; the failure to designate industrial zones in Arab localities and the relatively small per capita allocation of state aid to Arab local authorities.[23]

Both public and private economic sectors maintain the stagnation of the Arab economy by ensuring an allocation of Arab resources which is most beneficial to the national economy. Through this double-edged strategy of passive neglect and aggressive containment, the Arab community has been largely bypassed in the four decades of impressive economic growth and institution building in Israel. Whether there exists a conscious collusion between the state and the Jewish business sector towards Arab citizens is immaterial. The effective coincidence of interests has ensured a successful implementation of what can be termed a strategy. While there has been an evolution of official policy since 1948 determined by the imperatives of Zionist interests and those of national economic growth, it cannot be said that there is one all embracing (or all inclusive) policy towards the Arabs of Israel. This has been well documented by Richard Weimer in his study of policy towards Israeli Arabs.[24] As he points out, 'to characterise the "Arab problem" as an "unseen question", as "colonialism" or as "modernisation-versus-traditionalism" neglects the fact that Zionism itself is neither static nor does it end in 1948, but continues to be one of the ideological pillars of the State of Israel, subjected to the socio-economic realities of the state'.[25]

The Arab experience in Israel has shown that there are limits to the state's ability arbitrarily to deprive, coerce and subjugate the Arab population and its needs. This can be seen in the strong Arab commitment to the remaining land and to maximising its productive potential; the strong desire for educational advancement and acquisition of much demanded skills, however relatively inferior to those of the Jewish work force; the stubborn insistence of localities to obtain the 'modern conveniences' of electricity and water, usually at their own expense and effort; the examples of individuals, though relatively few, who found ways around restrictions to establish successful businesses and small industries. Overall, the Arab population has learned to resist to the greatest extent possible further encroachments on their rights and property. At the same time, this has entailed a learning process of how best to utilise the existing legal system to their advantage and at least to minimise its use against them. As a natural community response to relative state neglect and discrimination, this constitutes an incentive to growth; this dynamic has had an important role in defining and shaping a distinct Arab economy in Israel.

3. Social change in the Arab community

There are four main axes along which Arab social change operates which have a bearing on the process of economic development. Arab society is differentiated geographically on several levels: between villages and large towns such as Nazareth or Um al-Fahm; between the three main geographic areas of the Galilee, the Triangle and the Negev; between the predominantly rural Galilee and Triangle and the urban Arab population of the mixed cities. The separation of Arab population centres is in itself a barrier to balanced and comprehensive economic development. Further, the minimal intra-communal market and labour linkages, and the more recent phenomenon of rural-urban migration attest to a more complex internal structure than might otherwise appear to be the case.[26] Ignoring specifically Arab areas of the economy has been an important aspect of the approach of Israeli policy makers and academics keen to demonstrate the success of a (non-existent) policy of integration and equality between Jewish and Arab citizens.

Another axis is the religious composition of Arab society which has also been exploited as a source of blockage to development. The fact that members of the Druze community serve in the military has given them the opportunity to receive preferential treatment in some respects, but has not exempted them from discriminatory treatment in general (for example, in matters related to land expropriation) on account of their not being Jewish. The same holds true, although to a much lesser extent, for certain sectors of the Beduin and the small Circassian communities.

Another issue of relevance is the extent to which state policies of control, co-optation and integration of local elites and traditional leaders have succeeded in fragmenting Arab society along ideological and political lines:[27] groups co-opted into state or Zionist political interests and who actively collaborate in return for favours; those who have been unconsciously co-opted but are indifferent, having abandoned any specifically Arab identity or commitment; and the vast majority who are primarily concerned with the immediate problems of providing basic welfare for their families. As with other obstacles to cohesive development, reactions to this type of social differentiation can also have an unexpected unifying effect as the crude mechanisms of co-optation become increasingly obsolete and ineffective in the face of broader levels of social and political consciousness.

The growing political awareness and organisation of the Arab population and its identification with Palestinian aims and aspirations have shown themselves to be the greatest challenge to the system by which this national minority is ruled. In the sphere of social structure, therefore, the barriers to development also carry the seeds of development.

4. The Arab community and national economic activity

The Arab economy in Israel is naturally most importantly influenced by the national economy. The strengths and weaknesses of the Arab economy follow lines established by the national economy's overall development path and the specific dynamic of the national-communal relationship. The past period of Israeli economic growth has been highlighted by clear structural trends in each of the main economic sectors.[28] They can be construed as barriers to Arab development in so far as they are linked to the interests of national economic goals and predicate the close involvement of state and Jewish institutions as prime guarantors for their achievement.

They can also spur certain innovations and responses in Arab economic patterns which do not necessarily follow those established nationally. In addition to structural economic determinants, there are four aspects of the current Israeli economic policy and conditions which have a central effect on the Arab community. One is related to attempts to cut state expenditure which hits Arabs hardest, whether in terms of social services, state aid to local authorities or infrastructural investment. Though already relatively low, decreased state aid means fewer approvals of town plans and industrial zones, more strict allocations of development zone funds and tighter credit facilities.[29] The continuing economic crisis will lead to greater unemployment and consequently more unemployment of Arabs as they are the most expendable part of the work force.[30] As well as increasing economic hardship this might encourage greater labour mobility (both geographic and occupational/sectoral) thus maintaining relatively low skill development. The high rate of inflation and government austerity measures have already adversely affected the Arab population disproportionately because of existing low income levels and relatively fewer assets and savings upon which to fall back.

The Arab population has had to respond and adapt itself to national trends without seeing most of the benefits of these developments within its own community. The import substituting textile industry, for instance, employs significant numbers of Arab women, but at appallingly low wages and in virtual sweatshop conditions. Palestinian Arabs work in certain of the highly skilled new industrial branches (electronics, for example) without any of those concerns being Arab-owned, managed or located. Arabs have, in principle, had access to agricultural technology and have had to compete with its use in the Jewish sector. They have not, however, been able to make the large investment that successful application of this technology requires. This distorted pattern of sharing in the benefits of national economic development, often associated with a proportionately equal distribution of costs, is yet another illustration of the emerging picture of national communal inequality and in particular, of the conditions under which Arab economic development in Israel must labour.

III. THE STRUCTURE OF THE ARAB ECONOMY IN ISRAEL

I shall examine the Arab economy in Israel through reference to the three issues of greatest concern: the position of the agricultural base between continuing decline and self-generated growth; the three main forms of Arab industrial activity and the role of entrepreneurship; the role of Arab labour in the national economy.

1. Agricultural structure and activity[31]

(i) Land and production

Arab peasants and farmers cultivate a relatively small proportion of the national arable land (18 per cent of the total, or 10 per cent if the dry farmed land in the Negev is included). The total Arab arable area in 1981 was 756,700 dunums, of which almost half is in the Negev. However, Arabs cultivate more intensively than the national level: the Arab cropped area is 96 per cent of arable land compared to the national level of 92 per cent.

Field crops accounted for 68 per cent of the Arab cultivated area in 1981, 13 per cent of the national output, 3 per cent of their value, 2.8 per cent of gross value added and 13 per cent of the total Arab agricultural production. Vegetables and melons were the most significant crops. They took only 10 per cent of the cultivated area but provided 14 per cent of national output of these products, 15 per cent of the value, 15.5 per cent of the national value added and 28 per cent of total Arab agricultural production. Non-citrus plantations accounted for 21 per cent of the Arab cultivated area, 8 per cent of national non-citrus fruit output, 11 per cent of the national branch output and 30 per cent of the value of Arab agricultural production. Arabs cultivate an insignificant proportion of the national citrus output. Livestock, which accounts for 27 per cent of the value of communal agricultural production, is almost entirely concentrated in lamb and goat meat production, with Arabs producing 41 and 82 per cent of national production in those two areas respectively and 40 per cent of the national gross value added in both. Other crops in which the Arab community produces significant quantities are: barley (accounting for 31 per cent of national output and 77 per cent of the national crop area); tobacco (100 per cent and 54 per cent); cucumbers (40 per cent and 44 per cent); marrows (30 per cent and 62 per cent); beets (46 per cent and 46 per cent); strawberries (41 per cent and 66 per cent); melons (35 per cent and 36 per cent); olives (65 per cent and 81 per cent); cabbage and eggplants (combined totals of 16 per cent and 17 per cent).

These figures exhibit the relative significance of certain Arab produce to national agricultural output as compared to their relative importance to the community's economy. They also make clear the volume/value productivity differentials between Arab and national agriculture. Arab agriculture is 24 per cent as productive in value/ dunum terms as national agriculture and 19 per cent as productive in volume/dunum terms. The differential is greatest in field crops (10 per cent and 12 per cent of production respectively), in non-citrus fruit (19 per cent and 21 per cent) and in vegetables and melons (57 per cent and 44 per cent).

Ownership of land is almost entirely private. Only 1 per cent of Arab farm area in 1981 was on 'national land' compared with a figure of 81 per cent for Israel as a whole. Plots are mostly small and fragmented, often to the point of making cultivation uneconomic. Whereas 61 per cent of the national cultivated area is in farms of 500 dunums or more, only 14 per cent of the cultivated Arab area is in farms of that size. And in that same category, the average number of dunums per farm nationally is 3,265, while for Arabs it is 866. Most farming takes place in family units with a certain amount of leasing from Arab and (to a lesser extent) from Jewish owners. Jewish farming is almost totally organised in co-operative or collective production (moshavim and kibbutzim). To date there have been no successful Arab co-operatives. One central reason for this is the exclusion of Arabs from the national Histadrut-affiliated Farmers Union which plays a central role in representing farmers' interests at the national level.

The quality and distribution of the main agricultural production factor, land, is an essential determinant in the performance of Arab agriculture. There are sharp discrepancies in the quality of available arable land between the two main Arab cultivation areas in the central Triangle and the Galilee.[32]

The most detrimental factors determining the quality of land left to Arab cultivators is of course the effect of land expropriations. These have been applied on a wide scale since 1948, have often targeted the best quality land and have left farms divided into disparate plots. Arab inheritance patterns have also affected the distribution of land, lowering the relative size of Arab farms. The average size of Arab farms in 1981 was under 50 dunums of arable land per owner, compared with a figure for Jewish owners of 120. The fragmentation not only reduces the potential for economic farming, but also breaks up the better quality land. The 'hand and foot' inheritance division pattern splits plots between the better and poorer quality land, or divides holdings into long narrow strips. Irrigating a 1,000 by 10 metre strip requires pipes so long as to make the enterprise uneconomic. Problems remain in making the best use of consolidation through capital and technological innovation.

(ii) Water resources and utilisation

Access to national water resources is restricted by the policies of the state water authority.[33] Though it is the source of only 59 per cent of all domestic, industrial and agricultural water,[34] the Israeli Water Commission, Mekorot, is responsible for allocating water quotas from wells, even the private artesian wells which are prevalent in the Triangle.[35] The Triangle has always been more advanced agriculturally and obtained permits to dig wells in the early 1950s, before the authorities began to implement more stringent restrictions on water distribution and storage. Once dug, the Commission measures the capacity of a well and determines how much can be pumped out of it and for what period. Sometimes it will also specify on what crops the water can be used. There are no other significant water sources except for the few springs which do not provide large quantities.

Excluding the Negev, only 16 per cent of Arab cultivated land was irrigated in 1981, compared to 56 per cent nationally.[36] Arab irrigated land makes up only 2.6 per cent of the national total; of this total only 2 per cent is in the Galilee.[37] Arab agriculture consumes only 2.2 per cent of all water supplied to agriculture.[38] Irrigation methods which do exist are generally less sophisticated than those in Jewish agriculture. In general, irrigation is used on crops with high export value. The main system used in Arab villages is the furrow method. Cisterns are also used and water is distributed from them to fruit trees and some vegetable crops. Sprinklers have been introduced, but careful attention must be paid by the user to strength of pump motors, soil type, wind, etc. The most recent innovation, found on a small number of holdings, is drip irrigation.

The value productivity of a unit of water in Arab agriculture was almost double that in the Jewish sector in 1981/2,[39] despite the fact that Arabs possess less than 3 per cent of the capital stock in irrigation equipment.[40] This clearly exhibits an efficiency which goes well beyond anything created by Israeli-sponsored 'modernisation'. While there is nothing unexpected in the state policy of water distribution, Arab expertise in utilising a resource which is even more scarce for them than it is nationally illustrates tenacity and ability.

(iii) Labour, mechanical and chemical inputs

Arab agriculture suffers a technological gap compared to Jewish agriculture because of the high price of chemical and biological inputs. Jewish growers organised in the co-operative sector receive government subsidies for these items. This situation is further aggravated by the need for such inputs to be used in conjunction with the proper equipment and other inputs such as soil and water types, the absence of large-scale holdings on which these inputs can be most efficiently applied, and the lack of a thorough and comprehensive agricultural advice and extension service in the Arab agricultural sector. Arab holdings of agricultural machinery are relatively less than the proportion of land they own: Arabs own only 8 per cent of all self-propelled agricultural machines, of which 92 per cent are wheeled tractors which are mostly used to pull manual implements.[41]

Within the national economy labour is considered a scarce and relatively expensive resource. The crops which have expanded most recently are those most amenable to mechanisation. Labour intensive crops demand close observation and timely attention to detail, which is not compatible with mechanisation. One observer of Israeli agriculture has noted that

> ...family labour on a smallholding is a low-cost and flexible commodity since it is rarely counted and costed very carefully, is available for long periods each day and 'rests' at low cost at other times. Furthermore it tends to become more intimately involved in making a success of a particular crop since the family's standard of living depends directly on it.[42]

Most Arab agricultural wage labour works in Jewish agriculture, though Arab farmers with large units will often hire labour at harvest or ploughing time. In 1981, only 10 per cent of the total man-years worked in Arab agriculture was on other than the labourer's own holding.[43] This is also shown in the annual fluctuation of the proportion of self-employed and family labour on Arab farms, between 55 and 70 per cent in the period 1977 to 1984,[44] while the national average has been constant at just over 60 per cent. These forms of self-employment are obviously the safest and most cost-efficient for Arab farmers given the particular constraints within which they operate. It allows the concentration on the labour intensive crops that Arabs have tended to produce in the past few years. This tendency reflects an Arab preparedness to perform the tedious and menial tasks these crops require, a result of the division of agricultural labour. Of the labour input into national agriculture in 1981, 11 per cent was provided in the Arab sector (i.e. not including Arab labour in Jewish agriculture), while Arabs constituted 16 per cent of the national agricultural labour force.[45]

Arab self-employment also minimises the relative losses incurred from non-mechanisation and less intensive application of chemical and biological inputs as compared to Jewish agriculture. A policy of pursuing the 'comparative advantage' of labour intensification has allowed Arab agriculture to survive absolutely, and to thrive relative to the extent of subsidisation afforded to the Jewish sector. While this has been a sort of safeguard for the continuation of Arab agricultural activity in Israel, it will not necessarily continue to be the case.

(iv) Organisation of processing and marketing

The marketing of Arab agricultural produce is carried out through seasonal contracting to national agencies which set a price growers must usually accept. Whatever surplus remains is sold locally, though this is usually small as there is no organised Arab regional marketing network. This system is not mandatory but farmers deal with these agencies in the absence of any alternative. The absence of Arab-owned cold storage facilities, quality control and other ancillary establishments increases Arab dependence on national agricultural institutions. In certain branches, particularly vegetables, some Arab produce is exported through national export agencies.

Most Israeli agriculture is organised in the co-operative sector and regional groupings linked to Tnuva, the Histadrut-owned national co-operative operating in wholesale, processing and distribution. Tnuva handles some 75 per cent of all farm output: 'With much of the trade monopolised by statutory or quasi-statutory bodies there is little room for alternative channels to become established and growers must, perforce, use the existing facilities.'[46] Though the regulation of agriculture has eased in recent years it is still the rule rather than the exception.[47] The production and marketing boards include representatives of all branches of production and distribution in all regions as well as of consumer interests. The boards advise the government and communicate to growers what they consider the total acreage of particular crops should be, based on an analysis of market preference for varieties, sizes and qualities. Against this background, individual producers make applications to plant new crops.

In the past the process has been co-ordinated by the Ministry of Agriculture and national priorities were used to determine the amount of crops to be planted, by village. The guidelines are now more flexible and growers, including Arabs, are more or less free to plant what they want, except that certain cash crops such as tomatoes, cucumbers and strawberries are subject to acreage quotas. With most other crops farmers know roughly how much they will be able to sell and therefore plant accordingly. However, some branches such as poultry, dairy farming and certain fruit crops have remained closed to Arab farmers through continued state intervention. Determination of export crops is the responsibility of the export company, Agrexco, which is jointly owned by the government and the boards. Agrexco is not always responsible for harvesting decisions as the precise arrangements and degree of prior involvement with the producers vary from crop to crop.

The prerequisite for any successful marketing effort is a quality grading and packing process. Quality control takes place at the producer/owner packing houses and later at export points by Ministry of Agriculture inspectors. Arab farmers deal with their nearest station, usually part of a Jewish settlement, which grades the produce and then distributes the villages' output among the three main markets of Haifa, Jerusalem and Tel Aviv. Arab farmers sometimes grade their produce and take it to the markets themselves.[48]

The boards issue licenses for the movement of wholesale produce to market, with the power to regulate quality standards and prevent price reductions. The need to get a license as a merchant effectively restricts distribution to existing channels, reducing the number of new and competing businesses. In addition to selling to packing houses, some Arab farmers sell to buyers who come to the villages; others occasionally wholesale or retail directly. Recent deregulation measures have enabled farmers in principle to sell their produce wherever they wish.

Prices for locally sold produce are established in the retail markets and in the three main wholesale centres – farmers can sell at any price they can get. Sometimes minimum price guarantees are underwritten by the government. This does not apply to export crops which move through Agrexco. It determines the purchase price before planting and contracts for quantities on a seasonal basis. The farmer can choose to accept the price or not. Prices are set according to dollar rates and are translated to the official price at the time of agreement, offering some protection against the adverse effects of unfavourable currency movements.

The existing market arrangements have succeeded in binding Arab farmers to a market system within which they have no influence, whether through the regulatory agencies or the market. While the statutory nature of these arrangements has loosened recently, this will only lead to further fragmentation and isolation of individual Arab producers within the market. More than any other producers, Arabs are victims of a monopolised market and have little or no leverage. This stage of the agricultural process perhaps plays the greatest role in the expropriation of Arab value added. Data on the change in value added in agriculture between 1971 and 1981 indicate that while national agriculture increased value added by 186.8 index points, Arab agriculture lagged behind at 170.3.[49] The differential was greatest in field crops (362.2 nationally to 157.6 regionally), poultry (108.6 to 53.6) and vegetables (179.4 to 160.9).

(v) Capital and credit

In 1981, Arabs held 6 per cent of the national capital stock in agriculture.[50] The Arab share by type of stock was mainly in fruit orchards (15 per cent of the national total), livestock (12 per cent) and agricultural equipment and machinery (8 per cent). Together, these three types of assets accounted for 88 per cent of all Arab capital stock, with irrigation systems and greenhouses making up most of the rest (the Arab share of these assets was nationally insignificant at just over 2 per cent). In 1981, Arab agriculture contributed 6 per cent of national gross value added in capital stock.[51]

Some of the reasons for this low level of capitalisation have already become evident: if it cannot be effectively applied there is little point in accumulating capital stock. The Arab sector is largely bypassed by development funding that exists for agriculture, because of exclusion from the benefits the Jewish co-operative systems obtain. There are three types of state investment in agriculture:[52] commercial infrastructure – irrigation equipment, roads, co-operative grading, packing and marketing facilities (none of these facilities exist in Arab villages); the building of production units on individual holdings (this favours the kibbutzim and moshavim); some working capital.

Credit can be obtained in the form of seasonal grants from the Ministry of Agriculture through any bank. The criteria for eligibility are the quantity and nature of crops being grown. The interest rates on these credits are usually low. Additionally, development loans are given by the Israel Bank of Agriculture for improvement of irrigation facilities, construction of greenhouses, further development of avocado and grapefruit plantations, livestock breeding and for packing and trans-shipment of export crops. These are obtained from banks upon Ministry of Agriculture approval which is of course crucial: no Arab farmer, for instance, has yet obtained any support for poultry breeding.[53] The same applies to citrus growers and livestock breeders, but only through a very complicated system of application; both are almost exclusively in the domain of the kibbutzim and moshavim. There are also loans available for the drainage of lands which have a natural outlet but need some slight improvement such as levelling to facilitate drainage.

The production of intensive crops for export is highly capitalised. Through the supervised credit scheme (initiated by the Bank of Agriculture), the central authority exercises a virtually controlling influence over this type of development. Grants and loans on favourable terms are only available for projects 'approved' through a complicated procedure. Therefore, given the existing limited Arab capital accumulation in agriculture and the difficulty in obtaining state support, the Arab farmer has little recourse to increased capitalisation via the state. Until now, this has not proved too great a problem, in view of Arab agriculture's labour-intensive bias. This situation is one that is forced on Arab agriculture, however, and not one of choice.

2. Industrial-commercial-financial structure

(i) State industrial development policy[54]

Despite the virtual absence of any development-oriented activities in the Arab sector, state industrial and business development policy has an important influence in defining the scope of Arab economic activity. This is the case not only for the reasons discussed earlier but because of the specific Arab business and industrial forms that have evolved in the absence of state involvement. The relatively high profile of private Jewish capital in Arab areas is a significant part of the resultant structure. Here, however, it will be sufficient to outline the way in which state policy promotes an urban Arab productive and service structure with its particular rigidities and flexibilities.

The Law for the Encouragement of Capital Investment emphasises the need to increase employment in development areas and raise foreign currency earnings through exports and tourism. There are three development zones of different priority which are eligible for benefits depending on the content and aim of specific projects. An approved project can obtain the status of any of the following: approved enterprise; recognised enterprise; approved investment; approved loan; approved property. Areas covered by the law include industry, tourism, construction and real estate. Theoretically, an approved project in the top priority zone needs to provide only 25 per cent of the fixed asset investment to start out and can obtain soft loans on 40 per cent and government grants on the rest, with several years' subsidised operation to follow.

There is nothing in this law or in overall industrial investment policy guidelines which explicitly or otherwise excludes Arabs from benefits. Discrimination can, however, occur as a result of a conscious policy decision to refuse to approve even the most eligible Arab project if it is deemed politically necessary; ultimately the investment centre, which decides on all projects, has complete discretion in the matter. However, the 'A' development zone comprises some 28 Arab localities with a population of 66,000 and the 'B' zone 47 localities with 104,600 inhabitants.[55] Together these 75 localities in the top priority zones contain almost 60 per cent of the rural Arab population. There is little evidence that they have benefited at all from their presence in a development zone.

The other important aspect of industrial/business policy originating in state and affiliated bodies is that of the Histadrut which regularly assumes some moral responsibility for the encouragement of Arab development. Its 1983 Congress, for instance, passed a lengthy resolution highlighting the importance of the Arab regional activities of the Histadrut banking and marketing agencies and the need for intensification of the activity of the Histadrut holding company, Hevrat Ovdim, in Arab communities. These activities were aimed at 'establishment of industrial plants in Arab and Druze (sic) villages... and expansion of services provided by Hevrat Ovdim companies in the Arab sector'.[56] Specifically, Hevrat Ovdim was instructed to

> attempt to influence the government to provide the status of development region to industrial zones in the Arab and Druze villages and to prepare an industrial base inside these villages...such ventures to be carried out along with Arab and Druze workers, investors and initiators...Hevrat Ovdim will also work to absorb...a group of academics and skilled Arab and Druze workers and elaborate a plan for administration and the social training of this group to make them qualified to play a role in the industrialisation of the Arab and Druze villages.[57]

The initial results of the new strategy were given prominence by Hevrat Ovdim sources in 1984 with the implementation of a field survey of existing Arab industrial potential, the co-optation of sympathetic Arab elements, establishment of its first Arab-area based joint industrial venture and discrete efforts at establishing partnerships with Arab businessmen while also encouraging private Jewish capital towards the same.

(ii) Strength of national capital penetration

While public sector capital is not invested in Arab projects, there has been an increasing level of Jewish private capital deployment in the region, in addition to the Histadrut initiative. This private initiative arises partly out of the open field for cheap labour exploitation created by the absence of a state development policy and an untapped and flexible labour market. It is also a natural function of the private sector (primarily the textile industry) aiming to reap superprofits in an era when the highest growth is promised in the new, capital intensive industries.

The form of penetration has mostly been of a subcontracting nature, transferring labour intensive stages of the labour process to areas where abundant and cheap female labour can easily be mobilised. It has either involved establishment of wholly Jewish owned subsidiaries or joint ventures with local subcontractors. As a result, of the 410 industrial plants said by Hevrat Ovdim to exist in the Arab region in 1983, 16 per cent were non-locally owned.[58] This is not an especially high proportion and the figures do not exist to show how much of the Arab labour force was employed in these enterprises and which industries are non-Arab owned. It can be assumed, however, that they are likely to be those with a direct link to the Jewish economy: textiles/clothing, food processing, chemicals and plastics and possibly some jewellery/ornament plants. As it is doubtful that private investment would be made in small-scale units in any of these branches it is likely that most of the non-locally owned factories are larger scale (which means in this framework that they employ more than 10 workers). Given the predominantly small-scale nature of Arab industry, a substantial part of the larger units are therefore likely to be non-locally owned.

While direct Jewish control and the extraction of value added was predominant in the past decade, recently new patterns of the co-optation of local capital into private Jewish investments have begun to emerge. One example is the reported agreement between Jewish and Arab venture capitalists to build a factory for the production of prefabricated industrial buildings, with an initial capital of US$ 2 million split on an equal basis.[59] The preference for this joint investment might reflect Jewish hesitation about new substantial commitments in the Arab areas, especially in the prevailing recession. But it is also a function of the needs for the expansion of Arab commercial capital into continuously profitable spheres.

Histadrut-sponsored projects in industry, banking and marketing complement this private sector thrust into the Arab area. The new 'Company for the Development and Industrialisation of the Arab and Druze Sector', launched in 1983/4 under Jewish management and with Arab collaboration, has initiated 'a number of projects based on joint Hevrat Ovdim and Arab funding... among them a tehina factory in Um al-Fahm at a cost of US$ 300,000'.[60] This much heralded factory, employing 20 workers and under local Arab management is a fifty-fifty joint venture and may indicate a pattern for future investment. To date, that is the only reported industrial enterprise launched under this initiative; the present economic conditions in Israel have apparently slowed the momentum of the drive. Five supermarkets are planned for Arab areas in the near future with a total capital investment of US$ 3.5 million, serving a population of 130,000 and employing 300 workers.

This new Histadrut approach, despite the potential for furthering dependent Arab integration into the national economy, should be viewed in relation to the degree of Histadrut activity in the Jewish sector.[61] In 1982, of the 14 large supermarkets (Hamashbir) in the Galilee (an area approximately 50 per cent Arab), only one supermarket was in an Arab locality; of the 20 Hapoalim banks only three were in Arab towns. And while the Hevrat Ovdim had established 73 industrial projects in the region by 1982, none were in Arab localities.

The penetration of the Arab sector by Jewish public and private capital, small and reluctant as it is, has its negative consequences. It strengthens the pattern of enforced dependent integration of Arab capital and productive capacity into national projects, when and if expedient. On another level, the expansion of large-scale Jewish marketing can seriously threaten the livelihood of traditional Arab commercial sectors without offering alternative sources of work or security (except perhaps as supermarket employees). And the establishment of partially Jewish financed medium-to-large scale enterprises in traditional Arab production branches tends to squeeze out the remaining smaller scale Arab producers in those fields.

(iii) Industrial mix, structure and scale

Textile/clothing and construction material manufacture dominate the Arab industrial scene.[62] The other two branches where there is a proliferation of small, often self-employed production units are wood and metal working. There is a problem in grouping within the same figures self-employed production units and those larger scale production processes which involve greater application of fixed and variable capital (such as clothes factories, cement or tile factories and heavy metal works).

If we differentiate between units with one self-employed operator and those with at least one employee, the situation becomes clearer. The first group includes some 200 units, all in the carpentry and metal working branches, producing primarily for local individual customers, but also undertaking subcontracting orders for larger Arab or Jewish concerns in the same or complementary branches (especially construction). The second group is dominated by clothing and construction materials manufacture, but also contains some large metal and wood working plants. There are smaller proportions of plants producing food, plastics and chemicals and paper and printing materials. Forty per cent of the plants in this group employed over ten workers, 31 per cent employed between five and nine and 29 per cent between one and four.

This group (food, plastics, chemicals etc.) employed over 8,000 workers in 1983, constituting some 30 per cent of the Arab industrial labour force.[63] Seventy-one per cent of those locally employed were women, mainly in the textile and clothing branches, the branches which also had the highest levels of Jewish capital penetration. It can therefore be assumed that a majority of Arab industrial workers are employed directly or indirectly by Jewish capital.

The prevailing industrial mix is determined by two factors: the extent of public and private Jewish capital penetration and the remaining scope for individual Arab business initiative which prevailing skill levels and capital ownership permit. In a few individual cases, Arab entrepreneurs have succeeded in combining these two factors and have expanded their industries (for example, metal work and stone cutting) through linking to Jewish capital and markets. The main market for Arab industrial production is Jewish, except at the extremes of the scale. The smallest producers' output is consumed locally and the largest concerns sell both to the sectoral and national markets. There is nothing in the actual distribution of capital investment between branches that is in itself an obstacle to growth. Despite much fascination with capital intensity and technological processes in Israel and elsewhere, there is no clear evidence that more traditional, labour-intensive processes have less value adding capacity. On the contrary, some recent analyses of industry in the occupied territories indicate the opposite.[64]

(iv) Arab industrial/business outlook and practice[65]

The level of Arab entrepreneurial activity is influenced by the constraints imposed by Jewish capital penetration, the market and resource options open to business initiation and existing patterns of capital accumulation. These barriers have an effect at all levels of activity. Their perpetuation is primarily a function of the segmentation of Arab society, the isolation and individualisation of enterprises and the minimal business experience that has been acquired (except on the most specific and local of levels).

On their particular level and within their different horizons, the strata of self-employed craftspeople and artisans, industrialists, traders and other entrepreneurs naturally have their own goals and strategies. However, in most economies, these different initiators have an overall common interest and even a common consciousness. Indeed, the existence of professional associations, chambers of commerce and specific sectorally oriented business services testifies to this. In addition to sharing a common interest, the components of the business sector in any country have, at different stages and in different ways, a common strategy with regard to relations with consumers, government, labour, financial sources, trading partners and so forth.

Israel is no exception to this pattern, but its Arab business sector is. It might be argued by proponents of state policy that small-scale businesses, Arab or Jewish, have common goals while larger concerns have theirs. But this is fallacious since all elements of the Arab business sector, even to an extent the co-opted ones, are dealt with by Jewish public and private capital as the 'Arab sector'. Furthermore, our analysis has shown a distinctly Arab pattern of industrial and business formation, with only a few exceptions, that has very little in common with any existing Jewish patterns. The metal and wood working, sewing and building businesses and even the car maintenance garages of the Arab region share wider similarities with their counterparts in the occupied territories much more than with those in the Jewish sector.

The absence of common Arab industrial goals and strategies encompasses two more specific weaknesses in the pattern of industrial activity. On the one hand, it is only very recently that the possibilities of intra-entrepreneurial integration have been raised. So far, this has been on the level of horizontal links between wealthy capitalists and businesspeople, with an eye to establishing a joint venture Arab commercial project. There does not appear to have been any general emergence of an Arab business/industrial 'class consciousness'. This leads to the second consequence of the absence of a sectoral strategy. There have been no attempts to date within the Arab business community to identify and mobilise potential intra-sectoral or inter-sectoral linkages, an important characteristic of Israeli economic structure and activity. The whole sphere of subcontracting within the clothing industry and, to a lesser extent, wood and metal working trades is a practice essential to the dynamic of Jewish involvement. Examples exist of such methods, for instance, in the construction sector, where builders subcontract out doors and window frames to local craftspeople. This practice, however, has not been the result of a clear strategy to cut costs most efficiently and raise profit margins. Nor has there been any significant attempt to invest in food processing industries (except in the case of olive oil and some dairy produce) which would have an assured Arab source of supply. The absence of intra- and inter-sectoral linkages not only helps to maintain the fragmentation of Arab producing power nationally, but also restricts entrepreneurial contact and mutual learning and accumulation of comprehensive experience in production and marketing techniques. Most importantly, it slows potential expansion of the sector as a whole which remains dependent on existing and established sources of materials and lines of marketing.

There are other weaknesses apparent in the path of Arab industrial growth. These include the low level of management and administrative expertise, insufficient absorption and utilisation of new technologies (even simple ones), a reluctance to invest and tie up liquid commercial capital in productive spheres, and the virtual absence of any inclination to export or benefit from Israeli strength in the science-based industrial sector. None of these is necessarily the 'correct' thing for the Arab industrial sector to be doing. The Arab sector does not lack the potential, required experience, capital, technical expertise, labour or social structure to ameliorate these conditions of business activity. It has, however, until now lacked the institutionalisation and co-ordination of its accumulated resources and experience that could more efficiently and successfully mobilise that potential to the benefit of entrepreneurs and labour alike.[66]

(v) Financial patterns: constraints and new formations

Traditionally, private Arab savings have been low, because of low incomes, and directed to residential building, real estate, occasional small commercial ventures and conspicuous consumption. The use of savings to improve basic living standards through, for instance, the purchase of consumer durables, is not uncommon. Nor is the need to compensate for the absence of state subsidies on land and residential construction by investing in home building. Any remaining savings are not deployed in business ventures either because of traditional fear of risk among the older generation which largely possesses this capital, or simply because of the serious lack of opportunities within the Arab business sector.[67] It is safer and easier to leave savings in a bank in long term deposits, to lend it locally, or even to put it into stock market speculation than to invest in a weak, informal and disorganised Arab industrial and business sector.

Income, expenditure and savings figures for 1979/80 show some of the disparities between Jewish and Arab households.[68] Average national income is 1.4 times that of the average Arab household, national consumption expenditure is 1.5 times Arab consumption expenditure, national taxation levels are almost double and national savings seven times that of the Arab household savings. In fact, Arab households dissave by over 1 per cent of their monthly income. It should be remembered here that average Arab households are significantly larger than the national. This helps explain the fact that 84 per cent of monthly Arab income goes to consumption expenditure and 19 per cent to non-consumption expenditure (taxation and transfers).

While the 'average' Arab household will not be the usual industrial or business investor, these figures highlight the narrow capital base which exists in the Arab community. The main examples of substantial Arab capital accumulation are found not in private family savings patterns but in the instances of individual entrepreneurs who amassed wealth (industrial, marketing or other business) through inheritance, land originating capital, or through collaboration with and deployment of Jewish capital. Successful examples of the independent path of Arab industrial investment and production are few and far between: they too either benefited from a specific Israeli market (such as the Kadamani metal works contracts with the Ministry of Defence) or through a specific advantage in raw material or skills (such as that held by the Boulos marble and granite works).

(vi) Private and institutional entrepreneurship and initiative

Without recourse to the extensive theoretical literature on entrepreneurship, and with the limited data at hand, an initial profile of Arab entrepreneurial types in Israel can be drawn. It serves the purpose of better classifying existing groups which have undertaken economic initiatives of some sort. The specific nature of Arab entrepreneurship, not even common in the West Bank or Gaza Strip experience, is rooted in the historical circumstances of its evolution. In fact, it is significant that it is even possible to talk of Arab entrepreneurs in Israel in light of the fact that they almost all arose from nothing.

The expulsion of the bulk of Palestine's industrial and commercial elite and the isolation of the rest outside the reach of Arabs in Israel had a devastating effect on social and economic structures. The work process of mobile labour within the Israeli economy, though a hard path, laid the foundations for the emergence of individual entrepreneurial experiences. Increasingly, Arab contractors and subcontractors develop their own contacts, directly initiate employment, are equipped to finance and compete, refuse to accept cut-rate work, have their own means of production and long experience in product handling and holding market concessions.[69]

The most obvious, somewhat traditional, form of Arab entrepreneurship is that of the few large capitalists and businessmen. They are active in commerce, industry and agriculture as wholesalers, commercial agents holding concessions, large-scale industrialists and modern capitalist farmers and landowners (especially in the Triangle). This form of entrepreneurship is defined primarily by the combination of its own inherited or accumulated wealth (originating, for example, in real estate or land) with a working relation with the state and Jewish capitalist concerns. This relation usually involves investment by the latter in the form of capital, management and technical expertise or distribution networks; otherwise, legal and political facilities or cover is provided in return for political collaboration and support. The relation of this group to its capital is individual and personal and rarely through the intermediary of a large limited share company or other institutional arrangement. Even when this exists (as with the Boulos enterprises), the personal stake in the concern is considerable.

A second entrepreneurial stratum can be discerned in the widespread practices of smaller scale intermediation between Jewish (and sometimes big Arab) capital and Arab consumers and labour. This group is active primarily in commerce, wholesaling on a small scale and retailing in an attempt to fill the gaps in distribution linkages in the Arab community and between it and the Jewish economy. It engages as well in regional subcontracting in industry, through own-production, others' production or providing labour for Jewish capital. This group of entrepreneurs also works in providing labour for export from Arab to Jewish concerns outside, along with Jewish labour contractors and enters financial spheres, engaging in illicit and exploitative usury, drawing on its readily available liquidity. They might have links with the first group, in a mediatory role with other entrepreneurs. This group has an aggressive and ambitious view of its potential, always seeking new ways to make a quick and substantial profit at minimal risk. This is arguably the most parasitic and dependent form of entrepreneurial activity within the Arab community.

The third type is that of the smallest scale, usually (but not always) self-employed entrepreneurs in agriculture, industry, construction or commerce. This group includes individual craftspeople and artisans, small construction contractors and small consumer goods retailers, of the so-called workshop economy. They also provide professional, community and private services or production. The outlook of this group is limited, with little confidence in their ability to expand or break out of established productive routines, though they are not averse to doing so if the means are made available. It is capable of initiative and development of new skills and techniques, but operates under too many constraints to be able to afford the time and financial expense.

There also exist three types of local institutions which play key roles in development in the Arab economy.[70] Those with the greatest interest in economic development are probably the Arab co-operative societies, though the scope of their interests is very localised. The vast majority either provide drinking water or irrigation water to more remote localities, while others provide electricity and other infrastructural services such as housing and transport. There are only a few consumer and credit co-operatives and a small number of general agricultural and marketing co-operatives. Secondly, Arab local authorities, though not even having the resources to cater for the basic infrastructural needs of the inhabitants they serve, have a degree of jurisdiction in economic development areas. The third and final category of institutions involved in development is the range of more informal local or regional interest groups which bring together people of a similar profession, area, religion or interest. They are usually voluntary bodies with minimal organisational capacities and material resources. Their primary strength lies in their ability to highlight a seriously perceived public need and possibly to mobilise popular pressure.

Each of these three types suffers from its own problems and weaknesses or is legally or institutionally bound to state and affiliated interests; none has explicit strategies for their own development, much less for the Arab community as a whole.

3. Arab labour in Israel: its contribution to national growth[71]

Despite the higher proportion of the Arab population aged 14 years and over, the Arab rate of participation in the labour force is significantly lower than the Jewish rate: 39 per cent compared to 52 per cent. This is due to the relatively low participation of Arab women. However, the trend of greater Arab participation in labour has meant a rising overall Arab rate in the labour force.[72] Generally, unemployment is more prevalent among Arabs and hits them harder than Jews. The national rise in the number of unemployed between 1979 and 1984 of 131 per cent (from a rate of 2.9 per cent to 5.9 per cent) was mostly borne by the Arab sector. The number of unemployed Arabs rose three-fold (from a rate of 2 per cent to 6.6 per cent). Arabs formed 12 per cent of the labour force but a higher proportion of the unemployed in 1984.

The sectoral composition of the employed Arab labour force has changed radically since 1948. Agricultural employment declined to 15 per cent of the work force by 1980[73] and to only 9 per cent by 1984. Construction absorbed increasingly more Arab employees, its share having risen from 19.5 to 21 per cent in the same period. Industry, electricity and water accounted for 21 per cent of those employed in 1980. There was a small decline in employment in these areas in 1982 (20 per cent of the total employed), but by 1984 they were the largest overall employers taking 22 per cent of the Arab work force. Public service employment consistently rose until 1982, since when it has been on the decline, largely reflecting public sector cutbacks in the Arab sector. At the same time personal service sector employment was on the decline until 1982; subsequently it has started to grow again. A notable development has been the rise in the share of commerce in total Arab employment; up from 10 per cent in 1980 to 13.5 per cent in 1982, a level it has maintained since. Public services and industry absorbed the greatest proportion of labour in 1984 (26 per cent and 21 per cent respectively), commerce maintained its share at between 11 and 12 per cent, while agriculture and construction continued to decline and are currently the smallest sectors (approximately 5 per cent each).

More recently available figures indicate that labour leaving agriculture has gone mainly to industry and construction. Over the period 1978 to 1984, industry and construction were the two sectors which lost the most labour to other sectors and seemed to have the largest labour turnover. The sector with the greatest stability of tenure was public services, while transport, commerce and finance all contained in 1983 the greatest proportions of workers who had previously been employed in other sectors. These trends among Arab workers contrast with the structure of the national labour force.

The occupational characteristics of Arab labour reflect its position as a largely manual, low skilled production force. While 27 per cent of employed Arabs are in the academic, professional, administrative, clerical and sales (the so-called white collar) categories, over 57 per cent of Jews are in those occupational levels. Though 62 per cent of employed Arabs are production workers, the corresponding national proportion is 30 per cent. The proportion of skilled workers is 40 per cent among Arabs, as compared to a national level of 23 per cent. The trend has, at times, been towards a narrowing of these differentials, but in recent years there has been increased divergence.

There is startling new evidence of a 'de-skilling' process at work in the Arab labour force. Of the 9,900 unskilled production workers in 1983, almost 10 per cent had been classified as skilled in 1978. Of the 27,900 skilled workers in 1983, only 4 per cent had been unskilled in 1978. A large proportion of service workers (8 per cent) and sales workers (10 per cent) in 1983 had been skilled production workers in 1978. Those two occupational categories had by 1983 also absorbed significant proportions of 1978 unskilled production workers. On the whole, there appears to be minimal occupational mobility from the 'blue collar' to the 'white collar' categories except to the sales and service sectors, which in the case of the Arab labour force are mostly manual labour processes anyhow.

Arabs' status at work as employees does not differ significantly from the national proportion (77 and 79 per cent respectively in 1982). However, the proportion of Arabs who are employees has been rising due to a drop in self-employment and unpaid family labour, primarily in the declining agricultural sector. The number thus employed in agriculture fell from 12,000 in 1969/70 to 8,000 in 1983/4. An important and striking feature of Arab labour in Israel is its high level of mobility: in 1984, 53 per cent of employed Arabs worked away from their place of residence. This proportion has fluctuated between 54 and 45 per cent since the 1970s, increasing in times of economic recession and with the decline in local employment opportunities. This is a phenomenon which is almost non-existent in Jewish localities and is indicative of the Arab economy's crucial role in fuelling Israeli economic development.

V. CONCLUSIONS

The future prospects for the Arab economy in Israel cannot be clearly outlined. The range of features which constitute that economy can be interpreted both as incentives and barriers to growth. However, these are not static features and each year witnesses changes in established trends or accentuations of their path. While these factors might have contributed to the establishment of an unequal relationship between the Arab and the national economies, their dissolution or weakening could reverse existing patterns and trends.

For example, a change in state resource distribution, an alleviation of political grievances that have provided a focus for crystallisation of the Palestinian Arab identity, continued convergence of demographic trends, the breakdown of patterns of geographic and residential segregation (e.g. through the Arab population spilling over into Jewish areas or the successful 'Judaisation of the Galilee') are all developments which would decrease divergences. Additionally, the effect of the various barriers to autonomous development remains formidable and the established patterns of integration and subservience attest to the success of national policy. In this case, future growth could well maintain its current path of distorted national patterns and prerequisites.

On the other hand, increased Arab success in agricultural innovation, more aggressive and innovative entrepreneurship, or the beginnings of significant private Arab capital accumulation and investment would help the emergence of a more pronounced Arab economic profile in Israel. As regards growth prospects in the light of these possibilities, the relative homogeneity of sources and modes of production, consumption and income, the localisation of economic activity and the response to external factors, especially state policy, provide the basis for the crystallisation of internal dynamics of growth.

NOTES

1. The terminology used in the description of the different national groups in Israel is highly contentious and often confusing. Israeli officials often refer to the Arab population as 'Israeli Arabs'; official statistics refer to 'non-Jews'; the population itself would, by and large, refer to itself as Palestinian Arab, or simply Palestinian. The use here of 'Arabs' should be understood as referring to 'Palestinian Arabs', but this usage should not be understood as implying any specific political opinion. Similarly, the use of the term 'Jews' refers to 'Israeli Jews'. In official terminology these can be Jewish citizens of the State of Israel or any of the various permanent resident categories.

2. These issues are discussed in depth in R. Khalidi, *The Arab Economy in Israel: Dynamics of a Region's Development* (Croom Helm, London, 1988), chapter 1.

3. Central Bureau of Statistics, *Statistical Abstract of Israel*, 1985 (Central Bureau of Statistics, Jerusalem, 1985), pp. 32,52,703. This, the only comprehensive statistical source available, includes East Jerusalem and the Golan Heights populations in all figures for non-Jews and legally and administratively these territories occupied by Israel in 1967 are treated as part of the state. Therefore, however unfortunately, it is impossible to avoid inclusion of these areas in our discussion of the Palestinian Arabs in Israel.

Data from here on include East Jerusalem unless otherwise stated.

4. See also K. Nakhleh, 'Anthropological and sociological studies of the Arabs in Israel: A critique', *Journal of Palestine Studies*, vol. 6, no. 24 (1977), pp. 41-70.

5. United Nations Economic Commission for Western Asia, *Summary of the Final Report on the Economic and Social Situation and Potential of the Palestinian Arab People in the Region of Western Asia* (UNECWA, Baghdad, 1985), p. 25.

6. See, for example, I. Lustick, *Arabs in the Jewish State: Israel's Control of a National Minority* (University of Texas, Austin, 1980), chapter 7; M. Tessler, *Arabs in Israel* (American Universities Field Staff Reports, Hanover, 1980), pp. 13-24; K. Nakhleh, *The Two Galilees* (Association of Arab University Graduates, Belmont, 1982), pp. 3-9.

7. Khalidi, *The Arab Economy in Israel*, chapter 1.

8. Central Bureau of Statistics, *Statistical Abstract of Israel*, 1985, p. 32.

9. Unless otherwise indicated all figures in this section on demographic and geographic indicators are derived from the results of the 1983 Census of Population and Housing which can be found in Central Bureau of Statistics, *Statistical Abstract of Israel*, 1985, pp. 32-79.

10. Central Bureau of Statistics, *Agricultural and Rural Census, 1981 - Provisional Results* (Central Bureau of Statistics, Jerusalem, 1983), pp. 208-96.

11. The second largest Arab locality, Um al-Fahm, only received municipal status in 1985 and is the first Arab municipality to come into existence since the establishment of the State of Israel. The other two, Nazareth and Shafa 'Amr, have been municipalities since Palestine was in the Ottoman Empire.

12. Figures in Central Bureau of Statistics, *Statistical Abstract of Israel*, 1985, pp. 56-7, indicate that only 4 per cent of the Arab population were living in another locality in 1978, compared to 13 per cent of the Jewish population. As regards the relatively small Arab inter-district migration balance, they indicate that the Northern District (especially the Nazareth area) was the main source of migration, while the Haifa, Hadera and Beer Sheba sub-districts absorbed most of the Arab migration flow between 1978 and 1983. As regards the type of localities affected by Arab population movements, it can be seen that there was a negative balance in the rural localities (under 2,000 inhabitants) and the Arab urban localities (Nazareth and/or Um al-Fahm) and/or the mixed cities and a positive migration balance especially in the 'small urban' localities (2,000-9,999 inhabitants) but also in Haifa and Tel Aviv/Jaffa.

13. H. Rosenfeld, 'The class situation of the Arab national minority in Israel', *Comparative Studies in Society and History*, no. 20 (July 1978), p. 389.

14. R. Kislev, 'Land expropriations: history of oppression', *New Outlook* (September/October, 1976), pp. 27-32; S. Jiryis, 'Legal structure for the expropriation and absorption of Arab lands in Israel', *Journal of Palestine Studies*, vol. 2, no. 8 (Summer 1973), pp. 82-104; Lustick, *Arabs in the Jewish State.*

15. B. Abu Kishk, 'Arab land and Israeli policy', *Journal of Palestine Studies*, vol. 11, no. 1 (Autumn 1981), pp. 125 and 128.

16. Lustick, *Arabs in the Jewish State*, pp. 196-7; B. Abu Kishk, *al-aradi fi al-wasat al-'arabi: ahdaf isti'maluha wa-al-mashakil allati ta'uq*

tatawwuraha (Land in the Arab sector: the aims of its use and the problems blocking development) (The Popular Council for Social Renewal, Arab Affairs Department, Nazareth, 1976); M. Bayadsi, 'The Arab local authorities: achievements and problems', *New Outlook*, vol. 18 (October/November, 1975) pp. 58-61; Jerusalem Post, 20 December 1985.

17. See for example, W. Lehn, 'The Jewish National Fund', *Journal of Palestine Studies*, vol. 3, no. 4 (1974), pp. 74-96.

18. N. Makhoul, 'Employment structure of the Arabs in Israel', *Journal of Palestine Studies*, vol. 11, no. 43 (Spring 1982), pp. 107-115; G. Waschitz, 'Commuters and entrepreneurs', *New Outlook*, vol. 18, no. 7 (October/November 1975), pp. 45-9; E. Farjoun, 'Palestinian workers in Israel - a reserve army of labour', *Khamsin*, no. 7, pp. 120-2.

19. Y. Ben Porath, *The Arab Labour Force in Israel* (Maurice Falk Institute, Jerusalem, 1966).

20. Abu Kishk, *al-aradi fi al-wasat al-'arabi.*

21. This was highlighted in the results of a sample survey of two Arab farming localities, Jatt in the Triangle and Shafa 'Amr in the Galilee, conducted in 1985 by R. Khalidi and Z. Sabbagh, 'Survey of agriculture in two Arab villages', (unpublished), in which the highest proportion of farmers complained about the restriction of irrigation water quotas of 500 cubic metres/dunum as opposed to the higher quotas given to Jewish settlements.

22. A decision to admit Arabs to the Histadrut-sponsored National Farmers Union was only taken at the Histadrut convention in 1985; it will be four years before the decision takes effect.

23. Lustick, *Arabs in the Jewish State*, pp. 188-9.

24. R. Weimer, 'Zionism and the Arabs after the establishment of the State of Israel' in A. Scholch (ed.), *Palestinians Over the Green Line* (Ithaca Press, London, 1983).

25. Ibid., p. 58.

26. It has not been possible fully to benefit from the interesting work recently conducted on industrialism and entrepreneurship in the Arab region by D. Czamanski and M. Meyer-Brodnitz, 'Industrialisation in Arab villages in Israel', draft in R. Bar-El (ed.), *Industrialisation in Rural Israel* (forthcoming). In their contribution, they have analysed the Hevrat Ovdim data in industrialisation, in the light of past state development efforts and relevant theories of entrepreneurship.

27. Lustick, *Arabs in the Jewish State*, chapter 6.

28. A source of regular, authoritative and up-to-date information on Israeli economic and technological developments and events can be found in the monthly *Israel Economist*.

29. Regional Committee of Arab Local Councils, which groups all Arab municipalities and local councils, undertook several strikes commencing in late 1985 to protest against the failure of the government to award them the US$ 6 million due them as state grants (see *Jerusalem Post*, November and December 1985).

30. Y. Arnon and M. Raviv, *From Fellah to Farmer: A Study of Change in Arab Villages* (Settlement Studies Centre, Rehovot, 1980), pp. 14-5 and 26.

31. Unless otherwise mentioned, agricultural data refer to the agricultural year 1980/1, the year for which the fullest data are available from Central Bureau of Statistics, *Agricultural and Rural Census 1981*. Data on area are

calculated from the same source; data on volume and value are from Central Bureau of Statistics, *Statistical Abstract of Israel*, 1983 (Central Bureau of Statistics, Jerusalem, 1983), pp. 419-21; data on value added are from Central Bureau of Statistics, *Statistical Abstract of Israel*, 1985, pp. 412-15.

32. B. Abu Kishk, interview with the author, London, 1985.

33. U. Davis, *Comparative Study of Land, Labour and Citizenship Control in Israel, South Africa* (UN International Conference on the Question of Palestine, Paris, 1983).

34. Central Bureau of Statistics, *Statistical Abstract of Israel, 1985*, p. 452.

35. According to Abu Kishk in an interview with the author, London, 1985.

36. Central Bureau of Statistics, *Agricultural and Rural Census 1981*.

37. Ibid.

38. Central Bureau of Statistics, *Statistical Abstract of Israel*, 1985, p. 452.

39. Ibid., 1983, pp. 414-7, 419.

40. Central Bureau of Statistics, *Statistical Abstract of Israel*, 1984 (Central Bureau of Statistics, Jerusalem, 1984), p. 422.

41. Calculated from Central Bureau of Statistics, *Agricultural and Rural Census 1981*.

42. A.R. Hunt, *Production of Fruits and Vegetables in Israel* (Anglo-Israel Association, London, 1974), p. 17; see Amon and Raviv, *From Fellah to Farmer*, for further details on labour input.

43. Central Bureau of Statistics, *Statistical Abstract of Israel*, 1985, pp. 414-5.

44. Ibid., p. 398.

45. Ibid., p. 414.

46. Hunt, *Production of Fruits and Vegetables*, p. 20.

47. Ibid.; Abu Kishk interview with the author, 1985.

48. Abu Kishk interview 1985.

49. Central Bureau of Statistics, *Statistical Abstract of Israel*, 1985, op. cit. pp. 412-3.

50. Ibid., 1984, p. 422.

51. Ibid., 1985, pp. 412-3.

52. A. Szeskin, 'The rational way to use capital in Israel', *Agriculture in Israel* (Summer, 1979), pp. 29-45.

53. B. Abu Kishk interview with the author, 1985.

54. See Bank Leumi Ltd, International Consultants Guide, *Trade and Investment in Israel: A Businessman's Guide* (Bank Leumi, Tel Aviv, 1979); *Israel Economist*, 1981; K. Keim, *Overseas Business Reports: Marketing in Israel - No. OBR 80-24* (Department of Commerce, Washington D.C., 1981).

55. Calculated from Central Bureau of Statistics, *Agricultural and Rural Census 1981* and Bank Leumi Ltd, *Trade and Investment in Israel*.

56. Hevrat Ovdim Council, *Resolutions* (Hevrat Ovdim, Tel Aviv, 1982).

57. Ibid.

58. D. Czamanski et al., *Employment Potential of University Graduates in the Arab Localities in Israel* (Technion Centre for Research of City and Region, Haifa, 1984).

59. R. Jobran, 'The Arabs in Israel: their demographical and economical structure and entrepreneurial activities' (unpublished), p. 7.

60. Ibid.

61. Hevrat Ovdim, *Resolutions*.

62. Czamanski et al., *Employment Potential*.

63. Central Bureau of Statistics, *Statistical Abstract of Israel,* 1984, p. 350.

64. Mattin, untitled, (unpublished, Ramallah, 1985).

65. See note 26.

66. A field survey of Arab entrepreneurs, businesspeople and industrialists conducted in 1984, R. Khalidi, 'Survey of business projects and potential in the Arab region in Israel' (unpublished, 1985) reveals an apparently high level of motivation and initiative to innovate as well as a pronounced local/regional understanding of their position and role. However, there are no strong indications of a view towards common pooling of efforts and resources in any formal manner, except at the level of large-scale industrialists and businesspeople. Another sample survey conducted in 1984/5 of industry in Um al-Fahm and Nazareth, R. Khalidi and Z. Sabbagh, 'Survey of industrial enterprises in Nazareth and Um al-Fahm' (unpublished, 1985), confirmed that small-scale industries had a fairly narrow and local scope of activity, in terms of capital equipment and raw material sources, markets and labour inputs.

67. Arnon and Raviv, *From Fellah to Farmer*, p. 223.

68. Central Bureau of Statistics, *Statistical Abstract of Israel*, 1981 (Central Bureau of Statistics, Jerusalem, 1981).

69. Rosenfeld, 'The class situation of the Arab minority', p. 399.

70. See also G. Weigart, 'The Arab co-operative movement in Israel', *Kidma*, vol. 4, no. 3 (September-December 1977), pp. 29-33; Bayadsi, 'The Arab local authorities'.

71. Figures in this section, unless otherwise stated, were calculated from Central Bureau of Statistics, *Statistical Abstract of Israel*, 1985, chapter 12 and Central Bureau of Statistics, 'Labour Force Survey, 1984', *Monthly Bulletin of Statistics*, vol. 36, no. 3 (March 1985), and refer to 1984 data.

72. Central Bureau of Statistics, *Statistical Abstract of Israel, 1980* (Central Bureau of Statistics, Jerusalem, 1980).

73. Ibid., 1983.

4

The West Bank Economy: 1948-1984

Antoine Mansour

I. HISTORICAL BACKGROUND - WEST BANK ECONOMY 1948-1967

The establishment of Israel in 1948 led to radical changes in the basic economic relations and connections of the West Bank. Before the 1948/9 war the West Bank economy was fully integrated with the rest of Palestine. The war cut the region off from its major commercial and industrial centres which constituted the main market for its agricultural output. It also lost access to Mediterranean ports. The influx of refugees from the occupied part of Palestine to the West Bank increased economic difficulties and created acute problems of unemployment.

1. Population and employment

As a result of the flood of refugees from areas conquered by Israel in 1948/9, the population of the West Bank grew by 59.4 per cent during the period 1948 to 1952, an increase of 276,500. According to various estimates, the population of the West Bank changed little between 1952 and 1967, rising from 742,300 in 1952 to 803,600 on the eve of the 1967 war. This represented an annual growth rate of 0.54 per cent (Table 4.1). Migration from the West Bank, mainly to the East Bank of Jordan, was more intensive in the early 1960s than in the 1950s.

The high rates of emigration were the result of high rates of full and seasonal unemployment on the West Bank during the period 1948 to 1967. According to World Bank estimates, more than 50 per cent of the labour force was fully unemployed in 1954, and a further 20 per cent suffered seasonal unemployment. This difficult employment situation

Table 4.1: Population of the West Bank for selected years: 1946-1967 (in thousands)[1]

Year	Population
1946	465.8
1952	742.3
1961	801.4
31.5.1967	803.6

Sources: Estimates provided by Georges Kossaifi, 'Forced migration of Palestinians from the West Bank and the Gaza Strip', *Population Bulletin of ESCWA*, no. 27 (December 1985); International Bank for Reconstruction and Development, *The Economic Development of Jordan* (International Bank Reconstruction and Development, Washington D.C., 1957), pp. 5, 443.

was saved from becoming worse by the emigration of an estimated 350,000 Palestinian refugees to Transjordan in 1948, almost doubling the original population there of 375,000.[2]

The first Jordanian Census in 1961 indicated that about 37.6 per cent of the labour force was employed in agriculture, as compared with 11.5 per cent in industry and 10.4 per cent in the construction sector. The services sector was dominant, absorbing around 40 per cent of the total labour force (Table 4.2).

Table 4.2: Employment by major economic sectors: 1961

	Number	%
Agriculture	64,805	37.6
Mining and quarrying	4,416	2.6
Manufacturing	15,238	8.9
Electricity, gas and water	647	0.4
Construction	17,956	10.4
Services	69,075	40.1
TOTAL	172,137	100.0

Source: Department of Statistics, *First Census of Population and Housing* (Department of Statistics, Amman, November 1961), vols. 1 and 2, pp. 16-18.

2. Economic structure

The West Bank economy under Jordan remained largely underdeveloped, characterised by a large agricultural sector with a weak and underdeveloped industrial sector dominated by small-scale industry and handicrafts. It was heavily dependent on imports of manufactured goods. Estimates based on an economic survey of the West Bank conducted by the Israeli authorities in 1967 and using available Jordanian data indicated that the contribution of the industrial sector (mining and manufacturing) to total GDP was less than 9 per cent in 1966, while that of agriculture was about 27 per cent. The services sector dominated, contributing about 56 per cent of total GDP. This was due partly to the important role played by tourism in the economy (Table 4.3).

Table 4.3: Contribution of major economic sectors to total GDP: 1966 (percentage)

Sector	% of GDP
Agriculture	27.1
Manufacturing and mining	8.8
Electricity, gas and water	1.5
Construction	6.4
Services	56.2
TOTAL	100.0

Source: Economic Planning Authority, *Economic Survey of the West Bank (1967)* (Economic Planning Authority, Jerusalem, 1967) p. 7.

A report of the Central Bank of Jordan estimated that the West Bank had, on the eve of the June 1967 war, '46.9 per cent of total population and its manpower contributes a proportionate share to the economic activity of the country...It accounts for roughly 40 per cent of the GDP of the country, produces between 34 and 40 per cent of Jordan's agricultural production, accounts for about 20 per cent of Jordan's industrial output and generates between 53 and 60 per cent of the gross product of services in the Kingdom'.[3]

3. Investment

In 1950 the West Bank was more developed than Transjordan in almost every respect – economically, socially and in terms of human resources. By 1967 the East Bank had achieved better than parity. The large increase in the urban population, the development of the port of Aqaba and the fact that Amman became a political and commercial centre led to the rapid economic development of the East Bank. Most investments were allocated to the East Bank.

Investment in the West Bank was low. It was estimated by the Bank of Israel in 1969 that less than 14 per cent of the West Bank's GDP had been allocated to investment in 1965 (Table 4.4). The low rate of investment may be explained by the limitations of the market, the low levels of saving and the emphasis on East Bank development in the Jordanian budget.[4] Only one-third of total investment in Jordan was allocated to the West Bank.[5]

Table 4.4: Resources and uses of resources per capita in the West Bank: 1965 (in Jordanian dinars at 1969 prices)[6]

	JD
Private consumption	71.02
Public consumption	13.00
Gross investment	11.22
Exports	17.24
Total resource use	112.45
Less imports	32.24
GDP	80.20
Memorandum items (in per cent)	
Ratio of imports to GDP	40.3
Ratio of investment to GDP	14.0

Source: Bank of Israel, *The Economy of the Administered Areas in 1969* (Bank of Israel, Jerusalem, 1971), p.9.

Available data indicate that about two-thirds of investments in the West Bank went to the construction sector, which was confined largely to private housing. The building boom from 1948 to 1967 followed the net growth of the population and the increasing amount of remittances transferred by Palestinian workers, most of which went into building homes. Public sector investment was very limited.

Table 4.5: Distribution of gross investment by economic sectors: 1962-1965 (percentage)

Sector	1962	1963	1964	1965
Housing	58.8	72.1	73.1	73.5
Other Construction	8.8	10.3	10.5	10.8
Transport & other equipment	32.4	17.6	16.4	15.7
TOTAL	100.0	100.0	100.0	100.0

Source: Economic Planning Authority, *Economic Survey*, p.20.

Table 4.6: West Bank Trade by destination and by nature of product: 1966
(in thousands of Jordanian dinars and percentage)

	East Bank		Other Countries		Total	
	JD	%	JD	%	JD	%
Exports	2,000	100.0	2,300	100.0	4,300	100.0
Agricultural products	1,600	80.0	1,750	76.1	3,350	77.9
Industrial products	400	20.0	550	23.9	950	22.1
Imports	4,300	100.0	20,000	100.0	24,300	100.0
Agricultural products	300	7.0	2,000	10.0	2,300	9.5
Industrial products	4,000	93.0	18,000	90.0	22,000	90.5
Balance of trade	-2,300		-17,700		-20,000	

Source: Economic Planning Authority, *Economic Survey* pp. 27-8.

4. Balance of trade

Available data indicate that the West Bank had a large balance of trade deficit, the export-import ratio being less than 18 per cent. About 78 per cent of total exports were made up of agricultural products, mainly water-melons, melons, citrus, grapes and tomatoes; the main processed exports were olive oil, soap and marble. The East Bank absorbed about 46 per cent of total West Bank exports, while the bulk of the remaining exports went to Arab countries. The major portion (82.3 per cent) of West Bank imports came from outside Jordan and was composed mainly of industrial products, which accounted for 90.5 per cent of imports (Table 4.6).

5. Balance of payments

The West Bank trade deficit was partially met by the export of services, mainly tourism, and the rest more than covered by capital and unilateral transfers. These consisted of capital transferred by the government, UNRWA and other UN agency transfers, and private transfers, mainly remittances of former West Bank residents living abroad. After taking all factors into account and allowing for errors and omissions there was an overall surplus of JD 9 million in 1966.

Table 4.7: Balance of payments of the West Bank: 1966 (in millions of Jordanian dinars)

	JD
Trade balance	-20.0
Exports	4.3
Imports	24.3
Services (net)	17.0
Current deficit	- 3.0
Capital & unilateral transfers	12.0
Private transfers	2.0
Government	6.0
UNRWA & other UN agencies	4.0
Surplus	9.0

Source: Economic Planning Authority, *Economic Survey*, p.26

II. ECONOMIC DEVELOPMENT IN THE WEST BANK 1967 – 1984

Indicators such as GNP, per capita GNP, rates of investment, are not appropriate measures of the strength or weakness of the West Bank economy. These production linked concepts, which are devised to study productive economies, have little significance in economies dominated by transferred resources.[7] The West Bank economy enjoys an income disproportionate to its productive capabilities. It is heavily dependent upon funds transferred from abroad: revenues transferred from Arab labourers working in Israel, remittances from emigrants and Jordanian-Palestinian, Arab and international aid.

Data on national accounts indicate that uses of resources are much greater than the GDP, which means that investment is higher than savings. The deficit is covered by funds transferred from abroad (Tables 4.8 and 4.9). In fact, the ratio of resource deficit to GDP, which is equivalent to the ratio of net resource imports to GDP, is very high and ranged between 68 per cent and 78 per cent during the period 1968 to 1984.

The rate of investment (investment/GDP) is quite high. It increased, at constant prices, from 5.7 per cent in 1968 to 28 per cent in 1978 and to 33.6 per cent in 1980. It declined to 23.7 per cent in 1983/4, owing to the net drop in Palestinian and Arab aid to the West Bank. This ratio is not dissimilar to the rates of investment registered, at constant prices in Kuwait (27.5 per cent) and Syria (30 per cent) in 1981.[8] The rate of investment recorded in the West Bank was financed entirely by transfers from abroad. It cannot be considered an appropriate indicator of economic performance since the domestic saving rate is negative.

A clearer picture emerges from an examination of the way these funds are spent and the economic sectors that benefit from them. The West Bank economy suffers from a shortage of capital, the absence of adequate financial intermediaries, and the fact that a considerable proportion of local savings is transferred to the East Bank. Funds from abroad are invested mainly in the construction and services sectors. Investment in the commodity producing sectors has been severely curtailed during the occupation. There is a very high deficit in the area's balance of trade and the area is heavily reliant on imports from Israel.

Table 4.8: Resources and their uses in the West Bank in selected years: 1968-1984 (in millions of Israeli shekels at 1980 prices[a])

	1968	1978	1980	1983	1984
Total Resources	2,172.2	6,094.0	6,972.0	6,893.6	7,203.0
Gross domestic product	1,274.1	3,488.0	4,098.0	3,868.8	4,275.0
Imports	912.9	2,615.0	2,874.0	3,024.1	2,939.0
Total Uses	2,255.9	6,157.0	6,972.0	6,905.1	7,222.0
Private consumption expenditure	1,536.6	3,738.0	4,106.0	4,406.0	4,644.0
General government expenditure	239.9	375.0	394.0	421.1	432.0
Gross domestic capital formation	72.6	977.0	1,376.0	915.8	1,013.0
Exports of goods & services	406.8	1,067.0	1,096.0	1,162.2	1,133.0
Memorandum items (%)					
Ratio of imports/GDP	71.7	75.0	70.1	78.2	68.7
Ratio of capital formation/GDP	5.7	28.0	33.6	23.7	23.7

Note: a. Using Israeli statistics, estimates at 1980 prices were calculated for each component of expenditure and for total components on the basis of the annual quantity change. Hence, total expenditure is not identical to the sum of the expenditure components.

Source: Central Bureau of Statistics, *Statistical Abstract of Israel*, no.36, 1985 (Central Bureau of Statistics, Jerusalem, 1985).

Table 4.9: Investment and saving in the West Bank in selected years: 1968–1984 (in millions of Israeli shekels at 1980 prices)

	1968	1978	1980	1983	1984
National disposable income	1,811.6	4,846.3	5,442.8	5,527.1	5,853.0
Private consumption expenditure	1,536.6	3,730.2	4,098.7	4,406.7	4,644.0
General government expenditure	239 9	375.0	394.0	421.2	432.0
Total consumption expenditure	1,776 5	4,105.2	4,492.7	4,827.9	5,076.0
Memorandum items					
Savings (income – consumption)	35.1	741.1	950.1	699.2	777.0
Gross fixed capital formation	72.6	892.7	1,282.9	915.8	1,013.0

Sources: Central Bureau of Statistics, *Statistical Abstract of Israel*, 1985, pp 707-8; *Administered Territories Statistics Quarterly*, December 1985 (Central Bureau of Statistics, Jerusalem, 1985), pp.67-8.

1. Scarcity of capital and absence of financial intermediaries

(i) Absence of an adequate banking mechanism

The West Bank economy functions virtually without a banking system, an almost unique situation.[9] Arab and British banks, and Arab credit institutions, were closed in June 1967 and Israeli banks, which have enjoyed a monopoly since then, offer restricted services.[10] Deposits by Palestinians are limited and little credit is granted. Available data indicate that total deposits in Israeli banks were less than 4 per cent of GDP of the West Bank and Gaza Strip in the period up to 1975.[11] Before the 1967 war they were 29 per cent of GDP. In Israel the rate was 48 per cent.[12] The deposits are mainly made by merchants to finance commercial transactions with Israel. It is unlikely that the volume of deposits in the Israeli banks has changed substantially since 1975.

Credits offered by Israeli banks rose from IS 1 million in 1970 to IS 65 million in 1975, or 1.5 per cent of the GDP.[13] There has been no significant increase in loans granted to Palestinians since then because of Israeli constraints (for example, loans have to be approved by the Israeli military governor) and because of lack of trust on the part of the Palestinian population.

(ii) Savings transferred to Amman banks

The weakness of the Israeli currency and high inflation rates in Israel, especially in the early 1980s, have adversely affected the savings structure of the West Bank. The sole function of the Israeli shekel is to facilitate the exchange of goods and services. The loss of confidence in Israeli currency dates from the October 1973 war, and more particularly from the devaluation of November 1974, which was followed by a policy of 'creeping devaluation' in June 1975. Since then the Israeli currency has continuously lost value against major currencies although between 1968 and 1974 it was subject to only minor fluctuations. The major devaluation of November 1974 was accompanied by rising and until recently, accelerating inflation. The consumer price index in Israel rose by over two and a half times between 1973 and 1976, and by around 400 per cent between April 1984 and April 1985.[14] The West Bank was similarly affected. The West Bank price index rose by 360 per cent in the 1983/4 financial year.[15]

The instability of the Israeli currency and the lack of adequate banking services have led the Palestinian population to hoard their savings in Jordanian dinars. A considerable part of these savings is transferred to Jordan, either for deposit in Amman banks or investment in land and real estate. Savings in Amman are not redistributed as credit for West Bank concerns as entrepreneurs there cannot meet the guarantees and conditions demanded by Amman bankers.

The informal money market, mainly the money changers who play an active role in the economy, accept cheques drawn on Amman banks and transfer funds between the East and West Banks. But these have not been able to channel savings into investment credits.[16]

The West Bank economy therefore suffers from a substantial shortage of the capital required for the survival of industrial enterprises and agriculture, and the creation of new economic activities. According to a number of field studies the West Bank economy depends almost exclusively on self-financing. The investigation carried out by Bakir Abu Kishk on the industrial sector indicates that about 90 per cent of industrial firms in the West Bank stated that their investment had come from private funds or from partnerships.[17]

2. The domination of transferred resources

(i) Transfers from workers in Israel or abroad

According to Israeli sources, wages transferred from West Bank labourers working in Israel or abroad constituted 5.2 per cent of GNP in 1968, 23 per cent in 1976, 29 per cent in 1983 and about 27 per cent in 1984.[18] The Central Bureau of Statistics estimates that two-thirds of revenues transferred from abroad are the wages earned by West Bankers working in Israel.[19] About one-third of the West Bank labour force is employed in the Israeli economy; this corresponds to more than half of the total of wage earners.[20]

One of the main characteristics of the West Bank economy is the high rate of emigration and as a consequence significant remittances from abroad. Although rates of emigration during Israeli occupation are similar to those registered before 1967, the nature of the emigration in the more recent period is quite different. Emigrants leaving the West Bank can only return to their homeland with a 're-entry permit' issued by the Israeli authorities. These permits are granted under various types of restrictions applicable to different categories of the residents outside the West Bank. Moreover, the vast majority of people who were abroad during the 1967 June war have been refused permits and are therefore unable to return home. Another main characteristic of Palestinian migration from the West Bank after 1967 is that it affected entire families, not just men of working age.[21] Since

1967 military occupation policies have prevented development and maintained the pressure on people to look for work outside the region.

According to Jordanian sources, about 177,000 people were forced to emigrate during the three months following June 1967.[22] About 10,000 persons were leaving the West Bank annually between September 1967 and 1974, and the rate rose to around 15,000 per annum from then until 1982. The effects of emigration appear clearly in the low annual rate of increase of the population, which was only 0.56 per cent between June 1967 and 1982, while the natural increase was over 3 per cent per annum.[23] The rate of emigration declined after 1982 when Jordan introduced new measures to curb movement out of the West Bank and the decrease in oil revenues led to a drop in job opportunities in the Arab Gulf states.

No accurate figures are available on the amount of remittances transferred to the West Bank. The Israeli Central Bureau of Statistics underestimates earnings of residents working abroad,[24] since thousands of emigrants are no longer considered residents.[25] The fact that remittances are not channelled through a banking system creates another difficulty. The Central Bank of Jordan gives estimates for the total remittances of emigrants from both the East and West Banks. It is not possible, however, to estimate what proportion of this money crosses over to the West Bank. Central Bank figures are not comprehensive because a significant part of total remittances is transferred through money changers not banks. Furthermore, remittances by West Bank emigrants are not fully transferred to their families. Some of their earnings are deposited in accounts in Amman banks. However, total remittances channelled through the banking system from both West Bank and East Bank emigrants have increased considerably in recent years. According to the Central Bank of Jordan, total remittances jumped from JD 46.86 million in 1975 to JD 475 million in 1984.[26] With the significant falls in oil prices registered in the mid-1980s, however, this figure can be expected to have fallen.

(ii) Funds transferred from institutions and organisations abroad

The West Bank economy depends heavily on the aid provided from five major sources: the Joint Jordanian-Palestinian Committee for the Steadfastness of the Palestinian People in the Occupied Homeland, the Palestine Liberation Organisation, the Jordan Government and Arab and international aid. The total aid figure has dropped significantly since 1982. The Joint Jordanian-Palestinian Committee has been the most important source of investment from outside. Since it started operating in 1979 most of its funds have gone to social services, infrastructural and construction projects. Funds transferred to productive sectors are of little importance. Agriculture and industry were allocated 12.5 per cent of the Joint Committee aid between 1979 and 1985 as compared to 15.4 per cent for housing. The annual allocation of the Joint Committee to the occupied territories reached a peak of US$ 101 million in 1982. The budget has been reduced considerably over the last three years, as several Arab countries stopped contributing to the Committee's fund. Allocations for the years 1984 and 1985 dropped by 70 and 50 per cent respectively.[27]

Funds transferred directly by the PLO to the West Bank as well as the wages of government employees engaged before 1967 and grants to municipalities and co-operatives are not documented. Other Arab aid goes directly to Arab institutions and organisations, mainly municipalities, universities and charitable societies.

International aid comes from three main sources: the US government, the European Economic Community (EEC) and United Nations agencies. US government funds are disbursed through private voluntary organisations. Their purpose, according to a resolution of Congress in 1974, is 'to support projects and expand institutions in the occupied territories of the West Bank and Gaza to help build the socio-economic underpinnings necessary to preserve peace'.[28] Projects have to be approved by the US Agency for International Development (USAID) and thereafter the Israeli military authorities. The Israeli military authorities in turn distort the programme and aim it towards projects related to infrastructure and public works; thus less than one-third of the budgets of private voluntary organisations is devoted to economic development projects. The actual investment of USAID money between 1977 and 1983, after the approvals process was complete, was approximetely US$ 16 million.[29] Although these funds are limited in absolute terms and obviously have political objectives, they do make a positive, if not substantial, contribution to the improvement of socio-economic conditions.

European non-governmental organisations are also active in the occupied territories. Some of them are supported by the EEC which adopted a programme of direct assistance to the occupied territories at the end of 1981 and allocated to it ECU 2 million (European Currency Unit 1 = approximately US$ 1); annual allocations for this programme have been increasing steadily. This assistance has gone mainly to institutional support activities such as manpower training and support of agricultural co-operatives.[30]

United Nations agencies have been mandated by a UN General

Assembly resolution to find ways and means to improve the social and economic conditions of the Palestinian people. Their attempts to work in the occupied territories have been constrained by the Israeli government.

Only the UNDP programme has been tolerated by Israel and that after exhaustive negotiations. The special UNDP programme of development assistance to the Palestinian people has its origin in General Assembly resolution 33/147 (20 December 1978), which called the agency to set up concrete projects to improve the social and economic conditions of the Palestinian people. US$ 12 million, of which US$ 8 million was provided by governments and intergovernmental organisations, was allocated to the programme between 1982 and 1986. Projects completed or under completion are mainly in non-productive areas such as pre-primary education and health programmes with a few providing training in agriculture and industry.[31]

It is clear from the pattern of permit approvals that the Israeli authorities maintain a policy of steering aid money away from productive projects and into infrastructural works. They have been accused of using aid to free their own public funds for other purposes.

3. Weakness of the production sectors: economic structure and trends

The West Bank economy would have been even more adversely affected but for the link maintained with Jordan and the Arab region over the 'open bridges', and the work of international institutions and organisations. This link has mainly taken the form of an injection of funds and capital. Nevertheless, these funds do not compensate for the shortage of capital or the paucity of investment. Because foreign assistance has been devoted mainly to non-productive activities, agriculture and industry have been unable to respond to the constraints imposed by Israeli policy.

(i) Structure of the GDP

The services sector contributes the largest share to the West Bank GDP, ranging between 45 and 52 per cent during the period 1968 to 1983. The most significant change in the composition of GDP is the increasing importance of the construction sector. Its contribution has risen from 3.5 per cent in 1968, to 15.5 per cent in 1975 and 15.7 per cent in 1983. This increase has been at the expense of agriculture and industry. The contribution of agriculture to total GDP declined from 36.3 per cent in 1968 to 26.9 per cent in 1983. The contribution of mining and manufacturing was stable at around 8 per cent between 1968 and 1975 but fell to 6.9 per cent in 1983 (Table 4.10).

Table 4.10: GDP by major economic sectors at current prices (percentage)

	1968	1975	1983
Agriculture	36.3	30.3	26.9
Industry*	8.3	8.4	6.9
Construction	3.5	15.5	15.7
Services	51.9	45.8	50.5
TOTAL	100.0	100.0	100.0

Note: a. Mining and manufacturing.
Sources: Central Bureau of Statistics, *National Accounts for Judaea and Samaria, the Gaza Strip and Sinai for the Decade 1968-1977*, Special Series, no. 615 (Central Bureau of Statistics, Jerusalem, 1979); *Administered Territories Statistical Quarterly*, August 1976, no. 2 (Central Bureau of Statistics, Jerusalem, 1976); *Statistical Abstract of Israel* 1985.

The stagnation of the productive sectors has been reflected in sectoral shares of GDP. At constant 1975 prices, the West Bank's GDP grew by 0.2 per cent per annum between 1975 and 1981. The industrial sector did even less well and its share of GDP declined.[32] This is compared with the high annual growth registered in Jordan of 11.4 per cent for the GDP and 18.2 per cent for the industrial sector in the same period.[33]

(ii) Employment

The poor performance of the West Bank economy is also reflected in the levels of employment which, in contrast to most countries of the Arab region, dropped by 7.9 per cent during the period 1970 to 1975. It only returned to the level of 1970 in 1983 and grew by 5 per cent in 1984.

This phenomenon is explained by the number of West Bank labourers engaged in the Israeli economy and the high rates of emigration. In the West Bank there has been a shift from the productive sectors into services. The level of employment in agriculture declined by 30 per cent between 1970 and 1984 and the level in industry remained the same (Table 4.11).

Table 4.11: Distribution of employment in the West Bank by economic sector for selected years: 1970-1984 (percentage)

	1970	1975	1980	1983	1984
Agriculture	42.5	34.6	33.2	29.5	28.5
Industry[a]	14.6	15.8	15.2	16.1	15.9
Construction	8.4	8.4	10.7	11.0	11.3
Services	34.5	41.2	40.9	43.4	44.3
TOTAL	100.0	100.0	100.0	100.0	100.0
Total (in thousands)	99.8	91.9	94.3	99.1	104.0

Note: a. Mining and manufacturing
Source: Central Bureau of Statistics, *Statistical Abstract of Israel*, 1985, p. 725.

(iii) Investment

Most investment in the West Bank has been made by the private sector in infrastructure and construction. The share of the private sector grew from 44 per cent in 1968 to 91.2 per cent in 1980. It declined slightly to 76.5 per cent in 1984. The share of the construction sector in total private investments ranged between 70 and 80 per cent during the period 1975 to 1984 (Table 4.12). The minor share of the government and local authorities in total investments (equivalent to US$ 18.7 million in 1984, according to the official figures) is due to the absence of a national authority and the decreasing Israeli allocations to the West Bank since 1975. Israeli statisticians began including expenditure on infrastructure related to Jewish settlements and their needs in the statistics for the West Bank from the mid-1980s.

The interest in construction, particularly in housing, is linked to a social and political phenomenon which has become even more marked during the occupation. From their experience in 1948, Palestinians have learned the importance of remaining attached to the land, and of building so as to restrict as much as possible Zionist penetration around and close to Arab villages and towns. Israeli concern about the development of the construction sector in the West Bank resulted in a series of military orders being promulgated in the early 1980s to restrict home building. One of the measures, promulgated in August 1981, prevented West Bank municipalities and village councils from granting building permits without prior permission of the military governor. This measure applied to areas totalling 0.5 million dunums (approximately 9 per cent of the area of the West Bank) near

Table 4.12: Gross domestic capital formation by sector and type of assets for selected years: 1968-1984 (percentage)

	1968	1970	1975	1980	1984
Government and local authorities	56.0	38.9	17.4	8.8	23.5
Private sector: machinery, transport and other equipment	12.0	20.4	16.3	16.7	14.3
Building and construction works	32.0	40.7	66.3	74.5	62.2
TOTAL	100.0	100.0	100.0	100.0	100.0

Sources: Central Bureau of Statistics, *Monthly Statistics of the Administered Territories*, vol. 1, no. 8 (Central Bureau of Statistics, Jerusalem, August 1971), p. 97; *Administered Territories Statistical Quarterly*, no. 2, 1985 (Central Bureau of Statistics, Jerusalem, 1985), p. 70; *Statistical Abstract of Israel*, 1985, p. 710.

Jerusalem, Ramallah, Jericho and Bethlehem.[34] Another measure taken in October 1981 prohibited all new building in refugee camps. Until that date, UNRWA had been responsible for building in camps.[35]

Investment in the purchase of new equipment and machinery is minimal. The difficulties West Bank entrepreneurs encounter in competing with Israeli products and in obtaining credit and permits discourage investment in new economic projects.

4. Structure and trends in the production sectors: agriculture

(i) Diminution of the cultivated areas

The area under cultivation in the West Bank has declined continuously since 1967 because of confiscation of agricultural land, lack of water resources, reorientation of labour to Israel, lack of credit and Israeli constraints and competition.

According to Israeli sources, cultivated areas decreased by 15 per cent from approximately 1.86 million dunums in 1968/9 to 1.58 million dunums in 1983. This fall has mainly been at the expense of field crop areas which declined by 0.69 million dunums (64.3 per cent) during the period. In addition to Israeli expropriations, which affected arable land more frequently than orchards,[36] low productivity in field crops grown on rain-fed areas has also been a problem.

Table 4.13: Distribution of cultivated land according to the type of agricultural use in selected years 1964-1983/4

Type of Agriculture	1964 thousands of dunums	%	1968/9 thousands of dunums	%	1983/4 thousands of dunums	%
Field crops	1,128.1	52.0	1,072.1	57.7	382.5	24.1
Vegetables & melons	271.3	12.5	101.0	5.4	171.0	10.8
Fruit trees (including olives)	769.3	35.5	665.3	35.8	1,003.6	63.3
Citrus			20.0	1.1	27.2	1.8
Total	2,168.7	100.0	1,858.4	100.0	1,584.8	100.0

Source: Government of Jordan, *Agricultural Data on the West and the East Banks of Jordan* (1961-1967) (Ministry of Agriculture, Department of Agricultural Statistics, Amman, 1967); Central Bureau of Statistics, *Statistical Abstract of Israel*, 1972 (Central Bureau of Statistics, Jerusalem, 1972) and *Administered Territories Statistics Quarterly*, 1985.

There has been a significant increase in the area devoted to orchards and, much less significantly, to citrus groves. According to Israeli statistics the area planted with fruit trees increased by about 50 per cent between 1968/9 and 1983/4 to approximately 65 per cent of total cultivated area in 1983, as compared with 36.9 per cent in 1968/9. If we use Jordanian figures for the year 1964 as a base, however, the increase is only around 34 per cent (Table 4.13).

(ii) Agricultural production

There have been significant changes in agricultural production since the occupation. Table 4.14 shows that production of every commodity except citrus fell in the first five years of occupation compared with the last five years of Jordanian rule.[37] Production of field crops and melons dropped respectively by 39.6 and 69 per cent during the period 1977 to 1981 compared with the period 1961 to 1966. Production of vegetables, olives and fruit has increased continuously since the occupation. The 21.7 per cent increase in vegetable production is due to the expansion of the area used to cultivate winter vegetables under plastic covers and more efficient use of irrigation. Fruit production rose as the significant areas of new orchards planted just before the occupation came into production over the next decade and continued to be expanded. Israeli officials estimated in 1970 that 46 per cent of the citrus area and 29 per cent of the almonds were planted between 1963 and 1966.[38]

Table 4.14: Average annual agricultural production in selected periods: 1961-1981 (in thousands of tons)

Periods	Field Crops	Vegetables	Melons	Olives	Citrus	Other Fruit
1961-6	65.9	128.8	70.0	43.8	23.5	76.4
1967-71	39.4	80.0	18.4	39.4	36.6	48.8
1972-6	44.4	133.4	24.0	41.6	66.8	73.4
1977-81	39.8	156.8	21.6	73.2	77.6	94.8

Sources: Data compiled from B. Abu Howaj, *Agricultural Atlas of Jordan* (Ministry of Agriculture, Amman, 1973) and Central Bureau of Statistics, 'Accounts of the agricultural branch in the administered territories 1979/80' (in Hebrew), *Administered Territories Statistical Quarterly*, 1981, no. 1 (Central Bureau of Statistics, Jerusalem, 1981); *Statistical Abstract of Israel*, no. 35, 1984 (Central Bureau of Statistics, Jerusalem, 1984).

There have been no radical changes in the type of crops grown since 1967. Olives are still the main crop; their contribution to total production ranged between 20 and 50 per cent, depending on weather conditions. The other main crops are fruit and vegetables. There has been, however, a certain specialisation in products enjoying a market in Israel. In fact, Israeli military regulations concerning agriculture and restrictions on imports has encouraged Palestinian farmers to grow crops such as tomatoes and cucumbers for processing in Israeli factories or sale to Israeli exporters. This accounts for Israel's increasing share of West Bank agricultural exports, which rose to 33.7 per cent in 1984. Trade across the bridge to Jordan and the Arab world still accounts for the bulk of agricultural exports however.

(iii) Stagnation of industrial production

The stagnation of industrial production is reflected in the decline of the contribution of the industrial sector to GDP, as indicated above. In Jordan, in contrast, the share of industry in total GDP rose from 10.3 per cent in 1970 to 22 per cent in 1981.[39] In the West Bank, the number of manufacturing establishments (excluding olive oil presses) dropped from 3,261 in 1967 (according to Jordanian estimates) to 2,380 in 1984 (according to Israeli estimates), most of which are still small workshops employing small numbers of people. They clearly cannot overcome the restrictions outlined above and compete with the relatively sophisticated Israeli industrial sector.

There has been no significant expansion of exports across the bridge because regulations of the League of Arab States Special Bureau for Boycotting Israel confine manufactured exports to those relying on inputs available locally or imported through Jordan. Israeli regulations bar most imports from Jordan. Industrial exports to Jordan consist almost exclusively, therefore, of refined vegetable and olive oils and building stone and marble. Table 4.15 shows that no radical change has occurred in the West Bank manufacturing structure. Food, beverages and tobacco are still the main sectors although their share of total income declined from 67.5 per cent in 1969 to 55 per cent in 1984. Olive and vegetable oils (*samneh*) and chocolates constituted the major exports of the West Bank to Jordan. Exports of food products have constituted, since 1968, half of the total industrial exports to Jordan and, including olive oil, 75 per cent of the total.

The decline of the share of food products in total output has been offset by the growth in the manufacture of rubber, plastics and chemicals and non-metallic mineral products. Rubber, plastics and chemicals increased their share of manufacturing income from 8.7 per cent in 1969 to 17.8 per cent in 1984. This is explained by the growth of the pharmaceutical industry which has constituted the most significant development in West Bank industry since 1967. In contrast to most other firms, the nine relatively large pharmaceutical companies are highly capital-intensive. Many of the shareholders are doctors who prescribe their own company's products thereby nullifying the competitiveness of Israeli pharmaceutical products and allowing the industry to grow. The contribution of non-metallic mineral products to total manufacturing output increased from 1.4 per cent in 1969 to 4.5 per cent in 1984. Textiles and clothing, which occupy the third rank, contributed a steady 7 per cent between 1969 and 1984. The increased share of non-metallic mineral products in total manufacturing output is partly due to the growing demand for building materials in Israel. Textiles, clothing and leather products are labour-intensive industries mainly subcontracting from Israeli companies. Despite their importance in terms of the number of establishments and the fact that they employ one-third of all workers working in manufacturing, their position as subcontractors has reduced their contribution to total manufacturing income considerably. They have a very small value added.[40]

Table 4.15: Output by main manufacturing branches[a] for selected years: 1969-1984 (percentage at current prices)

	1969	1980	1984
Food, beverages & tobacco	67.5	61.3	55.0
Textiles and clothing	7.0	6.1	6.3
Leather and leather goods	1.8	1.6	2.1
Timber and wood products	3.2	2.7	2.8
Rubber, chemicals and plastics	8.7	14.8	17.8
Non-metallic mineral products	1.4	2.9	4.5
Basic metal products	5.4	6.3	5.3
Other industrial products[b]	5.0	4.3	6.2
TOTAL	100.0	100.0	100.0

Notes: a. Excluding owner operated workshops with no employees. b. Other industrial products include: paper and publishing, electrical and transport equipment.
Sources: Central Bureau of Statistics, *Monthly Statistics of the Administered Territories*, no. 3, March 1971 (Central Bureau of Statistics, Jerusalem, 1971); *Statistical Abstract of Israel*, 1981; *Statistical Abstract of Israel*, 1985.

5. Deficit in the balance of trade

The development of trade since the occupation indicates a continuous trend towards the increasing share of the Israeli market and the growing deficit in the balance of trade. This deficit is due to four main factors:

(a) The employment in Israel of over one-third of the Palestinian labour force and the emigration of skilled workers to the Arab Gulf States have led to a decrease in the productive capacity of the West Bank economy. This augments imports of merchandise and reduces exports, especially since at least a portion of this labour force was employed in the productive sectors of the West Bank economy.

(b) Israeli policy, and particularly the many constraints on trade with Jordan.

(c) The greater specialisation which occurred in West Bank agriculture and industry implied a higher import content in production and led to a net increase in trade with, mainly imports from, Israel.

(d) The structure of the West Bank economy being weaker and unable to withstand market penetration by the vastly more developed economy of Israel.

Table 4.16 shows that the overall trade balance for the West Bank has been negative throughout the period of the occupation. The ratio of total exports to total imports rose to 45.4 per cent in 1984. The trade deficit with Israel is even greater: exports to Israel are the equivalent of 27.5 per cent of imports. Israel's share of total West Bank trade rose to 78.3 per cent in 1984. West Bank imports from Israel increased from 80.3 per cent in 1969 to 89.3 per cent in 1984; and 36.5 per cent and 54.1 per cent of its exports went to Israel in the same years. Trade with Jordan and other countries has fallen throughout the period of occupation.

The West Bank has been made into a 'natural' market for Israeli products where there is free flow of goods, without customs barriers or licences, and where transport costs are low. The economy benefits from West Bank production because payments for West Bank products are made in Israeli currency whereas export earnings come in the convertible and more stable currency, the Jordanian dinar. The West Bank's surplus in its trade with Jordan throughout the occupation period is completely absorbed by Israel. The West Bank's deficit on trade with Israel exceeded at least three-fold the trade surplus with Jordan during the period 1970 to 1984 (Table 4.17).

Table 4.16: West Bank trade by partner country in 1969 and 1984 (percentage)

	Imports		Exports	
	1969	1984	1969	1984
Israel	80.3	89.3	36.5	54.1
Jordan	7.8	2.0	48.1	45.3
Other countries	11.9	8.7	15.4	0.6
TOTAL	100.0	100.0	100.0	100.0

Source: Central Bureau of Statistics, *Statistical Abstract of Israel*, 1985, p. 713.

Table 4.17: Foreign trade balance of the West Bank by partner country for selected years: 1968-1984 (in millions of US$)

Trade Balance	1968	1970	1975	1980	1984
Israel	−26.8	−38.4	−134.1	−239.2	−263.2
Jordan	9.6	10.2	29.7	70.5	75.3
Other countries	−6.6	−6.2	−16.7	−46.0	−34.4
Overall trade balance	−23.8	−34.4	−121.1	−214.7	−222.3

Source: Central Bureau of Statistics, *Statistical Abstract of Israel*, 1985, p. 713.

Israel maintains this trading position by military orders which prohibit many imports, impose higher customs duties than on imports through Israeli ports and strictly control imports over the Jordan river bridges. These 'security reasons' mean high costs and losses for Palestinian merchants and entrepreneurs. West Bank trade through Israeli airports or seaports must be undertaken through Israeli commercial agents.

Table 4.18 shows that industrial goods account for 83.5 per cent of the West Bank's total imports and 75.1 per cent of its total exports. Israel accounted for more than 88 per cent of West Bank imports in 1984, the Israeli market absorbed around 60 per cent of the much smaller West Bank exports. These exports are mainly products manufactured under subcontract: Israel absorbed 33.7 per cent of West Bank agricultural exports. Jordan takes around 66 per cent of West Bank agricultural exports and 38.3 per cent of industrial exports. Table 4.19 indicates the relative importance of industrial and agricultural products in West Bank trade with Jordan, Israel and other countries.

The deficit in the West Bank balance of trade has been increasingly covered by the export of services (especially wages

Table 4.18: Exports and imports of agricultural and industrial products by partner country: 1984 (percentage)[56]

	Agricultural Products Exports	Imports	Industrial Products Export	Imports	Total Exports	Imports
Jordan	66.3	0.1	38.3	2.4	45.3	2.0
Israel	33.7	93.3	60.9	88.4	54.1	89.3
Other	–	6.6	0.8	9.2	0.6	8.7
TOTAL	100.0	100.0	100.0	100.0	100.0	100.0

Source: Central Bureau of Statistics, *Administered Territories Statistics Quarterly*, December 1985, pp.6-7

Table 4.19: Exports and imports of the West Bank according to the nature of the product and by partner country 1984 (percentage)[57]

	Jordan Exports	Imports	Israel Exports	Imports	Other Countries Exports	Imports	Total Exports	Imports
Agricultural products	36.5	1.2	15.5	17.3	–	12.4	24.9	16.5
Industrial products	63.5	98.8	84.5	82.7	100.0	87.6	75.1	83.5
TOTAL	100.0	100.0	100.0	100.0	100.0	100.0	100.0	100.0

Source: Central Bureau of Statistics, *Statistical Abstract of Israel*, 1985.

Table 4.20: West Bank balance of payments in 1970, 1984 (estimates in millions of US dollars)

	1970[a]			1984		
	Debit	Credit	Net	Debit	Credit	Net
Merchandise	65.0	31.5	-33.5	411.0	190.0	-221.0
Services	20.8	28.9	8.1	144.9	286.2	141.3
Transportation	(2.2)	(–)	(-2.2)	(11.7)	(6.4)	(-5.3)
Insurance	(1.5)	(0.8)	(-0.7)	(8.5)	(4.2)	(-4.2)
Travel abroad	(6.4)	(2.7)	(-3.7)	(39.0)	(7.0)	(-32.0)
Investment	(0.1)	(0.9)	(0.8)	(0.8)	(–)	(-0.8)
Government	(1.7)	(–)	(-1.7)	(2.5)	(–)	(-2.5)
Other	(8.9)	(24.5)	(15.6)	(82.4)	(268.6)	(186.2)
Total Goods and Services	85.8	60.4	-25.4	555.9	476.2	-79.7
Transfer payments	4.1	40.7	36.6	41.4	88.9	47.5
Capital payments (net)	11.2	–	-11.2	–	32.2	32.2

Note: a. Converted from Israeli pounds to US dollars according to the average annual exchange rate in 1970: US$ 1.00 = I£3.50
Sources: Central Bureau of Statistics, *Statistical Abstract of Israel*, 1972; *Statistical Abstract of Israel*, 1985.

earned by Palestinian labourers working in Israel) and transfer payments. Table 4.20 shows that while exports of services covered only 24.2 per cent of the deficit in 1970, this ratio jumped to approximately 64 per cent in 1984, reflecting the increased number of labourers going to jobs in Israel. Transfer payments from abroad covered the remaining deficit. Capital movements, which were negative in 1970 grew to US$ 47.5 million in 1984. This figure includes, among other things, estimates of changes in the amount of Israeli, Jordanian and foreign currencies held by West Bank residents.

III. CONCLUSION

The West Bank has undergone two radical transformations of its economy since 1948. In that year the creation of Israel meant the destruction of the political, social and economic structure of Palestinian society. The West Bank, which had been completely integrated with the rest of Palestine, lost its markets and the severe economic problems which followed were compounded by an influx of hundreds of thousands of refugees. Economic relations between the West Bank and the East Bank developed and grew more complex between 1948 and 1967 as an integrated Jordanian economy emerged. Both parts of the kingdom relied heavily on imports from other countries. However, the West Bank remained relatively underdeveloped as the economy continued to rely mainly on the agriculture and services sectors. There were high rates of unemployment and emigration, and a low rate of saving and investment.

With Israeli occupation in June 1967 West Bank economic relations were ruptured again and new links had to be made, mainly with the Israeli economy. Israel became the area's major trading partner, but no radical changes occurred in its basic economic structures: agriculture and services still constituted the major economic sectors. However, the construction sector has taken a more important place in the economy due to the allocation of the bulk of investment to private housing. Savings have remained very low, but considerable investment has taken place of funds transferred from abroad. Despite aid provided to the West Bank, its economy has not only been increasingly subservient to the Israeli economy, it also faces the danger of stagnation and decline. Israel has followed a dual policy of (a) absorption of Palestinian Arab labour into the Israeli economy and total control of trade and (b) undermining potential growth in the Palestinian economy by the expropriation of land, severe limits on access to water resources, the denial of an adequate banking system and restrictions on economic development by military orders.

Although Arab and international aid has contributed to the improvement of the social and economic conditions of the Palestinian people in the West Bank, it has not been able to protect the productive economic sectors or prevent emigration. Protection of agriculture and the limiting of emigration should be the corner stone of any economic strategy in the West Bank aimed at staving off the destruction of the economy.

NOTES

1. The year 1946 is used because it is the year of the last British Mandate census. The West Bank, as a geographic unit, was not in existence at the time so population figures have to be estimated.

2. Y. Sayigh, *The Economics of the Arab World: Development Since 1945* (Croom Helm, London, 1978), p. 190.

3. Central Bank of Jordan, *Fourth Annual Report* (Central Bank of Jordan, Amman, 1967), pp. 5-6.

4. E. Kanovsky, *The Economic Impact of the Six Day War* (Praeger, New York, 1970), pp. 143, 365.

5. Economic Planning Authority, *Economic Survey of the West Bank (1967)* (Economic Planning Authority, Jerusalem, 1967), p. 20.

6. The exchange rate of Jordanian dinar/Israeli lira was calculated at 1 JD to 9.8 IL based on the official rate of IL per US$ published in Central Bureau of Statistics, *Statistical Abstract of Israel*, no. 21, 1970, (Central Bureau of Statistics, Jerusalem, 1970), p.478, and *Year Book 1986, International Financial Statistics* (International Monetary Fund, Washington D.C., 1986), p.422.

7. M. Chatelus and Y. Schemeil, 'Towards a new political economy of state industrialisation in the Arab Middle East', *International Journal of Middle East Studies*, no. 16 (1984), pp. 251-65.

8. United Nations Economic and Social Commission for Western Asia. Data compiled from national sources.

9. The only comparable instance of an economy existing without a banking system is Ireland between 1966 and 1977. There were three strikes in this period which closed the banks for a total of about one year. The longest period of closure was six months. See, for example, Antoine E. Murphy, 'Money in an economy without banks: the case of Ireland', *Manchester School of Economics and Social Studies Bulletin* (March 1978), pp. 41-50.

10. The Israeli authorities gave permission for a branch of the Cairo-Amman Bank to open in Nablus in late 1986. It is clear that it will be of limited capacity and capital and strictly controlled in its operations. See, for example, *Al Fajr Palestinian Weekly*, vol. 7, no. 330 (5 September 1986), p.1; *Jerusalem Post*, 18 September 1986, p.1.

11. Data on West Bank Palestinian deposits and credits are not available after 1975. The existing sources do not distinguish between branches of Israeli

banks in Arab towns and those in Israeli settlements.

12. A. Bregman, *The Economy of the Administered Areas, 1967-1975* (Bank of Israel Research Department, Jerusalem, 1976), p. 57.

13. Ibid.

14. Central Bureau of Statistics, *Statistical Abstract of Israel*, 1985 (Central Bureau of Statistics, Jerusalem, 1985) p. 265.

15. Ibid., p. 714. The national unity government which took office in Israel in 1984 managed, with increased financial aid and greater control of financial mechanisms, to bring inflation down. Few structural changes have been made, however, and the more stringent policies were soon relaxed. It is likely that similar economic problems will recur in the future. See George T. Abed, 'Israel in the orbit of America: the political economy of a dependency relationship', *Journal of Palestine Studies*, 61, vol. XVI, no. 1 (Washington D.C., 1986).

16. See Antoine Mansour, 'Monetary dualism: the case of the West Bank under occupation', *Journal of Palestine Studies* (Spring 1982); A. Mansour, 'Monetary situation: constraints and proposals for possible remedies', paper presented to the Seminar on Remedies for the Deterioration of the Economic and Social Conditions of the Palestinian People in the Occupied Palestinian Territories, organised by the United Nations Human Settlements, Vienna, 25-29 March, 1985.

17. UN ECWA, *Report on the Industrial and Economic Trends in the West Bank and Gaza Strip* (UN ECWA, Beirut, August 1981).

18. Central Bureau of Statistics, *Statistical Abstract of Israel*, 1984 (Central Bureau of Statistics, Jerusalem, 1984) p. 742; *Statistical Abstract of Israel*, 1985, p. 711; *Administered Territories Statistical Quarterly*, December 1985 (Central Bureau of Statistics, Jerusalem, 1985) pp. 71-3.

19. Central Bureau of Statistics, *Administered Territories Statistics Quarterly*, April 1983 (Central Bureau of Statistics, Jerusalem, 1983), p.725.

20. Central Bureau of Statistics, *Statistical Abstract of Israel,* 1985, p.725.

21. Georges Kossaifi, 'Forced migration of Palestinians from the West Bank and the Gaza Strip', *Population Bulletin of ESCWA*, no. 27 (December 1985).

22. Government of Jordan, *Report of the Joint Ministerial Committee for Relief* (Government of Jordan, Amman, August 1967).

23. Kossaifi, 'Forced migration'.

24. Central Bureau of Statistics, *Administered Territories Statistics Quarterly*, April 1983, p. 81.

25. Israel considers all persons absent during the 1967 census of population as non-residents.

26. Central Bank of Jordan, *Annual Report 1975* and *Annual Report 1984* (Central Bank of Jordan Department of Research and Studies, Amman, 1975 and 1984).

27. Estimates provided by the Joint Committee, Amman, 1985 (unpublished).

28. United States Congress, Committee on Foreign Affairs, *Economic Support Funds Programme in the Middle East* (United States Government Printing Office, Washington D.C., 1979).

29. Meron Benvenisti, *US Government Funded Projects in the West Bank and Gaza (1977-1983), Palestinian Sector* (The West Bank Data Base Project,

THE WEST BANK ECONOMY: 1948-1984

30. Antoine Mansour, *Palestine: une économie de résistance en Cisjorda-nie et à Gaza* (Editions L'Harmattan, Paris, 1983), p. 158.

31. UNDP, *Briefing Note on the Assistance to the Palestinian People Through the United Nations Development Programme* (UNDP, Geneva, February, 1984).

32. Growth rates have been calculated using the Least Squares Method. Source of the data on GDP and value added in industry: Hillel Frisch, *Arab and Jewish Industry in the West Bank* (The West Bank Data Base Project, Jerusalem, July 1983).

33. Based on data provided by UN ECWA, Baghdad.

34. *Haaretz*, 10 August 1981.

35. Ibid., 12 October 1981.

36. Land used to grow trees is less subject to confiscation than that in seasonal use.

37. In order to eliminate seasonal production fluctuations (West Bank agriculture is largely rain-fed), we compared the average annual production of the last five years with that of three previous periods (1961-6, 1967-71 and 1972-6).

38. Central Bureau of Statistics, 'Agriculture in Judaea and Samaria 1967/8-1969/70', *Monthly Statistics of the Administered Territories*, vol. 1, no. 8 (Central Bureau of Statistics, Jerusalem, August 1971).

39. Government of Jordan, *Five Year Plan for Economic and Social Development 1981-1985* (National Planning Council, Amman, 1980).

40. Central Bureau of Statistics, *Statistical Abstract of Israel*, 1984.

5

The Gaza Economy:
1948 - 1984

Ziad Abu-Amr

The Gaza Strip was an integral part of the southern province of Palestine until the war of 1948. The two districts of the Gaza Province, Gaza and Beer Sheba, were the poorest areas in the country. As a coastal area, Gaza district was a trade entrepot through which the products of the province, especially the wheat and barley of Beer Sheba, were exported. Gaza Province covered 13,688,501 dunums and in 1947 had a population of 303,500.[1] After 1948 all but 2.5 per cent of the province was lost.[2] This remaining area is the Gaza Strip. The Armistice Agreement between Israel and Egypt in 1949 recognised the Gaza Strip as a separate entity under Egyptian supervision. In the 1967 war the Strip was occupied by the Israeli army.

The Gaza Strip after 1948 was a separate economic entity cut off from the rest of Palestine. About 80 per cent of its population lost their livelihoods. An influx of refugees in the aftermath of the 1948 war tripled the population. Today, over 550,000 people live in an area of 360 square kilometres.

I. POPULATION

In 1948, the population of the Gaza Strip was approximately 280,000. At most, 90,000 of them were indigenous inhabitants. The rest were refugees.[3] The population increased steadily to 288,107 in 1950 and 373,292 in 1960, an average annual population growth rate of 2.7 per cent and a crude rate of 3.85 per cent.[4] The total population of Gaza in 1966 was between 400,000 and 455,000 inhabitants.[5] An Israeli census in September 1967 counted 354,000, the lower figure perhaps reflecting the collective deportations and waves of emigration immediately after the war.[6] Even at the lower estimate, the Gaza Strip is one of the most densely populated areas in the world; density in 1981 was estimated at about 1,400 persons per square kilometre.[7]

In 1984, 48 per cent of the population was fifteen years old or younger.[8] Large-scale adult male emigration has led to women outnumbering men in the 20-54 age group.[9] Table 5.1 indicates the distribution of the Gaza population by age group in selected years between 1967 and 1984.

Table 5.1: Population of the Gaza Strip by age group in selected years: 1967-1984 (in thousands)

Year	0-14	15-29	30-44	45-64	65+	Total	males/1000 females
1967	194.6	83.2	55.6	34.9	18.3	389.7	943
1969	174.0	87.3	49.7	13.6	14.6	362.2	946
1971	189.0	97.9	50.8	31.5	12.6	381.8	954
1973	197.5	107.5	50.4	36.2	13.8	405.4	974
1975	201.1	111.3	54.8	39.3	12.0	418.5	972
1977	209.1	123.1	50.3	43.9	14.9	441.3	980
1979	201.0	125.4	52.0	42.5	11.7	432.6	986
1981	210.4	130.5	56.2	43.9	10.4	451.6	988
1983	235.3	146.0	52.8	47.1	13.3	494.5	994
1984	243.4	148.9	55.9	47.9	13.8	509.9	996

Source: Gharaibeh, *The Economies of the West Bank and Gaza Strip* (Westview Press, Boulder, Colorado, 1985); Central Bureau of Statistics, *Statistical Abstract of Israel*, 1983 and 1984 (Central Bureau of Statistics, Jerusalem, 1983 and 1984).

II. LABOUR FORCE AND EMPLOYMENT

The labour force in Gaza has generally represented only a small percentage of the total population: about 15 per cent in 1968 and 18 per cent since 1974.[10] This is the result of a number of social and economic factors: the high percentage of the population under 15 years of age; the small number of men of working age; the emigration of adults; the high rates of school attendance; the limited economic resources and employment opportunities.

Unemployment has been high in the potential work force since 1948, particularly among the refugee population. Surveys made in 1960 indicated that in the indigenous Gaza labour force of about 69,000 people, 24,000 were unemployed. In the refugee population

11,550 had work and 64,500 were unemployed, 83 per cent of those of working age.[11] In 1966 it was estimated that 71,000 people in the Strip were at work. In 1968 the number declined to 45,000 as a result of the war which meant unemployment stood at 17 per cent for the non-refugee population.[12] Female participation in the labour force, which has been negligible at best, decreased to 3 per cent in 1982 in the face of increased competition for jobs from males.

In 1965, over a third of the work force was employed in agriculture. Since the occupation agriculture has ceased to be the largest employer, providing only about 18 per cent of total employment. However, it still accounts for 32 per cent of 'domestic' employment. Over 60 per cent of the labour force worked in services and construction in the 1960s; employment in industry was negligible.[13] In 1980, 40 per cent of the labour force was employed in services and the share in industry and construction increased to 20 and 25 per cent respectively.[14] The expatriation of skilled labour has lowered the overall standard of the Gaza work force to a pool of largely unskilled, manual labour. The impact of greater education has been limited because of expatriation.[15]

Since employment in Israel was opened to Gazans the number of workers going to Israel every day has jumped from 6,000 in 1969 to 36,000 in 1982, according to official estimates. Meron Benvenisti's West Bank Data Base Project report of May 1986 estimated that 45,000 Gazans work in Israel: 45 per cent of the total work force.[16] The labour black market is, according to official Israeli estimates, equivalent to 25 to 30 per cent of those legally employed.[17] The Gaza workers in Israel are concentrated in unskilled and semi-skilled jobs, primarily seasonal or temporary jobs in agriculture and construction. Most of these workers are the unemployed or the under-employed of the local agricultural sector. Since construction in Israel is a large employment sector, many workers in Gaza have found it to their advantage to learn minimal building skills.

III. SOURCES OF INCOME

Prior to 1967, the main sources of income in the Gaza economy, aside from the remittances from residents abroad, were from agriculture and fishing, trade and public services. Some sources estimated the per capita GNP in 1967 at US$ 80, one of the lowest in the world.[18] Table 5.2 indicates the distribution of the sources of income in the Gaza Strip in 1966. Since the Israeli occupation, work in Israel, the Jordanian-

Table 5.2: Sources of income in the Gaza Strip: 1966 (in millions of Egyptian pounds and percentage)

	£E millions	%
Agriculture and fishing	5.5	26.2
Industry	0.7	3.3
Building and public construction	1.0	4.8
Trade and personal services	4.3	20.5
Transport	0.5	2.4
Administration and public services	4.0	19.0
Gross Domestic Output	16.0	76.2
Transfers from abroad		
UNRWA and other public transfers	4.0	19.0
Remittances from relatives abroad	1.0	4.8
National Income	21.0	100.0

Source: Brian Van Arkadie, *Benefits and Burdens: A Report on the West Bank and Gaza Strip Economies Since 1967* (Carnegie Endowment for International Peace, Washington D.C., 1977), p. 31.

Palestinian Joint Committee and the money spent by private voluntary organisations have provided additional sources of income. The GDP of Gaza for 1984 at factor cost (current prices) was US$ 249.4 million and is divided as follows: agriculture, US$ 32.9 million; industry, US$ 29.0 million; construction, US$ 55.5 million; public and community services, US$ 75.7 million; transport, trade and other services, US$ 56.5 million. Taking into account factor incomes from abroad the Gaza GNP could be put at about US$ 500 million in 1984[19]

Table 5.3: Composition of Gaza GDP: 1984 (in millions of US dollars)

Sector	
Agriculture	32.9
Industry	29.0
Construction	55.5
Public and community services	75.5
Transport, trade and other services	56.5
TOTAL	249.4

Source: Central Bureau of Statistics, *Judaea, Samaria and Gaza Area: Statistics Quarterly*, no. 2 (Central Bureau of Statistics, Jerusalem, 1985), p. 79 (adapted)

and GNP per capita (at current prices) at US$ 980.[20] These figures indicate a dramatic shift in the economic picture. Agriculture has .been relegated to a secondary position behind transport, services and construction.

IV. ECONOMIC SECTORS

The Egyptians administered the Gaza economy as a unit quite distinct from their own. Between 1948 and 1967 there was a large imbalance between Gaza's plentiful human resources and its scarce material resources. There was an inadequate economic infrastructure and no integrated market. Yet, in the decade preceding 1967, the economic situation had improved somewhat. Mass education produced manpower for the Arab Gulf states and Saudi Arabia. Expatriate workers remitted money which was used to finance land reclamation, local trade and construction. As a result, agriculture, especially the citrus sector, expanded. The Egyptian authorities established a thriving free trade zone in the Gaza Strip and this generated substantial income and employment.

The 1967 war disrupted the already fragile Gaza economy. Existing problems were exacerbated by the reduction of remittances, and the loss of income derived from servicing the Palestine Liberation Army, the UN peacekeeping forces and from Egyptian tourists. Fishing was curtailed by Israeli 'security' measures. The Gaza economy came into direct contact with the larger and industrially more advanced Israeli economy and was also subject to military occupation policies which restricted independent development.[21]

1. Agriculture

From 1948 to 1967 agriculture was the main economic activity in the Gaza Strip, accounting for a third of all employment, 70 per cent of GDP and more than 90 per cent of all exports.[22]

Agriculture today in the Gaza Strip is in serious trouble. It is no longer an attractive source of employment to a substantial number of workers. As a result of Israeli expropriations less land is available. Citrus, by far the most important single sector, is under assault. Land holdings are increasingly fragmented. The marketing system is disorganised and dependent on Israeli permits and growers must sell their crops in competition with government-subsidised Israeli agricultural produce. The water supply is increasingly inadequate. Current financial and credit resources cannot meet the requirements of land reclamation, mechanisation and the introduction of modern irrigation techniques. After 1967 the number of agricultural workers domestically employed dropped steadily to 16,800 in 1970, 12,600 in 1977, 8,300 in 1982.[23] By 1984 only 7,800 people were employed in agriculture. In Israel, 7,900 Gazans were employed in agriculture in the same year.[24] The proportion of the Gaza Strip's GDP provided by agriculture declined rapidly to 28.4 per cent in 1968 and 12.6 per cent in 1984. Between 1967 and 1970 the average annual rate of growth in agriculture was 8.8 per cent. Between 1979 and 1981 it dropped to 0.9 per cent.[25] The decline continues.

Cultivated land in 1958 comprised 43 per cent of the total area of the Strip and 75 per cent of all arable land.[26] The total area cultivated in 1959/60 was 142,000 dunums yielding a crop valued at E£ 1.5 million.[27] By 1966 cultivated land had comprised 52.1 per cent of all arable land[28] and by 1968 it had risen to 55 per cent.[29]

An additional problem is the fragmentation of farm units. In 1968 almost 90 per cent of all farms were smaller than 50 dunums and 69 per cent were less than 20 dunums. This problem of small and scattered landholdings is certainly not unique to the Gaza Strip and is the result, in large part, of traditional Muslim inheritance patterns. It is a drawback to overall productive efficiency of available arable land.

Table 5.4: Land use in the Gaza Strip: 1984 (in dunums)

Category	Area
Construction and roads	41,000
Citrus	66,700
Fruit	60,000
Vegetables and other crops	57,000
Private barren land	8,000
Sand dunes (mainly government land)	77,000
Government land (acacia scrub)	40,000
Other kinds of land	10,000
TOTAL	359,700

Sources: Sharif Kan'ana and Rashad al-Madani, *al-istitan wa-musadarat al-aradi fi qit'a ghazza: 1967-1984* (Settlement and land confiscation in the Gaza Strip: 1967-1984) (Birzeit University Centre for Research and Documentation, Birzeit, 1985), pp. 9, 46; Eliyahu Kanovsky, *The Economic Impact of the Six Day War: Israel, The Occupied Territories, Egypt, Jordan* (Praeger, New York, 1970).

Table 5.5: Distribution of farm size in the Gaza Strip: 1968

Farm size in dunums	% of farms
Less than 10	46.3
10-19	22.4
20-49	20.1
50-99	7.1
100-199	3.0
200-plus	1.1

Source: Gharaibeh, *Economies of the West Bank*, p. 65.

Land has been made more productive, however, by the use of intensive irrigation and greenhouses. There were 570 dunums of Palestinian owned greenhouses in the Strip in 1986. Israeli settlers have an estimated 3,000 dunums.[30]

Citrus has been the main agricultural product since 1948. In 1960 about 16,000 dunums were planted with citrus trees, yielding 2.6 tons per dunum with a value of E £820,000.[31] In 1961 almost 21,000 dunums were planted with citrus and by 1966 the area had increased substantially to 68,000 dunums. Gaza became increasingly dependent on one crop. Growth of citrus cultivation was helped by private remittances flowing into the Strip.[32]

This expansion of the citrus crop in the 1960s was partly responsible for the improved economic conditions in the mid-1970s. Citrus trees planted in the 1960s began to bear fruit in the next decade. But overall the area planted with citrus declined from 70,000 dunums on the eve of the 1967 war, to 66,700 dunums in 1984 largely as a result of Israeli restrictions on water use and on marketing.[33] Vegetables, wheat, barley and corn were secondary crops and in most cases did not meet local demand before 1967.[34] In 1958 44,000 dunums were planted with vegetables. The area declined to 23,000 dunums in 1960.[35] Between 1954 and 1964 the proportion of land devoted to vegetable production declined from 65.4 per cent to 42.7 per cent as citrus cultivation expanded, reflecting a tendency among Gaza farmers to invest in an easily exportable cash crop.[36] Since occupation, the area of cultivated land has declined or, at best, remained fairly static: it was 170,250 dunums in 1966, 198,000 dunums in 1968 and had declined to 183,700 dunums in 1984.[37] Meron Benvenisti suggests slightly higher figures: 187,000 dunums in 1966, rising to 204,000 in 1967/8 and to 210,000 dunums in 1979.[38] The limited investment resources at the disposal of the Gaza farmers, political uncertainty concerning land tenure, the high cost of farm labour, poor returns, and the prospects of

107

higher incomes from employment in Israel have all contributed to agricultural stagnation in the Gaza Strip. While the number of landed farmers remained stable between 1970 and 1982 at 6,200, the number of farm labourers declined from 13,000 to 8,200.[39]

Since 1967 the most serious problem facing agriculture has been identifying and exploiting markets, particularly for citrus. Gaza traditionally marketed about 60 per cent of its production to the UK and Eastern European countries.[40] As these markets became no longer accessible, most of what is now a reduced citrus output is sent to the Arab world via Jordan. Uncertainty about marketing and inability to sell all their crop caused many growers to abandon their orchards. Israel makes the planting of new orchards, or even the renewal of old trees, difficult, citing water conservation as the reason.

About 32.5 per cent or 117,900 dunums of the Gaza Strip has been confiscated by the military occupation authorities for settlements and other restricted areas.[41] Israeli settlements in Gaza are based on irrigated farming and use large amounts of local water. Water resources, always scarce in the Gaza Strip, have come under even greater pressure since occupation. In 1984, between 30-60 million cubic metres of local water was put at the disposal of 2,110 Israeli settlers (5 per cent of the total population). In contrast, more than 500,000 Palestinians consumed 100 million cubic metres in the same year (irrigated agriculture takes up 85 per cent of this amount and the rest is used for domestic consumption). Thus, settlers consumed between 14,218 and 28,436 cubic metres per capita while each Palestinian was allocated less than 200 cubic metres.[42] The extensive Israeli use of Gaza water has put a strain on the Strip's agriculture. Over-consumption has caused a drop in the water table allowing sea water to seep in, thus increasing the salinity of the soil. The decline in citrus growing also stems in part from the scarcity and increased salinity of water. Irrigation is critical to agriculture in Gaza: approximately 90,000 dunums, 45 per cent of total cultivated area, is irrigated.[43] Traditionally, 75 per cent of the land under irrigation (about 40 per cent of all cultivated land) was rainwater fed. The remaining 25 per cent was irrigated by water drawn from artesian wells. Under occupation, the area of irrigated land has increased by only 5 per cent. This marginal increase could in fact be attributed to the reduction of the cultivated area because of Israeli land expropriation. The Israeli authorities actively restrict water use in the Strip. The digging of new water wells is forbidden and restrictions are placed on the amount of water which can be drawn from existing wells through the installation of meters. The municipalities face problems in their attempts to expand water supplies to meet increasing domestic demand. A number of wells have gone dry as the water table subsided and others have been shut down because of high salinity.[44]

The investment climate and credit availability in Gaza are also important factors working to the detriment of agriculture. Branches of Arab banks such as the Arab Bank Limited of Jordan, and the Egyptian Alexandria and al-Umma banks operated in Gaza only until 1967 when they were closed by the Israeli authorities. Their services had been, in any event, limited and focused mainly on trade as opposed to industrial or agricultural development projects.

In 1961 a local bank, the Bank of Palestine, was opened with a working capital of E£ 500,000. It was also closed in 1967. The Bank was reopened in 1982 on condition that it deal only in Israeli currency. Depositors were thereby effectively discouraged, because of the volatility of the Israeli shekel. The bank gives short-term credit to citrus growers at an interest rate of 18 per cent. Credits have also been extended to a few other industrial and commercial projects.

The Gaza fishing industry has also declined since 1967. Before the war, the Gaza fishing fleet supplied all local demand for seafood. Israeli military orders have severely limited the fishing area. Boats must stay 5 miles within both the northern and southern borders of the Strip and may not fish more than 12 miles out to sea. There is no modern port and boats must therefore be winched up on to the beach every evening. Rising fuel and maintenance costs and the difficulty of obtaining fishing licences have also contributed to the decline of the industry. The catch has fallen dramatically: from 3,800 tons in 1968 to 420 tons in the first eight months of 1985.[45] Furthermore, fishing like agriculture has suffered from constraints on marketing. The Israelis have forbidden the fishermen's co-operative to open a canning factory that would compete with Israeli plants.

2. Industry

The pre-1967 industrial sector in the Gaza Strip consisted mainly of owner-operated workshops geared towards meeting domestic demand. Industry accounted for only 4.2 per cent of GDP in 1967[46] and employed between 3,000 and 6,000 persons.[47] The only industries of any size were citrus related (Table 5.4). After the 1967 war, the number employed in domestic industry dropped to 2,700.[48] The development of industry in Gaza has been impeded by the absence of natural resources or sources of energy, a limited local market and a shortage of capital. Under Egyptian rule Gaza was in part a free port. This stimulated trade, but further hindered the development of industry.

There were two categories of pre-1967 industry in Gaza: those using local raw materials and those dependent on materials brought in from abroad. Industries based on Gaza resources were flour mills, olive presses, ice factories, soft drinks and sweet manufacturers, cigarette and tobacco processors, potteries, carpet weavers, citrus processors and organic fertilizer plants.[49] Woven and spun textile and soap making factories relied on imported raw materials. Industry was concentrated in Gaza City.

Immediately after 1948 weaving was the most important of the small industries in terms of output and employment. About two-thirds of all industrial firms in 1960 produced textiles and carpets.[50] The industry was based on the skills of the 2,000 weavers who came to Gaza in the 1948 refugee exodus.[51] In 1954 there were 2,200 owner-operated looms and one weaving factory employing 45 workers. Raw material was imported from Egypt. This industry declined rapidly, however, because looms could not be replaced or maintained and because lower priced textile imports came to dominate the local market. The number of weavers decreased from 2,500 in 1953 to 600 in 1960, employed in 500 workshops. According to another source there were only 50 looms still operating in 1957.[52] Soap manufacturing suffered similarly from lack of expertise, lack of availability of raw materials and from foreign competition.

A small number of workshops engaged in industries related to agriculture: maintenance and repair of agricultural and irrigation equipment and the manufacture of packing crates. In 1959 there were 139 such workshops employing 538 workers.[53]

Table 5.6 indicates the kind of industry that existed in the Strip in 1960, the manpower employed and the capital invested. The table shows a decline in the number of workers employed in industry. The 2,500 workers of 1953 decreased to 1,782 workers in 1960.[54]

After the 1967 war the share of industry in the GDP of the Strip increased to about 11 per cent. It remained, however, a rather small and constrained sector.[55] At the end of 1968, industry in Gaza began to expand rapidly as Israeli industrial firms set up subcontracting arrangements in the Strip.[56] The number of workers employed in local industry increased to 7,000 in 1968,[57] declined to 3,934 in 1969[58] and rose again to 6,000 in 1975. In 1984, 8,000 workers were employed in local industry and 7,300 had industrial jobs in Israel.[59] These figures clearly reflect the unstable conditions of Gaza industry. The number of workers in local industrial employment rose marginally to between

Table 5.6: Industries, manpower and capital in the Gaza Strip: 1960

Industry	No. of units	No. of workers	Average no. of workers/unit	Capital invested (in thousands of Egyptian pounds)	Estimated annual production (in thousands of Egyptian pounds)
Weaving	500	600	1.2	70.0	200
Carpets	8	85	10.6	15.0	25
Citrus packing	1	75	75.0	150.0	–
Soft drinks	5	80	16.0	43.5	40
Olive presses	12	65	5.4	10.0	12
Ice factories	4	30	7.5	7.0	15
Crop presses	5	15	3.0	4.0	2
Cigarettes and tobacco	4	35	8.0	8.5	40
Sweets	4	17	3.4	5.0	8
Bakeries/food industry	50	110	2.2	22.0	57
Soap	4	35	8.8	4.5	20
Clay	29	75	2.6	3.0	5
Workshops	143	560	3.9	30.0	95
TOTAL	769	1782	2.2	372.5	519

Source: Husayn Abu al-Namil, *qit'a ghazza: 1948-1967* (The Gaza Strip: 1948-1967)
(The Palestine Liberation Organisation Research Centre, Beirut, 1979), p.259.

6,000 and 7,000 by 1984.[60]

Between 1968 and 1975 industry's contribution to GNP increased from 3.7 per cent to 5.7 per cent.[61] The increase was mainly in local workshops which produced on contract for Israeli enterprises. Clothing and textiles have been the main industries in the Strip since 1967. Although subcontracting provided some employment opportunities, it has not produced any lasting industrial development or affected the structure of existing industries.[62] Israeli purchases have stimulated rapid growth in the manufacture of bamboo and straw furniture and Israelis living near Gaza provide steady custom for garages in the Strip. Table 5.7 shows the distribution of the 1,421 industrial establishments in the Gaza Strip by branch and employment in 1982.

The Israeli authorities have made no structural change in industry. Local industry receives no government assistance, subsidies, or credit. Development of infrastructure has been neglected. Israeli industry, with which the Gaza industry competes, is heavily subsidised by the Israeli government with selective taxation and generous investment incentives. These factors, in addition to political uncertainty and absence of adequate financial services, have made local and Israeli entrepreneurs reluctant to invest in the industrial sector in the Gaza Strip.

The outlook for Gaza industry is not good. It is dependent on and controlled by Israel which restricts independent industrial development. Infrastructural weaknesses, the absence of trade links, Israel's expropriation of basic resources and its protectionist policies, the lack of investment, the shortage of skilled labour, and dependence on imported raw materials all give little room for optimism for industrial development.

Table 5.7: Industrial establishments in Gaza by branch and size: 1982

Branch	No. of workers employed			
	1-3	4-10	11-20	21+
Food, beverages, and tobacco	154	40	5	3
Textile, clothing, leather and related products	306	160	45	12
Wood and wood products	128	75	4	5
Basic metal products	179	73	5	4
Others	102	112	6	3
TOTAL	869	460	65	27

Source: Gharaibeh, *The Economies of the West Bank*, p. 92.

3. Trade

Foreign trade before 1967 was of obvious importance. Citrus, other agricultural produce and wool rugs were the main exports. Imports included food, fuels, textiles, construction materials, pumps and other machinery. About 50 per cent of these imports came from Egypt.[63]

The Gaza imports were not, however, solely for the local market of 400,000 people. Gaza merchants and traders took advantage of the Strip's special relationship with Egypt (an Egyptian administration and a similar currency) and relaxed import policies to import such 'luxury' goods as batteries, whisky, radios, china and silverware for re-export to Egypt. To illustrate the relative volume of this kind of trade, Gaza food imports increased 3.81 times between 1954 and 1966, while imports of china and silverware increased 63.3 times during the same period.[64]

Table 5.8 shows the value of citrus exports *vis à vis* other exports in selected years. Citrus exports comprised 70 per cent of the Strip's total export in 1954 and had grown to 90 per cent in 1966.[65] The pre-eminence of this one cash crop is indicative of the skewed and fragile nature of the Gaza economy.

Table 5.9 shows the balance of trade and the trade deficit for selected years between 1950 and 1961. Remittances generally covered the deficits in the balance of trade.[66]

Before 1967 local trade flourished, stimulated by remittances and the active tourist business between Egypt and Gaza. The movement of Egyptians to Gaza to shop and Gazans to Egypt to sell was clearly strengthened by Gaza's low custom duties. Tourism ended with the 1967 war.

After occupation the Gaza Strip market was opened to the sale of Israeli products and the military authorities imposed high tariffs on foreign imports coming to Gaza.[67] Local trade was concentrated in the hands of a few large-scale wholesalers.[68] Trade with the West Bank and with Jordan was opened up. During the first year of occupation about 40 per cent of citrus exports went to these two areas. In the second year such exports fell to around 25 per cent.

Israel has become, by far, Gaza's largest trading partner. In 1982, 82 per cent of the Strip's total exports went to Israel. Jordan, the second major trading partner, received 16 per cent.[69] Concomitantly, the Gaza Strip imports almost exclusively from Israel; 91 per cent of Gaza's imports in 1982 came from Israel. Gaza and the West Bank combined are second only to the United States as importers of Israeli goods.[70] Table 5.10 shows Gaza's imports and exports in selected years between 1972 and 1982.

Table 5.8: Citrus exports of the Gaza Strip for selected years: 1954-1966 (in Egyptian pounds and percentage)

Year	Citrus exports	%	Other exports	%	Total exports	%
1954	298,557	70.5	124,981	29.5	423,538	100.0
1959	673,335	78.2	187,877	21.8	861,212	100.0
1962	1,006,000	81.9	217,756	18.1	1,223,756	100.0
1964	3,545,000	91.3	319,950	8.3	3,864,950	100.0
1966	3,887,000	89.4	462,000	10.6	4,394,000	100.0

Source: Abu al-Namil, *qit'a ghazza*, p.266.

Table 5.9: Balance of trade in selected years: 1950-1966 (in millions of Egyptian pounds)

Year	Imports	Exports	Balance
1950	0,988	0,137	-0,851
1953	1,189	0,272	-0,971
1955	1,662	0,429	-1,223
1958	2,750	0,696	-2,052
1961	3,950	1,100	-2,850
1965	10,674	4,297	-6,377
1966	11,995	4,349	-5,646

Sources: Muhammad 'Ali Khulusi, *al-tanmiya al-iqtisadiyya fi qit'a ghazza: 1948-1967* (Economic development in the Gaza Strip: 1948-1967) (United Commercial Printhouse, Cairo, 1967), p. 211; Abu al-Namil, *qit'a ghazza*, pp.266, 287.

The value of exports amounted to 38 per cent of the Strip's GNP in 1982, imports accounted for 64 per cent.[71] The balance of trade deficit is covered by the earnings of workers in Israel, remittances from abroad and other transfers.[72] It is evident from the table that Gaza continues to grow more dependent on Israel.

Table 5.10: Imports and exports of the Gaza Strip in selected years: 1972-1982 (percentage)

	1972	1974	1976	1978	1980	1982	1984
Imports	100.0	100.0	100.0	100.0	100.0	100.0	100.0
From Israel	88.8	89.2	91.3	90.7	89.0	90.9	91.9
From Jordan	0.1	0.1	-	-	-	-	-
From other countries	11.1	10.7	8.7	9.3	11.0	9.1	8.1
Exports	100.0	100.0	100.0	100.0	100.0	100.0	100.0
To Israel	47.3	60.8	64.3	65.8	76.2	81.5	83.4
To Jordan	10.2	18.4	23.4	27.1	17.7	15.7	12.9
To other countries	42.5	20.8	12.3	7.1	6.1	2.8	3.7

Sources: Gharaibeh, *Economies of the West Bank*, p. 109; Central Bureau of Statistics, *Statistics Quarterly*, no.2, p. 7.

4. Construction and services

Construction, mainly of private housing, contributed 6 per cent of the local GDP and provided employment for 4,000 workers before 1967.[73] Between 1968 and 1975 construction work increased by 30 per cent, but the number employed in this sector declined. Its contribution to GNP increased from 3.1 to 17.8 per cent during the same period.[74] Residential construction in the Strip has expanded for a number of reasons: limited alternative investment opportunities and a general predisposition to invest in home ownership both because it is more feasible and also as a sign of the people's determination to settle the land and thereby 'assert their rights to the land in the face of continuous threat of confiscations'.[75]

The services sectors in the Strip - transport, tourism, commerce and various public services - provided most of the remaining employment and accounted for over a half of the GDP before the war.[76] Income was derived from tourism, public services, transportation and the civilian staff servicing Egyptian, Palestinian and United Nations forces stationed in the Strip. UNRWA employed a large staff to run its refugee camps, schools and clinics.[77]

With the 1967 war, the Egyptian and United Nations troops left, the Palestine Liberation Army was disbanded, and tourism virtually ceased. After the occupation, the service sector's contribution to GDP continued however to be significant although the economic nature of these services changed. The services share fluctuated from a low of around 40 per cent to a high of 65 per cent. It provided just over half of GDP in 1982. Just over 20 per cent of the locally employed work force was in services in that year.[78]

V. CONCLUSION

The Israeli development strategy for the occupied territories can best be described as 'cosmetic'. Meron Benvenisti has described it as being by 'the initiation of change within the existing resource base and infrastructure rather than by efforts to transform the rural infrastructure through heavy capital expenditure, land reform, a move towards the processing of produce and improve structural support systems'.[79] In the best of circumstances, the Arab economy is permitted to develop only so long as its development does not compete or interfere with Israeli interests and broader objectives, or place a fiscal or economic burden on the Israeli system.[80]

Economic conditions and future economic developments in the Gaza Strip will be determined by both economic and political factors. Barring a major political breakthrough, the Gaza economy is unlikely to undergo significant changes. In the absence of alternative linkages it will remain structurally weak and highly dependent on Israel.

Subsidised Israeli products dominate the markets of the occupied territories. Movement of Palestinian agricultural and industrial output is strictly controlled. No authority exists to promote development, and growth linkages inside the West Bank and Gaza Strip economies, and between them, are vestigial. Such growth as there is in the Gaza Strip is determined by the level of wages of the 35,000-45,000 workers currently employed in Israel. Their higher wages have increased income and in turn spurred local consumption and related economic activity. However, with the economic crisis in the Israeli economy in 1984, recession set in in Gaza. Lack of investment both because of low incomes and occupation-related risks, will continue to be a major constraint on development. Tourism, a potential source of hard currency, has virtually disappeared.

The policy of integration with the Israeli economy, Meron Benvenisti suggests, has 'dealt a death blow to the economic viability of the Palestinians as a community'.[81] It remains a market for Israeli produce and a supplier of cheap labour. Demand for that labour has stabilised, following the 1983 economic crisis, at a lower level than previously. Productive economic activity in the Strip is therefore unlikely to expand in the near future. Water utilisation is at its limit and unless new sources are discovered or current lopsided distribution between inhabitants and settlers is altered there will be no expansion of agricultural output.

The lack of infrastructure, finance and investment and marketing opportunities condemn local industry to its current state. Existing trade patterns are unlikely to change as they have considerable benefits for Israel. New markets for Gaza products will have to be reached through Israel, Jordan or Egypt. None of these countries has so far shown willingness to address the urgency of the crisis.

In the words of one student of the economies of the occupied territories, the apparently unabashed objective of the Israeli economic policies in the Gaza Strip is to 'subjugate the Palestinian economy, to destroy its viability, to create economic hardships that would induce emigration (especially of men in their prime, the educated and the professionals), to exploit the natural and human resources of the territories, and thus to facilitate Jewish settlement and eventual annexation'.[82]

NOTES

1. Muhammad 'Ali Khulusi, *al-tanmiya al-iqtisadiyya fi qit'a ghazza: 1948-1967* (Economic development in the Gaza Strip: 1948-1967) (The United Commercial Printhouse, Cairo, 1967), pp. 40-41. The area of the southern province comprised about 51% of the area of Palestine. Its population comprised only 11% of the population. Jews owned 114,491 dunums in the province. The dunum is a unit of land area equal to 1,000 square metres, or about a quarter of an acre.

2. Ibid.

3. Ziad Abu Amr, *al-hijra min qit'a ghazza* (Emigration from the Gaza Strip) (The Centre for Rural Development, Al-Najah National University, Nablus, 1981), p.1.

4. Khulusi, *al-tanmiya*, pp. 51-3.

5. Fawzi A. Gharaibeh, *The Economies of the West Bank and Gaza Strip* (Westview Press, Boulder, Colorado, 1985), p. 29.

6. Elisha Efrat, 'Settlement Pattern and Economic Changes of the Gaza Strip: 1947-1977', *Middle East Journal*, no. 31 (Summer 1977), p.30.

7. Abu Amr, *al-hijra*, p.1. A report published in May 1986 by Meron Benvenisti's West Bank Data Base Project put the Gaza Strip population at 525,000 and the density per square kilometre at between 2,100 and 2,200 persons. See *Jerusalem Post*, May 25 1986, p. 1.

8. Gharaibeh, *Economies of the West Bank*, p.33.

9. Ibid.

10. Ibid.

11. Khulusi, *al-tanmiya*, pp. 61-4.

12. Gharaibeh, *Economies of the West Bank*, p.38.

13. Ibid., p.40.

14. Ibid.

15. Ibid., p.48.

16. Ibid; *Jerusalem Post*, 25 May 1986, p. 1.

17. Gharaibeh, *Economies of the West Bank*, p.50.

18. Meron Benvenisti, *The West Bank Data Project: A Survey of Israel's Policies* (American Enterprise Institute, Washington D.C., 1984), p.9.

19. Central Bureau of Statistics, *Judaea, Samaria and Gaza Area: Statistics Quarterly, no. 2* (Central Bureau of Statistics, Jerusalem, 1985), p.98.

20. Central Bureau of Statistics, *Statistical Abstract of Israel, 1985* (Central Bureau of Statistics, Jerusalem, 1985).

21. The total GNP of the West Bank and Gaza combined amounted to 2.6% of the Israeli GNP in 1967 and 5.2% in 1980. Benvenisti, *The West Bank Data Base Project*, p.9.

22. Van Arkadie, *Benefits and Burdens*, p.30; Khulusi, *al-tanmiya*, p.81.

23. Sharif Kan'ana and Rashad al-Madani, *al-istitan wa-al-musadarat al-aradi fi qit'a ghazza: 1967-1984* (Settlement and land confiscation in the Gaza Strip: 1967-1984) (Centre for Research and Documentation, Birzeit University, Birzeit, 1985), p.11.

24. Central Bureau of Statistics, *Statistics Quarterly, no. 2*, p. 168.

25. Ibid., p.15.

26. Khulusi, *al-tanmiya*, p.76.

27. Ibid., p.86.

28. Husayn Abu al-Namil, *qit'a ghazza: 1948-1967* (The Gaza Strip: 1967- 1948) (The Palestine Liberation Organisation Research Centre, Beirut, 1979), p.256.

29. Gharaibeh, *Economies of the West Bank*, p.62.

30. Ibid., p.65. In the Strip today there are about 570 dunums of Palestinian-owned greenhouses. Jewish settlers are estimated to have about 3,000 dunums.

31. Khulusi, *al-tanmiya*, p.78.

32. Remittances in 1959 were put at E£ 2.1 million and at E£ 3,364,439 in 1961. Additional sums were transferred unofficially. It has been suggested that the size of remittances was double the returns of citrus exports. Abu al-Namil, *qit'a ghazza*, p.254. In the mid-1980s remittances of Palestinians working in the Gulf states to their relatives in the Gaza Strip were estimated to be equivalent to a third of the GDP. Ann M. Lesch, 'Gaza: forgotten corner of Palestine', *Journal of Palestine Studies*, vol. 15 (Institute of Palestine Studies, Washington D.C., August 1985), p. 49.

33. Kan'ana and al-Madani, *al-istitan*, p.9.

34. Van Arkadie, *Benefits and Burdens*, p.30.

35. Khulusi, *al-tanmiya*, p.80.

36. Abu al-Namil, *qit'a ghazza*, p.256.

37. Kan'ana and al-Madani, *al-istitan*, p.9.

38. Benvenisti, *The West Bank Data Base Project*, p.13.

39. Gharaibeh, *Economies of the West Bank*, p.61.

40. Eliyahu Kanovsky, *The Economic Impact of the Six Day War: Israel, The Occupied Territories, Egypt, Jordan*, (Praeger, New York, 1970), p. 40.

41. Interview with Meron Benvenisti, *Qol Israel* (The Voice of Israel), May 25, 1986.

42. Kan'ana and al-Madani, *al-istitan*, p.11.

43. Gharaibeh, *Economies of the West Bank*, p.62.

44. Ibid., p.63.

45. *Jerusalem Post*, 26 May 1986, p.1.

46. Gharaibeh, *Economies of the West Bank*, p.85.

47. Kanovsky, *The Economic Impact*, p.176.

48. Elias H. Tuma and Haim Darin-Darbkin, *The Economic Case for Palestine* (Croom Helm, London, 1978), p.65.

49. Abu al-Namil, *qit'a ghazza*, p.260.

50. Gharaibeh, *Economies of the West Bank*, p.88.

51. Abu al-Namil, *qit'a ghazza*, p.260.

52. Ibid., p. 259; Khulusi, *al-tanmiya*, pp.156-7 gives the lower figures.

53. Khulusi, *al-tanmiya*, pp. 159.

54. Abu al-Namil, *qit'a ghazza*, p.259.

55. Gharaibeh, *Economies of the West Bank*, p.85.

56. Kanovsky, *The Economic Impact*, p.181.

57. Tuma and Darin-Darbkin, *The Economic Case for Palestine*, p.65.

58. Kanovsky, *The Economic Impact*, p.181.

59. Tuma and Darin-Darbkin, *The Economic Case for Palestine*, p.65; Central Bureau of Statistics, *Statistics Quarterly*, no. 2, p.168.

60. Official figures and those of independent researchers vary. See for example, Central Bureau of Statistics, *Statistical Abstract of Israel* and Sara

Roy, *The Gaza Strip Survey* (The West Bank Data Base Project, Jerusalem, 1986), p.58.

61. Tuma and Darin-Darbkin, *The Economic Case for Palestine,* p.65.
62. Gharaibeh, *Economies of the West Bank,* p.92.
63. Khulusi, *al-tanmiya,* p.226.
64. Abu al-Namil, *qit'a ghazza,* p.269.
65. Ibid., p.266.
66. Ibid., p.255.
67. Van Arkadie, *Benefits and Burdens,* p.35.
68. Benvenisti, *The West Bank Data Base Project,* p.14.
69. Gharaibeh, *Economies of the West Bank,* p.168.
70. Ibid., p.110.
71. Ibid., pp.110, 112.
72. It is estimated that about US$ 50-60 million has been transferred from the Jordanian-Palestinian Joint Committee to the West Bank and Gaza since 1979. Ibid., p.115.
73. Ibid., p.95.
74. Ibid., p.25; Tuma and Darin-Darbkin, *The Economic Case for Palestine*, p.66, gives figures of 4.8% and 10.4% for the two years.
75. Gharaibeh, *Economies of the West Bank,* p.97.
76. Ibid.
77. Van Arkadie, *Benefits and Burdens,* p.31.
78. Gharaibeh, *Economies of the West Bank,* pp.25, 98, 99.
79. Benvenisti, *The West Bank Data Base Project,* p.14.
80. Ibid., p.9.
81. Ibid.
82. Ibid., p.11.

6

Israeli Policy Towards Economic Development in the West Bank and Gaza

Mohammed K. Shadid

The problems of economic development in a third-world nation are considerable under normal circumstances; the economic development of a people subject to foreign occupation presents a far greater challenge. In this case the evaluation of economic development should not be limited to measuring conventional determinants such as long-term increases in per capita income. Healthy economic development requires innovations to preserve national institutional infrastructure and vital national resources while the struggle to end occupation continues.

Since Israel occupied the West Bank and the Gaza Strip in 1967 it has established over 150 settler colonies on confiscated Palestinian land. They are inhabited by an imported civilian population enjoying the separate legal, economic and judicial systems by which Israel also seeks to control the human and material resources of the occupied territories. The professed 'security' reason for the Israeli occupation appears secondary to the obvious economic and political value of the occupied territories to Israel: the nature of Israel's economic relations with the areas under its military control can best be explained by examining trends in the economic development of the West Bank and Gaza.

Given the current structural weaknesses and vulnerabilities of the Israeli economy, the resources of the occupied territories play a specific and not insignificant role in helping the Israeli economy deal with these weaknesses and vulnerabilities. The occupation has helped transform Israel into a state with an imperial economy, relying for its well-being on the captive human and material resources of the occupied territories. Unlike the European empires of the past two centuries, where the metropolitan centres received economic resources

121

from all over the globe, the Israeli imperial economy is based on a geographically contiguous area, making pacification easier, more efficient and perhaps less obvious.[1]

As Israel's economic crisis has worsened over the past decade its reliance on the occupied territories has grown. Inflation seemed to be out of control, rising steadily from 39.7 per cent in 1975, to 373.8 per cent in 1984 before its decline to 304.6 in 1985. It was growing at an average of 16 per cent per month before a strict wage and prices freeze was imposed. Relative stability was achieved at the expense of living standards and employment and the export markets and cheap labour of the occupied territories became even more essential.[2] Unemployment has been particularly high in Israeli development towns and among Oriental Jews with middle sector jobs. They often prefer drawing unemployment benefit to doing 'Arab work'. As a result of the economic crisis, wages for Arab workers have fallen and the number of jobs in construction has decreased. There have not been, however, the massive lay-offs of Palestinian workers predicted at the outset.

Israel's trade and payments deficits continue to deteriorate (see Table 6.1). The crucial importance of the occupied territories to Israel's economy can be seen in the volume of Israeli exports to the West Bank and Gaza (Table 6.2).

Table 6.1: Israel's trade and payments deficits: 1977-1985 (millions of US dollars)

Year	Trade Deficit	Payments Deficit
1977	1,759.7	2,382.0
1978	1,914.1	3,119.0
1979	3,083.1	3,657.0
1980	2,553.8	3,775.0
1981	2,485.8	4,335.0
1982	2,924.6	4,824.0
1983	3,491.6	5,039.0
1984	2,449.7	4,893.0
1985	1,940.5	3,972.0

Source: Central Bureau of Statistics, *Statistical Abstract of Israel*, no. 37 (Central Bureau of Statistics, Jerusalem,1986), pp. 196, 210.

Table 6.2: Israeli exports by destination in selected years: 1970-1985 (millions of US dollars)

Year	USA	West Bank & Gaza	United Kingdom	South Africa
1970	149.1	73.9	81.4	10.7
1975	307.5	367.7	169.3	34.7
1980	953.9	571.6	465.5	79.2
1982	1,117.7	639.6	416.5	74.2
1983	1,329.2	680.5	412.9	82.8
1984	1,638.0	649.9	481.5	104.4
1985	2,138.0	611.4	477.0	63.8

Source: Central Bureau of Statistics, *Statistical Abstract of Israel*, no. 35 (Central Bureau of Statistics, Jerusalem, 1984), pp. 213, 225, 227. The data for South Africa are believed to be underestimates.

These figures are taken from the *Statistical Abstract of Israel*, which excludes East Jerusalem and its 130,000 Arab inhabitants from the rest of the West Bank.[3] The addition of East Jerusalem would have led to an even more striking picture; goods and services supplied by Israel to East Jerusalem are not included in the statistics for the West Bank and Gaza. It has been estimated that they are equivalent to 25 per cent of Israeli exports to the West Bank and the Gaza Strip. The adjusted figure for 1985 would therefore be US$ 764.3 million instead of US$ 611.4 million.[4]

The occupied territories are Israel's second most important export market after the United States, being equivalent to 160 per cent of Israel's exports to the United Kingdom, Israel's third largest customer (Table 6.2). An indication of Israel's tight control over the economies of the occupied territories is the fact that 90.7 per cent of their imports originate in Israel.[5]

I. AN OVERVIEW OF ISRAELI ECONOMIC POLICY FOR THE OCCUPIED TERRITORIES

Israeli policy towards the occupied territories since 1967 has been governed by the common, though occasionally contradictory, interests of Israeli entrepreneurs and political strategists. They are forcefully protected by military orders regulating the indigenous Palestinian economy. The occupation authorities have sought to integrate the economies of the West Bank, the Gaza Strip and the Golan Heights[6] into that of Israel. The nature of this colonial relationship is most obviously revealed in the seizure of land and water, but it equally dominates trade, labour and industry.

The Israeli Ministry of Defence, in its report on 'Development and the Economic Situation' in the occupied territories, summarised the economic relationship between Israel and the captured areas quite candidly: 'The areas are a supplementary market for Israeli goods and services on the one hand and a source of factors of production, especially unskilled labour, for the Israeli economy on the other.'[7]

1. The industrial sector

The industrial sector's contribution to the GDP of the West Bank actually fell from 9 per cent in 1968, to 8.2 per cent in 1975 and 6.5 per cent in 1980.[8] GDP per capita is twice as high as that of Egypt but the contribution of industry to GDP is only a quarter the size.

The industrial sector in the West Bank and Gaza consists mainly of small and medium-sized workshops, 92.3 per cent of which employ between one and nine workers.[9] These establishments are un-mechanised and operate mainly in the processing of primary goods – food, beverages and tobacco. Textiles production and manufacture of clothing are also important (Table 6.3).

Table 6.3: Distribution of industrial firms by the size of their labour forces: 1978

Number of Workers	Number of Firms	% of Total
1-9	2,784	92.3
10-19	145	4.6
20-49	74	2.5
50-55	7	0.2
100 and more	7	0.2
TOTAL	3,017	100.0

Source: Hisham Awartani, *A Survey of Industry in the West Bank and the Gaza Strip* (Birzeit University Publications, Birzeit, 1979), p.25.

Pickled olives, olive oil and oil-based soap exported to Jordan and the Arab world account for nearly 90 per cent of all industrial sales.[10] About half the cement blocks, floor tiles, bricks and stones for construction produced in the occupied territories is sold to Israeli companies.[11] Sales of other products such as clothing (subcontracted from Israeli firms), wood products, wicker and other furniture, woven textiles, plastic household products (mattresses, sandals, etc.), fluctuate depending on the level of demand in the Israeli market.[12]

There is little investment by Arab entrepreneurs because of the high risks involved. Israeli capital is absent except in the form of subcontracts, particularly in the textiles and clothing sectors. Seventy per cent of all textiles firms were established after 1967.[13] It is 'the lowest paid industry in the West Bank and the Gaza Strip'.[14] Ninety per cent of textile workers are women earning less than 60 per cent of the wages paid for similar jobs in Israel.[15]

In the areas of industry, finance and agriculture, Israel has discouraged the establishment of a strong and independent infrastructure for the region. The flooding of the West Bank and Gaza Strip markets with subsidised foodstuffs and manufactured foods from Israel drives out Palestinian products. Discriminatory policies and practices militate against Palestinian businesses becoming viable. Palestinian manufacturers, for instance, are charged a 15 per cent production tax as laid down in Jordanian law.[16] This tax is not applied to Israeli manufacturers, either inside the Green Line or in the settlements. Value added tax of 15 per cent is also levied by the occupation authorities and a tax of 38.5 per cent on net assets is imposed at the end of the fiscal year. Israelis also pay these taxes, but there is discrimination in the method of calculation. Palestinians are taxed in stable Jordanian dinars, the Israelis in devalued Israeli shekels despite the fact that they both buy and sell their goods in shekels. On the whole, Palestinian manufacturers pay 35-40 per cent more tax than their Israeli counterparts. This makes their production costs higher and would undermine their ability to compete even if they had equal access to the market. The primary concern of the Palestinian manufacturer has become survival rather than development.

At the same time Israel is promoting a far-reaching plan for Jewish, rather than Arab, industrial development in the West Bank. By 1983 six Jewish industrial zones had been constructed in the West Bank:[17] Shaked, 40 dunums; Barkan, 300 dunums; Ma'ale Ephraim, 70 dunums; Karne Shomron, 150 dunums; Ma'ale Adumim, 650 dunums; and Kiryat Arba, 50 dunums. The aim is to have a total of 1,650 dunums of industrial development zones.

Plants in these zones employ some 2,500 workers, 70 per cent of whom are Jewish; the remainder are Palestinian Arabs who are assigned primarily unskilled jobs.[18] The authorities are promoting capital intensive industries to reduce the need for settlers to commute to cities inside Israel, and limit Arab employment. A 1982 World Zionist Organisation plan to settle 100,000 Jews in the West Bank by the year 2010 calls for the establishment of seven more industrial parks.[19] The total area designated for industry in the plan is 15,000 dunums. It predicts 83,500 new jobs for Jewish industrial workers with 25,000 unskilled and semi-skilled jobs for Palestinians.[20]

Israeli researchers estimate that by 1986 an additional 8,750 Jewish and 2,200 Arab industrial jobs will have been created. Investment in the new Jewish industrial parks is estimated at US$ 250 million over five years (US$ 60-100 million for infrastructure and the rest for 10 per cent government equity participation). Existing investment in Jewish industry in the West Bank is valued at US$ 328 million.[21]

2. Labour

After 1967 Israel invested heavily in industry to diversify from its dependence on agriculture. Profitability was increased by the availability of a large pool of unskilled labour in the occupied territories. Table 6.4 shows the increase in the number of Palestinians employed in Israel since 1970.

Table 6.4: Distribution of workers in the occupied territories by place of work in selected years: 1970-1985

Year	Total (thousands)	Number Working in Israel	% in Israel
1970	173.3	20.6	12.0
1973	194.7	61.3	31.5
1974	210.4	68.7	32.6
1975	204.9	66.3	32.2
1976	205.8	64.9	31.5
1977	204.4	63.0	30.8
1979	212.1	74.1	34.9
1980	215.7	75.1	34.8
1981	215.9	75.8	35.1
1982	222.7	79.1	35.5
1983	232.5	87.8	37.8
1984	241.3	90.3	37.4
1985	241.9	89.2	36.9

Source: Central Bureau of Statistics, *Statistical Abstract of Israel*, no. 37, 1986, p. 705

Israeli statisticians calculate the number of workers from the occupied territories through its labour offices. Official figures do not include people denied work permits, or workers who do not seek them. There are an estimated 20-25,000 Palestinians working in Israel without permits. They are privately employed by Israelis, either from Arab labour contractors or through unofficial labour exchanges (or 'slave markets' as they are known). Payment is in cash and neither side pays taxes or insurance.[22] A more realistic figure for the number of workers from the occupied territories employed in Israel in 1985 is 109,200 (89,200 legally plus 20,000 illegally), or 45 per cent of the total work force.[23]

Palestinian workers are confined to certain sectors in the Israeli economy, primarily construction (which takes 50 per cent of the illegally hired workers), agriculture and services.[24] They are paid lower wages than Israelis for the same job.[25] Many Israeli entrepreneurs have moved businesses to the occupied territories to exploit the labour market. Subcontracting exploits women's and children's labour which is even cheaper than Palestinian men's.

3. Agriculture

Before 1967, the West Bank was the breadbasket of Jordan. It is not even self-sufficient now. Occupation policy has transformed Palestinian agriculture so that it fulfils the function of supplying other factors of production and serves Israeli market strategies.

In the months immediately following the war, the Israeli authorities announced an 'open bridges' policy. West Bank farmers received permits to truck their agricultural surpluses (and manufacturers their products) across the Jordan River bridges to the East Bank. If the produce had been left unsold, the economy of the West Bank would have collapsed; the resistance of the population might have intensified and the provision of basic necessities by the occupation forces would have drained the Israeli economy. If West Bank fruits and vegetables had been allowed onto the Israeli market they would have undercut Israeli produce by 20-25 per cent.[26]

The Israeli army delayed access to the Israeli market for occupied territories agricultural produce by introducing military orders requiring permits and health checks on processed foods and certification that the produce would not cause Israeli surpluses.[27] Israeli farmers, on the other hand, had unrestricted access to the West Bank. In the first year of occupation the Israeli Ministry of Agriculture established a general policy for West Bank agriculture which aimed to reduce the area's pre-war dependence on trade with the East Bank and to introduce crops which would complement Israel's own and would either be exported

127

to Europe or processed in Israeli factories.[28] The exports over the bridges prevented the West Bank produce from glutting the Israeli market or remaining unsold, and brought in hard currency which improved Israel's financial situation.

Today about a third of West Bank agricultural output is marketed in Jordan.[29] The bridges are 'open' in one direction only; agricultural imports from the East Bank are not permitted. The 'open bridges' are an economic conduit to Jordan and the Arab world. Initially, Israel hoped to use the conduit for its own goods and it still entertains hopes of gaining access to the vast markets in surrounding countries.

In light of the growing importance of foreign currency earnings to Israel's ailing economy, there are clear advantages to Israel in promoting further development and expansion of agriculture in the occupied territories. In fact, the opposite has occurred and restrictions have caused stagnation. The registered increases in agricultural production were due to the introduction of modern technology, not to expansion in area. The actual area of land under cultivation in the West Bank and the Gaza Strip is smaller now than before the 1967 war (Table 6.5). There has been a drop in the number of people employed in agriculture, from 69,000 just prior to the war to 22,000 in 1983.[30]

Table 6.5: Area under cultivation in the West Bank in selected years: 1966-81 (in thousands of dunums)

Type of Land	1966	1968	1973	1974	1975	1976	1980	1981
Irrigated	100	57	82	81	83	89	92	98
Rain-fed	1,980	1,988	1,941	1,939	1,878	1,931	1,859	1,909
TOTAL	2,080	2,045	2,023	2,020	1,961	2,020	1,951	2,007

Source: Meron Benvenisti, *The West Bank Data Base Project* (American Enterprise Institute, Washington D.C., 1984), p. 13.

4. Land

Control of the land is the most vital issue in the development of the occupied territories and a point of violent confrontation between Palestinians and Israelis. Meron Benvenisti reported that 52 per cent of the West Bank land, including the most fertile areas, has been alienated from Palestinians through various techniques of land expropriation, no-construction orders, closures, demolition of houses, destruction of cultivated fields and armed terror against *fallahin*.[31]

This Israeli government policy of seizing the land and squeezing the population would, according to an extremist view articulated by current Israeli Knesset member and former Chief of Staff of the Israeli armed forces Rafael Eitan, cause Palestinians to 'run about like drugged cockroaches in a bottle'.[32]

5. Water

Immediately after the 1967 war, the water resources of the newly occupied areas were placed under the control of Israel's national water company, Mekorot. Since then, the authorities have permitted the drilling of only seven new wells to provide drinking water. Twelve irrigation wells have dried up, and many others, especially in the Jordan Valley, are becoming useless as the water table declines and salinity increases. Only two permits have been issued for Palestinians to drill wells on their own land for irrigation purposes and only one of these produced usable water.[33]

Over the same period Israeli settlements have drilled at least 17 wells: these wells, 5 per cent of the West Bank total, drew 14.1 million cubic metres of water, 30 per cent of the total for the West Bank. All 314 Palestinian wells drew 33 million cubic metres.[34] Israel helps itself to vital West Bank resources – ground water in the eastern drainage area of the Jordan Valley – while imposing draconian restrictions on water usage, especially of the western aquifers, by Palestinians on the grounds that it threatens salination of supplies inside Israel. Irrigation wells have been metered, and stiff fines imposed on users who exceed the limits imposed by the military authorities. Settlements, in contrast, are not restricted in their use of water for irrigation (even to fill swimming pools) while the majority of the West Bank villages, and some towns, suffer seasonal shortages.

In the irrigated regions of the Jordan Valley restrictions have been particularly harsh. Early in the occupation, the army destroyed 140 water pumps in the Gaza Strip and along the Jordan River and closed 30,000 dunums of agricultural land. In 1979, the authorities bulldozed the irrigation canal in the village of Jiftlik. Subsequently, land was confiscated and tenant farmers' homes destroyed and other areas closed to cultivation.

Israel's water policies have been a major impediment to any expansion or intensification of agricultural production in the West Bank. In the Jordan Valley, Mekorot's water plan calls for 36 wells by the late 1980s. This will extract half the available ground water for only 28 settlements housing 2,000 Israelis. Meanwhile, the subsistence of 14,000 Arab residents is threatened by dwindling water supplies.[35]

6. Israel's policy towards development projects

Indications of short- and long-term Israeli plans for the occupied territories are revealed in its decisions regarding development projects. This area has attracted public debate over the last few years because of conflict between the military authorities and a number of US private voluntary organisations (PVOs) over approval and implementation of development projects.

There are eight US PVOs with development and social welfare programmes in the West Bank and the Gaza Strip: American Friends Service Committee (AFSC), Mennonite Central Committee (MCC), American Near East Refugee Aid (ANERA), Community Development Fund (CDF), CARE, Catholic Relief Service (CRS), Holy Land Christian Missions (HCM) and American-Mideast Educational and Training Services (AMIDEAST). Only the first two, AFSC and MCC, do not accept US government funds. Programmes are usually proposed by the agencies, or by local Palestinians, or jointly. All individual development projects are subject to the approval of the Israeli military authorities.

7. US role and development funds in the occupied territories

US government economic aid to the Palestinian community in the West Bank and the Gaza Strip has become an important local and international political issue. This interest, generated by what had been a relatively low-profile US commitment, led to a new description of that commitment, by US Secretary of State George Shultz and later by Vice-President George Bush, as a policy redirection towards an 'improvement in the quality of life' for West Bank and Gaza Strip residents.[36] The US had been accused of joining Israel and Jordan in a policy of pacification, funnelling money to the West Bank via both governments in an attempt to increase their influence over the population. Bush announced in July 1986 in Amman that US$ 4.5 million of aid would, for the first time, be sent to the West Bank via the Jordanian government which almost simultaneously announced a five-year development plan of its own for the area. This kind of 'development' will complement the Israeli policy of permitting personal prosperity while forcibly restraining genuine social and economic development. Considering the small amount of aid the West Bank and Gaza Strip Palestinians receive compared with US aid to Israel (US\$ 14 million in fiscal year 1986 for the former and US\$ 4 billion for the latter), the US government clearly lacks any commitment to Palestinian development. Between fiscal year 1975, when the programme was authorised by Congress, and 1984, US\$ 51.6 million was allocated to the Palestinians. Over the same period the US provided Israel with a total of US\$ 24.3 billion in grants and low interest loans. In other words, for every US\$ 1.00 of aid to the Palestinians, Israel received US\$ 476.00.[37]

8. PVO development projects and Israeli policy

Before Bush's announcement, all US aid to the Palestinians was channelled through the six PVOs which accept US government funds, making these agencies potentially the direct instruments of US government policy. The US government does not, however, exert pressure on the Israeli military authorities to approve projects, leaving the agencies to negotiate alone. The 'new direction' in US policy towards 'improvements in the quality of life' by Israel, it is argued, does not differ substantially from the patterns of development both have shown themselves to favour for Palestinian residents of the occupied territories. An analysis by Meron Benvenisti of develop-ment projects submitted by the agencies to Israeli military authorities for approval provides further insight into Israeli policy in the area and how US funds are being used.

Three PVOs, ANERA, CDF and CRS fund development projects; AMIDEAST, HCM and CARE are involved in educational activities. Their work can be divided into three main areas: development and income-generating projects in agriculture and industry; social, educational, community and charitable work; public works such as the provision of water, sewage disposal, electricity networks and paved access roads.

Table 6.6 shows the relative importance given by the agencies to each area in terms of budgets and numbers of projects. Table 6.7 compares the number of projects and budgets submitted with those approved by the Israeli authorities. The preference for public works over economic development is clear.[38]

Table 6.6: Selected US private voluntary organisations projects in the West Bank: 1977-1983 (percentage)

Category	Submitted Project	Submitted Budget
Economic development	33.8	45.8
Social/educational	36.3	27.2
Public works	29.9	27.0
TOTAL	100.0	100.0

Source: Meron Benvenisti, *US Government Funded Projects in the West Bank and the Gaza Strip 1977-83* (Jerusalem: The West Bank Data Base Project, 1984), p. 7.

Table 6.7: US private voluntary organisation project submission and implementation: 1977-1983 (percentage)

	PVO Intention (Submitted)		Israeli Reaction (Actually Implemented)	
Category	Project	Budget	Project	Budget
Economic develop-ment	33.8	45.8	22.7	29.4
Social/educational	36.3	27.2	36.1	26.2
Public works	29.9	27.0	41.2	44.0
TOTAL	100.0	100.0	100.0	100.0

Source: Benvenisti, *US Government Funded Projects*, p.12.

Benvenisti's detailed analysis of 358 projects, involving a total budget of US$ 66 million, provided by the US government, administered by six PVOs and submitted to the Israeli authorities for approval and implementation shows:

(a) A third of the submitted projects and 45.8 per cent of the proposed budget were in the field of economic development; slightly more than a third of the proposals and 27.2 per cent of the proposed budgets were social, educational and charitable projects; almost 30 per cent of the projects and 27 per cent of the budgets were devoted to consumption oriented public works.

(b) Israeli intervention caused a major shift in the allocation of projects and budgets. The Israeli military authorities tended to disapprove of development projects and encourage public works. Consequently the share of consumption oriented public works in the projects actually implemented is 44 per cent. The proportion of the budget actually devoted to economic development projects was reduced from almost half of the provisional programme to less than a third.

(c) Israeli intervention alters the PVOs' emphasis and uses US economic aid in the occupied territories to implement its own economic policies (with US government acquiescence) which encourage individual prosperity and curb communal economic development. These economic policies are important components in the control of a hostile population. Curbing the development of a viable and independent economic sector forces the population to become more dependent on Israel, or alternatively Jordan. Continued individual prosperity usually militates against effective communal organisation and the pursuit of communal goals. In short, the actual contribution of US aid to the West Bank and Gaza has helped to strengthen the pacification programme pursued by Israel as well as relieving it of certain expenditures. (In fact, it has been estimated that Israel takes in – through VAT, tax on workers' wages, charges for utilities, etc. – far more than the amount it spends on services for Palestinian inhabitants of the occupied territories.)[39]

Despite the small size of the economic development programmes sponsored by the PVOs, Israeli officials are intent on control. General Ben Eliazer, the Israeli official in charge of project approval, when invited to comment on particular projects answered, 'I prefer not to answer specifically...I would like to give you the whole strategy...*no voluntary organisation has the autonomy to do whatever it wants in this part of the world. This is a place where there is law and order, and this is the place where there is an administration.*'[40] Another Israeli official in the West Bank military government was more direct in his reaction to certain economic development proposals. He said, 'Why should we assist towns like Halhoul and Dhahriyya where disturbances are commonplace and our forces are under attack?'[41]

West Bank and Gaza business people have discovered that their chances of obtaining approval of development projects are even smaller than those of the PVOs. Land reclamation project proposals are invariably rejected. Other major projects which have been rejected include: a cement factory near Hebron, a paint factory in Nablus and the expansion and modernisation of a flour mill in Hebron. Giving the reasons for rejecting the paint factory project, an Israeli official said, 'Why should we permit the building of a factory in Nablus while Israeli paint factories are operating below full capacity?'[42]

The fact that some projects are approved in one location or for a certain group, while similar ones elsewhere are rejected, indicates that political considerations are also important to the occupation authorities' approval or rejection of Palestinian development projects. People applying must be politically acceptable to the authorities. For example, when Israel was trying to promote the Village Leagues as an alternative to the PLO in the early 1980s, it allowed League members to distribute permits for road building and construction, exit, residency, and so on.

II. CONCLUSION

Responding to a request from the Israeli Citizen's Rights Movement for the relaxation of restrictions on development in the occupied territories, the Israeli Minister of Defence Yitzhak Rabin, replied: 'There will be no development in the occupied territories initiated by the Israeli Government, and no permits will be given for expanding agriculture or industry (there), which may compete with the State of Israel.'[43]

Israel, like other colonial powers, has profited enormously from the territories it occupied in war. The occupied territories have become markets for Israeli manufactured goods. The Israeli army has seized land and extracted raw materials, labour and taxes from the Palestinians who are militarily dominated, politically suppressed and economically dependent. Israeli policies are designed to maintain this status quo. Physically, Palestinian population centres are being restricted. The expansion of town and city limits is severely restricted, forcing the population into increasingly congested areas. Horizontal growth is permitted only to settlements which have been planned to encircle concentrations of Palestinian population.

Political suppression is equally evident. Gangs of armed settlers roam the streets of the largest cities of the occupied territories, supported and protected by the Israeli army. Collective punishments and detentions without trial are commonplace. Schools and universities are frequently ordered closed by the military; towns are placed under curfew; house arrests, house demolitions, forced resettlement and deportations are standard Israeli policy, and censorship is universal. These are also aspects of Israel's 'quality of life' programme.

Israel's economic policy for the occupied territories of no growth, no development and continued colonisation will not produce peace even if pacification is temporarily achieved with the support of the US.

The US Congress outlined its purposes in allocating aid to the Palestinians this way: 'It is the desire of the Congress to support projects and expand institutions in the occupied territories of the West Bank and Gaza to help build the socio-economic underpinnings necessary to preserve peace.'[44] US Consul-General in Jerusalem, Morris Draper, told an audience at the Hebrew University's Truman Institute in July 1986 that American aid would be forthcoming if 'movements' were made towards 'self-rule', a euphemism for autonomy, or toward confederation with Jordan. The new American policy of promoting private enterprise must be viewed as the de-emphasising of indigenous institution building which would give Palestinians some control over the planning and development of their future, a Palestinian national goal against which Israel's economic policies in the West Bank and Gaza Strip have fought for the last two decades.

For those Palestinians thirsty for any kind of development, no matter the political price, the immediate future seems manageable. Those Palestinians whose goal is political self-determination, in order to end the cycle of exploitation at the hands of those who control the direction of economic development, can expect an intensification of the kind of political suppression which the term 'quality of life' came to mean in 1986.

NOTES

1. Rami S. Khuri, 'Israel's imperial economics', *Journal of Palestine Studies*, vol. 9, no. 2 (Winter 1980), p. 71.
2. Central Bureau of Statistics, *Statistical Abstract of Israel*, no. 37, 1986 (Central Bureau of Statistics, Jerusalem, 1986), p. 250; *Jerusalem Post*, July 16 1985, p. 1.
3. Meron Benvenisti, *Jerusalem: Study of a Polarised Community* (The West Bank Data Base Project, Jerusalem, 1983), p. 71.
4. The population of East Jerusalem comprises about 10% of the total population of the West Bank and Gaza. The per capita income in East Jerusalem is higher than that in the rest of the West Bank; it has always been more affluent and therefore the volume of their imports is proportionally higher. Based on interviews with a number of West Bank importers from Israel, it is estimated that approximately another 15% of purchases by West Bank and Gaza Strip residents are made directly by individuals in Israeli shopping centres and these are not included in the official Israeli statistics. Thus 25% is a reasonable estimate of the amount which should be added to the official Israeli statistics.
5. Calculated from Central Bureau of Statistics, *Statistical Abstract of Israel*, 1984, p. 751.
6. The scope of this paper will be limited to a discussion of the West Bank

and the Gaza Strip. The Golan Heights merit special consideration that is not possible here.

7. Unit for Co-ordination of Activity in the Administered Areas, *Development and Economic Situation in the Administered Areas, 1967-1969: A Summary* (Ministry of Defence, Tel Aviv, October 1970); Sheila Ryan, 'Israeli economic policy in the occupied areas: foundations of a new imperialism', *MERIP Reports*, no. 24 (Washington D.C., 1974), p. 9.

8. Meron Benvenisti, *The West Bank Data Base Project* (American Enterprise Institute, Washington D.C., 1984), p. 15.

9. M.K. Budeiri, 'Changes in the economic structure of the West Bank and Gaza Strip under Israeli occupation', *Labour, Capital and Society*, vol. 15, no. 1 (April 1982), p. 55.

10. Hisham Awartani, *A Survey of Industry in the West Bank and the Gaza Strip* (Birzeit University Publications, Birzeit, 1979), p. 29.

11. Ibid., p. 28.

12. Budeiri, 'Changes in economic structure', p. 56.

13. Awartani, *A Survey of Industry*, p. 27.

14. Sarah Graham-Brown, 'The West Bank and Gaza: the structural impact of Israeli colonisation', *MERIP Reports*, no. 74 (Washington D.C., 1979), p. 12.

15. Awartani, *A Survey of Industry*, p.27.

16. Israel uses four types of laws and regulations in the West Bank: Jordanian Law (which is required by international law), the British Emergency Regulations of 1948 and Israeli Law. It uses one or more at a time as it suits its interests best. Whenever these laws are not 'adequate' the occupation authorities issue a military order.

17. Meron Benvenisti, *The West Bank Data Base Project*, p.17.

18. Ibid.

19. Ibid.

20. Ibid.

21. Ibid.

22. Joost R. Hiltermann, 'Mass mobilisation under occupation: the emerging trade union movement in the West Bank and Gaza', *MERIP Reports*, no. 136/137 (Washington D.C., 1985), p. 27.

23. Israeli statistics on the West Bank and Gaza exclude East Jerusalem; there are 24,000 Palestinian workers from East Jerusalem included in the Israeli workforce. A permit to work in Israel is not required for them. Therefore the total number of workforce in the West Bank and Gaza should be adjusted to 265,900. The figure for East Jerusalem is calculated from: Shimon Bigelman (ed.), *Statistical Yearbook of Jerusalem*, no. 3, 1984 (The Jerusalem Institute for Israel Studies, Municipality of Jerusalem, Jerusalem, 1986), pp. 176-178.

24. Central Bureau of Statistics, *Statistical Abstract of Israel*, no. 35, 1984, p. 763.

25. Hiltermann, 'Mass mobilisation', p.4.

26. Ryan, 'Israeli economic policy', p. 13.

27. Ibid.

28. *Jerusalem Post*, 22 October 1967.

29. Ryan, 'Israeli economic policy', p. 13.

30. Central Bureau of Statistics, *Statistical Abstract of Israel*, no. 35, 1984, p. 762.

31. Meron Benvenisti, *The West Bank Data Base Project*, pp. 21-2.

32. *Jerusalem Post*, 24 April 1983.

33. Raja Shehadeh, *The West Bank and the Rule of Law* (Law in the Service of Man, Ramallah, 1980), p. 66.

34. Joe Stork, 'Water and Israel's occupation policy', *MERIP Reports* no. 116 (Washington D.C., 1983), p. 22.

35. Ibid; Meron Benvenisti, *Interim Report No. 1* (The West Bank Data Base Project, Jerusalem, 1982) pp 20-1.

36. Meron Benvenisti, *US Government Funded Projects in the West Bank and the Gaza Strip 1977-83* (The West Bank Data Base Project, Jerusalem, 1984), p. 1.

37. *Washington Post*, 16 December 1984, p. A25.

38. Benvenisti, *US Government Funded Projects*, p. 7.

39. Meron Benvenisti, *West Bank Data Base Project 1987 Report: Demographic, economic, legal, social and political developments in the West Bank* (The West Bank Data Base Project/*The Jerusalem Post*, Jerusalem, 1987), pp. 30-2.

40. *New York Times*, 3 October 1980.

41. *Haaretz*, 13 April 1984.

42. Interview with Zafer Masri, Chairman, Chamber of Commerce, Nablus, 19 August 1985.

43. *Jerusalem Post*, 15 February 1985.

44. Benvenisti, *US Government Funded Projects*, p. 3.

7

Agricultural Development and Policies in the West Bank and Gaza

Hisham Awartani

I. INTRODUCTION

Changes in Palestinian agriculture in the West Bank and Gaza Strip have received special attention since the beginning of Israeli occupation in 1967. This interest has been partly motivated by agriculture's importance in the local economy. It provides 20-30 per cent of the occupied territories' Gross Domestic Product and employs a substantial part of the labour force. Agricultural development also has a sensitive impact on the question of food security for Palestinians under occupation. In addition to these factors, agriculture in the occupied territories commands a much greater significance because of its direct bearing on land and water use, both of which are at the root of the Arab-Israeli conflict. The importance of agriculture is further accentuated because of its profound effect on the occupied territories' trade relations with Israel and Jordan. Both countries adopt strongly protectionist import policies, especially in regard to farm produce.

This paper will explore the dynamics of change in agriculture, paying special attention to the political background and the ramifications of what may appear to be normal socio-economic transformations. Although most of the statistical data used in this paper relates to the West Bank, the resulting conclusions and recommendations apply in varying degrees to the Gaza Strip.

II. INCOME FROM AGRICULTURE

Agricultural output in the West Bank varies considerably from year to year, largely because of cyclical variations in the yield of olives and cereal grains which are extremely sensitive to changes in levels of

139

rainfall. Farm income has also been affected by the violent fluctuations in prices which have characterised local markets in recent years (Table 7.1).

Table 7.1 shows that the average value of income originating from agriculture between 1982 and 1984 was US$ 186 million per annum which amounted to 25.4 per cent of gross domestic product, and 18.5 per cent of Gross National Product. Though somewhat lower than is common in developing countries, the share of agriculture in the West Bank's GDP is noticeably higher than in both Jordan (6 per cent) and Israel (5 per cent).

Table 7.1: Income from agriculture in the West Bank: 1982-1984[a] (in millions of US$ and percentage)

	Income from Agriculture US$	GDP[a] US$	Share of Agr.(%)	GDP[a] US$	Share of Agr.(%)
1982	216	722	29.9	988	21.9
1983	194	738	26.3	1,037	18.7
1984	148	741	20.0	996	14.9
AVERAGE	186	734	25.4	1,007	18.5

Note: a. At factor cost and current prices.
Sources: Central Bureau of Statistics, *Statistical Abstract of Israel* (Central Bureau of Statistics, Jerusalem): 1984, p.251; 1985, p.254; 1986, pp. 241, 691.

The breakdown of West Bank agricultural income by source (based on 1983-5 averages) indicates that fruit accounts for 28 per cent of all income (see Table 7.2). Olive production is the single most important

Table 7.2: Agricultural output by source: average 1983-1985

	Millions of US$	% of Total
Crops	106.4	53.0
Field Crops	8.6	4.0
Vegetables and melons	41.4	21.0
Olives	18.5	9.0
Citrus	13.5	7.0
Other fruit	24.4	12.0
Livestock products	94.7	47.0
TOTAL OUTPUT	205.0	100.0

Source: Calculated from Table 28/27 in *Statistical Abstract of Israel*, 1986, p.713.

branch of farming with an average share of 9 per cent of income and 42 per cent share of total cultivated area. Citrus and grapes are also of great importance, especially as export commodities. Vegetable crops contribute 20 per cent of agricultural income, although their share in agricultural exports is considerably higher.

The livestock sector has markedly expanded in recent years. It provided 30 per cent of agricultural income 10 years ago, a share which rose to 46 per cent in 1983-5. Increased production of sheep and poultry account for most of the rise.

III. CULTIVATED AREA

The West Bank covers an area of 5,572 square kilometres (the Gaza Strip is 362 square kilometres). The breakdown of the area in terms of agricultural use is as follows: active cultivation, 2,000 square kilometres; grazing, 1,745 square kilometres; forests, 255 square kilometres; other uses, 1,772 square kilometres.[1]

The proportion of about 36 per cent of the West Bank under active cultivation is relatively high given the excessive gradients and the rocky nature of land. In fact an aerial classification of the West Bank conducted in 1968 showed that only 10 per cent of the area was suitable for irrigation and only 23 per cent could be used for rain-fed farming.[2]

It is clear from these figures, and supported by observation, that Palestinian peasants in the West Bank have practically reached the limits of cultivation possible within existing natural and economic constraints. Consequently, if a more extensive level of cultivation is sought, essentially for political reasons, it may not be deemed viable on economic grounds because of the high cost of reclaiming low quality land (US$ 170-450 per acre). Profit margins obtainable from cultivating such areas are currently so low that investment is rarely recovered within an economically acceptable time span. If wider cultivation is deemed necessary owners of such land will have to be effectively assisted. Not surprisingly, this has been precisely the Zionist policy on agriculture, not only during the early years of the struggle for land acquisition prior to the establishment of the state, but even today, as growers in Israel are still provided with massive subsidies to keep them in farming.

It is to be noted in this connection that a number of private voluntary organisations operating in the West Bank have sponsored a relatively large number of small but successful reclamation projects on marginal land which is usually planted later with fruit trees, most commonly olives. The subsidy component inherent in these projects has guaranteed their success.

IV. WATER

The West Bank receives more rainfall than most areas in the Near East. It is estimated that 68 per cent of its land surface receives an annual precipitation of over 300 millimetres, which is defined as the aridity threshold. The total amount of usable reserve is around 800 million cubic metres.[3] Two-thirds of that quantity flows into the coastal aquifers, thereby supplying about one-quarter of Israel's total water consumption, estimated at 1,920 million cubic metres in 1985.

Despite being relatively rich in water resources, West Bank Arab residents consume only 100-110 million cubic metres per annum, which amounts to 5 per cent of Israel's annual level. Table 7.3 indicates the wide gap in aggregate and per capita consumption of water between Israel and the West Bank for all major areas of water use.

Table 7.3: Water consumption in Israel and the West Bank: 1985 (millions of cubic metres)

	Israel	West Bank
Agriculture	1,389	80
Industry	109	5
Domestic	422	20
TOTAL	1,920	105
Memorandum Item (cubic metres)		
Per capita consumption	450	131

Sources: *Statistical Abstract of Israel*, 1986, p.8; Hisham Awartani, *Water Resources and Policies* (Jerusalem, Arab Thought Forum, 1980), p.10.

The two major sources of water supply in the West Bank are deep bore wells and springs. There are some 310 Arab wells which are estimated to discharge 35-40 million cubic metres per annum, and 300 springs providing a further 50-60 million cubic metres. Water catchment cisterns collect up to 6 million cubic metres per year.[4]

The politics of water use in the West Bank has received considerable attention in recent years. Israel has in effect imposed a ceiling on Arab water use, especially from deep bore wells, while maximising its own acquisition of West Bank water reserves. The Israeli water company, Mekorot, has drilled about 34 deep bore wells since 1968 with an annual discharge capacity of 30-45 million cubic metres, which amounts to over two-thirds of the volume taken from all 310 Arab wells.[5] Israel controls water use by Arabs through a series of policies and military orders which include, for instance, the almost total ban on permits for new wells, the imposition of a low ceiling on permissible water discharge and the obstruction of efforts to increase efficiency of surface water catchment.

The impact of the ongoing lopsided exploitation of West Bank water resources is pervasive and far-reaching. The current restrictive policies have severely restrained further expansion of the area of land under irrigation, which is estimated at about 5 per cent of the total cultivated area, as against 45 per cent in Israel. The subsequent dominance of rain-fed patterns of farming has rendered agriculture not only an excessively hazardous profession, but also reduced profitability to a minimum. This has accentuated the decline in the economic role of agriculture, whether measured in terms of employment capacity or its contribution to Gross Domestic Product.

A rather striking observation in this regard, however, is that Palestinian growers seem to have adapted their production operations to a level where they do not need water resources in excess of those available. An important reason for this adjustment bears, of course, on the widespread use of intensive patterns of farming and water-saving irrigation techniques. But this trend has been greatly reinforced and aggravated by the apparent drop in area under irrigation, which is precipitated by chronically poor profit margins. Mounting surpluses of major crops have resulted in greatly depressed sales prices. In these circumstances it could be assumed that non-availability of irrigation water is much less restrictive to growth of commercial patterns of farming than overriding economic constraints.

V. EMPLOYMENT IN AGRICULTURE

Employment in agriculture has declined steadily and substantially since June 1967. This has in fact become one of the most phenomenal transformations in the West Bank and Gaza following occupation. According to available data the number of workers employed in agriculture, whether hired or self-employed, has dropped from 49,000 in 1969 to 28,000 in 1985, a decline of 42 per cent in the West Bank (39 per cent in Gaza). In relative terms, the size of the labour force employed in West Bank agriculture has dropped from 45 per cent of total employed labourers in 1969 to 19 per cent in 1984

Table 7.4: Employment in Agriculture in the West Bank and Gaza: 1969, 1985

| | 1969 | | 1985 | |
	All employed (thousands)	Employed in Agriculture[a] (%)	All employed (thousands)	Employed in Agriculture[a] (%)
		thousands (%)		thousands (%)
West Bank	109.9	49.2 44.8	151.3	28.3 18.7
Gaza Strip	52.9	17.5 33.1	90.6	10.6 9.7
TOTAL	163.8[b]	66.7 40.7	240.9[b]	38.9 16.2

Notes: a. Only within the occupied territories. b. Includes Palestinian workers in Israel.
Sources: Central Bureau of Statistics: *Statistical Abstract of Israel*, 1971, p. 634; 1986, p. 705.

(Table 7.4). The drop in Gaza is similarly dramatic.

The decline in employment in agriculture is familiar to most developing countries. It is precipitated by a variety of factors, most notably the wider use of labour-saving machinery and the increased labour absorptive capacity of non-farm sectors. But the situation in the West Bank and Gaza is noticeably different. The drain of labour from agriculture in the occupied territories is almost entirely due to a severe decline in the profitability of all major production sectors. Farmers are being compelled by marginal profits and occasional substantial losses to make the 'rational' choice to give up farming and look for an alternative source of income. This trend has been accelerated by the sharp rise in the standards and cost of living, both in urban and rural communities.

The crux of the problem, in regard to profitability, stems from the fact that the price system for production inputs and farm produce has been radically restructured to the disadvantage of farmers. The costs of such major inputs as labour, animal-ploughing and irrigation water have risen by 5-18 times, whereas the price of major products (for example, olive oil and oranges) has risen by 2-3 times. Most of the imbalance in the market structure is caused by the unrestricted entry of subsidised Israeli farm produce to the occupied territories' market, as we shall discuss in a later section.

The consequences of declining employment in agriculture are very grave. At a time when unemployment in the occupied territories is increasing rapidly, a growing number of farmers and farm workers are becoming blue collar workers, mostly in Israel. So instead of alleviating unemployment, transformations in agriculture are making the problem worse.

A policy aimed at halting this drain and even at generating a net expansion in agricultural employment should be regarded as a major priority for Palestinian planners.

VI. TRADE AND MARKETING

The terms of trade, both in the domestic and export markets, have been radically restructured since occupation. Until June 1967 West Bank surpluses enjoyed unconditional access to East Bank markets. A substantial proportion of these products was conveniently exported to neighbouring Arab countries. The flow of farm goods from other countries into Jordan was selective and did not impede the expansion of sectors with a positive growth potential, such as citrus, vegetables, poultry and dairy cattle.

Immediately after occupation local markets were unconditionally opened to Israeli production, and the flow of Arab goods into Israel was subject to restrictions. As a result of this colonial subjugation of their economies to that of Israel, the West Bank and Gaza have become the second most important single export market to Israel, after that of the United States. Israel's exports to the occupied territories (including East Jerusalem) amounted to US$ 800 million in 1983, equivalent to 20 per cent of all its non-military exports, including diamonds. Not surprisingly, therefore, Israel's policies in the occupied territories are designed to maintain and develop its lucrative advantage.

The outcome of the restructured trade patterns can be clearly perceived from the figures showing the size and direction of the occupied territories' international trade. The West Bank and Gaza derive 90 per cent of their imports from Israel and send it 68 per cent of their exports. A commodity analysis indicates that 15 per cent of imports from Israel are agricultural goods.

1. The dynamics of agricultural trade

Alongside an alarming deficit in its industrial trade with Israel, the occupied territories suffer a substantial US$ 40 million deficit in agricultural trade. A large proportion of agricultural imports from Israel has displaced locally produced commodities. In dairy products, eggs, poultry, meat, beef and cereals, Israel's share of the local market ranges from 50 to 80 per cent. Israeli producers enjoy massive advantages over their Palestinian counterparts ranging from economies of large-scale production to direct subsidies. This lopsided confrontation has led to the collapse of some branches in the occupied territories, such as dairy farming, and the severe stunting of most others, such as poultry, citrus and vegetable production. This situation constitutes the most serious threat to the future of agriculture in the occupied territories.

The size of trade with Jordan, as shown in Table 7.5, is much smaller than that with Israel (equivalent to about 10 per cent) and its direction is diametrically different, as the West Bank and Gaza enjoy a steady surplus of around US$ 86 million. A major reason for this favourable balance stems from the restrictions imposed by Israel on all imports from Jordan. Table 7.5 shows that the value of exports from the occupied territories to Jordan amounted, during 1981 to 1985, to an

Table 7.5: Exports from the occupied territories to Jordan: average for 1981-5

Type of Commodity	US$	% of Total
All Agricultural goods	63,227	64.2
Olive oil	26,950	27.4
Citrus	17,850	18.1
Others	18,427	18.7
All Industrial goods	35,173	35.8
Samneh (ghee)	17,671	18.0
Soap	3,542	3.6
Stone and marble	10,629	10.8
Others	3,331	3.4

Sources: Central Bureau of Statistics, *Statistical Abstract of Israel*, 1985; *Judea, Samaria and Gaza Area Statistics*, 1985, vol.2, pp. 6-13.

average of US$ 101 million per annum and that 64 per cent of all exports were of agricultural origin.

The flow of West Bank and Gaza products into Jordan has been governed by policies laid down in Amman at senior levels of government and in co-ordination with the Arab League's Boycott Office. Through 1986 this policy was reflected in the following guidelines:

(a) No produce is permitted from the Gaza Strip other than citrus and guavas.

(b) Every effort is made to avoid permitting the entry of produce originating in Israel. This has been satisfactorily achieved through an elaborate set of measures.

(c) West Bank farm produce is permitted at a maximum rate of 50 per cent of estimated yields, assuming that a major proportion of production is disposed of in the domestic market. This assumption, however, disregards the obvious fact that Israel dumps its agricultural surpluses in the occupied territories, often at below market prices.

(d) Productivity estimates are in effect made by officials in Amman, and mostly at rates of one-half to two-thirds of actual yields. So by permitting only a maximum of 50 per cent of estimated yield the actual proportion of output permitted entry is in fact much less.

(e) The number of trucks which are licensed for operation between the West Bank and Jordan is limited to those which were in operation prior to June 1967 (around 400). This has created serious problems for exporters at times of peak production.

Despite their apparent rigidity, the regulations were enforced through the 1970s in such relaxed ways that they did not cause serious problems to Palestinian growers in the occupied territories. This policy has played a major role in initiating and sustaining a high rate of growth in certain patterns of intensive farming, and at the same time helped to meet soaring demand for fruit and vegetables in Jordan.

The problems encountered in exporting agricultural produce started in 1979. The Iran-Iraq war resulted in the abrupt closure of the Iranian market to Palestinian citrus. Iran had been taking approximately half of all citrus exports. This was followed by a sudden decline in exports to Syria and Iraq, though each for different reasons. The situation was made desperately worse by Jordan's mounting problems of excess production, which prompted a shift to increasingly protectionist policies. The tightening of entry regulations has substantially reduced the volume of farm produce exported to Jordan. It now rarely exceeds 30 per cent of output of a few products, mainly grapes, tomatoes, eggplants and melons.

2. Comparative advantage in export markets

The dilemma facing Palestinian growers in regard to the marketing of their produce raises serious problems and questions relative to the present and potential comparative advantage they enjoy in Arab markets. Until a few years ago local output of fruit and vegetables in those countries was much lower than domestic consumption, which gave ample opportunities for both Palestinian and non-Arab producers. Furthermore, productivity in the occupied territories, especially in intensive patterns of farming, was considerably higher than Jordan.

Since the late 1970s, however, the situation has been transformed to the 'disadvantage' of producers in the occupied territories. This policy has ultimately undermined the comparative advantage of the occupied areas' products in their traditional export markets. Such developments included the following:

(a) Local production of vegetables and fruit has risen sharply in most neighbouring Arab countries, especially in Jordan and Saudi Arabia, to the point where these countries experience little or no shortage of such major products as tomatoes, eggplants and cucumbers. Recently there have been complaints about chronic surpluses and the need to curtail output in these countries. Table 7.6 shows that the total output of major vegetable crops rose in Jordan by 83 per cent from 1970 to 1982, and in 1982 was 2.6 times that of the West Bank and twice the combined output of the West Bank and the Gaza Strip.

Table 7.6: West Bank agricultural co-operatives by type and period of registration as of 31 December 1984

	Period of registration		
Type	Before occupation	After occupation	Total
Credit	141	1	142
Livestock	7	14	21
Olive presses	9	13	22
Multi-purpose	11	-	11
Marketing	11	29	40
TOTAL	179	57	236

Source: Department of Co-operatives and Labour.

(b) Productivity of agriculture in neighbouring Arab countries, especially Jordan, has risen so markedly that it left no tangible advantage to growers in the occupied territories. Whatever productivity differential has remained is too insignificant to offset the differential cost of transport.

(c) The high cost of inputs used in agriculture entails further disadvantages for growers in the occupied territories. In Israel and Jordan some major cost items are heavily subsidised. Irrigation water, for instance, is delivered to producers in the East Jordan Valley at JD 0.003 per cubic metre, and in Israel at a price of about JD 0.020 per cubic metre. This is far lower than the ruling cost of around JD 0.100 per cubic metre in the West Bank. With a seasonal requirement of 600-1,000 cubic metres per dunum, the differential cost of irrigation is obviously very high.

(d) The quality of certain major products, like grapes and citrus, has not kept pace with the pronounced rise in consciousness for quality in the rich consumer markets of Jordan and the Gulf states. This deficiency has given a marked advantage to exporters from other countries with superior quality products.

These new problems do not lend themselves to easy short-term solutions. Unless producers in the occupied territories take active steps to correct deficiencies relevant to all these constraints, their marketing problems are bound to get worse and the agricultural sector will undergo a sharp decline. But as is argued later in this paper, this predicament is avoidable.

VII. AGRICULTURAL FINANCE

Sources of agricultural finance prior to occupation were gradually differentiated into a number of institutions, each with specific terms of reference. Medium- and long-term credit was handled by four regional branches of the Agricultural Credit Corporation (ACC), and production loans for seasonal purposes were advanced by the Jordan Central Co-operative Union (JCCU) through its three West Bank branches. Other sources of credit in agriculture included marketing middlemen and dealers in farm supplies, who most often gave loans in kind, and mostly for seasonal purposes. Commercial banks were also an important source of credit for certain types of farming operations. Total indebtedness from all these sources amounted in May 1967 to approximately US$ 11 million, about half of which was advanced by ACC.[6]

All lending institutions, official and commercial, were forced to close their branches in the occupied territories after June 1967. For about ten years after that Palestinian growers had no access to institutional sources of credit, other than the small-scale programme initiated by the military authorities in the early 1970s. Even that effort was short-lived and had minimal significance, because of its political nature. During that period, most capital outlay in agriculture had to be covered from farmers' savings, or through repayment facilities offered by suppliers of production requisites and marketing middlemen. Until the mid-1970s those sources met farmers' needs for short-term credit.

The capital market, however, tightened considerably in the late 1970s as Israel moved deeper into recession and inflation increased rapidly. Private lenders cut down drastically on their credit operations, for fear of possible losses as a result of the rapid devaluation of the Israeli currency. Because of reduced profitability and increased risk many farmers and entrepreneurs displayed a marked reticence to invest their own savings beyond imperative needs.

The Likud bloc, which came to power in Israel in 1977, introduced a strongly monetarist domestic economic policy and a more overtly repressive stance towards Palestinians. Both developments have seriously affected the capital market in the occupied territories. Sweeping restrictions were imposed on the flow of funds from outside sources, and as a result, the scarcity of finance has become one of the most important causes of the rapid decline in agriculture since 1977.

It was against this background that two major developments took place. The first was the formation of the Jordanian-Palestinian Joint Committee, with the proclaimed aim of channelling funds to eligible borrowers in the occupied territories. The second was the increase in number and mushrooming of activity of externally funded private voluntary organisations (PVOs) which provided assistance (often financial) to local communities.

1. The Joint Committee and agriculture

The Joint Committee commenced activity in 1979 with the ambitious aim of supplying a substantial proportion of the funds required for the rejuvenation of economic and social life in the occupied territories. The decision by the 1978 Arab Summit in Baghdad to raise for this purpose US$ 150 million per annum was a promising start. But the record of the Committee for the past six years leaves much to be desired, as indicated in the following observations:

(a) Out of a pledged funding of just over US$ 1 billion during the six years from 1979 to 1985, the Committee actually received a sum of just under US$ 400 million, about 38 per cent of that expected.
(b) As of the end of 1984, the Committee had channelled to agriculture a total of about US$ 31 million, equivalent to 8 per cent of its portfolio.[7]
(c) The policies and implementation procedures which were adopted by the Committee in connection with some of its assistance programmes inevitably led to a marked bias towards the wealthy and those with political influence. For many potential beneficiaries, especially those of limited means seeking smaller loans, the outlays associated with the obligatory travel to Amman and for administrative expenses constituted a built-in deterrent to the widespread use of the Committee's facilities.[8]

These are among the reasons why the Joint Committee's role in agriculture was one of its most striking failures.

2. PVOs and agriculture

The experience of PVOs in developing agriculture in the occupied territories has been notably heterogeneous. The total number of PVOs operating in the occupied territories is over forty. Those with a significant interest in agriculture are the following: Mennonite Central Committee (MCC), American Near East Refugees Aid (ANERA), Community Development Foundation (CDF), Catholic Relief Services (CRS) and the United Nations Development Programme (UNDP). All of these agencies are based in the West Bank itself. But there are a few other non-governmental organisations, which are also involved to some extent in agricultural development, but which are based abroad, most notably the Welfare Association.

Each of the above mentioned PVOs has its own objectives, sources of finance and terms of operation. It will therefore be difficult and certainly inaccurate to give a generalised evaluation of their record. Yet it is still possible to identify certain features which have been common to most of them to varying degrees:

(a) Notwithstanding their political affiliations and implicit objectives, PVOs operating in the occupied territories should be rightly credited for their endeavour and active interest in trying to arrest further deterioration in the social and economic base of the Palestinian society under Israeli occupation. Their efforts in trying to promote and initiate successful development projects commenced even before those of the Joint Committee.

(b) The volume of aid advanced by all major PVOs to agricultural projects, until the end of 1983, averaged around US$ 0.9 million per annum, far less than needed to salvage an economic sector which had been denied credit since 1967. That was a major reason why the aggregate impact of PVOs' aid to agriculture has been very small, despite numerous localised successes.

(c) The allocation of aid funds by most major PVOs has been the subject of bitter controversy. Until 1983 there was excessive emphasis on such areas as health, social services and public works, with only marginal interest in projects bearing on the local economic base, especially in agriculture. A detailed study by Meron Benvenisti of three major PVOs assisted by the US Agency for International Development (AID) has shown that only one-third of the projects submitted, representing 45.8 per cent of the proposed funds, has been directed to economic development.[9]

(d) The local staffs of most major PVOs are qualified to ascertain development priorities and define eligibility criteria. But for reasons relating to the politics of funding sources and the military authorities, many PVOs have failed to establish direct working relations with needy farmers, and resorted instead to dealing with agricultural organisations. Most local experts believe that aid advanced by PVOs to these organisations is aimed ultimately at cultivating a 'moderate leadership' which they hope will compete with or possibly replace the Palestine Liberation Organisation (PLO).

(e) The co-ordination between PVO managements and local experts is noticeably low key. Feasibility and progress appraisal studies of major projects are sometimes conducted without adequate sensitivity to the views of local experts. This is certainly an important cause of the appalling record of most major PVOs in agriculture.

(f) The tendency for some PVOs to build up fairly large staffs deserves special notice. It is hoped that by so doing they can indeed expand their reach and improve the level of their services. Such policies, however, raise concern that they would inadvertently undermine the prospects of building indigenous development institutions.

(g) The relations of PVOs with the Israeli authorities have borne heavily on all their activities, and for several years constituted their most serious constraint. All project proposals formulated by the US PVOs have to be submitted to the military occupation authorities for approval after they are completed. These authorities have a very different perception of priorities and eligibility criteria and have tried to reorient projects accordingly. After prolonged and often tedious deliberations many projects have been rejected, several others deferred for further study (possibly for several years), new projects imposed and some others approved as they were submitted. During the 1977 to 1982 Likud rule, the record of project approvals was strikingly low, as evidenced by Benvenisti's study. Only 40 per cent of projects in agriculture and 33.3 per cent of projects in industry were approved, compared to an approval rate of 100 per cent for public work projects which relieved Israel of its undeniable obligations to the occupied territories.[10]

(h) Any realistic assessment of the consequences of the financial role played by the Joint Committee and PVOs cannot ignore the psychological and social implications ensuing from a policy aimed at giving hand-outs to individuals and institutions. While by so doing they have not succeeded in solving the chronic problem of credit scarcity, their practices may have in fact made that job even more difficult. Selective subsidisation of individual entrepreneurs and institutions has sometimes distorted market forces and perpetuated management inefficiencies.

VIII. AGRICULTURAL EDUCATION AND RESEARCH

Immediately following occupation, the Department of Agriculture was placed under the direct jurisdiction of the military government. An Israeli officer at the Military Command was entrusted with the status of 'Minister of Agriculture', presumably as defined in Jordanian laws. Actual field work, however, was left to the Arab staff in the department through its six district offices. Each of these offices is staffed with between five and seven extension agents and an Israeli 'advisor' who acts as their liaison with the central office in the Civil Administration.

Until the beginning of the 1970s, the Department of Agriculture in the Military Administration pursued an active role in modernising agriculture in the West Bank and Gaza Strip. They recruited a large number of staff, organised demonstration plots, advanced credit to certain types of farming and enforced a relatively loose marketing policy. Coupled with other favourable transformations, the policies of the department led to accelerated modernisation in production practices and high growth rates in certain patterns of farming.

Official interest in the agricultural sector of the West Bank and Gaza proved to be short-lived. The policies of the first years of occupation were gradually phased out and superseded by others of a clearly restrictive nature. This change might have been initially motivated by Israel's own economic problems which emerged and started to snowball by the mid-1970s, thereby leading to a drastic curb in public expenditure. Furthermore, there was an increasing awareness among senior policy makers in Israel of the enormous economic gains which might accrue to Israeli producers if the local production base in the occupied territories could be circumscribed.

But the most important factor which precipitated the shift in official policies relative to agriculture seems to have been a steady and substantial change in Israel's political ambitions for the occupied territories. From the mid-1970s it became clear that partial or total annexation of these territories had become the ultimate goal of both major political blocs in Israel. So instead of developing agriculture, Israel's interests were believed to be better served by facilitating a reduction in the area under active cultivation and in the volume of water used in farming, as well as by curtailing all patterns of farming which entail visible and long-term attachment of farmers to arable land. Furthermore, a retarded agriculture would eventually facilitate the mobility of labour from rural communities to Israel or abroad, which has indeed become one of the most serious socio-economic consequences of occupation.

The practical manifestations of the reversals in agricultural policies have been numerous and drastic. The following is only a brief and partial list of the measures which were taken to serve the tacit goals described above:

(a) The budget of the Department of Agriculture has been reduced markedly in real value over the past ten years. Table 7.7 shows that the development budget for agriculture (at fixed prices) was slashed between 1968/9 and 1980/1 from IS 94 million to IS 11 million. There was a similar drop in the budget for research. On the other hand the regular budget which covers administration has been noticeably stable. Funds allocated for extension work and training in the 1981/2 budget amounted to 0.5 per cent of total expenditure. Salaries and administration consumed 95.6 per cent of the budget.

Table 7.7: Military government budget for agriculture in the West Bank and Gaza for selected years: 1968/9-1980/1
(millions of Israeli shekels at 1980/1 prices)

	Development	Research	Regular
1968/9	94.5	—	23.0
1971/2	49.1	1.166	23.0
1974/5	28.0	0.585	20.6
1978/9	16.0	0.318	20.6
1980/1	11.0	0.075	23.1

Source: Department of Finance, Bet El, quoted in David Kahan, *Agriculture and Water in the West Bank and Gaza 1977-83* (The West Bank Data Base Project, Jerusalem, 1984), p.55.

(b) The department's work force has been reduced by half, from 450 persons in 1976 to 229 in 1984.[11] Obviously, such a massive cut has entailed a serious contraction in the services of the department.

(c) The reduction in the number of workers has been effected arbitrarily, most commonly by closing whole departments (e.g. forestry and agricultural research) and by firings or forced resignations. This has intimidated remaining workers whose main concern now is to keep their jobs.

(d) Education, demonstrations and other field extension activities have been curtailed, so much so that extension agents are explicitly encouraged to spend most of their time in their offices. The annual plans laid down by senior officials instruct extension agents to minimise their activity in those sectors which are deemed undesirable by the senior Israeli officials, for either political or economic reasons. Areas of production where extension activities have been curtailed include olives and grapes, because of their land-intensive nature, and poultry, because it competes with an Israeli speciality.

(e) The massive decline in the services of the department is most visible in the area of agricultural research. The fairly developed research base built up before 1967 has been dismantled, presumably to increase Palestinian farmers' reliance on Israeli sources of technology. The long-term consequences of this process for agricultural development in the occupied territories, especially in the fields which are not of interest to Israeli researchers (for example, farming on marginal land) can be serious indeed.

(f) Agricultural education in government schools has almost totally collapsed. Until 1986, none of the local universities was permitted by the Israeli authorities to initiate an agricultural programme despite a remarkable expansion in all other fields of higher education. That has certainly been an important reason why graduates do not enter farming-related professions, and a reason for the perpetuation of a poorly educated farm labour force.

IX. CO-OPERATIVE SOCIETIES

Co-operatives in the West Bank date back to British Mandate days. The co-operative movement progressed rapidly under Jordan between 1948 and 1967. In December 1966 there were 176 agricultural co-operative societies with 9,000 members in the West Bank.[12] The majority (143) were merely small credit organisations with an insignificant scale of operation. The remaining 33 suffered complex organisational problems and had a marginal impact on the overall development of West Bank agriculture. The role of private firms, such as dealers of farm supplies and marketing middlemen, was much more significant.

After occupation all three West Bank branches of the Jordan Co-operative Organisation (JCO) were ordered to freeze operations by the Israeli military, though they remained officially in existence. Co-operative societies were also advised to freeze their activities until further notice. It was clear that the Israeli authorities could not decide whether to activate co-operatives or liquidate them.

But the situation has changed markedly since 1976. On the Jordanian and Palestinian sides, it became clear that because of prolonged occupation and consequent absence of a national authority, co-operative societies could play a major role as instruments or conduits of development. This line of policy was officially endorsed after the establishment of the Joint Committee which has since channelled most of its funding for agriculture through co-operatives.

The Israeli authorities have had an ambivalent attitude towards the revival of the co-operatives. It was clear at one point that they hoped co-operatives might be lured into a political role which would undermine the PLO's mounting influence in the occupied territories. On the other hand the Civil Administration was apprehensive that co-operatives could become centres for organised political resistance or, alternatively, endanger Israeli economic interests. Thus, the Civil Administration has permitted and sometimes even facilitated the reactivation of co-operatives, but insisted that all their activities are carefully vetted and approved by Israeli staff at Bet El (headquarters of the Civil Administration) in the West Bank.

Several new agricultural co-operatives have been registered over the last decade and a few of the old ones revived. The total number of registered co-operatives by the end of 1984 was 236, of which 57 were registered after occupation (Table 7.8).

Table 7.8: West Bank agricultural co-operatives by type and period of registration as of 31 December 1984

	Period of registration		
Type	Before occupation	After occupation	Total
Credit	141	1	142
Livestock	7	14	21
Olive presses	9	13	22
Multi-purpose	11	-	11
Marketing	11	29	40
Total	179	57	236

Source: Department of Co-operatives and Labour.

The number of functioning agriculture co-operatives is approximately 30; about half of these are olive press associations. The backbone of the co-operative movement lies in what are officially described as regional marketing co-operatives, each serving one district or sub-district. There are eight such co-operatives, all of which have been generously assisted by JCO and ANERA over the past seven years.

A critical evaluation of the record of agricultural co-operatives shows that so far they have succeeded in avoiding Israeli political pressure. There is, on the other hand, clear evidence that many co-operatives have been transformed into power bases serving the ambitions of local political leaders. In addition to violating basic co-operative ideology, the politicisation of co-operatives has greatly undermined their proclaimed economic objectives, especially in the areas of marketing and finance.

On the marketing side, which is supposedly their major area of operation, regional marketing co-operatives have been reduced to issuing the documents needed to channel produce to Jordan. They have done very little to open new markets, improve auxiliary marketing services or stabilise prices. Their role as a source of finance for member farmers has been limited to symbolic gestures.

The largely marginal role of co-operatives in developing agriculture in the West Bank and Gaza has been the outcome of complex factors, and is not the sole responsibility of their management staff. The literature on group work in rural communities in most Middle East countries shows clearly that farmers feel much more comfortable with individualistic approaches to problem solving and meeting felt needs. In this context it is not surprising that the co-operatives' record prior to occupation contained far more failures than successes.

The onset of occupation, and the subsequent dual affiliation of the co-operative movement, has created additional problems and bottle-necks which can be summarised as follows:

(a) The very slow and noticeably selective registration of new co-operatives. New applications for registration often remain at Bet El, presumably under consideration, for a very long time, sometimes up to several years. The political affiliations of applicants are carefully scrutinised before registration is approved.

(b) Strict and selective controls of finance. Each new project needs approval from Bet El before grants or loans can be solicited. These approvals are selective and often take a long time. Even after they are given approval the actual disbursement of funds remains subject to last minute changes in attitude at Bet El.

(c) There is an inadequate service infrastructure. Auxiliary services such as education, training, research and auditing have all sharply deteriorated under occupation and the abnormal working relations between the JCO and West Bank co-operatives has exacerbated the deterioration of services supportive to co-operative development.

(d) Because of fears that general assembly meetings of regional co-operatives may pave the way for the infiltration of 'collaborators' to boards of directors, these co-operatives have been advised by the JCO not to call such meetings and not to hold elections for management boards until occupation comes to an end. This measure has practically abolished the legal rights of members and given a free hand to ambitious local leaders to exercise uncontested authority.

X. DEVELOPMENT POLICIES

1. Objectives of an agricultural development strategy

The development of agriculture in the occupied territories should be given a high priority for both economic and political reasons. The following objectives could form the skeleton of an agricultural policy:

(a) Extensive expansion of land use, whether rain-fed or under irrigation.

(b) Raising the labour-absorptive capacity of agriculture to its limit within given constraints.

(c) Reducing dependence on Israel for food within a policy addressed to achieve greater food security for the West Bank and Gaza.

(d) Vigorous expansion of orchards to serve as a visible attachment to the land, in addition to their distinct economic advantages.

(e) Sustaining indigenous peasant forms of agriculture in areas where intensive patterns of farming are not feasible.

2. Land

(a) About two-thirds of West Bank land has such a low production potential that it often does not permit commercial patterns of farming. As the horizontal expansion of land cultivation is a major Palestinian priority the farming of marginal land should be conceived of as a national obligation, and not just that of landowners.

(b) The implementation of an expansionist land use policy could be expedited by arranging land reclamation projects at subsidised rates whether relative to fees charged or terms of repayment.

(c) Expanded cultivation of marginal land would be expedited by construction of new agricultural roads and rain water collection cisterns.

3. Water

(a) The twin objectives for a national irrigation water policy are the application of available water resources over the widest possible area and the exploitation of a larger share of usable water reserves.

(b) The first objective could be facilitated by a wider dissemination of modern irrigation techniques, thereby saving a substantial part of current water consumption. This step could be greatly accelerated by making credit available to eligible farmers.

(c) Owners of artesian wells should be assisted in modernising their pumps and in renovating the wells.

(d) Greater pressure should be exerted by high-level intermediaries for an equitable access of Palestinians to their water resources. This means, for instance, permitting the drilling of more wells, raising discharge quotas, and approval of viable surface water catchment projects.

4. Marketing

(a) Jordan should relax some of the restrictions on the flow of farm produce across the bridges. Current policies not only conflict with the organic ties which bind the two territories with the East Bank, but also endanger the very basis of steadfastness which Jordan and the PLO are trying so hard to preserve.

(b) It is clear that trade with other neighbouring Arab countries has been hampered by a number of political and economic barriers. The sanctions taken by the Arab League's Boycott Office have often backfired on the West Bank and Gaza, usually because of inaccurate information or the tacit national interests of member states. This situation is exacerbated by the absence of technical representatives from the occupied territories at meetings where their fundamental interests are being discussed. At a time when all Arab governments pledge unlimited support to the Palestinian cause, it is to be hoped that they would do something more tangible to facilitate the entry of some US$ 80-100 million worth of agricultural goods to their markets.

(c) Exports to Europe have been largely restricted to small quantities of Gaza citrus. In view of a number of comparative advantages which are enjoyed by local producers, and in the light of Israel's own successful export initiatives, it is recommended that Palestinian producers try much harder to explore export potential in Europe. Recent decisions by the European Community in this connection have been encouraging, but a more vigorous and institutionalised effort in the occupied territories is urgently needed. A Palestinian marketing firm should be established with the explicit objective of handling exports of farm produce to other countries.

(d) While it is true that the potential for large-scale agro-industries is currently limited, mainly because of competition with an extremely sophisticated Israeli food industry, it is certain that much could still be done in developing small-scale food industries which take advantage of cheap surpluses and abundant labour. The assistance which could be provided by an intermediate technology expert would be instrumental in realising this scheme.

(e) It is clear that some diversification in farming patterns is imperative. A vigorous effort should be made towards growing new products which are in strong demand at home and abroad (for example, avocadoes, persimmons, dates, strawberries). On the other hand, plantations of low productive potential should be uprooted or rejuvenated.

(f) It may be too optimistic to assume that Israel is likely to reconsider its terms of trade with the occupied territories, as long as these territories are under its control. But Palestinian and Jordanian politicians should insist on a radical reconsideration of terms of trade with Israel at an early stage of any forthcoming political dialogue.

5. Credit

(a) The continued absence of an indigenous agricultural credit institution, to provide eligible borrowers with loans on professional terms, remains one of the most pressing priorities. In view of the relatively flexible policies of the present Israeli government on development issues, its approval of the proposed project is not unlikely.

(b) Interest rates, security arrangements and repayment conditions will have to be on a par with the terms of agricultural credit in Jordan and Israel.

(c) The need for credit in the present setting is imperative if production is to be made more efficient, costs are to be reduced and the cultivated area, both irrigated and rain-fed, to be expanded. Ultimately, this will also increase the labour absorptive capacity of the agricultural sector.

(d) The Joint Committee is urged to reconsider its priorities. But while there is a lot it can and should do to rehabilitate agriculture, the Joint Committee should not be considered a substitute for a specialised credit institution based inside the occupied territories.

(e) Even if a credit institution is eventually established, PVOs can still render useful services to farmers in the occupied territories. It is gratifying to note some major PVOs have recently realigned their policies on more realistic grounds and in the light of intensive evaluation studies of previous achievements. It is hoped that PVOs will allocate more of their resources to development and employment-generation projects which are of a public or infrastructural nature. In contrast, grants to entrepreneurial projects should be minimised. PVOs are also urged to establish better co-ordination among themselves and more effective communication with local experts.

(f) Last, but most importantly, PVOs should be sufficiently sensitive to the volatile political environment in the area, and resist being used by funding sources in ways which could undermine the national aspirations of the Palestinian people.

6. Education and Research

(a) As it is inconceivable that the Department of Agriculture will be reactivated in the foreseeable future, a vigorous but low profile effort should be made to build up small extension service units in collaboration with regional marketing co-operatives. The implementation of this scheme, however, should be preceded by a detailed investigation of local needs.

(b) The extension staff in the Department of Agriculture should be given training opportunities in selected areas, something which they have been denied for a long time. This programme could be effectively handled by either AMIDEAST or UNDP.[13]

(c) The technical staff at the department would be more useful to the farming community if special collaboration arrangements were made with regional co-operatives. It is possible that the Civil Administration will not object to this kind of co-operation.

(d) Against a background of soaring unemployment among college graduates, the occupied territories need a carefully designed faculty of agriculture. The curricula should focus on qualifying graduates as farmers and agri-businessmen, and on initiating an active programme of adaptive research. Pressure would have to be exerted to secure Israeli permission to implement this project.

(e) The planning and implementation of development projects will be greatly expedited if an economic research centre is established. The proposed centre would provide feasibility studies for new projects and conduct progress appraisals for ongoing development activities. Furthermore, it could be of great help in supervising implementation of projects, should that be requested.

7. Co-operatives

(a) In the absence of a sovereign Palestinian national authority in the West Bank and Gaza Strip, co-operative societies should be conceived of as an important option still available for the revival of the local productive base. As such, every effort should be made to help expand and upgrade the services they render to farmers in various sectors.

(b) Because of numerous constraints it is not likely that regional co-operatives themselves will be able to provide real marketing or lending services to their members. Yet these co-operatives could act as catalytic intermediaries between their members and the specialised credit and marketing institutions proposed earlier.

(c) By virtue of their district-based mandate, regional co-operatives should undertake certain agricultural services of a collective nature, such as land reclamation and pest control campaigns. More importantly, these regional co-operatives could play a very helpful role in providing extension education to farmers and in lobbying for the interests of the farming community, both inside and outside the occupied territories.

(d) In order to meet the apparent needs for educational and research activities, and in order to disseminate a stronger understanding of co-operative ideals, it is recommended that an educational centre be established specifically for such purposes.

(e) The political context of co-operative work should be addressed at all levels. Elections should be held as stipulated in their by-laws and members thoroughly educated as to their rights.

8. Employment

(a) A halt in the further decline of agricultural employment and a subsequent expansion of the agricultural labour force could be achieved by the introduction of the above policies.

(b) Making credit facilities available to university and community college graduates at reasonable terms would help attract them to farming as a profession. The success of such new farmers will depend largely on the amount of training they receive and the level of extension services they are given.

(c) The most important prerequisite for expanding employment in agriculture is efficient marketing. Producers should be reasonably assured that they will be able to dispose of their goods at reasonable profit margins. Development policies related to credit and marketing have been discussed earlier.

NOTES

1. David Kahan, *Agriculture and Water in the West Bank and Gaza (1977-83)* (The West Bank Data Base Project, Jerusalem, 1984), p.20.

2. Unpublished report of the Department of Agriculture.

3. Rofe and Rafferty Consulting Engineers, *West Bank Hydrology* (Rofe and Rafferty Consulting Engineers, London, 1965), p.15.

4. Hisham Awartani, *Water Resources and Policies* (The Arab Thought Forum, Jerusalem, 1980), p.10.

5. Information obtained in private interviews with informed Israeli researchers in Jerusalem. Israel does not publish official statistics on water use in the occupied territories.

6. Hisham Awartani, 'Agricultural development in the West Bank' (unpublished Ph.D. thesis, University of Bradford, 1982), p. 161.

7. The Joint Jordanian-Palestinian Committee, *Financial and Banking Situation in the West Bank and the Gaza Strip* (The Joint Committee and the Royal Scientific Society, Amman, 1985), p. 108.

8. Hopeful borrowers have to make three trips to Amman before they receive the loans on which they pay interest at 2% per annum. About a quarter of those who apply receive loans.

9. Meron Benvenisti, *US Government Projects in the West Bank and Gaza (1977-83)* (The West Bank Data Base Project, Jerusalem, 1984), p.7.

10. Ibid.

11. Kahan, *Agriculture*, p. 51 and by personal contacts.

12. Mousa Arafah et al., *The Co-operative Movement in Jordan* (Jordan Co-operative Organisation, Amman, 1977), p.5.

13. American Middle East Educational and Training Services and the United Nations Development Programme.

8

Industrial Development and Policies in the West Bank and Gaza

Bakir Abu Kishk

I. INTRODUCTION

Industrialisation has been central in the planning and assessment of development of the developing countries despite the shift of emphasis during the second half of the 1960s towards the promotion of agriculture. In the occupied territories, however, neither the agricultural nor industrial sectors are progressing significantly either in terms of numbers employed or their contribution to Gross Domestic Product. Generally speaking, development in the West Bank and Gaza Strip is restricted, as the occupying authorities move towards annexing the territories to Israel, *de facto* if not *de jure*. As a consequence, there can be no implementation of comprehensive development plans in which the growth of the industrial sector would be used to stimulate other sectors and promote stable development. One Israeli researcher has described the West Bank economy as 'non-industrialised'.[1] This is a situation Israel inherited in 1967 and one it has basically maintained. While there has been growth in the economy overall, according to traditional indicators, industry has remained static. It has suffered with the downturns in the Israeli economy but not benefited when there has been improvement and expansion.

Taking this into account, the analysis of industrial development under prolonged occupation will be presented in four sections. The first will discuss industrial development prior to 1967. The second section is devoted to the analysis of growth, or lack of it, under occupation, and the third will present an approach to industrial development through the development of agriculture based industry. Section four will summarise the main findings and make recommendations.

165

II. INDUSTRIAL DEVELOPMENT PRIOR TO 1967 [2]

During the period 1948 to 1967 the West Bank and Gaza Strip were separately administered. The West Bank was under Jordanian authority and become part of the Hashemite kingdom in the early 1950s, while the Gaza Strip was under Egyptian administration. One thing common to both was the absence of long-term planning for industrial development.

The Egyptian authorities administered the Gaza Strip on a temporary basis and did not consider long-term industrial development plans. The Jordanian Government included the West Bank in its economic planning but did not accord industrial development a high priority nor did it allocate substantial official funds for it. Growth did occur in the two territories between the 1948 and 1967 wars, however, albeit in different ways.

1. The West Bank

The earliest statistical information available on West Bank industry is for 1954 when there were 254 establishments each employing four or more people. The total number of workers employed in industry was 3,562.

Most of the industrial units were little more than workshops producing handicrafts.[3] From the mid-1950s there was rapid industrial expansion and the total number of establishments rose to 3,716, with a total work force of more than 17,000 workers in 1965. In spite of this overall increase the overwhelming majority of the new units were still small-scale, employing less than four workers. The number of establishments with capital over JD 10,000 and employing 15 workers or more was very small; the most important are given in Table 8.1. The contribution of the manufacturing sector to GDP was estimated by Mazur to be 6.6 per cent or about a quarter of the contribution of the agricultural sector.[4]

Growth of the industrial sector was slower in the West Bank than in the East Bank during the period 1948 to 1967. The East Bank had no industry in 1950 but by 1965 it had 48 per cent of total units in the Kingdom. These were also somewhat better capitalised and more productive than those in the West Bank. Despite having 52 per cent of all factories, the West Bank's contribution to Jordanian industrial output was 28 per cent in 1966.[5] The average number of workers in factories employing more than 10 people was 19 for the West Bank, compared with 38 for similar units in the East Bank. Jordanian investment policy favoured the establishment of large-scale units in the East Bank. Only 15 per cent of total fixed investments was made in the West Bank.

Table 8.1: Major industrial establishments in the West Bank before 1967 (capital is in thousands of Jordanian dinars)

Name	Area	Capital	Number of Workers
Nabatin Oil Industry	Nablus	500	200
Silvana (chocolates)	Ramallah	100	100
Al-Jabshih (chocolate and sweets)	Beit Hanina	100	35
Jerusalem Cigarette Company	Al Azaria	200	100
Agricultural Industry	Hebron	80	20
Jordan Plastic Company	Beit Sahur	80	300
Al-Sharq Plastic Company	Jerusalem	45	62
National Beds Factory	Bethlehem	50	100
Al-Taqadum (industrial scales)	Hebron	10	15
Rabah Furniture Company	Ramallah	80	80
Zinc Factory Company	Nablus	—	40
TOTAL*		1,245	1,052

Note: a. K/L ratio for the above establishments = JD 1,183 per worker
Source: Rose Mosleh, 'Al-sina'a fi ad-daffa al-gharbiyya 1967-1979' (Industry in the West Bank 1967-1979), *Sh'un Filastiniyya*, no. 99 (Palestine Liberation Organisation, Beirut, 1980), p. 4.

The average investment per unit in the West Bank was less than JD 8,000 in 1965, compared with over JD 49,000 per unit in the East Bank. Industrial output per West Bank worker was JD 550.[6]

2. Gaza Strip

In contrast to the West Bank, the Gaza Strip was isolated. Cut off from its Palestinian hinterland after the 1948 war, it was separated from Egypt by the Sinai Peninsula. Development of the area was left to private investment, most of which, given the existence of water resources and the need for agricultural products, was concentrated in the agricultural sector. Industry remained a low priority and developed very slowly. The contribution of the sector to GDP was even less than that of the West Bank. It was estimated to be 3.3 per cent, or one-eighth of the contribution of the agricultural sector.[7] Gharaibeh gives a slightly higher figure. He estimated value added by industry in the Strip to be JD 0.4 million or 4.2 per cent of GDP.

It was the least important sector of the economy after transportation.[8] The number of people employed in industry in 1960 was 1,782 in 769 concerns. Only JD 300,000 was invested in industry and output per worker was JD 390. By 1967, the number of establishments had risen to 1,000. Table 8.2 lists those employing 10 or more workers.[9]

Table 8.2: Industrial establishments in the Gaza Strip employing 10 or more workers: 1967

Name of establishment	Number of Workers
Seven-Up and Happi soft drinks factory	112
Samir furniture factory	36
Ahmed Shurab Co., packing and exporting oranges	195[a]
Shunti Brothers Co., plastics	25
Amin Ahmed Al-Sharq, textiles	23
Halwiat Haj Sehwale, sweets	16
Al-Ishtirak al-Arabi	12
Aswan perfume factory	12
Jamil Abu Ghalune Factory, bricks	14
Jarallah al-Shik al-Khazindar Factory, bricks	15
TOTAL	460

Note: a. The work is seasonal.
Source: Field survey conducted by the author.

III. INDUSTRIAL DEVELOPMENT UNDER OCCUPATION

The 1967 war and the Israeli occupation brought severe economic disruption to the West Bank and Gaza Strip and fundamentally altered their established economic relationships with neighbouring economies. Initially there was some support for industry from the military authorities as the Israelis were concerned that unemployed workers from the occupied territories would flood their own labour market. They sought to stabilise the employment situation as quickly as possible. Investments continued for some years after 1967.[10] Small loans were made to existing factories to expand and retool. This phase continued until the mid-1970s, but by 1980 the military government had reduced its development budget to zero. The operating budget of the military occupation's trade and industry department is now entirely spent policing regulations on weights and measures and the enforcement of military orders dealing with industry.[11]

1. The West Bank

The 1967 war was a shock to the economy of the West Bank in general and to the manufacturing sector in particular. Many industrial establishments were paralysed in the general economic and political confusion. Imported raw materials were not available in sufficient quantities and productive activity was reduced. One-third of industrial

Table 8.3: Distribution of West Bank industries by standardised groups: 1967

No.	Major Group	Distribution of all establishments		Establishments with 10 workers or more	
		No. of units	No. of workers	No.of units	No.of workers
1	Stone cutting	110	1,725	85	1,562
2	Food manufacturing	1,050	5,013	31	762
3	Tobacco	3	229	3	229
4	Manufacture of textiles	53	685	19	511
5	Manufacture of clothing	421	1,465	5	62
6	Manufacture of footwear	463	944	8	126
7	Manufacture of wood excluding furniture	39	180	–	–
8	Manufacture of furniture and fixtures	746	1,892	10	215
9	Manufacture of paper and paper products	7	101	2	68
10	Printing and publishing	38	472	18	370
11	Manufacture of leather	35	73	–	–
12	Manufacture of rubber	24	53	–	–
13	Manufacture of industrial chemicals	42	852	19	748
14	Manufacture of non-metallic products	32	533	14	198
15	Manufacture of metallic products	495	1,493	12	233
16	Manufacture of machinery (excluding electrical)	1	16	1	16
17	Manufacture of electrical machinery	93	133	–	–
18	Manufacture of transport equipment	202	436	2	98
19	Beverages industries	5	126	4	126
20	Others	171	618	2	120
	TOTAL	4,030	17,039	235	5,444

Source: Mosleh, 'Industry in the West Bank', pp. 9-11.

Table 8.4: Distribution of West Bank establishments by major group and by size of work force[a]: 1979, 1982, 1983

Indus-trial Group	1979						1982						1983					
	Number of workers						Number of workers						Number of workers					
	1-3	4-7	8-10	11-20	21+	Total	1-3	4-7	8-10	11-20	21+	Total	1-3	4-7	8-10	11-20	21+	Total
Food	146	65	7	6	8	232	143	60	12	9	7	231	128	73	9	10	4	224
Textiles	302	107	26	40	10	485	263	111	31	34	17	456	281	120	32	33	18	484
Leather	179	52	1	1	-	223	135	61	4	1	1	202	168	73	8	1	1	251
Wood	365	59	7	6	-	437	358	70	10	6	-	444	411	74	5	7	-	497
Rubber	20	11	5	3	12	51	16	12	4	6	12	50	22	8	2	2	12	50
Metals	293	117	3	4	2	419	342	115	4	1	2	464	432	121	3	3	2	561
Minerals	36	63	11	10	2	122	47	73	17	7	2	146	64	69	16	11	1	161
Other	164	44	10	6	3	227	146	28	5	3	2	184	139	33	4	4	2	182
TOTAL	505	518	70	76	37	2,206	1,450	530	87	67	43	2,177	1,645	571	79	75	40	2,410

Note: a. Does not include East Jerusalem

Sources: Central Bureau of Statistics, *Statistical Abstract of Israel*, 1980 (Central Bureau of Statistics, Jerusalem, 1980), p.705; ibid., 1984, p.774

workers were made unemployed. In 1969, West Bank industries had recovered from the shock and the number employed compared to Jordan's projected figures for 1968. Thus 1969 may be a suitable base year for our analysis.

Table 8.3 shows the distribution of industrial establishments by major group, total workers employed and the number of establishments of each major group that employed ten or more workers. The table shows that only 5.8 per cent of the units employed ten or more persons, yet they accounted for 32 per cent of total employment in industry. There has been no progress in the industrial sector since then. In terms of the level of employment, industrial units continue to be small with the proportion employing more than ten workers declining. Table 8.4 shows that most factories, 94.8 per cent in 1979 increasing to 95.2 per cent in 1983, employed ten persons or less. The total number of establishments increased over the 1979-83 period by 9.2 per cent, but this rise was almost entirely made up of small establishments. The number of workshops with three or less workers increased for the same period by 9.3 per cent which underlines the decline in medium-sized establishments.

The large discrepancy in the basic data between the total number of establishments registered in Tables 8.3 and 8.4 is due to differences in coverage and in definition. The figures in Table 8.3 are drawn from both Israeli and Jordanian statistics and represent a comprehensive coverage of all establishments while those in Table 8.4 are from the Israeli *Statistical Abstract*. The latter probably represent incomplete coverage in general but also do not include East Jerusalem in the figures for the West Bank, while the data in Table 8.3 do. For example, Awartani, in his study of West Bank industry, registered 382 firms in East Jerusalem and its environs.[12] The UNIDO study by Sadler, Kazi and Jabr gives a figure of 92 establishments, employing 584 workers.[13]

As can be seen from the tables there is a large discrepancy in all categories except rubber, plastics and chemical products, non-metallic minerals and other mineral products. As Israeli statistics from 1977 have included in the industry section owner-operated workshops, it cannot be a discrepancy of size. Saket attributes the decline between 1969 and 1979 to the small workshops being driven out of manufacturing by Israeli imports. Given the high subsidies on basic foodstuffs in Israel in 1967 this could explain the decline in that sector.[14] Frisch notes the ability of the Israeli textile industry to move its subcontracts into or out of the occupied territories; this may explain other differences.[15] Israel also counts olive presses separately.

Table 8.5: Contribution of various sectors to the West Bank GDP: 1979, 1981, 1983 (at factor cost in millions of Israeli shekels at current and constant 1976 prices)

Sector	1979		1981		1983	
	Cur. Prices	Const. Prices	Cur. Prices	Const. Prices	Cur. Prices	Const. Prices
Agriculture, Forestry & Fishing	441.0	112.5	2,492.1	123.0	11,330.6	112.5
Industry	91.0	25.0	501.6	24.8	2,908.2	28.9
Construction	240.6	60.9	1,169.3	57.7	6,627.5	65.8
Services	167.9	42.5	1,014.0	50.1	6,148.0	61.0
Transport, Trade and Others	478.3	121.0	2,255.1	110.4	15,092.6	149.9
GDP	1,418.8	362.0	7,432.1	366.0	42,106.9	418.1
Memorandum Items %						
Share of the Industrial Sector	6.41	6.9	6.75	6.78	6.9	6.9
Share of Agricultural Sector	31.08	31.07	33.53	33.61	26.91	26.91

Source: Central Bureau of Statistics, *Statistical Abstract of Israel*, 1984, p. 175. Constant prices calculated using the Israeli Consumer Price Index, 1976 = 100.The shares of the agricultural and industrial sectors in the GDP are calculated.

It should be noted, however, that 1969 was a period of greater domestic industrial activity than the late 1970s and early 1980s when a large number of owner-managers of small establishments liquidated their businesses either because of Israeli competition or emigration in search of greater opportunities in the booming economies of the neighbouring Arab countries.

Table 8.5 shows that industry's contribution to GDP did not increase between 1979 and 1983, continuing at the 1969 level of below 7 per cent. In terms of numbers employed, the industrial sector did not expand either. On the contrary, the proportion of the

Table 8.6: Distribution of the labour force by location and major economic sector: 1978, 1981, 1983 (percentage)

Sector	West Bank			East Jerusalem			Gaza Strip			Commuters to Israel		
	1978	1981	1983	1978	1981	1983	1978	1981	1983	1978	1981	1983
Agriculture, Forestry & Fishing	27.8	24.1	22.6	4.6	4.5	4.6	21.9	17.3	18.0	14.8	12.7	12.1
Industry (mining & manufacture)	17.6	16.4	16.8	27.2	27.4	27.3	17.3	17.2	17.1	22.8	18.2	18.6
Construction (building & public works)	20.7	24.0	24.7	11.5	11.2	12.8	21.4	26.5	26.1	46.2	51.0	50.4
Commerce, Restaurants & Hotels	12.5	12.5	12.8	20.6	21.7	20.5	13.5	14.2	13.6	–	–	–
Transport, Storage & Communication	4.2	4.9	5.0	6.3	6.4	6.3	6.8	6.8	5.9	16.2	18.2	18.1
Public & Community Services	13.0	14.2	13.4	20.6	20.2	13.5	13.5	12.8	13.1	–	–	–
Other	4.2	3.9	4.7	9.2	8.6	5.6	5.6	5.2	6.2	–	–	–
TOTAL	100	100	100	100	100	100	100	100	100	100	100	100

Sources: Bakir Abu Kishk, 'The industrial and economic trends in the West Bank and the Gaza Strip', *United Nations Document* E/ECWA/UNIDO/WP.1 (Economic Commission for West Asia, Joint ECWA/UNIDO Industrial Division, Beirut, December 1981), pp. 8-28; Central Bureau of Statistics, *Statistical Abstract of Israel*, 1984, pp. 762 and 963.

Table 8.7: Distribution of Gaza Strip industrial establishments by major group and by number of employees: 1979, 1982, 1983

Indus-trial Group	1979 Number of workers						1982 Number of workers						1983 Number of workers					
	1-3	4-7	8-10	11-20	21+	Total	1-3	4-7	8-10	11-20	21+	Total	1-3	4-7	8-10	11-20	21+	Total
Food	151	36	4	5	3	199	154	39	1	5	3	202	151	40	2	3	2	198
Textiles	298	95	43	44	10	490	306	110	50	45	12	523	304	119	51	43	12	529
Wood	125	61	4	2	6	198	128	72	3	4	5	212	130	72	2	5	3	212
Metals	165	64	6	2	5	242	179	65	8	5	4	261	183	64	7	5	4	263
Other	91	88	11	10	6	206	102	96	16	6	3	223	103	90	16	5	2	216
TOTAL	830	344	68	63	30	1,335	869	382	78	65	27	1,421	871	385	78	61	23	1,148

Sources: Central Bureau of Statistics, *Statistical Abstract of Israel*, 1980, p. 707; ibid, 1983, p. 793; ibid., 1984, p.775.

Palestinian labour force working in industry declined between 1978 and 1983 not only in the West Bank, but also for those commuting to work in Israel. Table 8.6 illustrates this trend. Only construction increased its work force, particularly for commuters to Israel. Since the 1984 economic crisis, construction has stagnated in Israel and created a serious unemployment problem for commuters from the occupied territories.

2. Gaza Strip

The unimportance of the manufacturing sector relative to agriculture in the Gaza Strip meant that the immediate impact of occupation on industry was not as strong as it was on agriculture nor as powerful as it was on industry in the West Bank. Information on the distribution of establishments by major group is not available for the year 1969. The manufacturing sector employed 4,095 workers in that year. Table 8.7 shows the distribution of establishments by major group over the period 1979 to 1983. The table shows that the change between 1982 and 1983 was not significant in terms of total units, but there was a fall in the number of plants employing more than ten workers. About 38 per cent of all establishments are concentrated in textiles; these firms subcontract work from Israeli companies and do not contribute significantly to the permanent development of the area. In terms of the contribution of the industrial sector to GDP, Table 8.8 shows that its share declined from 11 per cent in 1979 to 9.9 per cent in 1983; in real terms the contribution declined by 26 per cent. Only the services sector increased its contribution in real terms during the period, when GDP declined by 10 per cent.

Table 8.8ᵃ: Contribution of various sectors to Gaza GDP: 1979, 1981, 1983 (at factor cost in millions of Israeli shekels at current and constant 1976 prices)

Sector	1979 Current	1979 Constant	1981 Current	1981 Constant	1983 Current	1983 Constant
Agriculture, Forestry & Fishing	150.0	40.2	689.9	34.5	2,696.4	25.0
Industry	77.9	20.8	290.3	14.5	1,655.7	15.4
Construction	160.3	43.0	791.4	39.6	3,973.4	36.8
Services	105.1	43.0	726.6	36.3	4,161.8	38.6
Transport, Trade and Others	152.6	40.8	872.1	43.6	4,296.6	39.6
GDP	645.9	187.8	3,370.3	168.5	16,756.9	155.4
Memorandum Items (%)						
Share of Industrial Sector		11.08		8.6		9.9
Share of Agricultural Sector		21.4		20.5		16.1

Note: a. Because of the exclusion of the Sinai Peninsula in 1982 and lack of information on that particular area, it is not possible to compare the same years as in Table 8.7.
Source: Central Bureau of Statistics, *The Administered Territories Statistical Quarterly*, vol. 14, no. 1 (Central Bureau of Statistics, Jerusalem, 1984), p. 175. Constant prices calculated by the author.

3. Obstacles in the way of industrial development under occupation

During interviews conducted in 1981 with managers of 276 randomly selected firms, more than 86 per cent of respondents expressed their desire to expand. When asked to indicate the reasons which inhibited them from doing so other than political factors, more than 60 per cent identified market size and competition with Israeli products. Others specified shortages of capital and qualified workers.

These answers touched on three sensitive areas: trade, finance and training, which are discussed below.

(i) Factors limiting industrial trade

Since 1967, the external trade of the occupied territories has been strictly controlled through a range of measures adopted by the Israeli military authorities. As in other areas of economic activity, a key instrument to achieve this has been the application of a series of military orders which restrict the movement of commodities to and from the occupied territories. These orders subject Palestinian exports and imports to complicated certification procedures, while also limiting the development of industry through specifying the types and quantities of raw materials that can enter the territories for use by the manufacturing industries.[16]

Restrictions on Palestinian trade have an especially debilitating effect in view of the relatively small local market and the difficulties in competitively producing those capital goods required for development of consumer goods in demand locally. An important structural determinant of the Palestinian economy's ability to develop trade is the physical barriers imposed by occupation separating the territories from their natural Arab hinterland. This has resulted in adding heavy costs to the trade process, in terms of time, transport and the cumbersome certification procedures.

These problems are complicated by the free flow of Israeli exports to the West Bank and Gaza Strip often in the form of 'dumping' low-priced agricultural commodities and poor quality, if not hazardous, industrial goods. Whereas the occupied territories cannot act to control or limit the unbridled entry of subsidised and protected Israeli agricultural and industrial goods, Israel strictly controls the import of Palestinian products. Virtually no Palestinian agricultural goods are exported to Israel, except for certain industrial commodities used in Israeli product processing (tomatoes and oranges). The most lucrative Palestinian cash crops are banned from entry to Israel. The export of Palestinian industrial goods to Israel is formally less restricted. However, as the major policy guideline in this area is 'protection of Israeli industries', the export of most Palestinian manufactures is thereby ruled out in effect. Only in the area of subcontracting is there a significant movement of Palestinian manufactured goods into Israel, though in this case the materials involved are initially imported from Israel and the only 'export' element is that of cheap Palestinian labour which goes into the assembly and finishing of Israeli goods. Recent Israeli military orders enforce complex labelling requirements on Palestinian products, adding further costs to an already overburdened manufacturing process.

Another significant constraint on the development of Palestinian industrial exports is the effect of the Arab Boycott provisions which prohibit the entry into Arab countries of any Israeli goods or products containing Israeli raw materials or materials imported via Israel.

Except for some recent exemptions, industries established on the West Bank since 1967 and not licensed by Jordan have not been allowed to export at all to Jordan. This has meant that the production of major Palestinian exports, such as soap, must use raw materials imported via Jordan, usually at relatively high costs. Expansion and industrial diversification is similarly limited since new equipment must also be imported from Jordan, at a cost substantially higher than would be the case if capital goods could be imported through (or from) Israel. The import of such goods from Jordan is further discouraged as a result of restrictions placed by Israel at bridge crossings and the heavy customs duties applied by Israel on most industrial imports.

The volume of trade from 1980-3 between Israel and the occupied territories is shown in Table 8.9. The occupied territories suffer from a chronic trade deficit which is growing annually and which stood at some US$ 400 million in 1983. The deficit is largest with Israel, which provides about 90 per cent of the total imports of the occupied territories, of which 87 per cent are industrial products. Industrial imports from Jordan are restricted because of the above-mentioned Israeli regulations as well as the high costs associated with movements of goods from and via Jordan. The occupied territories' industrial exports account for over 75 per cent of total exports, and are mostly destined for Israel, indicating the increased domination by the Israeli market of the territories' export capacity. Though this is partially offset by industrial exports to and through Jordan, these have accounted for a decreasing share of total Palestinian exports. Meanwhile, some 15 per cent of Israeli exports are destined for the occupied territories, rendering the Palestinian economy the second largest single Israeli (non-military) export market after the United States.

Restrictions on trade are further compounded by complex regulations affecting industrial licensing. To make sure military orders are followed rigidly, the military authorities issued order No. 184, dated 10 December 1967, to transfer the powers of the Jordanian government and local authorities to an authorised person appointed by the military governor. These orders have been used to discourage industrial development in the occupied territories and to restructure local industry according to the interests of the occupying power. Thus while small-scale textile and construction-related industries are allowed to operate in the occupied territories in accordance with the interests of Israeli subcontracting construction processes the establishment of industries which could compete with similar Israeli enterprises has been blocked.

Two examples show how projects have been denied permits, either outright or by procedural tactics. In the first, the Israeli military authorities in the Gaza Strip refused for several years an application for a permit to establish a citrus processing plant in Gaza City. A conditional permit was finally issued in 1986, but by then the conditions in the citrus industry and the prospects for available finances had changed considerably and adversely for the project. In the second, the military governor of the West Bank refused to issue a global permit allowing the cement industry to conduct soil surveys in the occupied territories to explore the extent of the availability of raw materials. The Arab Cement Company, instead of having a global permit to conduct the survey, was forced to submit a request for each individual location and has had to wait several months before obtaining a permit for any particular site. This had the effect of delaying the completion of the preliminary procedures for several years. In both cases, the justification provided by Israeli officials has been that cement and juice production capacity existed in Israel and there 'was no need for the creation of additional capacity in these fields'.

Another factor which has constrained the growth of markets for Palestinian industrial products arises from the application by Jordan of Arab Boycott provisions with regard to licensing of industries established since 1967. Accordingly, until 1979, only pre-1967 factories were allowed to export to Jordan, along the above-mentioned guidelines of Arab certification of origin. In 1979, the Jordanian Government agreed to award licenses to a number of factories (mostly larger soap, paper and vegetable oil industries) which had been established since occupation. This did not, however, provide a solution for the many smaller-scale industries whose future growth depends on expanding markets.

(ii) Finance

The economy of the occupied territories suffers from the absence of financial institutions on one hand and from the tight monetary policy administered by the Israeli authorities on the other. In 1967 all Arab banks operating in the West Bank and Gaza Strip were closed by Israeli military orders and their assets and liabilities were frozen or impounded by Israeli authorities. Subsequently, Israeli banks were allowed to open branches in the occupied territories, but their activities have been limited to daily and short-term transactions. The amount of credit extended to investors to encourage industrial development has been insignificant. Investors have been forced to look for private, and therefore more expensive, sources of finance.

These have been supplemented by external aid, from Jordanian, Arab or international sources.

Though foreign sources of finance have helped to alleviate the general lack of credit facilities, these cannot be expected to substitute for domestic resource mobilisation. This raises special problems in the context of the occupied territories in light of the restrictions placed by the Israeli authorities on capital inflows into the territories, the increasingly tight controls placed on foreign exchange dealings, and the complex provisions which govern loan procedures with Jordanian and Arab banks. There are no sources of credit available from Israeli government agencies, and branches of Israeli banks have also refrained from financing industrial or other productive endeavours. The main function of Israeli bank branches has been to syphon resources out of the occupied territories by maintaining large balances in banks in Israel.

Specialised credit institutions in Jordan, such as the Amman-based Industrial Development Bank, have acted cautiously with regard to extending credit to the occupied territories' borrowers. This is mainly due to the difficulty of appraising, monitoring and recovering loans. The Industrial Bank and other specialised credit institutions have, however, lent money for West Bank projects using funds placed with it by the Jordanian authorities or the Jordanian-Palestinian Joint Committee. Credit available from those institutions has been at low interest rates and flexible repayment terms, usually subject to Jordanian government guarantees, though the actual magnitudes have been generally small. Most Jordanian commercial banks do not provide credit to Palestinian businesses in the occupied territories unless the borrowers can provide collateral outside the territories.

Meanwhile, the efforts of local institutions have been directed to filling the resource gap, though with only limited impact. Small private credit and insurance companies have been established, while some co-operative societies, mainly engaged in agriculture, have attempted to provide credit, especially in rural areas. Other informal facilities, provided by private and individual sources such as moneychangers, money lenders and commercial agents, have concentrated on providing short-term, personal credit in addition to exchanging Jordanian and Israeli currencies. These activities have rarely spread to risky productive areas and remain primarily a channel of intermediation between local savings and commercial banks outside the occupied territories. In general, the cost of credit available from informal sources is high, both in terms of interest rates and guarantee conditions. While some informal sources of credit have been directed to the productive sectors, this has mainly been in agriculture, and in the form of short-term seasonal loans for purchase of inputs and payment of wages. The small-scale industrial sector has not benefited from similar arrangements.

(iii) Training

Vocational or on-the-job training opportunities are very limited. The lower productivity and poorer quality of products in the manufacturing sector of the occupied territories is partly attributable to the lower training and educational levels of the work force. In the responses to the questionnaires completed by managers and owners of firms cited above, it was found that about 34 per cent of the work force was considered skilled.[17] However, given that 69 per cent of all workers had less than nine years of schooling the degree to which this could be considered accurate was questionable. It was clear that there is a need for higher quality training programmes designed to attract more highly qualified students. Most vocational and technical training institutions and programmes are run by private voluntary organisations or by the UN. Most of them operate under severe financial handicaps and suffer from restrictions on expansion imposed by the Israeli authorities.

IV. INDUSTRIAL DEVELOPMENT THROUGH THE DEVELOPMENT OF AGRO-INDUSTRY[18]

The contributions of agriculture based industry to rural development are manifold. Agro-industries can increase rural production and productivity through, for instance, the manufacture and supply of productivity-raising inputs. The processing of agricultural outputs such as tomatoes, vegetables, citrus and other fruits also has a major impact on the rural economy. Rural industrialisation, by increasing economic activity, can also make a significant social contribution to the human resource base. Wider opportunities for entrepreneurial initiative, greater knowledge and awareness, upgraded skills, and additional means of realising increased expectations follow the expansion of the rural economy. Rural industrialisation development can bridge the gap between rural and urban communities and reduce the negative aspects of urban industrialisation which have contributed to highly unbalanced urbanisation.

In most developing countries, the population and non-agricultural sectors are not dispersed among cities of varying size, as in the developed countries, but are concentrated in a few large centres,

Table 8.9: Imports, exports and trade balances for the West Bank and the Gaza Strip: 1981-1983 (in millions of US dollars)

	1981			1982			1983		
	Import	Export	Deficit (-) or Surplus	Import	Export	Deficit (-) or Surplus	Import	Export	Deficit (-) or Surplus
Grand Total	690.06	367.50	-322.56	684.25	357.80	-325.70	668.70	326.50	-362.20
From and to Israel	618.40	265.09	-353.35	609.50	239.10	-370.40	624.70	238.60	-386.10
Agricultural production	84.01	41.69	-42.32	70.90	31.20	-39.70	78.40	33.70	-44.60
Industrial production	534.43	223.40	-311.02	538.60	207.90	-330.70	546.30	204.90	-341.40
From and to Jordan	6.87	94.61	87.74	8.44	113.80	105.30	5.90	81.10	75.30
Agricultural production	0.17	41.69	41.52	0.40	55.50	55.10	0.20	37.50	37.30
Industrial production	6.70	52.93	43.32	8.04	58.30	50.20	5.60	43.60	38.00
From and to others	64.75	7.80	-56.95	66.30	5.60	-60.70	58.10	6.70	-51.50
Agricultural production	4.65	6.42	1.79	10.10	4.80	-5.20	10.80	5.70	-5.10
Industrial production	60.10	1.38	-58.74	56.20	0.80	-55.40	47.40	1.00	-46.40

Source: Central Bureau of Statistics, *Statistical Abstract of Israel*, 1984, p. 751.

often only the capital. This situation creates a self-propelled process of concentration of population and industries. New industries find the advantages of infrastructure, markets, and labour supply in the existing cities. Labour migrates from the countryside to these cities in the expectation of finding employment, higher wages and better living conditions. The results are often the opposite.

Fortunately, cities in the occupied territories vary in size and are located at convenient distances from each other. Industrial zones between these cities would attract the labour force from nearby rural communities and at the same time be close to the markets of the major cities. Such development would have several benefits for the occupied territories. It would reduce the pressure on the cities to provide services to the newcomers from the rural communities and encourage people to stay in their villages and improve the infrastructure and services for the whole community. Rural industrialisation which complements the agricultural sector would prevent the formation of dual structures in the economy and create a balance between rural and urban communities.

A strategy of rural development must aim to increase the efficiency of existing industries and introduce new opportunities and instruments of development. Increased productivity is one necessity. It could be achieved by eliminating less productive tasks, increasing specialisation and better utilisation of raw materials. A more diversified rural sector, involving greater dispersion of economic activity and the expansion of non-farm activities, must be a primary goal. The major obstacle to such a development would be Israel's response to the resulting reduction in its exports to the occupied territories and the fall in availability of cheap, commuter labour.

V. SUMMARY AND POLICY RECOMMENDATIONS

1. Summary

Industry in the West Bank and Gaza Strip consists of primarily small-scale enterprises. More then 90 per cent of existing establishments employ less than ten workers. Comparison between industrial statistics for 1969 and 1983 shows no significant changes in the types of product made, total number and size of establishments, contribution to the GDP or employment level. The main reason for this stagnation is the occupation, which through its policies on production, investment and trade, and through the limitations it has imposed on financial intermediaries for development, has made it profoundly difficult for local manufacturers to maintain current levels of production in the face of Israeli competition, much less to initiate new industries and expand markets.

If industrial development in the occupied areas is to contend with existing military regulations and other controls imposed by the occupation authorities the prospects are not promising and the opportunities remain limited.

2. Policy recommendations

Formulation of policies and programmes for industrial development must be done with reference to the very special conditions imposed by a prolonged occupation. In the absence of Palestinian national sovereignty in the occupied territories, the development process has to involve much greater popular participation to be effective. Rural industrial development programmes should be integrated horizontally with agricultural and social development programmes and vertically with urban/industrial development programmes.

The starting point for industrial development has to be at the level of existing knowledge and understanding of industrial organisation and technology. Priorities need to be established on the basis of resource endowment, availability of raw materials, current and potential skills and the identification of market opportunities. Such priorities can only be properly established in the context of a full understanding of the local market and the nature of existing demand. Both forward and backward linkages within the economy will help to identify the main areas for specialisation.

The range of product possibilities for rural industrialisation programmes may be summarised as follows:

(i) Production of agricultural inputs
Feeds: Poultry farmers use pre-mixed feeds on their farms. Today there are ten establishments in the occupied territories, one of them in the Gaza Strip, producing food-stuffs for poultry. The capacity of these establishments is about 2,500 tons per month, which is one-third of the local market demand.

Hatcheries: In spite of the relatively sizable broiler chicken and egg production in the territories, there is no local hatchery to supply chicks. Hatcheries which operated prior to 1967 have gone out of business and all chicks are imported from Israel.

Other agricultural inputs: Total imports of the occupied territories of agricultural inputs were estimated at about US$ 250 million in 1983.[19] Import substitution should be investigated particularly for mixed fertilisers and plastic products for growing vegetables under cover.

(ii) Processing of agricultural produce
There are a number of options in this sector including the production of fruit and vegetable juices, milk and milk by-products from fresh or dry milk and the expansion of vegetable processing beyond olives.

(iii) Production of building materials
This includes, in addition to the existing quarries, stone-cutting and concrete block production, the production of metal door and window frames and processing of timber for construction.[20] Feasibility studies need to be undertaken to assess the viability of this and other possibilities.

(iv) Traditional handicrafts
In addition to the local traditional dresses and handmade straw items, there is the handicrafts and souvenir industry. This trade is well established especially in Hebron and Bethlehem but depends heavily on imported raw or half-processed materials. The value of imported clay and other inputs would justify the establishment of a factory in the occupied territories, provided that the producers of these items could organise themselves co-operatively.

(v) Planning recommendations
(a) Agriculture based industry should be moved away from large cities to rural areas. Because of differences in local factor endowment an even pattern of development between rural and urban areas or between rural areas might not be feasible. Fortunately, in the case of the occupied territories, where the total area is relatively small, the distances between the major cities are not a limiting factor. It is possible to think of establishing an industrial zone or zones between the major cities that would serve the rural areas in the vicinity and yet benefit from the nearby urban centres.

(b) Greater emphasis should be placed on the promotion of small and medium-sized firms to create jobs and to further regional dispersal.

(c) Technology that is appropriate for the prevailing conditions in the occupied territories should be selected.

(d) Research needs to be undertaken on the improvement of the quality of products, commercial distribution inside and outside the

Table 8.10: Geographical distribution of establishments by location and major group: 1980

Group	Jerusalem A	Jerusalem B	Hebron A	Hebron B	Ramallah A	Ramallah B	Nablus A	Nablus B	Tulkarm A	Tulkarm B	Jenin A	Jenin B	Bethlehem A	Bethlehem B	Jericho A	Jericho B	Gaza Strip A	Gaza Strip B*	Total A	Total B
Food	24	2	12	-	38	6	61	7	17	-	15	-	17	1	11	-	75	-	270	16
Beverages	-	-	-	-	2	1	-	-	-	-	-	-	2	-	1	-	3	-	8	-
Tobacco	-	-	-	-	3	2	-	-	-	-	-	-	1	1	-	-	-	-	4	3
Textiles	-	-	73	13	26	9	91	16	14	13	6	2	36	13	-	-	215	-	416	66
Leather	2	-	5	-	-	-	1	1	-	-	-	-	-	-	1	-	3	-	11	-
Shoes	14	-	184	6	3	-	47	2	11	-	10	-	20	-	-	-	29	-	279	8
Wood	15	-	-	-	7	3	53	-	-	-	9	-	61	-	10	-	34	-	259	3
Furniture	-	-	123	3	21	-	8	-	-	-	-	-	1	-	-	-	26	8	150	11
Paper etc.	1	-	6	-	2	1	1	-	-	-	2	-	2	-	1	-	5	-	16	1
Printing	5	1	3	-	4	1	8	-	-	-	-	-	8	-	-	-	12	1	37	3
Chemicals & chemical products	-	-	-	-	11	7	15	3	-	-	-	-	-	-	-	-	4	2	38	12
Rubber	1	-	-	-	-	-	-	-	-	-	-	-	-	-	-	-	-	-	1	-
Pottery etc.	2	-	-	-	-	-	2	-	-	-	-	-	35	4	-	-	3	-	43	4
Glass etc.	-	-	6	1	-	-	-	-	-	-	-	-	-	-	-	-	5	-	11	1
Minerals	4	1	150	4	33	-	33	-	22	1	12	-	14	2	4	-	100	14	372	22
Non-ferrous metal	-	-	1	-	-	-	-	-	-	-	-	-	-	-	-	-	-	-	1	-
Fabricated metal	21	-	126	2	22	-	50	2	28	-	35	-	11	1	-	-	90	-	383	5
Machinery	-	-	-	-	-	-	-	-	-	-	3	-	2	-	11	-	2	-	16	-
Electrical machinery	-	-	2	-	-	-	-	-	-	-	-	-	2	1	-	-	2	-	6	1
Other	1	1	-	-	-	-	3	-	12	-	2	-	8	-	1	-	6	-	33	1
TOTAL	90	5	691	29	172	34	373	34	104	14	94	2	219	33	42	-	614	40	2,399	160

A = Total units   B = Units with 10 or more workers

Note: a. Figures for Gaza are not available

Source: Abu Kishk, 'Industrial and economic trends', pp. 103-10

occupied territories and industrial management.

(e) Feasibility studies should be conducted in existing establishments to discover whether or not they can be expanded and to what extent this is possible.

(f) Studies should be undertaken to delineate industrial zones and to determine the type of industries appropriate to each zone before investment is made in infrastructure.

(g) The shift from traditional labour intensive to modern capital intensive industries and technology reduces the capacity of the industrial sector to absorb the surplus labour. Labour intensive industries should be favoured wherever possible.

It is obvious that the list is long and some of the suggestions may not be permitted by the Israeli authorities. It should be noted, however, that thus far, the Israeli authorities have not generally opposed the expansion of the existing establishments. Expansion could take place, therefore, on the basis of the current industrial stock. Table 8.10 shows the geographical distribution of all units, and of those the ones employing more than ten workers, in the various major industrial groups. The table shows that there are 160 larger firms in the West Bank and about 40 in the Gaza Strip. These 200 firms should be used as a starting point for an industrial expansion programme in areas where the occupied territories have shown a clear comparative advantage.

This approach is possible under present conditions because these firms are already in the market and the production technology is known to the management. There is a strong potential for improvement in most of these industries.

NOTES

1. Hillel Frisch, *Stagnation and Frontier: Arab and Jewish Industry in the West Bank* (The West Bank Data Base Project, Jerusalem, July 1983), p. 11.

2. The first and second sections of this paper draw heavily on my previous paper, Bakir Abu Kishk, 'The industrial and economic trends in the West Bank and Gaza Strip' *United Nations Document* E/ECWA/UNIDA/WP.1 (Economic Commission for West Asia, Joint ECWA/UNIDO Industrial Division, Beirut, December 1981), pp. 8-28.

3. International Bank for Reconstruction and Development, *The Economic Development of Jordan* (Johns Hopkins Press, Baltimore, 1957), pp. 10, 66-8.

4. Michael Mazur, 'Economic development of Jordan' in C.A. Cooper and S.S. Alexander (eds), *Economic Development and Population Growth in*

the Middle East (Elsevier, New York, 1972), pp. 211-78.

5. Fawzi A. Gharaibeh, *The Economies of the West Bank and Gaza Strip* (Westview Press, Boulder, 1985).

6. Gharaibeh, *The Economies of the West Bank and the Gaza Strip.*

7. Economic Planning Authority, *Israel Economic Survey of the West Bank* (Central Bureau of Statistics, Jerusalem, 1967), p. 81.

8. Gharaibeh, *The Economies of the West Bank and the Gaza Strip,* p.85.

9. Ibid., p.87.

10. Jan Metzger, Martin Orth and Christian Sterzing, *This Land is Our Land* (Zed Press, London, 1983), chapter 4.

11. Frisch, *Stagnation and Frontier,* pp. 63-8.

12. Hisham Awartani, *A Survey of Industries in the West Bank and the Gaza Strip* (Birzeit University, Birzeit, September 1979) pp.17-18.

13. P.G. Sadler, U. Kazi and M.H. Jabr, *Palestine: Development of the Industrial Sector* (London, 1983), p.35. But other figures quoted in Sadler et al. would suggest that there are 784 industrial concerns in East Jerusalem. They give a total number of 2,991 factories in the West Bank including East Jerusalem (p.19) and a figure of 2,207 for the West Bank excluding East Jerusalem (Table 1.2, p.24).

14. Bassam Saket, *al-qit'a al-sana'iyya fi al-munatiq al-muhtalla: al-daffa al-gharbiyya wa qit'a ghazza* (The industrial sector in the occupied territories) (Arab Industrial Development Organisation, Baghdad/Economics Institute, Amman, May 1982), pp.13-19.

15. Frisch, *Stagnation and Frontier*, pp.52-7.

16. Abu Kishk, 'Industrial and economic trends', p.11. These orders include: (a) Military Order No. 49, dated 10 July 1967. It is illegal to take out of or bring into the occupied territories any commodity without a permit signed by the authorised persons. (b) Military Order No. 411, dated 15 December 1971. (i) It is illegal to bring into the occupied territories any commodity without a permit from the authorised person. (ii) It is illegal to take out of the occupied territories any commodity without the permission of the authorised person. Military Order No. 653, dated 15 April, 1976 will illustrate this point: Order No. 653: It is illegal to do the following without the permission of the authorised person: (i) It is illegal to open any place to produce commodities which are subject to control. (ii) It is illegal to bring into the occupied territories, or take out of the territories, any commodity which is subject to control. The list of controlled items includes the following: mixed fertilisers with a high proportion of ammonium nitrate, herbicides which contain a high proportion of sodium chlorate, and aluminium powder. A full analysis of Israeli military orders can be found in Raja Shehadeh, *Occupier's Law: Israel in the West Bank* (Institute of Palestine Studies, Washington D.C., 1986).

To make sure these orders are followed rigidly the authorities issued order No. 184, dated 10 December 1967, to transfer the authority vested in the Jordanian government and local councils to authorised persons appointed by the military governor. The authorised person has used these orders to discourage the economic development of the occupied territories.

17. Abu Kishk, 'Industrial and economic trends', p. 67.

18. The general ideas on rural development were taken from various United Nations documents, mainly: *Industry and Development No. 5*

(UNIDO, ref ID/SER. M/S, Vienna, October, 1980); *Industrialisation and Rural Development,* (UNIDO, ref ID/215.ID/WG.257/23, New York, 1978), *Industry and Development No. 6,* (UNIDO ref ID/SER.M/G, New York, 1981); *Small-scale Industries in Arab Countries of the Middle East,* (UNIDO ref ID/21, New York, 1970).

19. This figure was found in the Israeli *Statistical Abstract* in Israeli shekels. The values were then divided by the US dollar exchange rate for 1983 to get the value of imports in US dollars.

20. The amount of wood consumed in the occupied territories means that the development of a building timber plant should be seriously considered. In Israel there are five factories and the occupied territories import about one-quarter of their production.

9

Money and Finance with Undeveloped Banking in the Occupied Territories

Laurence Harris

When the West Bank and Gaza were occupied by Israel in 1967 one of the first actions of the new administration was to demolish the existing Arab financial and monetary institutions. In the West Bank, for example, the earliest military orders closed the 31 branches of Amman-based and other banks, imposed the authority of the Bank of Israel over all banking matters, made the Israeli pound (later the shekel and then the new shekel) legal tender (jointly with the Jordanian dinar) and imposed Israeli foreign exchange controls.[1] These actions to repress Arab financial institutions and to exercise Israeli authority in areas formerly controlled by the Central Bank of Jordan have had profound effects on subsequent financial and monetary conditions in the occupied territories and, through them, on their 'real economy' (in the sense of real saving, investment in physical capital and growth).[2] There is, however, little systematic knowledge of what those effects on the monetary and financial system have been. In this paper I consider some aspects of them. In section I, I describe the monetary and financial system that does exist; in section II, I outline an existing theoretical framework for analysing 'financial repression'; in section III, I relate the occupied territories' experience to that theoretical framework and examine the problem of money and finance in the West Bank and the Gaza Strip.

I. THE OPERATIONS AND INSTITUTIONS OF THE FINANCIAL SYSTEM

The occupied territories' financial system is built around a number of distinct institutions and agents:

(a) The Arab money changers have a key role for the whole system. Their operations, which are largely illegal under occupation law but not generally repressed, are relevant for the internal transactions of the economies but are most significant in the relations between the occupied territories and other economies;

(b) Branches of Israeli banks which are (almost) the only legal banks in the occupied territories;

(c) Permitted Arab financial institutions of which the most significant is the Bank of Palestine (in Gaza);

(d) Merchants and landowners who provide agricultural credit on an unofficial basis;

(e) Finance emanating from Amman.

Although these institutions have distinct characteristics they are partially linked in an interdependent financial network. This chapter describes and analyses each in turn.[3] In this analysis, a distinction is made between monetary activities and financial intermediation. The former involves dealing in money - foreign exchange dealing, transfer of funds, clearing of cheques etc. - whereas the latter refers to borrowing and lending. The two may overlap in practice but remain distinct in principle. In this chapter the institutions concerned with giving grants are not described except to the extent that grant finance overlaps with credit and financial intermediation.

1. Money changers

Money changers operate in every town in the occupied territories with, in most cases, a shop front, kiosk or counter which carries out the most obvious part of their work, the exchanging of one currency for another. All engage in foreign exchange dealing at this level, but the most important fact is that many have also developed a wide range of banking functions. They operate as banks (or constrained embryo banks) by taking deposits, transferring funds, clearing bills and cheques and giving loans.

There are, however, different types of money changers. They differ as to whether they are located in the West Bank, Jerusalem or the Gaza Strip, whether they were established before 1967 or subsequently and whether they concentrate wholly on financial transactions or combine these with commodity dealing. Those which have in effect developed into banks are the largest; they were established before 1967, are based in the West Bank or Jerusalem, and generally hold only financial assets rather than non-monetary commodities. To analyse their significance

I examine each aspect of their business in turn.[4]

(i) Currency exchange

Exchanging one currency for another is the foundation of the money changers' business. It has flourished particularly because they disregard all exchange controls and are therefore able to deal in foreign exchange with Israeli citizens, residents of the occupied territories and others, all of whom have been formally constrained by Israeli or Jordanian exchange regulations to varying degrees at different times since 1967. A second reason for the money changers' strength as foreign exchange dealers is that the high rates of inflation in Israel during the early 1980s gave rise to a situation where the shekel price of the US dollar in the money changers' free market generally diverged significantly from the official rate and thereby attracted much foreign exchange business to them.

As far as pure currency exchange is concerned, money changers deal principally in cash with some business, especially in tourist areas, in travellers' cheques. But because this business is linked with their wider banking role, currency exchange also involves receiving and disbursing debits (cheques and drafts) on the bank accounts of customers and money changers in Amman.

The most substantial part of currency exchange is illegal in terms of the occupying authorities' law. Authorised money changers in the West Bank are permitted to buy and sell the two currencies which are legal tender there, the Israeli shekel and the Jordanian dinar, but transactions in US dollars, which are a major element, are illegal as are transactions in other currencies. In Gaza, even the exchange of shekels for dinars is illegal for the money changers. In East Jerusalem, where Israeli foreign exchange regulations are considered to apply to the annexed city, unlike the West Bank and Gaza, there is nevertheless a position more like the West Bank regarding the ability to deal in Jordanian dinars because of a commitment at annexation to permit the continuation of pre-1967 activities.

In fact, however, the illegal currency dealing of the money changers is not normally prevented by the occupying authorities. But they do use the position of tolerated illegality to take action against money changers either on an arbitrary basis or in connection with Israel's macroeconomic policy. Examples of the former in recent years include the temporary arrest in Nablus of the West Bank's largest money changer and the confiscation of US dollars from time to time (one such incident is said to have occurred in Jerusalem in the summer of 1985). An example of the latter was the temporary closure of the

193

open transactions in dollars of Jerusalem money changers when Israel tightened its monetary policy and foreign exchange restrictions (although examples exist of transactions continuing through clandestine arrangements at that time).

Money changers determine their own exchange rates taking into account local market conditions and current and expected conditions in the foreign exchange markets of Europe and elsewhere. The current exchange rates on the world's foreign exchange markets provide the benchmark for the money changers' daily rates but they diverge from them in response to two other forces: expected changes in the world market rates and the current balance of demand and supply for individual currencies in the local market. The system by which large money changers set prices in line with these three forces is as follows: the day's exchange rate for spot transactions on international foreign exchange markets is obtained. Because, under occupation, it is impossible for money changers (in the West Bank at least) to obtain telex facilities or high technology links to market information services, they obtain the market rate from other sources, in particular the world radio services such as the BBC. The rates at which they buy and sell are then set at a premium (or discount) in relation to the international market's rates to anticipate expected changes in the latter over the next one or two days, this being the length of time it usually takes the large money changer to transfer surplus funds to (or deficits from) the international centres. Finally the premium (or discount) is adjusted in response to any large imbalances in the local demand and supply for currencies at those international rates. A common method by which money changers take expectations and local conditions into account is to adjust their prices in the same direction as international market prices with a lag after a change in the latter.

In setting exchange rates the large money changers determine their own spreads as well as premiums; the relation between their spreads and international markets' spreads is determined by similar factors to the above.[45] Exchange rates for particular currencies, for example, between the Israeli shekel and the Jordanian dinar, are determined as cross rates in relation to their individual exchange rates *vis-à-vis* the US dollar. All exchange transactions are conducted without documentation or record keeping and, in contrast with foreign exchange purchases made by Israeli bank customers, without taxation.

Exchange rates are determined in this way by a small number of large money changers. It appears that smaller money changers follow their rates.

(ii) Money transfers

The transfer of funds among the occupied territories, Amman, and foreign countries is integrally linked with the money changers' currency exchange and has been so since before the Israeli occupation.

The largest money changers have branches in the occupied territories, Amman and the Gulf. (Money changers permitted by the Jordanian authorities to operate in Amman are in two categories: those which are permitted to have foreign bank accounts and those which, without such permission, can only deal in bank-notes.)[6] In addition, they have a network of correspondents and agents which extends at least to the international financial centres in Europe and the USA. These branches, correspondents and agents are the channel for the money changers' money transfers. The transfers they make between centres outside the occupied territories (from the Gulf to Amman, or from Amman to Europe for example) are carried out through normal banking mechanisms, debiting and crediting the money changers' accounts with banks there. But net transfers between Amman and the occupied territories take place by carrying or smuggling cash over the bridges, the crossing points into and out of the occupied territories. In general, there is a net flow into the occupied territories from Amman because the occupied territories have a balance of trade surplus with the East Bank. It is estimated that US$ 170 million crossed the bridges into the West Bank in the five months from March 1985.

Carrying or smuggling cash between the occupied territories and Amman is the only way in which the money changers can carry out net transfers between those places, for occupation itself has broken the formal channels. Since 1967 it has closed all the branches of Jordanian (and other Arab) banks formerly operating in the occupied territories, there are no relations between Jordan and the Israeli banks in the occupied territories and Israeli foreign exchange controls and controls on the amounts of cash that can be carried across the bridges (controls that are relaxed and tightened at different times) give currency smuggling its role as the main means of transferring net balances between Amman and the occupied territories.

Only net balances give rise to cash movements between Amman and the occupied territories; money changers in the occupied territories receive both debits and credits on Amman and only have to move cash to the extent that these are unbalanced. Thus, for example, a person in the West Bank wanting to transfer money from Amman will obtain the cash from a money changer in return for a cheque on his or her bank account in Amman. If another person deposits an equivalent amount of cash with the money changer for transfer to his or her account in Amman no cash need cross the border. In that example the transactions may be closed by the money changer paying the first person's cheque into his account in Amman and (by unwritten agreement with the second person) instructing his Amman branch to pay a cheque from his Amman account to the second person's Amman account. Alternatively, the money changer may simply give the second person the first person's cheque (originally drawn in favour of the money changer). In that case, if the standing of the person who drew the cheque is high enough, the cheque is sometimes passed on again in settlement of another transaction and, to a certain extent, therefore circulates as money.

Transfers between the occupied territories and Amman are an important feature of the occupied territories' monetary system since Amman is in effect the local banking centre for the occupied territories.[7] But to a large extent the transfers effected by the money changers are over a much wider area and Amman is a staging post. Much money transfer business emanates from inflows from the Gulf and elsewhere to Amman, or to the occupied territories via Amman, as Palestinian workers employed in the Gulf and elsewhere send their earnings as remittances to their accounts in Amman or to their homes. Similarly, money changers handle the significant outflow of funds from families in the occupied territories to children studying abroad and also carry out many of the transfers that arise from the occupied territories' imports and exports.

The money changers' role in transferring funds depends on the existence of a high degree of trust and confidence. Agreements are oral and undocumented and, in any case, would not be legally enforceable; an individual who gives the money changer cash for transfer to his or her bank account or to a third party can only do so on the basis of trust; and equally the money changer accepts cheques in settlement on the basis of trust. This requirement limits the money changers' ability to expand or match the breadth that banks have in economies with similar levels of development but different political frameworks.

(iii) Deposits and loans

The money changers' money transfer activities give rise to financial intermediation which, although limited and partial, is similar to the financial intermediation banks carry out. That is, the large money changers take deposits (borrow) and lend.

In its most basic form, the use of borrowed funds is acquired by money changers simply as a result of the time lag necessarily involved in transferring funds from one centre to another. Thus, when a person in the West Bank pays cash to a money changer for transfer to his or her bank account in Amman, the money changer has the use of that money, interest free, for the time that it takes for instructions to be given to the money changer's Amman office and the payment made from that office's bank account into the person's bank account.

But money changers also attract deposits more actively, paying interest on deposits in Jordanian dinars and foreign currencies with them (although some depositors place funds with money changers without requiring interest). In the third quarter of 1985 the interest paid on short-term Jordanian dinars was between 15 and 18 per cent per annum at a time when Amman banks were paying 8.5 per cent per annum. For short-term deposits in foreign currencies large money changers pay interest rates above the short-term interest rates on credits in those currencies on international markets; in the third quarter of 1985 they paid 2 or 3 per cent per annum more than the international rates.

These high deposit rates are determined by competition for funds between different money changers and banks. They would not be sustainable if the borrowed funds were used for lending in the organised international markets. In fact, however, they are used for two forms of more profitable business: providing funds for the activity of money changing and money transfer and lending within the occupied territories. Money changing and money transfer yields profits in the form of commission (which is between 1 and 1.5 per cent on large transactions in notes) and spreads. Lending yields profits in the form of interest.

Money changers lend short-term at rates of up to 3 per cent per month for merchants and small businesses.[8] The loan arrangements vary but none is based on formal documentation. One type of arrangement is for a money changer to lend money to a merchant secured only by a post-dated cheque on Amman (dated 30 days later, for example) but that small degree of documentation is the maximum. Money changers' lending is mainly confined to 30-day loans, but some loans for several months are given with repayment being by instalments.

(iv) Evaluation of money changers

Since the occupying forces in 1967 closed Arab banks in the West Bank and Gaza money changers have carried out many of the functions of banks. The largest money changers, established before 1967, carry out a wide range of banking functions including currency exchange, money transfers and borrowing and lending. Because of the undocumented character of their business and its generally illegal nature in terms of the occupying power's regulations, several functions of banks have not been developed by money changers; for example, they do not issue letters of credit or take on contingent liabilities such as guarantees (although there is at least one recent example of a money changer being willing to guarantee a client's credit).[9] But currency exchange, money transfer and borrowing and lending are simultaneously well developed and subject to severe limits, a combination which justifies money changers being seen as 'constrained' or 'embryo banks'.

In currency exchange, the large money changers in the occupied territories are the market makers and price setters for Israeli shekels, Jordanian dinars and US dollars. In money transfer they transfer funds for clients in large and small amounts among the occupied territories, Amman, the Gulf States, the US, Europe and other centres. In relation to these transactions money changers also accept deposits and make loans extensively. Nevertheless, the conditions of occupation set severe practical and formal limits on the extent to which money changers develop banking functions. The absence of a legal authority for most money changers' operations and the fear of both money changers and clients that documented transactions of any kind will be interrupted by the occupying authorities lead to money changers' transactions being undocumented and based on oral agreements. This, together with the impossibility of resorting to courts for legal remedies against default, means that their business depends on a high degree of trust and personal knowledge which acts to limit it.[10] Large money changers do compete with each other and their exchange rates and interest rates are constrained by this competition; each competes for business throughout the occupied territories (sometimes using the branches of Israeli banks to transfer funds to their own accounts from clients based in other parts of the occupied territories). But, although that competition exists, each money changer's business is constructed around a network of clients who know and trust the money changer's business honesty. Clan and historical relationships play an important role in underpinning a money changer's business and therefore limiting its expansion. These relationships are only unimportant for transactions such as over-the-counter currency exchange where little trust is involved, hence small money changers with little historical record have been able to proliferate since 1967 by confining themselves mainly to such transactions.

The importance of trust and personal knowledge, rather than legally enforceable documentation, severely limits the ability of money changers, even as embryo banks, to meet the financial needs of Palestinian development. The risk in such transactions gives rise to high-risk premiums on interest rates which can hinder investment in working capital and fixed capital. In the occupied territories even the relatively high interest rates on deposits with money changers have not enabled them to attract the small savings of peasants and others outside their established network of clan-based or other relationships of trust. Indeed, many ordinary individuals who are not engaged in trade or handling large sums are unwilling even to take the risk of entrusting funds to money changers for the transfer of funds. Thus, the money changer's ability to mobilise domestic savings as an element in economic development is severely limited by the risky environment.

2. Israeli banks

After the occupying power closed the branches of Arab banks in the West Bank and Gaza, Israeli banks opened branches in the area. In 1982 there were 27 such branches.[11] They are not widely used by the Palestinian Arab population. Palestinians would choose only to accumulate bank deposits in Jordanian dinars (which has been the strongest currency in the occupied territories) but are unwilling to do so because of the danger that assets held in Israeli banks may be seized and partly because of the tax charges imposed on the use of such accounts. Assets and liabilities of the Israeli banks are summarised in the Bank of Israel data reproduced in Table 9.1. The branches of Israeli banks do not act as financial intermediaries within the occupied territories in the sense of borrowing savings (accepting deposits) and lending them to businesses and people in the West Bank and Gaza. Thus in 1984 only 8 per cent of these branches' total assets were loans to the public and these were either to Israelis or short-term credit to Palestinian merchants. Instead of the deposits with these branches being part of a process of financial intermediation within the West Bank and Gaza, the bank acts as a channel to invest the funds in Israel itself: in 1984 60 per cent of these branches' assets were deposited by them in accounts in Israel (the figure was 70 per cent in 1980-2 with a further 8 per cent held in Israeli coins and notes).[12] This policy of using the Israeli bank branches to channel funds to Israel itself reinforces Palestinian Arabs' unwillingness to use them.

Although they do not carry out significant financial intermediation within the occupied territories, and although a significant proportion of their business is with Israelis in the occupied territories,

Table 9.1: Assets and liabilities of branches of Israeli banks in the occupied territories 1980-4 (excluding East Jerusalem) (in millions of Israeli shekels)

	Guarantees & other liabilities	Government ear-marked deposits	In foreign currency	In Israeli currency	Total	Guarantees & other assets	Other	From govern-ment ear-marked deposits	Total	Balances with branches in Israel	Coins & notes	Total
1980												
I	27.7	4.3	74.0	77.0	151.0	26.5	14.1	6.4	20.5	118.5	17.7	183.2
II	40.0	4.1	91.5	88.8	180.2	39.0	21.7	6.5	28.2	135.8	21.1	224.3
III	44.7	4.6	126.9	104.2	231.1	39.6	25.5	6.1	31.6	178.4	30.8	280.4
IV	50.5	5.1	186.8	127.7	314.5	41.7	30.0	4.7	34.7	262.7	31.0	370.1
1981												
I	81.5	4.2	217.6	153.4	317.0	57.4	43.3	5.3	48.6	310.4	40.3	456.7
II	102.9	3.8	328.0	192.9	520.2	81.2	67.2	5.0	72.2	427.3	46.2	686.9
III	149.7	3.6	432.5	215.2	647.7	121.3	85.1	5.5	90.6	531.0	58.1	801.0
IV	155.0	3.2	511.3	213.3	724.6	132.8	51.1	3.2	54.3	620.0	75.7	882.8
1982												
I	178.0	3.8	698.8	267.4	964.2	175.6	102.5	3.7	106.2	787.8	76.4	1,146.0
II	165.2	2.6	932.9	279.3	1,212.2	152.3	123.1	2.6	125.7	987.1	114.9	1,380.0
III	256.8	12.6	1,158.4	405.4	1,563.8	242.5	232.7	12.5	245.2	1,181.8	163.7	1,833.2
IV	351.1	9.9	1,269.9	527.4	1,797.3	303.8	217.9	9.9	227.8	1,489.6	137.1	2,158.3

1983												
I	312.0	3.1	1,399.0	571.2	1,970.1	261.4	286.9	3.1	289.9	1,491.2	243.1	2,285.5
II	582.0	3.6	1,827.0	698.2	2,525.3	510.9	437.6	3.6	441.2	1,775.5	383.2	3,110.8
III	1,025.5	6.8	2,553.9	818.5	3,372.4	823.0	661.9	7.4	669.3	2,298.1	614.3	4,404.7
IV	1,402.3	13.6	3,857.3	1,130.0	4,987.3	1,304.0	685.2	13.7	698.9	3,644.0	676.3	6,403.2
1984												
I	2,662.9	28.2	5,846.0	1,541.8	7,387.8	2,366.6	954.3	28.2	982.5	5,550.0	1,179.8	10,078.9
II	3,932.5	30.0	10,226.9	2,554.3	12,781.2	3,410.5	1,805.6	30.2	1,835.8	9,976.1	1,512.3	16,734.7
III	7,729.7	53.2	15,982.2	3,864.4	19,846.6	6,479.5	2,871.6	53.2	2,924.8	14,943.2	3,282.0	27,629.5
IV	11,142.2	66.2	26,028.5	6,798.3	32,826.8	10,554.2	3,459.6	66.2	3,525.8	26,429.0	3,526.2	44,035.2
Percentage change over preceding year												
1981	206.9	-37.2	173.7	67.0	130.4	218.5	70.3	-31.9	56.5	136.0	144.2	138.5
1982	126.5	210.1	148.4	147.3	148.0	128.8	326.3	210.1	319.5	140.3	81.2	144.5
1983	299.5	37.0	203.7	114.3	177.5	355.6	214.5	38.1	206.8	144.6	393.1	196.7
1984	694.6	386.8	574.8	501.6	558.2	662.6	404.9	383.2	404.5	625.3	421.4	587.7
Percentage of total assets/liabilities												
1980	13.6	1.4	50.5	34.5	85.0	11.3	8.1	1.3	9.4	71.0	8.4	100.0
1981	17.6	0.4	57.9	24.2	81.2	15.0	5.8	0.4	6.2	70.2	8.6	100.0
1982	16.3	0.5	58.8	24.4	83.3	14.1	10.1	0.5	10.6	69.0	6.4	100.0
1983	21.9	0.2	60.2	17.7	77.9	21.6	10.7	0.2	10.9	56.9	10.6	100.0
1984	25.3	0.2	59.1	15.4	74.6	24.0	7.9	0.2	8.0	60.0	8.0	100.0

Source: Examiner of Banks, *Annual Statistics of Israel's Banking System 1980-84* (Bank of Israel, Jerusalem, 1985), Tables 1-6.

the Israeli bank branches do carry out two functions in the Palestinian economy. They transfer funds and clear cheques for Palestinians whose income is paid in Israeli shekels (such as Palestinians employed by Israelis) and they provide facilities for Palestinian business imports and exports.

Arranging guarantees and letters of credit is an extremely valuable service to Palestinian importers and exporters over which the Israeli bank branches have a monopoly since money changers do not have the legal standing to be recognised by foreign banks in such business. From the banks' own point of view it is a significant and profitable part of their business and its significance has increased: the balance sheet item which incorporates these contingent liabilities rose from 14 per cent of total liabilities in 1980 to 25 per cent in 1984.

Nevertheless, Palestinian merchants state strongly that the Israeli bank branches give a poor service in arranging the finance of international trade. They quote many examples including banks' failures to arrange proper documents as agreed and delays which lead to demurrage costs. Similarly they claim that the branches of Israeli banks provide an inefficient service in operating accounts. Although the Israeli bank branches in the occupied territories as a whole have a monopoly of the lucrative commission business of formal financing of Palestinian international trade, and although each branch generally has a monopoly of bank business in its own town, their profitability is not assured. In the West Bank, the Israelis claim that branches have been operating at a loss (although some of the loss is attributable to foreign exchange movements); in Gaza, the Israeli bank branch (Bank Leumi) serving the important urban centre, Khan Yunis, closed on 1 May 1985 because it was making a loss. The occupying powers have used the Israeli branches' lack of profitability as an argument against permitting Arab banks reasoning that the latter would also be unprofitable. But the Israeli branches' low profitability stems from specific factors including both their inability to attract deposits on a large scale from Arabs for the reasons mentioned and their failure to carry out financial intermediation and make profits from loans on the public.

3. Permitted Arab financial institutions

The occupying authorities have permitted some Palestinian Arab financial institutions to operate including the Bank of Palestine Ltd (Gaza) and an Arab insurance company (West Bank). Money changers are also formally approved by the Israelis but since the main parts of their activities are not formally approved (and not all money changers have approval) they are treated (in section I) as being quite different from permitted Arab institutions.

(i) Bank of Palestine Ltd.

The Bank of Palestine is an Arab owned and managed bank in Gaza.[13] It was established in 1960 and began operations on 13 February 1961 with a capital of £E 500,000. It was closed by the Israeli occupying authorities but it obtained permission to reopen for business in 1981. Negotiations to reopen the bank were unsuccessful until then but finally succeeded after the bank took its case to the Israeli High Court. The court rejected the objections of the occupying authorities (which centred on the bank's use of the name 'Bank of Palestine') and ordered negotiations among the bank, the occupying authorities and the Bank of Israel (represented by its Examiner of Banks).

An agreement was signed in 1981 but it has not been implemented in full. Although the Bank of Palestine did reopen as a commercial bank in 1981, the agreement to permit operation of 'normal banking business' was abrogated even before the opening, the authorities having prohibited all foreign exchange business. Thus all the bank's business is in Israeli shekels, although customers' loan repayments are indexed to the US dollar, and Egyptian currency is used as the unit of account for calculating the bank's annual balance sheet and revenue accounts. Moreover, the agreement permitted the reopening of the Gaza City headquarters and branch with a commitment to future consideration of reopening the bank's branches in Khan Yunis and Rafah. In the event, permission has not been given for the branches, although the closure of Bank Leumi in Khan Yunis has left that town without any banking facilities and, in that context, in September 1985 some citizens signed a petition demanding permission to reopen the Bank of Palestine branch.

Operating under these restrictions the Bank of Palestine has remained small. Its total assets were £E 4,677,855 at the end of 1984. Its deposits and other customer accounts (£E 3,230,753) were less than three times the bank's equity in capital and reserves (£E 1,245,760).[14] This is an extremely low ratio of deposits to capital for a commercial bank. For comparison, whereas the Bank of Palestine's ratio of deposits to capital was only 2.56, an accepted ratio in the USA is between 25 and 30.[15] This indicates that by 1984 the Bank of Palestine had not been able to attract deposits to the extent that a commercial bank operating without the restrictions of occupation is able.

Another indication of its inability to develop full banking functions is that it has not developed fully as a financial intermediary. In other words, it does not intermediate significantly between lenders and borrowers by lending a high proportion of the total deposits placed with it; its outstanding loans in 1984 (£E 1,700,730) were only 36 per cent of its total assets while its cash holdings were high at 48 per cent of assets (70 per cent of deposits). More fully developed financial intermediation would lead to a proportion of those cash holdings being used for loans; for comparison, the Israeli bank, Bank Hapoalim held only 15.5 per cent of its assets in cash in 1984.[16] One reason for both the bank's low level of deposits and its low proportion of loans is the prohibition on business in foreign exchange including Jordanian dinars. Since the bank reopened, the high rates of inflation and devaluation of the Israeli shekel have made it costly to hold bank accounts in shekels; since the bank can only take deposits in that currency, deposits with it are unattractive. Similarly, the restriction on foreign exchange business hinders the bank from lending to importers. The depression of the Gaza economy under occupation also restricts other lending opportunities.

The Bank of Palestine lends to industry, agriculture and other borrowers. All its lending is short-term with a maximum term of ten months and repayments by monthly instalments but the renewal of credit enables borrowers to obtain credit for periods of up to three years. The security taken for loans is three guarantees by persons (third parties) although it may require additional security on loans of over US$ 50,000. Although the Bank of Israel's supervisor of banks advises the Bank of Palestine to take mortgages as a security for a wide range of loans, it does not normally do so.

The Bank of Palestine gives some loans to agriculture at an interest rate of 12 per cent per annum which is less than half the rate charged by Israeli banks. With the very high rate of inflation existing until mid-1985 this represented a significantly negative real rate of interest. The Bank of Palestine reasons that loans at 12 per cent are justified since the opportunity cost of these funds is only 8 per cent; the latter is the yield that could be obtained if the funds were placed in deposits at the Bank of Israel instead of being loaned.

The Bank of Palestine regards its agricultural loans as serving the development of Palestinian agriculture in Gaza.[17] Recent examples are loans to finance new agricultural ventures: a nursery and seedling producer (approximately US$ 10,000); a rabbit farm; sheep farms. In 1983 the bank began to lend to citrus growers. Citrus production in Gaza has declined severely. Whereas the output through the Gaza Citrus Growers Union was 250,000 tons in the mid-1970s, it was 168,000 tons in 1980/1 and by 1983/4 it had declined to 146,000 tons before recovering to 161,700 tons in 1984/5.[18] The decline was due to many factors, especially the obstacles the Israeli occupying power places in the way of exports; one factor is probably the absence of development finance for citrus growers, and the start of the Bank of Palestine's credit programme for citrus growers in 1983 was probably one contributory factor behind the recovery in 1984/5. Nevertheless, there is considerable diversity in both the cost and availability of its credit to farmers.

To summarise the Bank of Palestine's position, it operates under severe difficulties which prevent it from expanding and make it impossible for it to develop properly either in the sphere of money dealing and money transfer or in financial intermediation (borrowing and lending). The prohibition on foreign exchange dealing and on opening new branches (or reopening old ones) has impaired the bank's development in each of these fields, and the obstacles the Israeli occupation has created for Gaza economic development in general have further hindered it by restricting the economic environment within which the bank works.

In addition, the occupying authorities have taken direct actions to hinder the bank. For example, in July 1985, the Bank of Palestine attempted to triple its capital by selling 100,000 shares to the public. Although, according to its officials, it had complied with all the legal requirements, the military closed the bank on the day of public applications for the shares, posted soldiers at the door and erected notices warning the public not to buy shares. The authorities claimed that legal requirements had not been met, and the action had the clear but unjustified implication that Gazans should not have confidence in the bank.

(ii) Arab insurance

One Arab-owned insurance company has been permitted to operate in the West Bank since the mid-1970s. Its principal business is general insurance, especially vehicle insurance to meet the legal requirements for vehicles, rather than life insurance. Its general insurance is secured by reinsurance in London.

Despite the low proportion of life insurance business, the company does carry out some financial intermediation by lending surplus funds. Its policy is to concentrate on short-term credit (as short as 30 days) but examples also exist of it giving medium-term credit for up to three years. Its interest rates vary from 15 per cent to 25 per cent per annum.[19]

4. 'Informal' sources of rural credit

Peasants in the West Bank and Gaza have had access to short-term credit from merchants and landlords. To a very large extent this credit is organised around merchant and marketing operations. Together with any money changers' credit to peasants these traditional sources comprise a network similar to the 'informal' or 'unorganised' credit markets that researchers have described in peasant societies throughout the world.[20] Short-term credit is connected to two uses which are distinct but sometimes overlap: seasonal credit to obtain inputs for the agricultural cycle and consumption credit to obtain necessities in difficult times.

Merchants provide seasonal credit through a variety of relationships. Commission agents are a significant type in some areas; they are big merchants who sell the small farmers' produce on the wholesale market and take a commission as a percentage of their net sales.[21] The commission agent supplies the farmer with credit in kind (seeds, seedlings, fertilisers and other inputs) and money at the start of the season as part of the arrangements under which he sells the subsequent crop for the farmer on the market. In one study of agriculture in part of the Jordan Valley it was found that the commission agent's 'normal' profit came in the form of a 7 per cent deduction from the net proceeds of the farmers' crop, but it may have been increased by charging high prices for the inputs provided. (In other parts of the Jordan Valley the agents' share is different.) This transaction involves no separate interest charge for the credit; interest is implicitly incorporated as one element in the total commission. However, delay in the commission agent recovering his loan leads to an explicit interest charge which may be as high as 30 per cent per annum on the loan. The arrangements between a farmer and a commission agent are frequently incorporated in a written contract.

In many cases the commission agent is also the landlord. In other cases, absentee landlords renting to tenant farmers or to sharecroppers also provide credit to those tenant farmers. Until 1948, big landowners also accumulated large estates through lending to poor owner-cultivators to enable them to buy seeds and other inputs, taking land as collateral and obtaining ownership of the land after poor harvests led to defaults.[22] The present study has no information on whether land is used as collateral for rural credit in present circumstances, but the law since 1948 and conditions of the military occupation have been against it.

In addition to commission agents' credit to peasant farmers, a significant form of credit associated with marketing consists of seasonal loans provided by marketing cooperatives. In the West Bank 18 per cent of farmers belong to co-operatives.[23] The largest is the Jericho Marketing Cooperative, an organisation which has two main functions: certifying that crops exported to Jordan are not of Israeli origin and providing seasonal credit for the production of such crops. Its funds for this credit programme come from finance provided by Jordan's central co-operative organisation: in 1984/5 it received approximately JD 0.75 million from this source and provided short-term loans at low interest rates (interest rates as low as 3 per cent have been quoted).

The Jericho Marketing Cooperative's credit has not been sharply distinguished from grants or subsidies to its members for there has not been a strong management system of enforcing repayment in cases of default or delay.

A final element in the structure of rural credit associated with merchants and marketing consists of the village storekeepers who sell commodities for credit and give cash loans.[24] Their interest rates and conditions are not known, but in other countries such arrangements provide credit for people in great need at usurious rates.

5. Jordanian (East Bank) sources of finance

West Bank residents have access to some finance emanating from commercial banks and official sources operating through investment banks in Amman. These reflect the historical political circumstances of the West Bank and East Jerusalem in relation to the Hashemite Kingdom of Jordan and the Arab world's support for the policy of steadfastness in the occupied territories.

(i) Amman commercial banks

Since the occupying authorities closed the branches of Amman banks in the occupied territories in 1967, the headquarters of these banks have continued to pay salaries to employees in the area.[25] The main function these employees can carry out, however, is to assist potential new customers in completing the documents and arrangements for opening accounts in East Bank branches and transmitting them. In some circumstances they also finance exports to Amman by paying the West Bank exporter locally in Jordanian dinars and arranging for the Amman branch to collect payment from the importer in Amman.

Nevertheless, many residents of the occupied territories have accounts with Amman banks on the East Bank but they have limited access to loans from this source. The Amman banks regard loans to residents of the occupied territories as relatively risky since they cannot be monitored easily and action to recover debts is impossible. They require a West Bank borrower to offer two or three guarantees from residents of the East Bank and that is a difficult condition for the borrower to meet, either because of lack of personal knowledge between communities on the East and West Banks or because of economic risks.

(ii) Housing Bank

The Housing Bank is a specialised Jordanian bank, established in 1974 to give construction loans to building firms and owners.[26] Its loans on the East Bank are mainly secured by mortgages. It also finances foreign trade and carries out foreign exchange dealing. The bank has a large branch network and retail deposits, including remittances from workers overseas, are its major source of funds.

On 20 September 1981 the Housing Bank and the Jordanian-Palestinian Joint Committee signed an agreement to arrange facilities for lending to residents in the West Bank. Between September 1981 and the beginning of September 1985 the Housing Bank has arranged 2,150 loans to the West Bank totalling JD 13.8 million.

The Housing Bank's loans to West Bank residents are of three types:

(a) Construction Loans. These are up to a maximum of JD 7,000 for a maximum period of 15 years with a two year period of grace before repayments start;

(b) Construction Finishing Loans. These are up to a maximum of JD 3,500 for 15 years;

(c) Repair Loans. These are up to a maximum of JD 2,000 for 20 years with a one year period of grace.

The Housing Bank is effectively acting as the administrative agent of the Joint Committee in channelling finance to the West Bank and the credit should, therefore, be regarded as an element in the policy of support for steadfastness rather than an aspect of normal, commercial financial intermediation. The finance for the Housing Bank's loans to the West Bank is provided by Jordan's Central Bank rather than from the Housing Bank's own resources. The borrower arranges the loan through the Joint Committee which issues the authority for the Housing Bank to lend the funds. No interest is received by the Housing Bank. Although these loans are secured by guarantees from an East

Bank employer or merchant the Housing Bank itself would not be willing to give credit to West Bank residents as part of its normal business as a result of the occupation. The absence of a branch network in the West Bank prevents it from having knowledge of borrowers or monitoring the credit. The occupation prevents recourse to the Jordanian legal system for contracts and the occupying power's land appropriations prejudice the value of property as collateral.

(iii) Industrial Bank.

The Industrial Bank was founded in 1965 and began operations in 1966 with the objective of financing industrial and tourist developments on a long term basis.[27] It also has special credit facilities for small businesses (for which the maximum size of each loan is JD 4,000 and the interest rate is 6.5 per cent per annum). It does not accept retail deposits.

At the beginning of the Israeli occupation in 1967 the Industrial Bank had approximately JD 450,000 in outstanding loans in the West Bank, nearly all of which has not subsequently been repaid. In the present circumstances the Industrial Bank is not willing to lend to West Bank residents as a normal part of its business because of the difficulty of appraising credit applications, monitoring credit use and recovering debts under the occupation.

However, the bank does lend money for West Bank projects, including hotel development, using funds placed with it for this purpose by the Jordanian authorities and allocating the credit in accordance with the authorities' directions. In addition, the Industrial Bank is now to receive a European Economic Community loan of ECU 2 million (European Currency Units) for lending to small-scale projects on the West Bank. All loan agreements with West Bank residents are secured by guarantee from persons on the East Bank.

II. MODELS OF FINANCIAL REPRESSION

In one sense, the occupied territories' experience is an extreme form of 'financial repression'. This concept has been applied by many writers to the financial systems of third-world countries where the state has intervened in banking and finance to set interest rates, direct credit and regulate it in other ways. In these paragraphs I set out the basic framework of the theory that has been constructed around that concept to analyse the effects of financial repression in third-world countries (the McKinnon-Shaw model).[28]

The McKinnon-Shaw theory emphasises that financial intermediation can make a significant contribution to economic growth if the state permits it to operate in competitive conditions, in particular if financial intermediaries such as banks pay interest rates on deposits and charge interest on loans which reflect market conditions. Third-world economies are seen as having a capital shortage in the sense that there are many high yielding investment projects that entrepreneurs in agriculture, industry and other sectors wish to undertake but have been unable to because of uneven access to finance and a low level of national saving overall to generate finance. If financial intermediaries' interest rates were to reflect market conditions, this capital shortage would cause them to be high in order to attract scarce savings and lend them on to high-yielding projects, but financial repression occurs when the state sets interest rate ceilings which frustrate this process.[29]

The general character of financial repression is that

(a) it restricts the growth of financial intermediaries (most significantly banks) by preventing them from paying interest to attract increased savings into deposits;

(b) in restricting the interest rates financial intermediaries (especially banks) can charge to borrowers, borrowers demands for credit are increased;

(c) discouragement of savings and encouragement to borrowing leads to an excess demand for credit (a reflection of capital shortage);

(d) the state acts in this way in order to enable it to control the direction of credit, instructing the banks which sectors and firms should receive priority in the allocation of scarce credit and providing finance for investment projects from public funds;

(e) if the state were to lift or change its regulations, interest rates would rise which would lead to increased funds being channelled through intermediaries from savers to enterprises with investment projects and the high rates would ensure that they are directed toward high-yielding projects.

The Israeli authorities' regulation of the Arab financial system in the occupied territories may be considered as an extreme form of financial repression; but it does not have all the characteristics described by the general concept. Its most extreme element has been the closure of Arab banks and the fact that the branches of Israeli banks and the reopened Bank of Palestine are (for different reasons) not able to act effectively as banks for the Arab residents. Thus, one writer notes, 'the West Bank economy is virtually without a banking system' and 'this situation is almost unique';[30] and the position in Gaza is not very different. This restriction of the banks' activity is a much more extreme hindrance to financial intermediation than the limitations which the theory ascribes to interest rate controls. On the other hand the model's assumption that restrictions on the banking system have their counterpart in state control of investment funds is only partly true, for although the occupying authorities have administrative controls to refuse or permit any significant credits, they do not themselves disburse significant funds to finance Arab investment projects.

One of the strong implications of the financial repression concept is that markets for financial capital are highly fragmented; indeed, in McKinnon's treatment this appears almost as a central characteristic of financial repression and is paralleled by fragmentation in all aspects of the economy. Fragmentation means that credit does not flow freely enough through the economy, so that savings and finance in one area or sector stay within it even though higher yields may be available on investment projects in other areas.[31] Fragmentation means that some borrowers have privileged access to credit while others have none and it is claimed that it exists in financially repressed third-world economies because of three processes linked to the restriction. First, the state is supposed to use its control of funds to favour particular borrowers (creating the possibility of corruption). Second, the banks (and other financial intermediaries) ration their scarce credit by favouring particular sectors, firms and individuals. Third, the restrictions on banking stimulate the development of informal and often illegal financial activities such as rural money lenders which, by their nature, are local and based upon specific social groups. Fragmentation is one of the most significant aspects of the occupied territories' economies and particularly its financial system. In the absence of effective banking within the Arab economy or significant investment funds injected by the Israeli state, financial fragmentation originates from other sources. In the next section I outline the causes of this fragmentation and the general relation between the financial repression model and the situation in the occupied territories.

Another implication of the theory of financially repressed economies is that where financial intermediation is restricted there is also a low demand for money relative to output and income or, in other words, a high velocity of money. In one version of the model this arises because the demand for money is highly elastic with respect to real rates of interest, so that if low or zero interest is paid on bank deposits (and zero interest on cash) the demand for money in those forms as an asset will also be low. Thus, interest rate restrictions on financial intermediaries reduce the demand for money since banks are the most significant forms of intermediary and the controls reduce the attractiveness of bank deposits. This effect is intensified by inflation: for if nominal interest rates on money are low or zero, high rates of inflation make real interest rates negative. The corollary of this is that if constraints on interest rates are lifted, the demand for bank deposits will rise and this increase in the stock of deposits means that the real stock of money increases in line with the expansion of the banks' financial intermediation.[32] In the occupied territories, too, there are grounds for thinking that there is a low demand for money and low real stocks of money although the reasons are largely specific to the local circumstances.[33]

III. WEAKNESSES IN THE FINANCIAL AND MONETARY SYSTEM

The financial and monetary systems of the occupied territories consist of a set of arrangements that have developed within the political economic constraints of occupation. As a result they are underdeveloped compared with the financial and monetary arrangements of other poor economies, but considering the severity of the constraints – the Israeli occupation authorities' opposition to any significant Palestinian financial and economic development – money and finance have been developed remarkably strongly in some directions. Nevertheless, the dominant aspect of the monetary and financial system is that its weaknesses are severe and make it unsuitable for the long-term development of an independent Palestinian economy. Its weaknesses also create a risk that in the near future the system will encounter severe problems even in continuing to service the occupied territories at the existing level. In this section I consider the main weaknesses and relate them to the financial repression model.

1. Fragmentation

The dominant characteristic of the monetary and financial system is that it is accommodating. It has developed to finance the existing structure of the Palestinian economy, therefore it accommodates the patterns of trade and production that have arisen under occupation. One corollary is that unless appropriate changes are introduced the systems cannot provide the financial basis for the development of an autonomous Palestinian economy. A second is that because the system is accommodating it is fragmentary in two senses.

First, it is fragmentary in the sense that the 'real economy' of Palestine is fragmented and the financial and monetary arrangements reflect this. Thus, the fragmentation of the labour force since 1967 has been centrifugal with an initially high level of net emigration of workers; the workers' remittances that resulted (accounting for an estimated 32 per cent of GNP in 1982)[34] have been a significant element in the growth of money changers. Similarly, the obstacles to the integrated development of the domestic economies of the occupied territories have given rise to a high level of dependence on imports and exports and a high level of trading activity rather than productive activity; the operations of money changers, banks and other financial agents are similarly strongly characterised by their relation to trade.

Second, it is fragmentary in the purely financial sense. That is, it is a segmented and divided system which, depending to a large extent on personal trust, is built on networks of personal relations. Currency exchange is not greatly fragmented since it requires little trust, but money transfer and borrowing and lending are, with the result that the scope for financial intermediation is limited. Thus, savings in one circle are not generally transmitted through the financial system to finance investment in another.[35]

The financial fragmentation is the outcome of two forces: first, it reflects and accommodates the fragmentation of the real economy and, second, it results from the specific policies of the occupation directed at repressing the Arab financial system. Both have stimulated the growth of informal monetary and financial arrangements such as those of money changers and rural merchants (such as commission agents). In this respect, the financial fragmentation of the occupied territories is more complex than the standard McKinnon-Shaw model, for in the latter the fragmentation of the financial system is seen as the effect of specifically financial policies with a determining influence running from the financial system to the real economy: if financially repressive policies were ended, the model argues, the new cohesion of the financial system would bring cohesion to the real economy. In the West Bank and Gaza, by contrast, the restrictions on trade, production and social conditions imposed by the occupation ensure that even if Arab banking were allowed to develop, fragmentation would remain and the informal financial networks based on personal knowledge and trust would continue to have a role.[36]

Finally, in comparing the fragmentation of the financial system in the occupied territories with that described in the 'financial repression' model I have noted above that in the former it does not originate in interest controls over local banks (for an effective banking system is prevented more directly from operating) nor from privileged access of some Palestinians to investment funds injected by the Israeli state (since funds do not directly enter the Arab economy in any significant amounts). In the West Bank and Gaza the differential access to credit which is the mark of fragmentation relates to differential access to the networks within which money changers lend, borrow and transfer money; secondly it relates to state and quasi-state funds from the East Bank (both grants and the East Bank sources of credit identified above) since different social groups have different degrees of access to such funds for housing construction, seasonal agricultural credit or industry.

2. Money holdings

These forms of fragmentation have the effect that the economy has a distorted monetisation. In one sense the Palestinian economy is highly monetised in comparison to other poor economies: for a very high degree of agricultural production is for sale rather than subsistence; a high proportion of personal income comes from working for money wages (locally, in Israel, in the East Bank or elsewhere); foreign trade for cash is a high proportion of economic activity. Moreover, residents of the occupied territories have a high degree of familiarity with dealing in different currencies (Israeli, Jordanian, American) and using shekels, dinars and dollars as units of account. But this high degree of use of money is distorted in several senses. It is not generally associated with large holdings of money within the occupied territories; it is not associated with a high degree of financial intermediation; there is no single monetary standard.

There are no reliable estimates of the stock of money in the occupied territories and none can be produced without major fieldwork. But on the basis of *a priori* reasoning and casual evidence it is possible to reach some judgements regarding it. On balance it appears that holdings of money balances (in real terms, in terms of the goods they can buy) are lower than would be expected for another country with similar GNP.

Both demand and supply factors have to be considered in reaching this judgement, but the initial problem is to define the money supply in the circumstances of the occupied territories. Here, it will be defined as cash, demand deposits in banks and time deposits in banks owned by residents of the occupied territories. Since three main currencies are in use, the definition should include cash and deposits denominated in Israeli shekels, Jordanian dinars and US dollars. No firm principle can establish whether the definition should include bank deposits held in Amman, in Israel (excluding East Jerusalem) or in foreign centres elsewhere.

The most crucial determinant of money holdings in the occupied territories is the demand for money. There is no state authority or central bank with a monopoly of the money supply or control of it and capital flows into and out of the occupied territories directly relate to cash flows. Therefore, the nominal stock of money in the occupied territories (or defined to include deposits in Amman) is generally demand determined. However, there are periods when these demand forces are thwarted by exchange controls, increased regulation of cash flows across the bridges or other interruptions. Thus, at times there may be an excess supply of money in the occupied territories (or an excess demand); the Central Bank of Jordan believed at one time that there was a danger of an excess supply of money ('a liquidity over-hang')[37] in the West Bank itself but considers that this was gradually eliminated between 1975 and 1982 by increased capital flows from the West Bank to Amman.

There are strong reasons for thinking that the demand for money, and hence the amount of money held by residents of the occupied territories is low compared to other economies at similar levels of development. The factors influencing the demand for bank deposits and those behind the demand for cash are best considered separately, but in each case the relevant consideration is the attractiveness of this as compared to other assets such as jewellery, land and housing and, as with all forms of money, a major element in that is its liquidity. Bank deposits with Israeli banks are relatively unattractive partly because of the difficulty of operating dinars accounts with them and the rapid depreciation of shekel accounts until mid-1985, but mainly because of the danger that the Israeli authorities may freeze or confiscate such deposits as a political act. Bank deposits in Amman have their attractiveness reduced by the absence of a branch network giving local access to them in the occupied territories, by the incompleteness of access to money changers who can transfer funds to and from Amman and by the risk of interruptions to cash flows across the bridges. Cash holdings of Jordanian dinars and, to some extent, US dollars have not suffered through depreciation but they do not yield interest, they carry the risk of theft, loss and deterioration, and their international acceptability (which is an important consideration if money is considered as a liquid hoard to be used if the owner is forced to become a refugee) may be regarded as less secure than other assets such as gold.

These arguments suggest that the demand for money in the occupied territories and, hence, its stock is relatively low. A low level of liquid assets is also suggested by the fact when an Israeli imposed curfew interrupts the ability of a town's population to go to their jobs or farms, sales of basic necessities such as food are immediately cut through absence of funds, and shopkeepers' credit to individuals without money quickly expands.[38]

Related to distorted monetisation and low holdings of bank deposits is the fact that the institutions and agents surveyed in section I provide a low degree of financial intermediation in the occupied territories. Financial intermediation involves agents in borrowing the savings of some sectors (by accepting deposits in the case of banks) and lending these funds to borrowers.[39] The deposits taken by branches of Israeli banks are not used to a large extent for lending within the occupied territories. The Bank of Palestine has a low ratio of deposits to capital and a low proportion of loans to total assets. The amounts involved in deposits with money changers and their loans to borrowers is not known, but in view of the undocumented nature of transactions with money changers, their illegality in the authorities' view and the need for a high degree of personal knowledge and trust, it is probable that their financial intermediation is not quantitatively great.

Other sources of credit in the occupied territories are not generally financed by funds the lender has borrowed. Some, such as merchants' credit to village households or commission agents' seasonal credit to farmers, are financed out of the lenders' own capital. Others, such as the credit advanced by the (Amman-based) Housing Bank for house construction, are financed by outside funds provided as part of the 'steadfastness' policy.

Low money holdings and low financial intermediation appear to correspond to the McKinnon-Shaw model's predictions. In that model, however, the explanation for low money holdings would lie partly in the high rates of inflation in the West Bank and Gaza Strip which have produced negative real returns on some money holdings. But this argument does not apply directly to the occupied territories because a special characteristic of their monetary system is that they have a plural monetary standard, with both Israeli shekels and Jordanian dinars being widely used.[40] In addition, US dollars circulate widely.

In part this is the effect of the occupation regulations governing legal tender, for both Jordanian dinars and Israeli shekels are counted as legal tender in the West Bank. But the plural standard applies also in Gaza and East Jerusalem where the occupation authorities recognise only the Israeli currency as legal tender. It reflects, therefore, an unwillingness to use Israeli shekels as the only form of money partly because it is the currency of the occupying forces and partly because of the frequent depreciation of the Israeli currency in the 1970s and 1980s. The weakness of the shekel has led to the widespread use of US dollars within Israel itself; within the occupied territories it has led to the wide use of both dinars and dollars.

Israeli shekels are used as a medium of exchange for everyday small transactions and they are received in wage payments by Arabs working within the Israeli economy. Jordanian dinars and US dollars are regarded as stores of wealth, able to retain their value over time. They are also used as the medium of exchange in large transactions and a wide range of medium and small transactions. For example, some olive growers in the West Bank only accept payment in Jordanian dinars for olive oil, partly because the proceeds of such sales are an important source of savings.[41] Thus, there has been wide use of currencies with stable real values in the face of local inflation and low money holdings within the occupied territories, largely the result of other factors.

3. Absence of central banking

In other countries the monetary and financial system is under a central bank or central monetary authority which is an arm of the state. Its central bank provides implicit or explicit guarantees of the system's stability through measures encompassed in the broad term 'lender of last resort'. The counterpart is that it supervises the safety of the banks' and finance houses' operations ('prudential regulation') and it regulates their effect on the economy's total money supply or credit ('monetary control'). The occupied territories do not have such credit authority.

The Bank of Israel exerts the authority of the central bank over the Israeli banks with branches in the occupied territories. It also supervises and regulates the operations of the Bank of Palestine although it is doubtful whether it would act as lender of last resort to ensure that bank's stability. But the money changing and money transfer system in the occupied territories, and the major sources of credit, are outside its control. The Central Bank of Jordan has some authority over money changers to the extent that it is the licensing authority with power of enforcement over their Amman branches, but this has only a marginal effect, if any, on operations within the occupied territories. The occupation prevents the Central Bank of Jordan exerting any direct control, regulation or supervision of the monetary and financial affairs of the occupied territories.

The absence of a legitimate state with a monopoly of authority over the monetary and financial system (through its central bank or central authority) is the most fundamental obstacle to the system operating effectively. Muhammad Talat-Harb expressed very strongly the need for a central bank in furthering national economic development and national independence (in the context of Egypt in 1920): 'Each country must pursue its own financial policy, must win its economic independence and preserve it. In every country in the world, the task of directing this policy and preserving this economic independence falls to a national bank, whose privilege it is to issue banknotes and to stand above the competition between all other banks, to supervise their activities, to help them with loans when the need arises, to solve and, where possible, prevent crises...Such a bank is the supreme arbiter of financial credits and business confidence...Every government takes care that no foreign hand can regulate the affairs of the national bank...'[42] The occupied territories do not have such a central bank.

Without a legitimate state authority and central bank acting as supervisor and lender of last resort, the financial institutions are inherently less secure than they would otherwise be and, therefore, have difficulty in developing financial intermediation. They are relatively less attractive as repositories for savers' assets, and their willingness to lend instead of holding high reserves is low. Thus, even if other obstacles to the establishment of financial institutions were removed, the absence of a legitimate state with financial authority would hinder the development of financial intermediation. Moreover, a state which itself borrows from the financial system would provide it with assets (bonds, bills or direct loans to the state) which are secure and yield a profit and the absence of this deprives the financial system of a source of security.

The absence of a state with responsibility for economic development as a whole means that the credit that is available under the present system is not directed toward areas of need identified as priorities for comprehensive development. An independent state's development plan would, by contrast, be able to guide credit to areas which are judged to have a high priority. In this respect, the implication of the 'financial repression' model that the free development of a banking system could allocate financial capital more rationally than the state is inappropriate. The scale of economic transformation required in an independent Palestine can only be co-ordinated through development planning. The absence of a unified monetary standard for the Palestinian economy is a severe obstacle to economic development which is a direct corollary of the absence of an independent state and central bank.

First, the economy's reliance on the circulation of two or more currencies leads to a diversion of resources toward the business of money changing. Although this is carried out with a high level of efficiency, the resources used by the money changers themselves and by other enterprises (their customers) calculating their best monetary deals are considerable. Moreover it can encourage a business orientation which sees the possibility of making money out of money-dealing as more significant than the possibility of profiting from producing and investing in production: a mentality in which knowledge of the exchange rate acquires greater significance than calculations of productivity rates.

Second, if there were a unified national currency with an independent state controlling it, that state would be able to use the 'seignorage' from it to finance development projects. That is, by issuing currency itself (or creating bank deposits by borrowing from the central bank) the state would gain command over the resources for development. In making this comparison between a plural and a unified monetary standard, a single unified money would only serve development better if, unlike the Israeli shekel, it was relatively stable.

The potential role of financial intermediation depends in part on the economy's savings. Estimates of savings can be made on the basis of past and current experience, although they are not reliable. The increase in private saving associated with an increase in the Gross Domestic Product (the Marginal Propensity to Save, or MPS) has been estimated at 25 per cent of the latter. The increase between 1968 and 1973 appeared to be at an MPS of 0.25 (in relation to personal disposable income rather than GDP) while for 1981 and 1982 MPS has been estimated at 0.28.[43] A UNIDO report on manufacturing industry's potential for growth[44] uses an estimate of 0.15 for the MPS which appears to be an underestimate. That assumption, together with an assumed increase in per capita income of 2.5 per cent per annum leads to an estimate of the real value of savings to the end of the 1980s, as shown in Table 9.2.

Table 9.2: Estimate of savings in the occupied territories to the end of the 1980s (millions of US dollars)

1986	1987	1988	1989	1990
47	50	54	57	53

The level of savings is itself affected by the existence of financial intermediaries and it would be higher if the weaknesses in the existing financial system were overcome.

IV. CONCLUSION

In conclusion, the occupation of the West Bank and Gaza has affected their money and finance, key elements in the Palestinian Arab economy. For years, the policy was to eradicate Arab banking. Although Israeli banks were encouraged to operate in the occupied territories, the policy was not wholly designed to integrate Arab financial and economic life with Israel's as a subordinate but profitable annex; it was principally designed with a political aim to weaken and undermine independent Arab economic development. Nevertheless, Arab financial operations have survived, been transformed and developed with great strength in particular fields. However, the financial development that has occurred has been partial and distorted.

NOTES

1. Military orders 7, 9, 21, 33, 76, 83, 93, 94, 295, 299 and 823 relate most directly to the occupying power's control of finance.

2. The principal concern of this paper is the financial and monetary system and its effect on the 'real economy', but the relationship is two-way with the 'real economy' also influencing monetary and financial developments.

3. The analysis in this section is based on interviews conducted in Jordan, the West Bank, the Gaza Strip and Jerusalem in September 1985. The fieldwork was related to a study conducted in that month under the auspices of the British Council.

4. The information on which this section's description of money changers is based was obtained from independent interviews with two large money changers and one medium-sized money changer in the West Bank and Jerusalem. It was supplemented from interviews with business people who are their customers, with M. Shukri, Deputy Governor of the Central Bank of Jordan and others.

5. A money changer, believed to be the largest in the West Bank, gave the following description in mid-September 1985: 'If today's Dollar-Deutschmark

($/DM) rate in Europe is 2.84, I would deal at a $/DM rate of 2.86-2.87 (a one point spread).'

6. Interview with M. Shukri, Deputy Governor of the Central Bank of Jordan.

7. Egypt has played some historic role as a local banking centre for residents of Gaza, but its significance in this respect is small compared with Amman.

8. This interest rate was noted by an industrialist who had borrowed from a large money lender. However, the money lender himself had said in a previous interview that his lending rates are between 1 and 1.5% per month. It is probable that different rates are applied to different loans.

9. Interview with Wahid al-Masri; example given of money changer being willing to give a guarantee from his East Bank office for a development loan from a third party.

10. For a general analysis of the limitations of financial systems based on personal trust see R.I. McKinnon, *Money and Capital in Economic Development* (Washington D.C., 1973).

11. The figure of 28 branches in 1982 is quoted in Dan Zakai, *Economic Development in Judea, Samaria and the Gaza District 1981-82* (Bank of Israel, Jerusalem, 1985), p.67. However, his data appear to include the Bank of Palestine which, in the present report, is not included as an Israeli bank. Note that this total does not include the branches of Israeli banks in East Jerusalem.

12. These data are drawn from the Examiner of Banks, *Annual Statistics of Israel's Banking System 1980-84* (Bank of Israel, Jerusalem, 1985), p.26.

13. The following information comes from interviews with Mr Rushdi T. Sakallah, General Manager, and Mr Hashim Ata Shawwa, Chairman, Bank of Palestine Ltd.

14. Bank of Palestine Ltd, *Balance Sheet, Gaza* (Bank of Palestine Ltd, December 1984).

15. The 1984 consolidated balance sheet of Bank Hapoalim shows a ratio of 68.8. Ibid., p.28.

16. Ibid.

17. Interview with Hatam Ata Shawwa.

18. Data supplied by Hatam Ata Shawwa from the records of the Gaza Citrus Growers Union.

19. Interviews with Mr. Hadi, representing the company, and other industrialists.

20. The classic study of 'unorganised' markets is U. Tun Wai, 'Interest rates outside the organized money markets of underdeveloped countries', *IMF Staff Reports*, vol. 6, no. 1, pp.80-125.

21. The information on the role of commission agents is based on S. Tamari and R. Giacaman (eds), *Zbeidat: The Social Impact of Drip Irrigation on a Palestinian Peasant Community in the Jordan Valley* (Birzeit University and Documentation and Research Centre, Birzeit, 1980).

22. S. Tamari, 'Building other people's homes', *Journal of Palestine Studies*, no. 41 (Autumn 1981), p.44

23. Interview with Mr. Shehadeh Dajani.

24. S. Tamari, 'Building other people's homes', p.57.

25. The information in this section is based on interviews with Mr. Kemal, General Manager of the Arab Bank, Nablus; Mr. Mihdat Kanaan, General Manager of the Cairo-Amman Bank, Nablus and Mr. M. Shukri, Deputy

Governor of the Central Bank of Jordan.

26. Information from an interview with Mr. Abd al-Rahman Saleh, Housing Bank, Head Office, Amman.

27. Information based on interviews with Mr. Ziad Annab, Industrial Bank, Amman and Mr. Shehadeh Dajani, Community Development Fund, Jerusalem.

28. The classic statements of the theory of financial repression are in R. I. McKinnon, *Money and Capital.* Derivative readings are collected in W.L. Coats and D.R. Khatkhate (eds), *Money and Monetary Policy in Less Developed Countries* (Pergamon Press, London, 1980). There are variations in different formulations of the model and the outline presented here is a synthesis.

29. The general thrust of the argument is that a competitive banking system should be permitted. If, however, the banks are monopolistic or state regulated, the administered interest rates should reflect market conditions by being raised to a presumed equilibrium level.

30. A. Mansour, 'Monetary dualism: the case of the West Bank under occupation', *Journal of Palestine Studies,* no. 43, pp.103-16.

31. In McKinnon's theory, capital market fragmentation is indicated by a simultaneous existence of widely different rates of return on investment projects in different sectors. Or it would be if such returns were quantified.

32. Empirical evidence on the interest-elasticity of the demand for bank deposits is discussed in Coats and Khatkhate, *Money and Monetary Policy.*

33. The grounds for believing that the demand for money is low in the occupied territories are set out below. This conclusion differs from Mansour's assumption ('Monetary dualism') that the velocity of money is low in the West Bank. The differences may be attributable to the fact that Mansour is referring to an earlier period when other financial conditions prevailed.

34. Zakai, *Economic Development,* Tables II-1 and V-3.

35. See McKinnon, *Money and Capital,* for the general effects of such fragmentation.

36. In part, the fragmentation of the credit system related to the underdeveloped state of commodity markets which gives particular agents such a monopolistic position which they reinforce through giving credit on a client basis.

37. Interview with Mr. Shukri, Deputy Governor of the Central Bank of Jordan.

38. Evidence that this has been the effect of curfews in Hebron is based on interviews with Mr. K. Ossaily and Mr. Natshe.

39. The classic definition of financial intermediation in these terms is that of J. Gurley and E. Shaw, *Money in a Theory of Finance* (Brookings Institute, Washington D.C., 1960).

40. See Mansour, 'Monetary dualism', for one perspective of this plural standard.

41. Tamari, 'Building other people's homes', p.52.

42. Mohammad Talat Harb, speech at the inauguration of the Misr Bank, 7 May 1920, reprinted in English as 'An Egyptian bank for Egyptians only' in A. Abd al-Malek, (ed.), *Contemporary Arab Political Thought* (Zed Press, London, 1983), pp.55-7.

43. See Brian Van Arkadie, *Benefits and Burdens: A Report on the West Bank and Gaza Strip Economies Since 1967* (Carnegie, New York, 1977) and Zakai, *Economic Development,* Table ii-1.

44. UNIDO, *Survey of Manufacturing Industry in the West Bank and Gaza Strip, Interim Report* (UNIDO UC/PLO/80/231, June 1984), chapter 7.

10

Jobs, Education and Development: The Case of the West Bank

Atif A. Kubursi

I. INTRODUCTION: THE ECONOMIC SETTING

Unlike the global empires of the past, where the imperial centre relied on economic resources shipped from colonial outposts thousands of miles away, the 'Israeli Imperial Economy' is based on resources and markets located in geographically contiguous areas, making the process of political subjugation and economic domination easier, more efficient and less obvious.[1]

Although Israel's economic domination and exploitation of the occupied territories is subtle on account of their geographical proximity, it is deliberate, calculating and systematic. It rests on mechanisms that are well co-ordinated and synchronised. Control of water use severely limits agricultural production and economic life in the occupied territories. The proletarianisation of farmers and agricultural labourers has driven many of them either to work in Israel for low wages or to leave the area altogether. Induced emigration, actively sought by Israel, has a number of consequences: first, it depopulates the occupied territories and facilitates Israeli expansion and creeping annexation; second, it reduces the potential for industrialisation as markets shrink and resources are depleted; third, emigration of persons of working age reduces the productive capacity of the occupied territories and increases their dependence on the Israeli economy. The remaining pool of human resources serves as a buffer stock that absorbs the major burdens of Israeli economic adjustments, easily utilised or discarded depending on the state of the economy.

Palestinian workers could theoretically find employment in other sectors of the occupied territories' economy, such as industry. But West Bank and Gaza industries have stagnated or declined. This is in large part due to direct restrictions on licensing, capital mobilisation and markets, but also due to indirect influences such as the increase in the cost of labour and competition from subsidised Israeli products. Most of the industries in the occupied territories are therefore confined to small-scale operations with limited production capacities and capital, often employing only members of the owners' families.

There is some subcontracting activity from Israel to the West Bank, but it is based on exploiting the cheap labour of Arab women. Because subcontracting involves labour-intensive steps in industrial processes originating and subsequently completed in Israel, its contribution to the industrial development of the occupied territories has been, and will remain, minimal.

In 1983, after 16 years of occupation, there were only seven firms in the West Bank employing over 100 workers and seven firms employing between 50 and 99 workers. Most were founded before 1967.

There is no capital market in the occupied territories. Domestic savings are either drained by higher taxes, invested in the construction of family dwellings or placed in liquid funds in Jordanian dinars in Jordan. All organised financial institutions which existed in the West Bank and Gaza before 1967 remained closed until 1982 when, after a drawn-out legal battle, the Bank of Palestine in Gaza was allowed to resume some limited operations. Of special note here is the absence of specialised credit institutions that would normally channel funds into agriculture, industry and housing and thereby underpin development-oriented, as distinct from strictly commercial, activities. Furthermore, military orders require that all outside sources of funds be declared to the occupation authorities. Although generally ignored, such restrictive policies limit large-scale investment in the occupied territories as well as increasing the risks.

Dumping by Israeli industries has severely restricted competition. Expensive raw materials – which must be acquired exclusively from or through Israel – have raised the cost of production to a point where many existing firms have become non-viable. Over 90 per cent of West Bank and Gaza imports come from Israel. In 1968, Israel's trade surplus with the West Bank and Gaza was approximately US$ 9.7 million. By 1978, it had reached approximately US$ 248 million and by 1983 there was over US$ 428 million. Industrial imports constituted over 87 per cent of the total imports of the occupied territories from Israel.[2]

Israel has undermined the capacity of local authorities to carry out basic planning and infrastructural investments, thereby thwarting the potential for community-based development. Research centres are harassed and closed and university faculty and students arrested and detained, often without specific charge.

II. THE MANPOWER-EDUCATION SYSTEM: THE ISSUES

This paper deals with the problems of manpower under the most unusual of circumstances. The population in the occupied territories grows, the school-age population and school attendance expand, large and increasing numbers of students enter higher education and in due course graduate, but, and here is the twist, the local labour market remains absolutely stagnant. In the higher skilled and professional categories, the employment opportunities continue to shrink. Hence one confronts the peculiar situation where education and employment become, in a perverse way, negatively correlated in the occupied territories. In the words of one student of this situation, 'an analysis of employment rates in correlation with education levels indicates that, unlike the situation among the Jewish population of Israel, the employment rate in the administered areas (*sic*) goes down as the level of education (measured in years of schooling) rises. This may be attributable to the paucity of suitable jobs for educated workers.'[3]

In general, and abstracting for the moment from the situation at hand, the lack of synchronisation between the labour market and the education system is symptomatic of some fundamental problems in either or both. The educational system may be deficient in quality or it may be producing the wrong proportion of skilled workers. Alternatively, the labour market may be inadequate and deficient in providing sufficient new employment. It is rarely the case in developing countries that the fault is in one system. It is generally the case that the two systems are not fully coordinated.

In the case of the occupied territories, this lack of synchronisation is fundamentally aggravated by the impact of Israeli occupation policies and practices in relation to economic development, as noted earlier. The normal process of social and economic transformation that would create expanding opportunities for absorbing graduates of the educational system is distorted and stunted by restrictions on industrial and technological development. The primary objective of development in the West Bank and Gaza must remain the achievement of genuine and self-generated social and economic change in the context of the Palestinian people's right to self-determination in their own homeland. Under the present circumstances, only partial, and for the most part, temporary solutions can be sought. In this rather limited, and largely artificial, context the first concern of manpower and educational planning would be to link the two systems to each other and to establish a smooth interface between the economy and education.

Human resource planning has two broad objectives. First, manpower and educational planning seeks to provide an expanding economy with the requisite number and quality of human resources and skills capable of sustaining expansion and growth. In the absence of a sufficient supply of job opportunities, due to lack of investment and growth, qualified manpower will be forced to remain unemployed, accept lower wage rates in the local economy or seek employment elsewhere (e.g. in the case of the occupied territories, either in Israel or by emigrating). In either case the development process is retarded and growth of indigenous output is sacrificed. Second, human resource planning seeks to ensure a stable but dynamic balance between the supply of skills that is produced by educational and training systems on the one hand and the demand for such skills in the economy on the other. In the absence of such equilibrium (balance between supply and demand) there will either be a shortage of certain skills with the subsequent emergence of bottlenecks and constraints on growth, or there will be surpluses of certain skills and, consequently, a waste of resources.

Manpower and educational planning is therefore an integral part of overall social and economic planning. This is particularly the case when growth and development require a co-ordinated set of economic and social decisions and transformations to bring about an outcome of the economic process that is different from that which would emerge spontaneously from the operation of market forces or from the imposition of artificial constraints on the growth of work opportunities.

Manpower and educational planning in the occupied territories is counter-productive unless it is geared to and promotes economic and political independence. In the absence of a national Palestinian sovereign authority, planning could be exercised first in the micro-units of the economy and only later made to expand to higher operational units. Although this is the reverse of customary planning models, the experiences of workers' councils in Yugoslavia and village councils in Algeria suggest that voluntary micro-units could perform critical and important planning tasks. They may be able to co-ordinate with one another perhaps more successfully than under a monolithic central planning authority. In any event, in the case of the occupied territories, it is a matter of necessity.

This paper seeks to develop an integrated model which connects manpower requirements, educational system operations and economic development and policy priorities into a coherent system. Because of data problems only the economy and the education systems of the West Bank are modelled. The main objective is to answer two basic questions: first, what economic configurations are necessary to generate a situation of near full employment of available manpower in the West

Bank? Or, alternatively, what level of economic activity would permit reabsorption of the workers currently employed in Israel back into the local economy? Second, what changes in the education system in the West Bank would be necessary to produce the right mix of skills that could respond best to the current economic requirements of the West Bank under the prevailing, hopefully transitional, constraints of occupation?

III. THE MODEL

Recognition of the important contribution that education makes to economic growth and development has heightened the interest of economists and social planners in the development of national economic models for the efficient allocation of resources in the educational system and for the optimal utilisation of the human resources it produces.

In this section a general-manpower-educational-economic model is constructed to integrate the demographic, educational and economic sub-systems.

The basic structure of the model involves a flow of input data, in a simultaneous process, to three sub-models: the Labour Force Model (LFM), the Manpower Requirements Model (MRM) and the Educational Simulation Model (ESM). The LFM is in turn linked to the MRM and both are linked along with the ESM to the Manpower Policy Model (MPM) system (Figure 10.1).

Figure 10.1. A schematic outline of the model

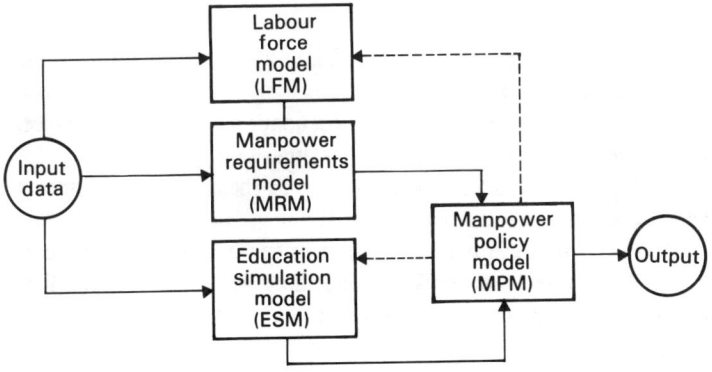

227

The model adopted here is a special adaptation of the World Bank Compound Model.[4] It uses the basic framework of the Compound Model but adjusts its structure and objectives in light of the special and specific conditions of the West Bank.

1. The labour force sub-system (LFM)

Each sub-system of the model performs a special function and is integrated in the sequential hierarchy with the other sub-systems. We begin with the LFM.

The LFM accounts, at the beginning of each year, for the available labour force by sector (i) and occupation (j). Since some labourers emigrate, retire or die they will not be available in later years. However, through the supply of output from the educational system and return of migrant workers, additional resources become available. The stock of manpower available to the system will be updated accordingly each year.

Two basic categories are distinguished here: West Bank labour and the non-West Bank Palestinians. The basic technical relationships governing these two sub-systems are the following:

(1) $LF_t(i,j) = BLF(i,j)$

where $BLF(i,j)$ is the base year West Bank labour force stock by sector and by occupation.

(2) $LF_t(i,j) = [LF_{t-1}(i,j)(1-a_{t-1}(j))] + ESM_{t-1}(i,j) + MPM_{t-1}(i,j)$

for $t \geq 2$

where $LF_t(i,j)$ is the West Bank labour force at the beginning of year t in sector i and occupation category j.

$a_t(j)$ is the attrition rates vector by occupation for West Bank labour. It is assumed that $a_t(j) = a_{t-1}(j)$ unless otherwise stated.

$ESM_{t-1}(i,j)$ is the labour force supplied by the educational system in year t–1, for sector i and occupation j.

$MPM_{t-1}(i,j)$ is the net exportation or importation of West Bank labour. When non-West Bank labour is included, the following functional relationships would be identified.

228

(3) $LF_t^N (i,j) = BLF^N (i,J)$

(4) $LF_t^N (i,j) = [(LF_{t-1}^N (i,j) (1-a_{t-1}^N (j)))] + MPM_{t-1}^N (i,j)$

for $t \geq 2$

$MPM_{t-1}^N (i,j)$ is the net importation or net exportation of non-West

Bank labour.

2. The manpower requirement sub-system (MRM)

This sub-system accounts for the total manpower requirements by sector and occupation to achieve given output targets taking into account labour productivity in each sector. The net manpower requirements are also identified within this sub-system by comparing the total manpower requirements and the available manpower stock.

To determine sectoral output, several options are open.

Option one
Choose a constant growth rate of sectoral output on the basis of historical trends.

(5) $X_t (i) = [X_{t-1} (i)] [1 + \alpha_i]$

Option two
Choose flexible growth rates of sectoral outputs such that the total output growth is consistent with full employment of local manpower. These targets could be derived from an optimisation model which will be shown later.

(6) $X_t (i) = [X_{t-1} (i)] [1 + \alpha_t (i)]$

Similarly rates of growth of labour productivity may be assigned to different sectors. The two options above in terms of productivity growth rates would appear as follows:

(7) $P_t (i) = P_{t-1} (i) (1 + \overset{t}{B} (i))$

and

(8) $P_t (i) = P_{t-1} (i) (1 + B_t (i))$

229

when $X_t(i)$ and $P_t(i)$ are given, then employment estimates $E_t(i)$ are derived by (9).

$$(9) \quad E_t(i) = \frac{X_t(i)}{P_t(i)}$$

for $P_t(i) > 0$.

If one or both of $X_t(i)$, $P_t(i)$ is/are missing, $E_t(i)$ must be given.

The employment estimates by sector can easily be converted into employment by sector and occupation using a sector/occupation matrix (SOM). This is most commonly obtained from cross-sectional analysis of international comparative data or from time-series data for one or more countries having an economic structure similar to that of the economy under study.[5] Alternatively, and if planners' preferences can be ascertained, the coefficients of the SOM may be derived from a priority matrix. Because of the very special conditions governing the economy of the West Bank, comparisons could be misleading, and the latter approach is employed. The typical element of the SOM is s_{ij} with the following properties:

$$(10) \quad \sum_j s_{ij} = 1.0$$

$$(11) \quad 0 \leq s_{ij} \leq 1.0$$

Let q_{ijt} be the elements of $L_t(i,j)$ where $L_t(i,j)$ is the manpower requirements in sector i of occupation j needed to achieve the expected output target $X_t(i)$.

Let e_{it} be the elements of $E_t(i)$, s_{ijt} be the elements of SOM_t then $q_{ijt} = e_{it} \times s_{ijt}$ with the following properties:

$$(12) \quad \sum_j q_{ijt} = \sum_j e_{it} \times s_{ijt} = e_{it} \sum_j s_{ijt} = e_{it}$$

where $\sum_j q_{ijt}$ is the total manpower requirements for sector i at time t and $\sum_i q_{ijt}$ is the total manpower requirements for occupational category j at time t. Thus,

$$(13) \quad \sum_j \sum_i q_{ijt} = \sum_j \sum_i LF_t(i,j) = \sum_i E_t(i)$$

whereas, net manpower requirements $NMR_t(i,j)$, is

(14) $NRM_t(i,j) = L_t(i,j) - LF_t(i,j)$

3. The education simulation model (ESM)

The ESM simulates the flows of students and trainees through the system on the basis of initial enrolments in the base year and assumptions about participation rates, drop-outs, repetition rates and promotion rates.

Participation rates are the percentage of students from a given age cohort.

Repetition, drop-out and promotion rates, by definition, add up to unity. But drop-outs are split into two groups, those leaving at the end of the year having successfully completed the year and those who have not successfully completed the year.

These parameters can be changed to reflect educational policies such as: higher participation of girls in a given programme, increased flows from secondary to vocational and technical training, or specification of particular proportions of upper secondary school entrants to literary and science oriented courses, and the introduction of automatic promotion into higher grades, or the limiting of repetition to a maximum number of attempts.

The ESM is based on a model by the same name originally developed by the United Nations Educational, Scientific and Cultural Organisation (UNESCO). It has, however, been significantly modified for use as part of our model.

One such modification permits streaming control, a feature allowing for feedback adjustments between the economy and the educational system. For as long as it is important that the educational system does not produce more students in any discipline over and above the number needed to meet the manpower requirements, a feedback mechanism is required so that the ESM, while taking into account repetition, drop-out and promotion rates in various grades, can readjust its intake to post-primary levels in order to meet the manpower requirements that are in accordance with developmental priorities (as defined by a predefined priority matrix).

Another modification incorporates special conditions regarding age and labour force participation such as when certain school leavers may not be able to join the labour force because of a minimum age stipulation or some other externally imposed sanctions.

Finally, the ESM is adjusted to take account of those who never received any form of schooling but who ultimately join the labour force.

The following input requirements are defined:

$UAS_0(c,a)$ = the existing cumulative underage school leavers by course c and by age a in the base year.

Let AA = the minimum legal age to work minus one.
BB = the minimum age allowed to attend any school.

$FIL_t(c)$ = rates of graduates from course c, in year t, to participate in the labour force.

$EQM_t(c,i,j)$ = entrance qualifications matrix for graduates from course c into sector i and occupational j in year t.

(15) $UAS_t(c,a) = UAS_{t-1}(a,i) + SAL_t(c,a)$

defined for all c which satisfies the constraints $BB \le a \le AA_{-1}$
and $UAS_t(c,BB) = SAL_t(c,BB)$ for all c.

It is to be noted that $UAS_{t-1}(c,AA)$ will be allowed to join the labour force in year t.

Let us define $LG_t(c)$ = the number of graduates of course c who will be eligible to participate in the labour force after they are filtered by matrix $FIL_t(c)$ as

(16) $LG_t(c) = FIL_t(c) \times G_t(c)$

where $G_t(c)$ = the number of graduates from course c in year t.

Thus,

(17) $MSE_t(i,j) = \sum_c (i,j) = \sum[EQM_t(c,i,j)] [LG_t(c) + UAS_{t-1}(c,AA)]$

where $MSE_t(i,j)$ = manpower supplies of the ESM to go into the labour force in sector i and occupation j in year t.

It is noted that

(18) $ESM_t(i,j) = MSE_t(i,j)$.

4. The manpower policy model (MPM)

The basic function of the MPM is to allocate the output of the educational system, the existing labour force and newcomers to the overall SOM in accordance with the specific priorities of the economy and society.

In the context of the occupied territories, the highest priority of MPM should be to employ the graduates of the educational system and to find alternative employment for those now working in Israel. In the areas where supplies are greater than requirements, two types of adjustments may be necessary. First, investment and exports should be treated as free variables whose magnitudes should be contingent on the maximum absorptive capacity of the economy. Second, at the same time adjustments in participation and repetition coefficients in the ESM will have to be made.

The allocation of graduates of the ESM and returnees from employment in Israel will be conducted on an optimal basis determined by a linear programming model.

Two major inputs are required: the priority matrix $PM(i,j,p)$ assigns a priority p to given sector i and occupation j. The manpower supplies from the ESM will be allocated to each sector/occupation in accordance with the priority matrix $PM(i,j,p)$.

In PM (i,j,p)

$p = 0$ implies low priority
$p = 1$ implies higher priority
$p = 2$ implies the next higher priority and so on up to 9;

Then the manpower requirements for ESM by priority p and by sector i and occupation j in year t will be

$$AD_t (i,j) = [NMR_t (i,j)] [I_{ij} (k)]$$

where $\quad I_{ij} (k) = 1, \quad$ if $k = p$ in sector i and occupation j

$\qquad I_{ij} (k) = 0, \quad$ if $p = k$ in sector i, occupation j

Namely, $AD_t (i,j)$ is the additional national manpower required to be absorbed from those working in Israel in sector i and occupation j having priority p.

Turning to the linear programming model, one of many which can be used in the current context, the objective is to maximise employment opportunities within the economy given other resources and technical constraints on the economy.

Maximise $Z = \sum_i \sum_j q_{ijt} = \sum_i \sum_j \lambda_{ij} X_{it}$ subject to

(1) $\sum_i X_{it} = Y_t$
(2) $C_t + I_t + G_t + E_t - M_t = Y_t$
(3) $\sum_i k_i X_{it} \leq K_t$
(4) $K_t (1-\Sigma) + I_t = K_{t+1}$
(5) $C_t - \Theta Y_t = 0$
(6) $M_t - E_t \leq F_t$
(7) $M_t - \Theta_2 Y_2 = 0$
(8) $\sum_i \lambda_i X_{it} \leq LF_t$

where

Y_t =   the GDP of the occupied territories in the year t.
X_{it} =   the GDP originating in sector i in year t.
k_i =   the capital/output coefficient in sector i.
K_t =   the total capital stock in year t.
Σ =   the depreciation rate of the capital stock.
c_t =   private consumption in year t.
Θ_1 =   the marginal propensity to consume.
M_t =   the imports of the territories in year t.
E_t =   the exports of the territories in year t.
F_t =   net factor payments from abroad in year t.
Θ_2 =   the marginal propensity to import.
λ_i =   the labour/output ratio in sector i.

Before discussing the results of implementing the model, a general description of the educational and manpower situation in the occupied territories is necessary to provide a background to the conclusions and recommendations of the paper.

IV. THE EDUCATION-MANPOWER SYSTEMS IN THE OCCUPIED TERRITORIES

A number of distinctive characteristics of the demographic education-manpower sub-systems in the occupied territories render the task of modelling them a complex undertaking. The following is a brief account of some of these characteristics.

(a) The percentage of persons below 19 years of age is disproportionally high. In 1985, more than 76 per cent of the total population of the

Figure 10.2: Framework of the model

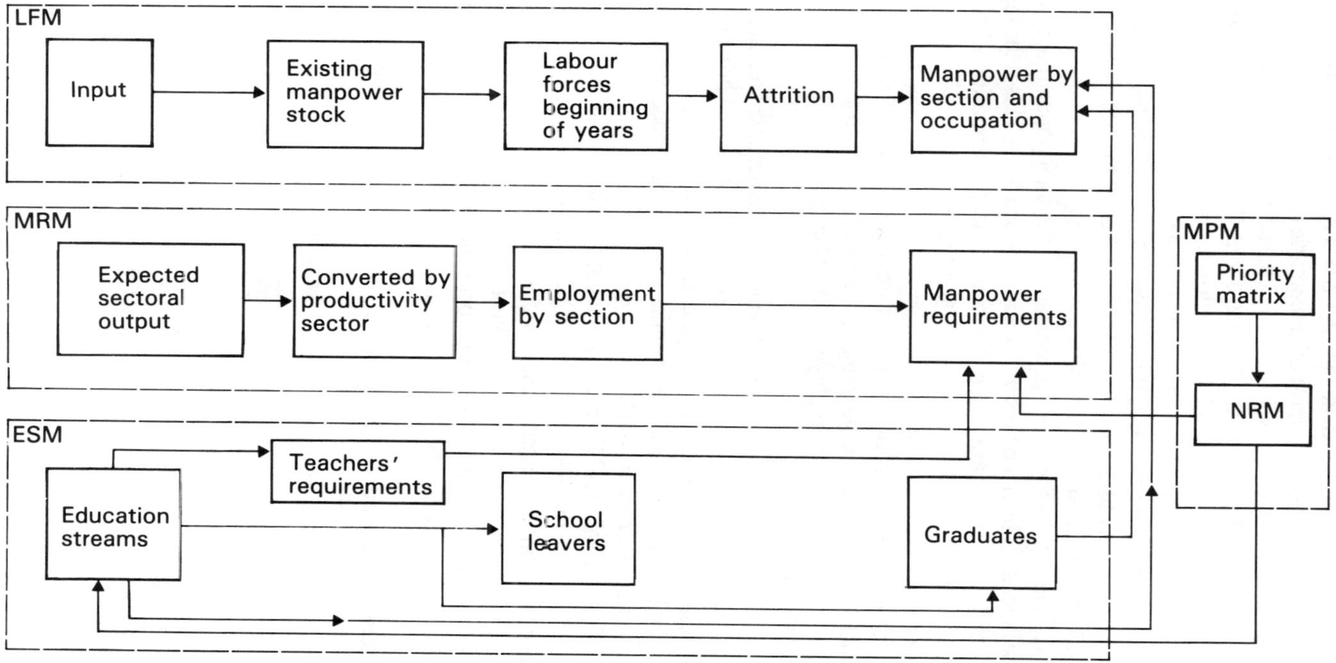

occupied territories was in the age bracket of 0-19 years. This is significantly higher than most other countries and is at least 6 percentage points above what it was in 1967. Those 14 years old and younger were about 47.1 per cent in 1983 and about 48.5 per cent in 1967.[6]

(b) The natural population growth rates are high indeed, but the effective growth rates (when adjusted for net emigration) are modest for most years except 1983. Population growth rates in the Gaza Strip are significantly higher than those for the West Bank because of more restricted emigration opportunities.

(c) The labour force as a percentage of the total population is very low indeed for both the West Bank and the Gaza Strip. This is the result of the low participation rates of women, the concentration of 'emigrants' in the working age groups and the high share of the young cohorts in the total population.

(d) The proportion of the labour force from the occupied territories which works in Israel is very high. It represents over 45 per cent of the total number of people employed in the Gaza Strip and 33 per cent in the West Bank.

(e) The overall rate of unemployment in the occupied territories is determined by the lack of investment and growth caused primarily by the restrictions of the occupation policies, but the variability in this rate is highly correlated with economic activity and hence with labour market conditions in Israel.

(f) A total of 311,243 students was enrolled in schools, colleges and universities in the West Bank in 1981/2. This represents over a third of the corresponding population.[7]

(g) The literacy rate of the West Bank labour force is high by international standards. Only 16.6 per cent were illiterate, another 16 per cent had 1 to 6 years' schooling, about 10 per cent had 7 to 8 years,

Table 10.1: Labour force by years of schooling in the West Bank: 1984

Years of Schooling	Labour Force
0	25,700
1-6	24,400
7-8	13,700
9-12	26,800
13-plus	9,400
Total	100,000

Source: Government of Jordan, Ministry of Education.

and a surprising 18 per cent had 9 to 12 years, and about 10 per cent had over 13 years. These rates appear even more impressive when taken in the context of the perverse relationship between educational attainment and employment noted earlier and the high concentration of educated manpower among those who emigrate (see Table 10.1).

(h) There was a total of 166,584 students in the Gaza Strip in 1985/6; the majority were enrolled in United Nations Relief and Works Agency (UNRWA) Schools (52 per cent). Almost all the others (43.5 per cent) attended public schools.[8] Few students were in post-secondary schools (there is only one small institution of higher learning in Gaza). A larger proportion was at the secondary level, particularly in public schools, as UNRWA education ends at the ninth grade.

(i) There are very few students in vocational schools in the West Bank and Gaza. The vast majority of students, 96.3 per cent, are in academic streams (see Table 10.2). This contrasts strikingly with the situation in Israel and in industrial or industrialising countries.

(j) The educational parameters of the system are symptomatic of high drop-out rates and inefficiencies within the educational system. Although the parameters presented here were calculated from data pertaining to the West Bank only, it is our judgement that they apply, perhaps even more strongly, to the case of the Gaza Strip.

(k) There were six degree-granting institutions of post-secondary education in the occupied territories in 1986. Five of them were on the West Bank and one in Gaza. Al-Najah National University in Nablus had the largest enrolment with 3,007 students, Birzeit had around 2,404 and Hebron and Bethlehem Universities had 1,746 and 1,197 students respectively. There were 4,570 students in Gaza and 1,420 in Jerusalem. The total enrolment for the 1985/6 academic year was 14,344 students. There were also 15 community colleges, all of them in the West Bank, with a total enrolment of 5,505 students in the same academic year. This gives a grand total of 19,849 post-secondary students.[9]

Employability of university graduates in the occupied territories has been limited, with the consequence that a large proportion of them remain unemployed or emigrate. There were at least 5,376 unemployed graduates in the West Bank and 2,699 in the Gaza Strip in 1986, and the situation appears to be worsening. This number is quite possibly an underestimate given that it represents only those who register with the Graduates Club in Jerusalem. Just over half are from universities, the rest holders of the teaching or vocational certificates.[10]

About 40 per cent of university students in the West Bank and Gaza are women. About a third of the student body were registered in the arts faculties, 17.7 per cent in the sciences, 15 per cent in commerce, 13.7 per cent in education, 13.5 per cent in law and Islamic studies, 4.5 per cent in engineering and 1.7 per cent in nursing and medical laboratories.[11]

Table 10.2: School enrolment in the West Bank: 1982/3 – 1983/4

Cycle	1982/3	1983/4
Kindergarten	13,041	15,665
Primary	192,836	194,042
Middle	64,495	67,726
Secondary Academic	37,382	36,610
Secondary Vocational	1,442	1,673
Community Colleges	2,272	4,773
Universities	8,343	9,891
Total	319,811	330,380
Memorandum Item Share of Population (in per cent)	35.9	36.2

Source: Government of Jordan, Ministry of Education.

V. THE SIMULATION RESULTS

The model described in Section III was tailored to the extent possible to fit conditions in the West Bank. Many adjustments had to be made to render it operational. This involved a number of aggregations and the borrowing of parameter values from neighbouring countries. The simulation exercise should therefore be treated as exploratory and the results as preliminary.

It is also important to recognise that the adopted model is too complex a system to be undertaken by a single research paper. Further work needs to be done and should involve a number of researchers including economists, programmers, demographers, statisticians and educationalists. However, a number of interesting results emerged from even this preliminary treatment of the model. Some of these are shown here starting with the linear programming system working backwards.

The following system was finally used:

Maximise

$$0.745V_1 + 2.931V_2 + 1.65V_3 + 0.778V_4$$

subject to

$-V_1 - V_2 - V_3 - V_4 + Y = 0$
$.78Y - E \leq 33.8$
$.3Y - I \leq 0$
$.68Y - I - E = -20.8$
$V_1 \geq 30.05$
$V_2 \geq 5.68$
$V_3 \geq 14.83$
$V_4 \geq 45.71$
$0.745V_1 + 2.93V_2 + 1.65V_3 + 0.778V_4 \leq 150.2$

The national accounts and the labour force data are all for the West Bank in 1983. The value added figures are in constant prices of 1968 and are expressed in millions of Israeli shekels (IS).[12]

The coefficients of the objective function are derived as follows:

Agricultural: $22.4/30.05 = 0.745$.

That is 745 jobs are needed to sustain one million Israeli shekels of value added in agriculture in 1968 prices. Similar calculations are made for the rest of the sectors.

Industry: $16.65/5.68 = 2.931$
Construction: $24.48/14.83 = 1.65$
Trade and Services: $35.57/45.707 = 0.778$

The marginal (average) propensity to import $= \dfrac{M}{Y} = \dfrac{75.0}{96.3} = 0.78$

where $Y = $ GDP
Exports = IS 27.1 million in 1968 prices
Net factor incomes from abroad = GNP− GDP = 132.1−96.3 = IS 33.8 millions in 1968 prices.

Marginal Propensity to Consume = Average Propensity to Consume
$= \dfrac{\text{Consumption}}{Y} = \dfrac{105.5}{96.3}$
$= 109.6$

Labour force = 150.2 thousand persons.

1. The findings

The optimisation experiments revealed a number of interesting results.

(a) The West Bank could easily employ all of its labour force were exports to rise to IS 55 million and investment to IS 43 million in 1968 prices. This represents a doubling of exports and the raising of real investments by 70 per cent over their 1983 levels.

The engine of growth and absorption of the surplus labour (the unemployed and those crossing the 'green line') is the industrial sector. The optimal value added in this sector rises to IS 23.1 million in 1968 prices. This represents an almost fourfold increase over current values. Other value added contributions are left by their solution at their prevailing values in 1983. The selection of the industrial sector is based on its high labour/output ratio.

As these changes may be viewed as drastic, the experiment was run incrementally. Exports were increased in steps of IS 5 million (in 1968 prices) until their value reached the value the solution assigned to it when it was determined endogenously. The shadow price of a unit of exports is equal to 3.76 and it represents the additional jobs which would emerge if exports were to rise by IS 1 million. Their value was derived as follows:

An increase of IS 1 million in exports allows an increase in income of $1.0/0.78 = 1.282$ because this increase in income is the one allowed by the balance of payments constraint such that exports are equal to imports. The increase of 1.282 units in income will come from the industrial sector which is the most efficient in generating jobs. Thus $(1.282)(2.93) = 3.76$.

(b) The shadow prices on the other sectors' value added represented the loss of jobs that would emerge if income were to be increased say in agriculture instead of in industry. For example, the shadow price on the lower bound on agricultural output is 2.185. This number is the difference between the labour/output coefficients of the industrial and the agricultural sectors $(2.185 = 2.93 - 0.745)$.

(c) The maximum income attainable when employment is maximised approaches IS 113.7 million in 1968 prices. In other words, full employment in the economy would raise the GDP by 18 per cent. This is not a great deal and is perhaps the result of the relative openness of the West Bank economy, meaning that export-driven increases in GDP also lead to rising imports which dissipate a large portion of added income. It is also an indication that the industrial sector is efficient in generating jobs, but not very efficient in generating income.

(d) When the objective function is changed and income instead of employment is maximised, the value of optimal GDP rises to IS 136.5 million, 42 per cent higher than 1983 values. Employment rises to almost 130,000. In other words, not all the labour force could be utilised domestically. Value added in agriculture rises to IS 70.3 million, or more than 2.3 times the prevailing values in 1983. In this case, exports would have to rise to IS 72.7 million in 1968 prices or increase by about 268 per cent.

The model is structured on an aggregate basis. This macroeconomic structure conceals and sidesteps the input-output structure of the economy. If this were to be incorporated, two basic changes are likely to appear: (1) increases in the value added in one sector are not possible without increasing value added in other sectors. Thus, the simple relationships identified here are only indicative of general tendencies but are not strictly accurate; (2) the most binding constraint on agriculture in the occupied territories is lack of water which is functionally dependent on the policies and practices of the occupation authorities.

2. The implications

The implications of these results for the educational system are significant. Below are some tentative suggestions of changes needed to reorient the system to an acceptable degree of harmony with the projected economic conditions.

(a) There will be a strong demand for technicians and vocationally trained people to serve the needs of agriculture and industry where most of the new jobs would be created. Thus, the prevailing emphasis on general education would have to be re-evaluated.

(b) The expansion of industry takes time and requires a long gestation period. Switching labour from Israel to the West Bank would be easy during the construction phase. When production comes on stream a different mix of skills is required. Training and re-training labour may become an important function of the educational system.

(c) The efficient allocation of resources within the educational system requires the expansion of primary and middle level cycles and improvements in the linkages between the vocational and technical cycles.

(d) Unemployment among university graduates could be reduced once investment and exports increased. Some retraining and under-employment may be unavoidable at the outset, but the connection at earlier stages of the educational cycles and in structure and level of economic activity could absorb resulting excess supplies in the near future.

241

VI. CONCLUSIONS

The recognition of the important contribution that education makes to economic growth and development has heightened the interest in the examination of the efficient allocation of resources in the educational sector and in the optimal utilisation of the human resources that education produces.

The West Bank is encumbered in its efforts to synchronise the manpower and the educational systems by the inability of the Palestinians in the occupied territories to control either of these two elements and hence to reorient both systems towards national, self-reliant development. Without a sovereign authority, the chances of reforming education and stemming unemployment remain severely constrained. But what it takes to achieve better synchronisation between the economy and the educational system, and thereby achieve higher employment and growth, is clear and modest in terms of the resources for investment. Exports need to be increased substantially and investment must flow into the productive sectors, especially industry. Vocational and technical education should absorb higher proportions of secondary school graduates. Furthermore, and in light of the heavy dependence of the West Bank and Gaza on trade, measures must be taken to ease current marketing constraints. Arab markets could be opened selectively and consistently to absorb additional outputs of industry and agriculture from the occupied territories.

NOTES

1. R.G.Khouri, 'Israel's imperial economics', *Journal of Palestine Studies*, vol.9, no.2 (Winter 1980), p.71.
2. The Arab Fund for Social and Economic Development et al., *The Joint Arab Economic Report, 1984* (Arab Fund for Social and Economic Development, Amman,1984).
3. Brian Van Arkadie, *Benefits and Burdens: The West Bank and Gaza Strip Economies Since 1967* (Carnegie Endowment for International Peace, New York, 1977), p.67.
4. See Ismail Serageldin, 'The modelling and methodology of manpower planning in Arab countries' in N. Sherbiny (ed.), *Manpower Planning in the Oil Countries* (JAI Press, Greenwich Conn., 1981), pp. 55-90.
5. See G.T. Abed and A.A. Kubursi, 'A macroeconomic simulation model of high level manpower requirements in Iraq' in Sherbiny, *Manpower Planning*, pp.145-71.
6. Central Bureau of Statistics, *Statistical Abstract of Israel, no.35, 1984* (Central Bureau of Statistics, Jerusalem, 1984), p.742 (these figures do not include East Jerusalem).

7. Central Bureau of Statistics, *Palestinian Statistical Abstract, no.4,* 1982 (Palestine Liberation Organisation, Damascus, 1982), pp.81, 88. These figures include East Jerusalem.

8. Central Bureau of Statistics, *Statistical Abstract of Israel, no.37,* 1986, p.732.

9. Executive Committee of the Council for Higher Education, *al-dalil al-ihsa'i li-al-jami'at al-filastiniyya* (A statistical guide to the Palestinian universities), (Council for Higher Education, Jerusalem, 1986), pp.33-5; UN ESCWA/Arab Labour Organisation, *al-'adad al-midani fi al-daffa al-gharbiyya wa-al qit'a ghazza* (Technical training in the West Bank and the Gaza Strip) (UN ESCWA/Arab Labour Organisation, Baghdad, 1987), p.22.

10. Ishan Atiya *et al., Unemployed Graduates in the West Bank and Gaza* (Arab Graduates Club, Jerusalem, 1985), pp.156-7.

11. Central Bureau of Statistics, *Palestinian Statistical Abstract, no.4,* 1982, pp.88, 97.

12. These data were obtained from Bakir Abu Kishk, *The Palestinian Economy and the Prospects for the Future* (forthcoming), chapters 2 and 4.

11

Society and Change in the Northern Jordan Valley

Alex Pollock

It is the aspiration of most development plans to achieve not just broad macroeconomic objectives such as improvement in the Gross National Product, but also to ameliorate the condition of producers themselves. In the occupied territories this has been particularly the case. With no national authority to consult, development agencies have had a close and direct relationship with peasant farmers and plans introduced in the region have aimed to improve both the productivity of the land and the living standards of those who work it.

In this paper I shall examine the failure of development plans to bring about any fundamental change in the material conditions of life in one of the most intensively developed areas of the West Bank – the northern Jordan Valley. The area studied includes the seven villages of Bardala, 'Ain al-Beda, Marj Najeh, Zbeidat, Jiftlik, Frush, Beit Dajan and 'Ain Shibli.

Salim Tamari and Rita Giacaman, in their 1980 study of Zbeidat, stated, '...the Zbeidat community, perhaps one of the most underdeveloped in the Middle East – lacking in health services, electricity, running water and schools – has acquired one of the most developed systems of agricultural technology in the world'.[1]

Their observations, which apply equally to the other six villages in the region, are confirmed by a 1983 Arab Thought Forum (ATF) survey of the area[2] and point to an acute degree of poverty and underdevelopment.

For example, there is a general adult illiteracy rate of 48 per cent in an adult population of 2,667 (30 per cent of adult men are illiterate and 64 per cent of the women); 60 per cent of adult women have had no formal schooling. Overcrowding is chronic, with an average family size of eight and an average living density of five persons per room.

Forty-eight per cent of houses consist of one room; 43 per cent of households have no kitchen; 67 per cent no latrine and 77 per cent no running water. Women have to carry domestic water from wells often a considerable distance from their homes. Eighty per cent of homes have no electricity.[3]

The statistical indicators describe a peasant community suffering a severe degree of economic and social hardship. How can one of the most technologically developed sectors of West Bank agriculture provide such minimal, if not completely inadequate, living conditions for the peasant producers?

The answer to this paradox is complex and lies in the colonial nature of Israel's domination of the economy of the occupied territories, the impact of this domination on the social relations of the area and the failure of economic development plans introduced by external agencies significantly to challenge these structural determinants. Two theoretical perspectives can inform an analysis of this phenomenon: nationalist inspired dependency theory and Marxist class theory. I would argue, however, that taken independently they do not provide an adequate explanation of social relations in the Jordan Valley.

Dependency theory describes social relations where one dominant nation, state or ethnic group expropriates a significant portion of the economic surplus of the indigenous economy at the expense of the subordinate nation, state or ethnic group. This model conceives of social change and the creation of poverty as an externally generated process, the result of economic exploitation and political oppression of the subordinate by the superordinate.[4]

The main shortcoming of this theory is that it fails to explain relations of economic exploitation which are established within the structure of the subordinate state/nation and coexist with external economic and political control. Although dependency theory only provides a partial explanation of social change and the creation of underdevelopment it is an important tool in the formation of development policy and strategies. One of dependency theory's most appealing political features is its utilitarian nationalist propaganda function which underscores nationalist anti-imperialist and anti-colonial struggles, ideologies and development policies.

Marxist class theory focuses on relations between economic classes in which one socially dominant class (or its state representatives) economically exploits and politically oppresses another social class which is the primary producer of goods and services. Economic exploitation occurs not between nations *per se* but between classes. In Marxist schema, exploitation and oppression between nations is facilitated through existing class relations within the dominant nation.

At the level of prescribed political struggle the differences between Marxist and dependency theory are telling. Dependency theory normally proposes a united national anti-imperialist or anti-colonial struggle in which progressive elements of the national bourgeoisie provide the intellectual and ideological leadership.[5] Some Marxists view this prescription as a misguided panacea. They argue that the anti-imperialist and anti-colonial struggle has to be fought on class lines and that an alliance should be formed between all objective anti-imperialist and anti-colonial forces but that within this alliance a political and ideological campaign has to be fought to unite all progressive forces in a socialist movement. Unless this is achieved, these Marxists argue, a social revolution will only succeed in replacing colonial or imperialist exploitation with national bourgeois class exploitation and oppression.

These two theoretical perspectives articulate distinct pro-grammes of social transformation and economic reconstruction. In terms of explaining social processes, however, they should not be viewed as mutually exclusive. In order to arrive at a detailed explanation of underdevelopment and poverty in most third-world countries a synthesis of dependency and class theory is required. One possible way of constructing such a synthesis is to conceive of depend-ency among nations, states and ethnic groups as a conditioning structure which sets structural limitations on the form of class relations which develop. For example, the colonial, political and economic domination of the West Bank has set limitations on the internal development of the economy and the forms of class relations which underpin it.

Taking this as my starting point I shall describe a number of external factors which impose structural limitations on the development of the Jordan Valley economy. Next I shall consider the way the productive forces, and the class relations of production and distribution, developed in the area during the period from 1975 to 1984.

I. STRUCTURAL LIMITATIONS IMPOSED BY ISRAEL ON THE AGRARIAN ECONOMY OF THE NORTHERN JORDAN VALLEY

Occupation dominates all aspects of the political and economic life in the West Bank. The Israeli military government imposes a series of deleterious conditions on the development of Palestinian agriculture. Some are designed to prevent Palestinian agricultural output competing with Israeli agricultural produce, others are related to the Zionist programme of colonial expansion. Their impact on socio-economic conditions in the Jordan Valley falls in five main areas:

(a) In the Allon Plan, the first post-1967 plan for the future of the occupied territories and the basis of the Israel Labour Party colonisation plan for the Jordan Valley, the region was designated an area of strategic importance to the Israeli state. Military planners say the Jordan rift provides the Israeli heartland with geographic depth, which would provide an early warning of military strikes from Jordan. A series of Nahal posts were established along the valley in 1968 followed, from 1969, by a number of civilian agricultural settlements.[6] The establishment and expansion of Israeli settlements have meant that Palestinian farmers and Beduin herders have been continually subject to land expropriation and seizure of livestock since 1969.[7] Ibrahim Matar estimates that two of the settlements, Mehola and Argaman, were constructed on 13,100 dunums confiscated from the villages of Bardala, 'Ain al-Beda, Zbeidat and Marj Najeh.[8] The legal situation of local Palestinian farmers is not made any easier by the fact that much of the land in the region – apart from the area around Jericho – is not registered in the Tabu or the Ottoman Land Register.

Widespread land expropriation and absence of officially recognised land registration documents have been significant factors in blocking the development of a real estate market in farm land. This clearly inhibits the development of capitalist agriculture in the Palestinian sector.

(b) The Israeli military authorities have imposed strict controls on Palestinian water utilisation, through the expropriation and destruction of artesian wells and limitations on well depth which has a direct bearing on water quality. Palestinians can excavate wells only up to 120 metres in depth and no permit has been granted for a new well in the Jordan Valley since 1967.[9] The Israeli water authorities and the settlements are allowed to drill deeper wells. These wells provide good quality water while water from the Palestinian wells is highly saline. Water and ground salinity restricts the type and variety of crops Palestinian peasant farmers can grow. Bananas and citrus fruits, for instance, will not grow under saline conditions. Saline water also imposes severe natural restrictions on farm ecosystems and Palestinian farmers are largely restricted to vegetable and field crops.

Moreover, the quantity of water which Palestinian farmers are allowed to pump from their wells is tightly controlled by metering and penalties for breaking restrictions are punitive. The ATF survey found 36 per cent of all farmers reported water shortages.

(c) The West Bank is seen by Israel as a legitimate extension of its own market and as such consumes a large amount of Israeli produce. Since Israeli agriculture is highly subsidised their produce often enters the West Bank market at prices below comparable Palestinian crops. Trade between Israel and the West Bank is almost all one-way. Palestinian access to the Israeli market is extremely restricted. In 1984, for example, four tons of tomatoes from the whole of the Jordan Valley was officially allowed to enter Israel. The result is that if Palestinian farmers want to increase their income they have to look to exports via Jordan. This strategy is fraught with difficulties as the Jordanian authorities control movement across the bridges for their own economic and political interests.

(d) Since the beginning of 1983 the peasant farm communities of the Jordan Valley have been subject to Military Orders 1015 and 1039 restricting the planting and production of commercial vegetables and fruit.[10] Grapes, plums, tomatoes and eggplants are the crops particularly affected. Tomatoes and eggplants are the most important sources of income for the Jordan Valley farmers. Since 1983 no farmer has been allowed to grow these crops without first obtaining permission from the Israeli authorities.

(e) Finally, the Israeli military authorities have refused, except for one or two special cases, to allow farmers in the Jordan Valley to construct adequate and permanent dwellings. During 1984 the military authorities destroyed the homes of 73 farmers in the Jiftlik region, claiming they were unlicensed.[11] This creates instability and makes it very difficult for farmers realistically to plan a long-term future. At present they live on a day-to-day basis and hope that their conditions will not deteriorate too drastically.

II. DEVELOPMENT OF THE PRODUCTIVE FORCES

The northern Jordan Valley has a number of features characteristic of a regional export-enclave economy. It specialises in the production of vegetables for the internal West Bank market and export via Jordan. The seven villages studied in the ATF survey have a total of 17,389 dunums under production, 72.3 per cent (12,566 dunums) being cultivated with vegetables. Tomatoes are grown on 40 per cent (4,965 dunums); another 18 per cent (2,196 dunums) were under eggplant production. The overall importance of these two crops is further

249

highlighted by comparisons with the total number of dunums under eggplant and tomatoes for the whole of Israel. During the 1982/3 season Israel grew tomatoes on 61,600 dunums. The seven Jordan Valley villages harvested an equivalent of 8 per cent of this total. The figures for eggplant production are far more revealing. During the same period Israel had 5,300 dunums of eggplant while the seven villages produce the equivalent of 41 per cent of the total Israeli dunumage.[12] These two crops are the most important sources of export revenue for the villages. Fifty-two per cent of all tomatoes and 25 per cent of all eggplants are exported (250,000-300,000 tons of tomatoes and 17,000-20,000 tons of eggplants) giving a regional export income of between JD 6.25 and 7.5 million.

The reason for the heavy preponderance of tomatoes and eggplants is simply explained. During the early 1970s a number of foreign non-governmental aid organisations became interested in establishing a drip irrigation project with the aim of offsetting backward rural production and poverty in the Jordan Valley.[13] These agencies were motivated by commendable humanitarian values and, often, by ideological commitment to alleviating the worst aspects of Israeli colonial rule. However, the manner in which they sought to make their intervention was modelled on classical diffusionist lines.

The diffusionist model of agrarian reform views the problem of rural poverty and underdevelopment as essentially stemming from technological backwardness. The main policy initiatives which flow from this assumption are based on the belief that poverty and underdevelopment can be checked by sending agricultural extension agents into the countryside to diffuse the backlog of technological knowledge about new equipment and plant species.[14] This equipment is then made available through international aid transfers and grants. The approach is rationalised by technological determinism which is technocentric and thus fails to consider that existent social relations might themselves be part of the problem of poverty generation. Social groups whose exploitative influence such a policy should aim to curb soon adopt the same technologies.

In the Jordan Valley the combined efforts of the aid agencies, large landowners and commission agents in implementing the process of technology transfer led to a virtual agrarian revolution in the mid-1970s. This revolution was biochemically based and augmented by plastic water conservation systems. There was a major change from traditional earth-furrow irrigation systems to plastic pipe drip irrigation. High-yield hybrid strains with saline-resistant properties replaced older breeds and inorganic fertilisers were introduced.[15] The improvements which occurred can be classified as a vegetable crop variation of the field crop 'Green Revolution' which swept through South East Asia and Latin America between the mid-1960s and early 1970s. It was based on high-yield varieties of rice and wheat augmented by forms of intermediate technology.[16] The technology transfer in the Jordan Valley had low capitalisation costs since the technology was intermediate and did not directly consume energy. It did, however, significantly increase annual production input costs which are recurrent and subject to inflationary spirals due to world market pricing. At the time of their introduction these improvements were within the foreseeable financial capacity of the majority of peasant farmers in the region, although in order to purchase the equipment they had to raise money through foreign-funded aid grants, savings, loans and credit.

The most important effects of these transfers were:

(a) The technology introduced was labour-saving in the early and mid-season. Labour time was thus saved in field preparation, weeding and irrigation preparation. Because drip irrigation is water conserving and because the military authorities' water restrictions refer to volume and not area under irrigation, farmers were able to bring most, if not all, of their arable land under irrigated production. Drip irrigation can also be used in hilly areas which permitted an increase in the area of irrigated land.

(b) Because there are acute problems with water and ground salinity in the region, tomato and eggplant specialisation became inevitable. These are the two vegetables with high-yield varieties which are at the same time resistant to saline conditions.

(c) The introduction of intermediate drip irrigation technology, chemical fertilisers and hybrid plants increased crop tonnage per dunum of tomatoes and eggplants by between 500 and 800 per cent. This initially made farming very attractive to peasant farmers, landlords and commission agents alike. In the early phase of these introductions farming was both more profitable and more productive.

(d) The 'Green Revolution' in Jordan Valley agriculture, as well as making it one of the most developed regions in the Middle East, has made peasant farmers much more dependent on the market. The number and extent of market transactions has intensified and all farm inputs now have to be purchased at international prices. Previously, most seeds, fertilisers and simple equipment would have been produced on the farm or bought in the vicinity.

(e) Output as well as input costs have increased with improved productivity. Transportation, labour, packaging and exportation costs have all risen.

It was hoped by developmentalists that the increase in productivity, trade and capital flows engendered by technological improvements would begin to offset the worst aspects of poverty and underdevelopment. And in Zbeidat, at least, during the period 1980 to 1981 it appeared outwardly that important steps in the eradication of rural poverty were under way. During this period the villagers increased their disposable income considerably. They were able to raise enough money, and to get permission from the Israeli authorities, to build larger houses with bedrooms, kitchens and, often, inside toilets. Plans were well advanced for the introduction of a gravitational piped water system which would supply all houses in the village. Electricity supply was also updated and improved by the purchase of a new generator.

Improvements could not be sustained, however. When I made a field visit to Zbeidat in May 1984, local farmers reported the season had been the worst in living memory. They received only IS 60-5 for a 15 kilogram box of tomatoes and IS 30 for a similar crate of eggplants.[17] Farmers were not allowed to sell any of their produce in Israel and exports through Jordan were held up until February by Jordanian import restrictions. By the time the Jordanian market opened up, Zbeidat eggplants and tomatoes were beginning to rot in the fields. Farmers lucky enough to sell their produce in Jordan received only JD 0.030 for a 12 kilogram box of tomatoes. A number of farmers I interviewed said they had exported 1,200 kilograms of tomatoes to Amman on which they made a net loss of JD 10 after transport, marketing and porterage costs.

The reasons for such poor returns were partly climatic. The 1984 season finished two months earlier than usual due to adverse weather conditions. There was a negligible amount of rainfall during the growing season and this affected plant quality. Further, the Jordan Valley dried out faster than is normal because the previous winter was warm and dry. In a normal season farmers would be harvesting plants until April or May. However, eggplants and tomatoes rotted because of the combined heat and aridity whose effects are intensified by salinity.

Because of the disastrous season farmers became indebted once more. One informant, a tenant farmer, showed me bills and receipts for over JD 1,000 which he had to repay to the region's largest landlord, a Nablus-based merchant. The bills covered all farm inputs: fertilisers, insecticides, plastic sheeting, drip irrigation equipment and the hire of tractors for ploughing and the laying out of plastic sheeting. This particular farmer considered himself lucky to owe so little. Other farmers owed as much as JD 3,000 and most were indebted to the tune of around JD 2,000. The farmers we spoke to said that in previous bad seasons when they used the old techniques they had accumulated debts of around JD 200. A debt of JD 2,000 was previously unheard of and almost unimaginable.

All the farmers were deeply concerned about the implications for the future, since they claimed that they did not have enough money to support their families, let alone pay off their debts. The fears were well-grounded. In the 1985 season a small independent farmer working 40 dunums could expect to make a profit of approximately JD 4,000. This may sound quite substantial but it should be remembered that this sum has to be shared in a household containing betweeen four and six adult members. Moreover, Zbeidat farm units are on average around 20 dunums. More importantly, Zbeidat farmers are not independent smallholders. The majority are involved in sharecropping compacts which means they have to pay 50 per cent of their net yields to landlords. Thus, unless repayment of these loans is met from hidden sources the farm income of Zbeidati sharecroppers is unlikely to be adequate to repay their loans fully. Structural indebtedness is the likely outcome.

This cautionary tale is not unfamiliar. There is a great deal of literature on the aftermath of the 'Green Revolution' from South East Asia and Latin America, which relates a series of similar cases. It clearly shows that the 'Green Revolution' technology has brought economic benefits to a limited group (by and large the middle peasantry, large landlords and agrarian merchant capitalists) while the long-term effect on the small peasantry has been the intensification of poverty, de-peasantisation and proletarianisation.[18] A familiarity with this literature on the part of the development agencies working in the West Bank would certainly not have solved the situation in the Jordan Valley, but it could have curbed the worst excesses of their policies and allowed them to focus more clearly on existing social relations as the root of the problem of poverty and underdevelopment.

III. PEASANT CLASSES, MERCANTILE CAPITAL AND THE EXTRACTION OF ECONOMIC SURPLUS

I have referred to the peasantry throughout this paper as if it were a homogeneous social group. This is a useful shorthand but the peasantry is not a single classification. It includes a number of distinct forms of relations of production and class. In the Jordan Valley there are three forms of land tenure: small holding, cash tenancy and sharecropping, which for all practical purposes we can treat as three forms of class relations of production. Each type of tenure has distinct ways in which the economic surplus is transferred from one class to another within the actual relations of production. These processes are conventionally referred to as economic exploitation, i.e. exploitation mediated through the relations of production.[19]

In small holding production there is no economic exploitation at the level of production relations *per se*, since there is no transfer of surplus product between social classes. The small holding family does not pay rent or service dues and works its own land. Exploitation occurs inside the household and is based on the sexual division of labour and patriarchal control of property.

In cash tenancy a portion of the farm product is syphoned off in the form of rent. This form of exploitation is properly termed rentierism. Rentier capitalism has largely failed to develop in the Jordan Valley for the reasons mentioned above, namely, the absence of a real estate market in farm land. Such rentierism as does exist is diffuse and there is no extensive land renting by large private owners. The major rentier in the north Jordan Valley is the Israeli military government which, for very specific historical reasons, rents lands to the village of Zbeidat at nominal rates.[20]

In sharecropping there is direct economic exploitation and economic transfer at the level of production relations.[21] Sharecropping is a contractual relationship between the peasant producers and their landlord. Historically there were significant variations in the forms which sharecropping took in Palestine but today we can identify three distinct forms of contract:

(a) The most widespread form is where the sharecroppers provide their own and their families' labour and additional wage labour if needed during the harvest season. The landlord provides land, water, water pump (if required) and fuel for the pump. Seeds, fertiliser, insecticides, drip irrigation equipment and all other inputs are purchased jointly. The final crop is shared between the landlord and the tenant on a fifty-fifty basis, normally set at the market price. The ATF survey showed that 85 per cent of sharecroppers in the villages of the northern part of the Jordan Valley had this form of contract.

(b) Nine per cent of sharecroppers in the valley have a contract in which they provide their own and their families' labour plus wage labour if required and the landlord provides all inputs. Under this type of contract the tenant receives one-third and the landlord two-thirds of the final crop.

(c) In this form of contract the landlord only provides the land and the sharecropper finances all inputs and labour. On the basis of this contract the landlord receives 15 per cent and the sharecropper 85 per cent of the net yield. The ATF survey revealed only one farmer with this form of contract.

In the seven villages studied the ATF found a total of 566 individual land tenures: 72 per cent of these were shareholdings, 17 per cent small holdings, 8 per cent cash tenancies and 3 per cent shepherd holdings. These figures refer to tenures and not individual farmers. It is often the case that one individual may occupy more than one tenure or agrarian class location. In Zbeidat, for example, it is common for a peasant to be a cash tenant and a sharecropper simultaneously, renting land from the Israeli Department of Absentee Property for cash payment and sharecropping for an absentee landlord.

It is my contention that, by and large, although economic relations of exploitation and transfers of economic surplus through class relations exist at the level of economic production, and the level of exploitation is particularly intense in sharecropping, this is not the main mechanism of surplus transfer and exploitation in the Jordan Valley. The main beneficiaries of technological improvement and increased productivity have not been the peasantry or their landlords, but urban-based mercantile capitalists. Therefore, by implication, the most important mechanism of surplus transfer and economic exploitation is mercantile control over agrarian markets. The most intense form of exploitation of the peasantry occurs when they act as consumers and sellers, rather than in their role as economic producers. I showed previously how technological transfers increased the degree of commoditisation, inasmuch as the peasants' market relations as consumers and as producers of goods for market sale have become both more extensive and intensive. Almost all farm production now enters the market and there is a minimal amount of household subsistence production. The manner in which the economic surplus is transferred from the peasantry to mercantile capital is as follows: at the end of the crop cycle the peasant encounters mercantile capital in the form of the commission agent, who operates as a wholesaler and auctioneer in the *hisbeh* (fruit and vegetable market). These markets are located in the urban centres. The commission agent sells the crop at auction and receives between 5 and 12 per cent of the price. The agent also provides a number of other services which serve to bind the peasant. For instance, tomatoes sent to sale have to be packed in regulation boxes which the commission agent sells to the farmer for IS 40 and buys back for IS 35 at the end of the season. In the course of

255

a season the IS 5 profit per box is multiplied hundreds of thousands of times for the larger merchants. Commission agents are, too, the main transport hauliers and peasant farmers also have to pay porterage costs. The big commission agents are also the main dealers in seeds, fertilisers, insecticides, plastic sheeting and drip irrigation equipment. These market relations are often reinforced through patronage and patriarchal networks.

In the Jordan Valley there is a visible trend towards the horizontal integration of the market and sales functions in a number of powerful merchant families. This is particularly the case for one such family whose key members are commission agents for 26 per cent of all farmers in the Jordan Valley. This horizontal integration incorporates the auctioning of crops, provision of transport and packing services, sale of agricultural inputs and the renting of farm machinery. Merchant capital, therefore, profits from every peasant money transaction.

Although the process of horizontal integration is well established, monopoly pricing does not occur as long as the peasants remain independent of direct control by their commission agents. If they are not subject to direct control they can sell their produce through the agent from whom they get the best commission and buy their inputs at the lowest price.

Recently, however, there has also been a much more pernicious development – the combination of horizontal and vertical integration. The commission agent is becoming the landlord to a significant number of tenants. In this process the market and production relations of exploitation become interlocked and the peasants' room for manoeuvre in the free market is curtailed. The commission agents use their position as landlords to force their tenants to buy only from them. Under these conditions the monopoly pricing of farm inputs above free market prices becomes established. The agents have also exploited their dual positions as landlords and suppliers to develop a series of semi-legal mechanisms to drain the peasantry's financial resources. One example is the system of 'enforced credit' where the peasant has to buy goods on credit even if they can afford to pay cash. They therefore have to pay premiums in the form of interest rates.

As long as these relations develop unchecked it is unlikely that the Jordan Valley peasantry will break out of the cycle of poverty and underdevelopment. The poverty cycle is not a natural catastrophe over which there is no social control. The poverty of the majority in the Jordan Valley, as elsewhere in the third world is the obverse side of the wealth of a powerful few. Poverty and wealth are interrelated aspects of economic and social class relations. Any serious challenge to the causes of poverty must take into account that it will inevitably come up against powerful vested interests who will not wish to see their ability to control capital accumulation diminish.

These last points take discussion of genuine social and economic development far beyond the traditional diffusionist agrarian reform strategy. They also take the debate beyond nationalist liberation ideology and its political strategies which seek to put off discussion of economic change and transformation until after the liberation struggle had been won.

If development is to promote the transformation of agrarian poverty and underdevelopment it must challenge both conditions and causes simultaneously. This means challenging colonialism and class exploitation. Because of the mutually reinforcing relations between colonialism and class structure, this struggle cannot be put off until the creation of a national state but has to be fought simultaneously and in the context of a national liberation programme. It must also constitute the basis for a genuine and effective development strategy.[22]

NOTES

1. S. Tamari and R. Giacaman (eds), *Zbeidat: The Social Impact of Drip Irrigation on a Palestinian Peasant Community in the Jordan Valley* (Birzeit University Documentation and Research Centre, Birzeit, 1980).

2. The statistical information in this paper was gathered in the course of an ATF development survey (unpublished) carried out by the author and Mary Hovsepian in 1983. Statistical abstracts of the survey will be published at the end of 1986. Much of the non-statistical data was gathered by the author on field visits since that time.

3. ATF statistical abstracts (forthcoming).

4. Ian Roxborough, *Theories of Underdevelopment* (London, 1979), pp. 42-59.

5. Ibid., pp. 30-1. Some Marxists, particularly in the Latin American communist parties in the 1960s, had similar strategic agendas in which a leading role was assigned to the national bourgeoisie, with a bourgeois-democratic revolution being seen as a necessary stage on the road to socialism. See Andre Gunder Frank, *Capitalism and Underdevelopment in Latin America* (New York, 1969), p. 225.

6. W.W. Harris, *Taking Root: Israeli Settlements in the West Bank, the Golan and Gaza-Sinai, 1967-1980* (Chichester, 1980), pp.105-23. 'Nahal' is the acronym of the Fighting Pioneer Youth, a division of the Israeli army which combines military service with agricultural training and is often deployed in new settlements.

7. For a general description of the situation see Ibrahim Matar, 'Israeli settlements and Palestinian rights' in N. Aruri (ed.), *Occupation: Israel Over*

257

Palestine (Zed Press, London, 1984), pp. 126-8, and Meron Benvenisti, *The West Bank Data Base Project* (Washington D.C., 1984), pp. 30-5.

8. Matar, 'Israeli settlements', p. 131.

9. Ibid., p. 129.

10. Translations of these military orders are available in English from the Palestinian human rights organisation Al-Haq (formerly Law in the Service of Man), P.O.B. 1431, Ramallah, West Bank, via Israel.

11. *Al Fajr Palestinian Weekly,* 9 and 16 November 1984.

12. These comparisons are made between ATF survey figures and official Israeli statistics.

13. For an initial appraisal of these projects see Peter Oakley, 'The Jordan Valley: drip irrigation for small farmers', *Reading Rural Development Communications Bulletin,* no. 5 (November 1978).

14. For a critical assessment of the diffusionist model see Alain de Janvry, *The Agrarian Question and Reformism in Latin America* (Baltimore, 1981).

15. Salim Tamari, 'The agrarian system' in Tamari and Giacaman (eds), *Zbeidat.*

16. For a clear account of the biochemical basis of the 'Green Revolution' technology which is accessible to the non-scientist see Terry Byres and Ben Crow, *The Green Revolution in India* (Milton Keynes, 1983), pp. 9-16.

17. During May 1984 £1.00 = IS 250.00.

18. The issue is considered in greater detail in A. Pollock, 'Some aspects of selected strategies for rural development and an outline of a socialist alternative', *Birzeit Research Review,* no. 3 (1986). See also Andrew Pearce, *Seeds of Plenty, Seeds of Want* (Oxford, 1980) and Keith Griffin, *The Political Economy of Agrarian Change* (London, 1974).

19. The theoretical basis of this approach is developed in A. Pollock, 'Sharecropping in the north Jordan Valley: social relations of production and reproduction' in Kathy and Pandeli Glavanis (eds), *Agrarian Relations in the Middle East* (provisional title) (London, forthcoming).

20. For details see Tamari, 'The agrarian system', pp. 3-9.

21. See, Pollock, 'Sharecropping in the north Jordan Valley', pp. 16-32.

22. For a discussion of the elements of a socialist development strategy see Pollock, 'Some aspects of selected strategies'.

12

Dispossession and Pauperisation: The Palestinian Economy Under Occupation

Yusif A. Sayigh

I. INTRODUCTION

This paper deals with the economy of those parts of Palestine which were occupied by Israel in June 1967, namely the West Bank and Gaza Strip[1] and attempts to identify and assess the overall economic impact of occupation. I propose to establish two central points:

(a) The economies of the occupied territories suffer from heavy, far-reaching and debilitating dependence on the Israeli economy. This dependence, however, is so special and atypical, and reaches so far beyond the specifications attached to the paradigm of dependency in the mainstream development literature, that it is imperative to qualify the notion heavily if it is not to be misleading, and to search for a more apt characterisation of the state of the occupied economies.

(b) The economies of the West Bank and the Gaza Strip have suffered pauperisation over the years, notwithstanding some outward appearances of prosperity and Israeli claims of economic well-being under occupation.[2]

II. DEPENDENCY AND BEYOND: THE POLITICS AND ECONOMICS OF DISPOSSESSION

Most of the surveys and analyses of the economies of the West Bank and the Gaza Strip explicitly or implicitly suggest the heavy dependency of these economies on the economy of Israel. Even some Israeli social scientists have underlined the state of dependence, with criticism of the Israeli motives and policies that have brought it about.[3] But frequently emphasis is placed by Israeli writers on the interdependence between the economies of the occupier and the occupied. This is understandable, as the notion of interdependence provides a convenient euphemism to sweep under the carpet the notorious aspects of dependence.

I will not describe here conventional theories of dependence. The ground has been well covered. It will be sufficient for present purposes to indicate below the main areas where the dependence of the occupied territories is most clearly observable. My concern will essentially be, first, to demonstrate those aspects and areas where the relationship between the economies of the occupied and the occupier radically deviates from the conventional pattern of dependence, and secondly, to identify the real relationship beyond dependence and its determinants.

1. Trade

This is perhaps the most obvious and measurable area of dependence which, together with the employment of Palestinians in the Israeli economy, has received most attention. The West Bank and Gaza Strip constitute a virtual 'captive market' for Israel's exports. For several years now, the occupied territories have been the second largest importer from Israel, after the United States. In 1983, these territories imported US$ 680.5 million worth of Israeli goods, while the United States imported US$ 1,329.2 million. (Israel's total commodity exports were valued at US$ 5,574.3 million.)[4] Commodity imports from Israel constitute just over 90 per cent of total imports to the occupied territories.

Significantly, industrial imports to each of the two occupied areas are roughly seven times as large as agricultural imports.[5] By itself, this fact suggests the extreme modesty and sluggishness of the manufacturing sector in the occupied territories. This verdict acquires greater poignancy when read against the background of deliberate Israeli policies and measures which block the expansion of Palestinian manufacturing industry, and make it extremely difficult for Arab importers to buy goods from other countries. On top of this, as Sheila Ryan says, the occupied territories market is 'a convenient dumping ground for shoddy Israeli industrial products which could not compete with the local manufacturers of the industrialised countries of Europe and North America'.[6]

Dependence in the area of trade can also be seen, though not as dramatically, with respect to exports from the occupied territories. Israel absorbs 73 per cent of the total commodity exports of these territories, with the value of industrial exports six times as large as that of agricultural exports.[7] However, the predominance of industrial commodities in the composition of total exports, like the proportion of these going to Israel, is misleading in itself and has led to the superficial assertion that the two parties to the exchange are interdependent. By far the largest part of Palestinian industrial exports consists of re-exported Israeli goods. These were originally imported by subcontractors in unfinished form. They are finally sold in the Israeli market or exported elsewhere. This exchange makes only a modest contribution to the manufacturing process in the West Bank and the Gaza Strip, and to the value added accruing to them. More seriously it constitutes misleading evidence of interdependence between the two parties concerned. It is even more misleading when interpreted as an instance of dependence by the occupier on the occupied, as it has been by some analysts. The former, through the subcontracting arrangement, essentially capitalises on the fact that labour is cheaper in the occupied territories than in Israel, and therefore takes more surplus value from the occupied economies as a result.

Two other relevant considerations stand out: first, that the West Bank and the Gaza Strip have very little choice with respect to the subcontracting and re-export relationship, having been deprived of most of their freedom of economic (and essentially, of political) decision making and action, and of inputs vital for the independent development of manufacturing industry; secondly, to the extent that the relationship is forced on the West Bank and the Gaza Strip, the structure of their economies is so distorted as to suit primarily the interests and priorities of the Israeli economy.

2. Labour

Because the occupied economies are forcibly restricted in size, range and rate of expansion, and their structure is deliberately warped to serve the purposes of the occupier, employment opportunities grow much more slowly than the labour supply. There are as a result several areas of structural deformation. These include:

(a) Agriculture, where land expropriation/confiscation and water appropriation and control by Israel have over the years forced a substantial proportion of the agricultural labour force out of agriculture.

(b) Handicrafts, where hundreds of craftsmen have had to give up their traditional occupations both because of the stiff competition of cheap Israeli manufactured substitutes, and because the Israelis have diverted a substantial part of the tourist business away from Palestinian markets and tourist sites.

(c) Manufacturing industry, a potentially significant labour-absorbing sector, whose growth and diversification have been severely blocked by restrictive Israeli policies.

(d) The civil service, which is now largely run by Israeli personnel.

(e) Construction, which would absorb a lot of labour were the occupation authorities to allow housing activities to expand in response to the pressure of the market.

Together, these structural deviations and distortions have resulted in the loss of work opportunities for roughly half the work force. The larger part of the shortfall - about two-fifths of the work force - has been absorbed in Israel. A total of 87,000 Arab workers from the West Bank and the Gaza Strip are officially reported to have been employed in 1983 in Israel. This constitutes 37.8 per cent of the 232,500 total of employed persons (32.7 and 46.5 per cent for the West Bank and Gaza Strip respectively).[8] But these data are widely believed to understate the facts. The migrant work force is engaged in menial, low-skill jobs in Israel; it comprises many teenagers; and it is either forced to commute back and forth between residence and place of work in great discomfort, or else to sleep illegally in Israel in squalid and unhygienic conditions, and thus to risk harassment by the police. That part of the labour supply not employed in Israel (or the occupied territories) tends to emigrate after exhausting its meagre savings and endurance while looking for gainful employment.

Some analysts see in the employment of occupied territories Palestinians by the Israeli economy a case of dependency by the latter on the West Bank and the Gaza Strip - a fact thought to balance the dependence of these territories on Israel. Others consider the employment an example of interdependence - indeed, some see it as a healthy development potentially conducive to peaceful co-existence and co-operation between Israel and a hoped-for Arab state.[9]

I consider these interpretations to be utterly fanciful, motivated at best by wishful thinking, if not a deliberate effort to confuse. The employment of Palestinians in Israel is of minor significance for the Israeli economy: it is not as crucial relatively speaking as the employment of some 40 per cent of its work force is to the economies of the West Bank and the Gaza Strip. Furthermore, none of the Palestinian labourers is engaged in the crucial, strategic branches of any sector, and none in a highly skilled capacity (except in construction). But to carry the argument for the employment in question to the realm of politico-economic problem solving, as Ja'far does in the *Khamsin* correspondence referred to (see note 9), or as Tuma and Darin-Drabkin do in their book when they investigate the feasibility of a Palestinian state in the West Bank and the Gaza Strip, is to ignore the moral and economic, as well as the national, implications of continued dependence of many thousands of Palestinians on the Israeli economy for work. In effect, this would codify dependence and endow it with praiseworthy virtues.

3. Finance

In typical instances of the dependency of peripheral countries on industrial countries at the centre, the former obtain a significant part of their investment finance and working capital from the latter. External finance is thus one of the symbols and bonds of dependence, and it constitutes one of the distinguishing developments of imperialism in Lenin's formulation.[10] However, one of the atypical aspects of the dependence of the occupied territories is that Israel provides virtually no investment finance. This is in spite of the fact that Arab banks in operation before June 1967 remain closed and only in the late 1980s have two been allowed to re-open and operate under especially restrictive conditions.[11] The economies of the West Bank and the Gaza Strip have had, therefore, basically to depend on financial flows from (the East Bank of) Jordan, the substantial inflow of remittances from West Bank and Gaza Strip residents working abroad to their families back home, and, since 1979, on aid from the Jordanian-Palestinian Joint Committee for the Support of Steadfastness (fed by a special fund established and financed by Arab governments). These flows, plus local savings, make up the resources available for investment and working capital. The instruments that manage the transfer and circulation of these resources fall into two categories: a large number of institutions (municipal councils, co-operative societies, and the like) through which funds are received and allocated; and a number of small credit and money changing businesses.

The stringency of financial transfers from Israel is a matter of policy. The observer is faced with a paradox here: on the one hand, the absence of Arab banks, and therefore the dependence of Palestinians, of necessity, on Israeli banks and on the other hand, the restriction by these banks of their operations in the occupied territories, through the application by Israel of quantitative and qualitative limits and very high charges and interest rates. A situation has deliberately been created where finance is restricted at both ends: the Palestinian and the

Israeli. In fact, Israel itself benefits from the outflow from the West Bank and the Gaza Strip into its money market of a significant portion of the foreign exchange coming in.

4. Infrastructural services

In terms of services the occupied territories basically have to depend on themselves, or suffer serious shortages. There is a wide discrepancy between the very limited road building or maintenance undertaken to serve Palestinian areas and communities, and the elaborate highway and road grid designed and built to connect the occupied territories, and especially the Jewish settlements there, with Israel, and to link the settlements together. The same can be said of the inadequacy of the water network serving Palestinian (especially rural) areas, compared with the water system that serves Jerusalem and the Jewish settlements. This is apart from Israel's takeover of Arab water resources as we shall see later. The occupying power follows a restrictive electrification policy which forces the occupied territories into total dependence on the Israeli grid.

Israel's negligence of the social infrastructure is even more glaring. It makes minimal efforts in the fields of education and health. But this does have the silver lining of promoting self-reliance. In order to maintain the facilities which existed before Israeli occupation, and to add to them, Palestinians have had to act independently with the financial help of Palestinians abroad and other Arabs, as well as some help from international bodies. The performance is more marked in the field of education than that of health. On balance, so far as physical and social infrastructural services are concerned, dependence is much less significant than expected. This is not because Israel does not want to subject the territories to extended dependence; it is rather because it wants them to go without much of the infrastructure input in question to the extent possible while making it difficult for them to undertake the provision of these services themselves to the extent desired.

III. DEPENDENCY AND DISPOSSESSION

1. The usurpation of power

The identification so far undertaken of the areas of dependency would, if taken by itself, suggest an overall state of partial or spotty dependence. But it would be erroneous to draw this kind of conclusion. For a balanced conclusion it is necessary to look at the global impact of Israeli intentions, policies and behaviour on the economies of the West Bank and the Gaza Strip in two respects: the degree of freedom available in economic decision-making, and the availability of the means needed to translate such decision-making into concrete programmes and projects aimed at far-reaching improvement in the economic performance of the population, and in consequence on its living standard and quality of life.

The weight of evidence shows that Israel has largely succeeded in its determined attempt to tie the economies of the occupied territories to its own. From the nature and extent of Israel's policies and actions, and more pragmatically by the results achieved, a three-faceted intention emerges: to severely restrict the expansion and diversification of the occupied economies; to keep the two areas as largely non-communicating entities; and to further fragment and segment each of them internally. In this way the stunted economies both complement the Israeli economy and are also heavily dependent upon it.[12]

The exploitation of the occupied territories is effected by Israel as an entire social formation – by its government, its capitalists and its labour alike. The shades of difference between the behaviour of Israeli management and labour only marginally qualify, but do not invalidate, this statement. The Palestinians, who suffered external colonialism under the British, suffered it again at the hands of the Zionist movement as an aggressive force from outside and now suffer it at the hands of the Israeli state as an occupier. But, in this last instance, and within the framework of Zionist ideology, they suffer it as internal colonialism beyond the purely military/political aspects of the occupation.[13] This internal colonialism is much more destructive than the normal form of external colonialism, since it has combined the uprooting, dispossession and displacement of the national population with the imposition of a stunting state of dependence on those who remain in the country. (Roughly half the Palestinians are now in the diaspora, after the Zionist takeover of most of Palestine in 1948, and of the rest of the country in 1967.) Israeli occupation has usurped the power of decision-making of the occupied through its effective and comprehensive web of policies, laws and regulations, measures and court rulings and orders. In addition, Israel tightens the noose around the economies of the West Bank and the Gaza Strip by withholding such essential means of economic growth as finance, capital goods, raw materials, licenses and vital infrastructural services.

2. The nature of Palestinian dependency

The usurpation of the power of economic and political decision-making is only one aspect of the particularity of dependence in the occupied territories. This particularity is important enough to deserve some discussion. I proposed in the Introduction that the paradigm of dependency does not adequately describe the case of the occupied territories. This is partly because this case has features that do not constitute components of the paradigm as generally established in the relevant literature (notwithstanding the special nuances of different subschools)[14] and partly because the case is one where the crisis of the occupied territories goes beyond dependence into outright, crude and brutal dispossession. Before discussing the nature and extent of dispossession in the last part of this section, we will now turn to an identification of those features of the present case which deviate widely from the recognised features of dependence.

The primary deviation, and the one with the most serious implications, is the fact that the peripheral entity is a part (and the smaller one at that) of the same geographical, and until fairly recently, the same political unit as the centre to which it is now tied with chains of dependence. In the latter part of the twentieth century, virtually all social formations that are likewise tied are sovereign states or at least on their way to political independence – all, except for the black majority of South Africa. Like it, the Palestinian community in the occupied territories is subjected to internal colonialism that has emerged from the roots of external colonialism, to forced dependence and to dispossession.[15]

This distinction is significant and ought to be recognised.[16] Dependence elsewhere is not today physically forced on the countries concerned, nor is dispossession or primitive appropriation of national resources and property practised, although historically they were in most instances. Current dependence is brought about through capitalisation on the historical process of colonialism and the ties it forged over generations or centuries in the areas of trade, finance, manufacturing, exploitation of natural resources, as well as the building of a dualistic structure – to say nothing of political, cultural and technological ties of bondage. The relationship has become *sui generis*, because of the continued dominance of the world capitalist system with its many strong tentacles of control: the power of inertia and despondency lulling the dependent countries into inaction or half-hearted action to pull themselves out of dependence and move gradually into self-reliant development, individually or regionally

and the collusion often worked out between dominant economic forces in the industrial capitalist country and the dependent country concerned.

The occupied territories do not have the option of action to free themselves of dependence. Consequently, their economies are twisted, distorted and stunted, not through the working of the invisible hand of market forces, but through imposition and the visible hand of the occupying power. This stands in sharp contrast with other cases of 'conventional' dependence where the industrial capitalist country has in most instances promoted the development of one or a few productive sectors and of some part of the physical infrastructure, even if within a dualistic framework and essentially to serve its own interests.

Another structural feature of the occupied territories which is not typical is the fragmentation or segmentation of each of the economies through the elaborate road and water systems; the interposition by design of Jewish settlements among population centres and across communication lines; the expropriation/confiscation of vast areas of land which shatters the unity of territory[17] and the blocking of free association, whether of companies into large economically viable groupings, or of labour and professional groups. At the macro-level, segmentation takes the form of restrictions that minimise sectoral complementarity and intensive interaction. Illustrations include the difficulties encountered in the establishment of agro-industries, of banks which could promote extensive sectoral linkages, of hospitals, co-operatives, laboratories, etc. which could absorb large numbers of trained personnel. To all this must be added the fact that occupation has cut the West Bank and the Gaza Strip off from other Arab countries, thus narrowing the economic base and compressing the size of the economy.

A paradox worth noting is that the economies of the occupied territories are dependent on an economy which is itself heavily dependent on an industrial country – the United States. Israel's dependence is mostly financial, but it has other economic and technological, but above all military, political and diplomatic aspects. Two observations are relevant with respect to the explanation of the paradox. The first is that Israel can enforce dependence on the occupied territories, in spite of its own dependence, only because of its overpowering military strength and the American support it gets, in the face of the absence of Arab unity and resolve. It thus barters military strength for economic weakness. Otherwise it would be unable to impose dependence on the Palestinian economy, or any other economy with as much dynamism and resourcefulness.

The second observation is that Israel tries to lighten its dependence, in its own eyes and those of the United States, by offering its services as the guardian of American interests in the Arab region, and by claiming that Arab alignment with America is in part a function of Arab fears of Israel's reaction.[18] In addition, Israel pays in kind from time to time, by passing on to the United States military and technological intelligence obtained from the field, mostly through the capture of Soviet arms or the decoding of electronic computer systems in Soviet rockets, tanks or planes. Through this two-way flow, the relationship tends to resemble some kind of interdependence rather than one-way dependence.

We have tried to show that countries suffering dependency in the contemporary world have basic political and economic features not shared by the occupied territories. These include sovereignty and self-determination; a large degree of freedom of decision-making; integration within the social formation; ability to develop structures and sectors in the manner thought best to serve national interests; ability to exploit natural resources; ability to nurture national culture and social organisation; a large measure of security and ability to draw up development plans and programmes as nationally desired with a large measure of freedom to implement them. The critical difference between countries enjoying such advantages and the occupied territories is the political, socio-cultural and economic dispossession to which the occupied territories under discussion have been and continue to be subjected. This is in addition to the particular brand of dependence forced on them by the occupying power. It is to be recalled that the term dispossession as used in this paper is meant to designate the syndrome of dispossession, uprooting and displacement in its entirety.

3. Dispossession

Crippling as the state of Palestinian dependency is, it is not as economically, socio-culturally and politically destructive as the dispossession which has been practised systematically and relentlessly by Israel since the start of the occupation as a continuous process rather than as a one-time act of vengefulness. This statement may seem harsh, but the record of Israel justifies it. Over the years of occupation, the Palestinians in the West Bank and Gaza Strip have been dispossessed and deprived of a large part of their national, collective and individual political, social and cultural rights and freedoms. Furthermore, the deprivation extends beyond current rights and freedoms to reach into the future. Hence the need to go beyond economic dispossession, which has received a large measure of attention so far, into non-economic areas.[19] After all, economic dispossession only became possible because of political and socio-cultural dispossession. And it is the latter that explains the particularity of Palestinian economic dependence on Israel, as we have indicated.

It is necessary at this point to emphasise that dispossession in its broad sense has been a central, crucial and persistent objective of Zionist and subsequently Israeli state policy, from the first Zionist Congress in 1897, down to Israel Koenig, Rabbi Meir Kahane, Yuval Neeman, Menachem Begin and other Zionist fundamentalists today.[20] The justification for reference to history is that the experience of the occupied territories since 1967 falls squarely within the continuum of long-term Zionist objectives and the policies that translate them from one phase to another. Yet, while these objectives and policies have never been secret, their self-centred nature has not deterred the Zionists, and now the Israelis, from claiming that they would be beneficial to the natives (in Herzl's terms) or to the non-Jews (in official Israeli terms). The next section will be devoted to an examination of the validity of this assertion, but for the moment we will focus on the locus of the major areas of dispossession:

(a) The denial of sovereignty with all that it implies for the individual Palestinian, for associations of individuals and for society as a whole. Through this denial, Israel usurps the Palestinians' power to take political decisions, without consulting them and against their basic rights, demands and interests. This is at the heart of all dispossession, but not the only expression of it. It involves Israel's power to approve or deny associations, to dissolve ones already in existence, to cancel the results of municipal elections, to bar political association and so on.

(b) The destruction of thousands of houses, and large areas of refugee camps, especially in the Gaza Strip, in individual or collective punishment for, or as a precaution against, security violations. This measure, which has uprooted many thousands and rendered them homeless, has led to social disruption, loss of roots and considerable anguish, in addition to the economic destruction involved and – above all – to the tangible degree of depopulation resulting.

(c) The deportation of thousands of Palestinians – union leaders, educators, politicians, mayors, professionals and activists in general.[21] The obvious and immediate aim is the depletion of leadership in the occupied territories; the longer-term objective is the gradual depopulation of the land. However, the process is always rationalised as one necessitated by security considerations (as we shall see, several measures operate together to promote depopulation).

(d) The harassment of educational institutions, from the intermediate level upwards.[22] This is only part of a comprehensive process of harassment which constitutes an incursion into the cultural heritage and institutions of the Palestinians, involving strict censorship and control of teaching and reading material, especially in Arabic. In many instances the harassment has taken the form of outright closure of educational institutions and of newspapers, as well as detention of individuals for long periods, with or without trial. Many Palestinians have found it impossible to bear the pressure and have left the country.

(e) The proletarianisation of a large segment of the population as a result of deliberate policies. Foremost among these in impact are: land expropriation/confiscation; the appropriation and control of water resources beyond what had been developed and used in 1967; the severe containment and stunting of manufacturing industry; the neglect of the institutions of technical training; the repressive control of the building industry; incursion into the Palestinian tourist industry; exposing Palestinian handicrafts to stiff competition from cheap Israeli goods, and denying them government support and, generally, the harassment of economic enterprise through deterrent licensing requirements, deliberate bureaucratic delays, restriction of trade union and other types of association and the stringent squeeze on financial inflows.

Together, these factors have meant the uprooting of scores of thousands of gainfully employed Palestinians from their chosen occupations or jobs, and in effect steering most of them into less desired and secure employment, much if not all of it in the Israeli economy itself.[23] In extreme cases, many of the newly proletarianised have left the country altogether, thus possibly becoming the largest single component of those who have been pushed into emigration.

(f) Depopulation has left a deep mark on the demographic structure of the occupied territories. We need not go into any detailed discussion of the surprising phenomenon of a drop in the absolute size of the population between the war of June 1967 and the end of 1982, which reflects a negative rate of population increase in a community known to have a natural rate of net increase of about 3.5 per cent per annum. The drop has resulted from the outflow of over 700,000 Palestinians to other Arab and non-Arab countries. This left the population at the end of 1982 50,000 smaller than it was in early June

1967.[24] The emigration has not been the consequence of innocent economic factors, but the deliberate, energetic and ruthless application of Israeli policies bringing about the operation of the factors in question.[25]

(g) Another form of dispossession is the denial of respect to the Palestinians as human beings. This is not merely a case of verbal excess, as when, for instance, Rafael Eitan, former chief of staff of the Israeli army, stated that the Palestinians would be made to 'run about like drugged cockroaches inside a bottle';[26] or when David Hacohen, chairman (in 1973) of the Knesset foreign affairs committee, told a British parliamentary delegation on the subject of Palestinian refugees, 'But they are not human beings, they are not people, they are Arabs.'[27] Instead, we refer here to a more serious and continuous current of belief and feeling, whereby the Zionists/Israelis claim superiority over 'inferior' natives. This is expressed in many ways, and with varying degrees of harshness and lack of concern for the dignity and self-respect of the Palestinians.[28]

(h) The expropriation/confiscation of Arab land is dispossession in its most naked form. The act itself is very painful, but it becomes even more so when coupled with thinly disguised excuses like the non-exploitation of the land (when frequently the Israeli authorities themselves impede exploitation by fencing land off for military or public purposes; or when they appropriate the water needed for irrigation). It is most painful when it is effected through fraudulent means and the forging of documents, with the connivance of senior Israeli officials.[29] Many holdings have been expropriated/confiscated because Arab claims of ownership have not been accepted by the authorities, mostly because of the non-completion of land settlement-of-title operations before the British Mandate came to an end. Large tracts have also been expropriated/confiscated because Israel considered them to be in the state domain and itself, therefore, the rightful owner, while in fact they had been for generations or centuries the collective property of villages. But Palestinian losses in immovable property go beyond land, and the destruction of thousands of houses, to include the total destruction of hundreds of villages. Though the vast majority of these were in that part of Palestine occupied in 1948, a number stood in the part occupied in 1967.[30]

(i) The establishment of settlements on expropriated Arab land (in violation of the Geneva Conventions to which Israel is a signatory), of which over 130 have come into being since 1967 in the West Bank and the Gaza Strip,[31] is one more measure to make the process of Zionist colonisation irreversible and to leave the dispossessed with no redress. This is apart from the military motive of segmenting what remains of Arab Palestine and accelerating the process of depopulating the land after dispossessing the people.[32]

(j) The final major instance of dispossession is the takeover of most of the water resources of the occupied territories and the control of Arab water use. The mechanism for the dispossession consists of strict prohibition of the development by the Palestinians of any springs or other surface or underground water reserves not already tapped and under utilisation at the time of occupation in 1967; the prohibition of the utilisation of any quantities of water in excess of those drawn and utilised in 1967 in already developed sources; the prohibition of the further development of wells already in use. All this is in spite of the expanding needs of agriculture especially in view of the urgency to resort to irrigation to make up for the loss of land area through expropriation, as well as the expanding needs for domestic consumption. The water thus appropriated comes under Israel's sole control for allocation or conservation. Thus, while villages are deprived of much of their vital well and spring water and underground reserves, and suffer the sight of their crops drying up and dying, or have to cut down their own fruit trees, neighbouring Jewish settlements, built on expropriated Palestinian land, enjoy the luxury of swimming pools and abundant piped water for agriculture, industry and domestic use.[33]

The various strands of dependence and dispossession are closing tighter on Palestinian society and economy as Israel pursues the primary Zionist objective of the takeover of as much of Palestine with as few of the Palestinians as is possible. It is limited only by what is politically advisable and militarily achievable in the present international context. This objective necessitates that the economic conditions of the Arabs who remain be such that the community can survive but not prosper. In other words, Israel should be able to point to some outward indicators of well-being, without allowing the possibility of enough economic prosperity and social and political relaxation to make the Palestinians feel the 'pull' of their homeland more strongly than the 'push' of the hardships generated by dependence and dispossession. There is every indication that Israel has succeeded in its objective. Nevertheless, there is still need to examine closely the second proposition stated in the Introduction: that occupation has led to the pauperisation of the inhabitants of the West Bank and Gaza Strip. We use the term 'pauperisation' to express economic stagnation resulting from an economic performance below what, in all likelihood, would have been possible without occupation.

IV. OCCUPATION: PROSPERITY OR PAUPERISATION?

It is claimed by Israelis and Zionists (and perhaps with particular vigour by gentile Zionists) that Israel has brought prosperity to the territories under its occupation – indeed that the prosperity would not have been achieved in equal measure without the occupation. One variant of the claim is that the inhabitants of the occupied territories are economically better off than the populations of East Jordan, Syria and Lebanon – the natural reference group for the Palestinians.

1. Data

To test the validity and tenability of the claim in question, we will present two sets of data. Table 12.1 relates to the year 1948 (or 1950 in cases where statistical and other information is not available for 1948). Table 12.2 relates to 1983 (the most recent year for which most of the information compared is available). Comparisons will be made between economic and social performance of each economy at the initial and the terminal dates, and between the economies at each of these dates. Ideally, the components of each set of data ought to include not only the level of income per capita (or GNP per capita, as the case may be), but also such indicators as rates of enrolment in educational institutions, health services available per unit of population, life expectancy at birth, housing space per person, calorie intake per day, durable household equipment owned per household and so on. Unfortunately, such varied information is not uniformly available for all the countries concerned for 1983. Consequently, only those items of information that are available, measurable and comparable will be presented.

National income and GNP will be used for comparison, though these concepts are not interchangeable. This is justified, since a rather broad order of magnitude is all that is required for our purposes. The currency unit used for measurement is the US dollar in all instances. The conversion from local currency to dollars will be at the official rate or market rate, whichever predominated in the particular country at the time. Owing to the wide difference in the methods and bases of price index preparation from one country to another, all income units will be at current prices. Finally, the sources of the data presented will be indicated in the notes in every instance. The sources for 1948 or 1950 are much more varied, less reliable and more dependent on

Table 12.1

Palestine [34]

National income for 1945 = £P 62.80 million, or US$ 251.2 million (at £P 1.00 = US$ 4.00).

Arab population for 1945 = 1.256 million.
Therefore income per capita = £P 50 or US$ 200.

National income projected for 1948 at 5% per annum = £P 72.7 million or US$ 290.8 million.

Population projected for 1948 at 3% net increase per annum = 1.37 million. Therefore income per capita for 1948 = £P 53.06 or US$ 212.24. (This level is taken to apply to the inhabitants of the West Bank and Gaza Strip for 1948.)

Transjordan/East Jordan [35]

National income for 1948 for Transjordan (before the merger with East Palestine, that is, the West Bank) estimated roughly at £P 5.63 million (£P 1.00 = JD 1.000), or US$ 22.52 million (£P 1.00 = US$ 4.00 in 1948).

Population for 1948 estimated at 375,000.
Therefore, income per capita for 1948 = £P/JD 15, or US$ 60.

National income for Jordan (East and West Bank together), for 1952 = JD 44.5 million, or US$ 112 million (JD 1.00 = US$ 2.80 in 1950 and 1952); discounted for 1950 by 10% from the level in 1952, income = JD 40 million, of which about JD 25.9 million was generated in the West Bank (a population of 460,000 with an income per capita of £P/JD 56.3 - projected from the level in 1948; see data on Palestine). This leaves an income of JD 14.1 million generated on the East Bank, or US$ 39.48 million.

Population estimated at 725,000 in the East Bank in 1950, including the refugee component. Therefore income per capita in the East Bank for 1950 = JD 19.45 or US$ 54.46.

Syria [36]

National income for 1953 calculated at £S 2,263.5 million, discounted by 15.75% to set it back to 1950, = £S 1,955.5 million or US$ 535.75 million (US$ 1.00 = £S 3.65.

Population for 1953 = 3.61 million, discounted by 8.42% for 1950 = 3.33 million.
Therefore income per capita for 1950 = £S 587.23 or US$ 160.88.

Lebanon [37]

National income for 1950 calculated at £L 1,042 million, or US$ 278.60 million (US$ 1.00 = £L 3.74).

Population estimated at 2.75 million for end 1974, discounted back to 1950 on the basis of a net rate of increase of 2.6% per annum, or a cumulative growth of 85% between the two dates. Thus population for 1950 = 1.49 million.
Therefore, income per capita for 1950 = £L 699.32 or US$ 187.

Table 12.2

	WB & GS	E.Jordan	Syria	Lebanon
GNP per capita, US dollars at current prices	687[a]	1,640	1,760	1,010
Enrolment rates at 1st & 2nd level schools, % of school age children (5-19)	81	92	79	82
Life expectancy at birth (years)	72[b]	64	67	65
Population per hospital bed	566	1,711	2,236	260
Daily calorie supply per capita	2,861[bc] 2,554[bd]	2,882[b]	3,040[b]	3,000[b]

Notes: a. Weighted average for West Bank and Gaza Strip.
 b. For 1982.
 c. For West Bank.
 d. For Gaza Strip.

informed 'guesstimation' than those for 1983, where more refined and reliable methods are used.

(i) The base, 1948-1950

The only items of information available for all the countries covered (Palestine, Transjordan/East Jordan, Syria and Lebanon) in this discussion of the base year are national income and population, from which income per capita is calculated. The presentation in Table 12.1 is made country by country.

(ii) The terminal year 1983[38]

The GNP per capita for Lebanon for 1983, as recorded in Table 12.2, would have been much higher (on the assumption of continued normal political conditions) had the rate of exchange between the local currency and the US dollar not moved against the former from US$ 1.00 = £L 2.25 in 1974 which was the last normal year before the civil war, to US$ 1.00 = £L 5.49 in 1983. Thus, national income per capita for 1974 was the equivalent of US$ 1,180.[39] Projected at a rate of growth of 6 per cent per capita annually (a very reasonable rate, given the record of the several years preceding 1974), income per capita at the 1974 rate of exchange would have risen to US$ 1,993 in 1983. GNP per capita would obviously have been still higher. This (hypothetical) high level, in excess of that of Syria for the same year, is theoretically tenable, considering the fact that the base from which Lebanon had started in 1950 was higher than that of Syria, and that the Lebanese people and economy displayed notable vigour and dynamism in the years following 1950, which were reflected in fast growth, economic diversification and qualitative improvement in production.

275

2. Commentary

Four comments will be made now, derived from the two sets of data presented above, and from the most salient consequences and implications of dependence and dispossession discussed in the previous section.

(i) Per capita national income data

In the base years 1948-50 per capita national income data show a clear advantage for the Palestinians over the Transjordanians, the Syrians and the Lebanese. In 1983, the ranking has been reversed, with the Palestinians in the West Bank and the Gaza Strip trailing the list. The drop in the rank of the per capita income/GNP of the Palestinians is even more significant in terms of welfare, if account is taken of the two distorting factors which Israeli occupation imposed after 1967. These are the galloping inflation and the many currency devaluations which have bedevilled the Israeli economy. In contrast, Jordan, Syria and Lebanon have suffered much milder inflation since 1967 and very modest devaluations of their currencies. While it is true that by converting values from local currencies into US dollars, the greatest part of the impact of inflation and devaluation has been adjusted for, nevertheless the devaluations in Israel, though frequent and far-reaching,[40] have fallen distinctly short of the extent to which inflation has increased. Although this paper does not include a rigorous calculation to show the net residual effect of the extent to which inflation has outdistanced devaluation, it is sufficient for present purposes to draw attention to the distorting impact of this residual on the level of GNP per capita.

(ii) Rate of growth 1950 –1967

The objection might be made that the retardation in the economic performance of the West Bank and the Gaza Strip compared with that of Jordan, Syria and Lebanon should essentially be imputed to the years preceding 1967, when East Jordan was responsible for economic policy in the West Bank and had distinctly favoured itself at the expense of the West Bank, and when the Egyptian administration in the Gaza Strip invested proportionately less effort and resources in the development of the Gaza Strip than of Egypt itself. Some Palestinian and other Arab writers have made this kind of observation. I believe that, while official Jordanian policy did in fact show favouritism towards the East Bank, this did not lead to retardation or even to stagnation in the economy of the West Bank: in fact, tangible growth and expansion was registered during the years 1950 to 1967, as we shall show. I am convinced that the imputations against Jordanian policies are made more on ideological and political than on economic grounds. According to one researcher, just before the June War in 1967, the West Bank had 7,300 industrial establishments in operation, or 48 per cent of the total for the Hashemite Kingdom. West Bank industry contributed before the war about 20 per cent of the aggregate GNP of Jordan. The overall performance of the West Bank economy generated a rate of annual growth of between 6 and 8 per cent per capita in the same period. Another researcher argues that the growth rate for the years 1954-66 averaged over 10 per cent per annum or a per capita rate of some 6.9 per cent. In absolute terms, the second writer estimated GNP at current market prices for both Banks to be US$ 512.85 million in 1967, just less than half of which was generated in the West Bank.[41] It is not clear what size of population is to be taken as a basis of calculation to derive the GNP per capita. Using the figure for the end of 1966, then GNP per capita would be about US$ 300; using the lower figure of the summer of 1967 (after the exodus of some 250,000 persons as an immediate result of the war), it would be about US$ 430. For GNP per capita in the West Bank to have risen from US$ 430 in 1967, to US$ 753 in 1983,[42] means a cumulative growth of 175 per cent, or an average annual compound rate of 3.5 per cent at current prices. This rate is half the average achieved over the period 1954 to 1966.[43] The retardation of the substantial rate of growth which characterised the period when the West Bank was still an integral economic part of the Kingdom must be attributed to the Israeli occupation. Data for the Gaza Strip are not available, making similar comparisons impossible. However, it can safely be argued that the Gaza Strip economy could not have been more seriously damaged or handicapped than that of the West Bank, since its performance under Israeli occupation is not very different (GNP per capita for the Gaza Strip for 1983 was US$ 583.3 against US$ 753.3 for the West Bank. The differential is explained by the much larger component of impoverished refugees in the Strip).

(iii) Disposable income

The claim of prosperity under Israeli occupation is often buttressed by reference to such tangible indicators of economic well-being as the increasing number of radios and television sets in Palestinian homes and figures for ownership of durable household equipment like gas ovens and refrigerators, bicycles and private cars. The building of new houses is also cited. That these indicators do exist is not deniable.

But the Israelis cannot claim credit for developing and implementing economic policies that generate the disposable personal income which makes it possible for the Palestinians to acquire the household goods. It would be more correct to say that what is being economically achieved is in spite of, rather than because of, Israeli policies. The personal disposable income of Palestinians in the occupied territories does not come solely from the GNP generated in the economy. To a substantial extent this GNP is supplemented by non-requited financial transfers through remittances sent by family members working abroad, by other non-requited transfers from Arab governments via the Joint Committee and by salaries paid by Jordan to thousands of West Bankers who were government employees before the 1967 war. The considerable combined inflow of financial resources tangibly increases the volume of disposable income, thus permitting greater expenditure on durable goods of all kinds, for day-to-day consumption needs, and also for investment and house building. The multiplier effect of consumption expenditure and the accelerator effect of investment outlays made possible through the inflows just cited, taken together, boost national product after a certain time lag. Indeed, Israel itself benefits from these inflows thanks to increased purchases of goods and services by the occupied territories and from the receipt of a large part of the foreign exchange transferred to the West Bank and Gaza Strip inasmuch as legally these have to go through the Israeli banking system.

Finally, we must bear in mind that a significant part of the wage component of national income in the West Bank and Gaza Strip is earned by Palestinians working in Israel.[44] To this extent, the component in question is not generated by the economies of the occupied territories strictly speaking: in fact, it is thus earned only because the West Bank and Gaza Strip economies are kept at a low level of activity by Israeli policies, to the point where they fail to generate job opportunities for a significant proportion of the labour supply.

(iv) Retardation

I trust that by now the Zionist claim that Israeli occupation has been beneficial to the West Bank and the Gaza Strip has been shown to be invalid: indeed, that the opposite is true, namely that the occupation has been an obstacle which has directly retarded the progress of the occupied territories, warped their structure, forced them into subservience to the Israeli economy and dispossessed them to a serious degree. This is all said within a purely economic context. The verdict would be much harsher if account was taken of the non-economic implications and consequences of the occupation, which I tried to establish in the first section of the paper.

Without repeating points already made, it is necessary to add that the pauperisation of the occupied territories is much more serious than the statistical indicators suggest. This is because dispossession strikes not only at the present capabilities of the population and the economy, but also at their potential and prospects. As a process, it increasingly and cumulatively threatens the future of Palestine and the Palestinians. By the same logic, it helps the Zionists/Israelis to consolidate their grip on the country and further to widen and deepen the agony of the Palestinians and their sense of loss and alienation.

V. CONCLUSION: THE OUTLOOK FOR DEVELOPMENT

The main conclusions of this paper have already emerged in broad outline from the examination of the two propositions which I set out to test. Nevertheless, it will be useful to state briefly how the conclusions impinge on the future development of the occupied territories under continued occupation, although the paper has not been designed to explore the outlook for development.

(a) Meaningful and far-reaching development cannot be achieved, or even sought, under the conditions of dependence-cum-dispossession. 'Dependent development' itself is not possible, since Israel's external-turned-internal colonialism blocks even capitalist transformation which mature capitalist industrial countries claim to promote in their relations with third-world countries.[45] This being the case, it is a futile exercise to speculate whether self-reliant development can be achieved in the occupied territories.

(b) Given present constraints, the economies of the West Bank and the Gaza Strip can only be maintained at a low level of economic performance, even assuming the same volume of external financial support. Even this will have to be predicated on the surrender of vital economic, socio-cultural and political desiderata.

(c) The third conclusion is operational. Given the special nature of dependence and dispossession suffered by the occupied territories, and the tight, wide ranging web of control the Israelis use, it is unrealistic to set out to design broad plans and programmes for development. Individual projects and restricted programmes should be chosen, which are thought to have a reasonable chance of getting through Israel's web. The projects thus targeted should, as far as possible, be made to fit into an implicit broader framework. This

279

cautious remark is made to save the would-be planners and programmers, and the people under occupation, unnecessary frustration and pain. An Arab proverb has relevance here: 'Frustration takes its magnitude from expectation.'

(d) Finally, given the trend of the analysis of this paper, and the nature and implications of the conclusions, it seems logical and defensible to assert that only after the disappearance of the occupation can nationally conceived and designed, well-integrated and energetic development be sought and pursued with a significant degree of hope.

NOTES

1. Israel also occupied the small Hamma area to the south-east of Lake Tiberias in 1967. It is not included in the discussion here.

2. A survey of developments in the occupied economies will not be attempted here as background, since there are already a number of general or sectoral surveys. In addition to those perused by me, I have learnt a great deal from some 35 interviews made with knowledgeable residents of the occupied territories during the spring of 1984, in the course of preparing a study of the programme of official Arab aid in support of the steadfastness of the Palestinians under Israeli occupation.

3. Meron Benvenisti is the author most widely quoted in this context. See, for instance, *The West Bank Data Base Project* (The West Bank and Gaza Data Base Project – Interim Report No. 1, Jerusalem, 1982). A revised and expanded printed edition appeared in 1984, published by American Enterprise Institute for Public Policy Research, under the title: *The West Bank Data Project: A Survey of Israel's Policies.*

4. Central Bureau of Statistics, *Statistical Abstract of Israel 1984, No. 35* (Central Bureau of Statistics, Jerusalem, 1984), Table VIII/1, pp. 212-3.

5. Ibid., Table XXVII/10, p.751.

6. Sheila Ryan, 'The West Bank and Gaza: political consequences of occupation', *MERIP Reports*, No. 74, January 1979, p.3.

7. Central Bureau of Statistics, *Statistical Abstract of Israel,* 1984, Table XXVII/10, p.751.

8. Ibid., Tables XXVII/19 and XXVII/20, pp.762 and 763.

9. See Muhammad Ja'far's reply to Salim Tamari in the exchange between them in *Khamsin,* nos. 5-8, especially no.7, p. 154. For a purely pragmatic view, see Elias H. Tuma and Haim Darin-Drabkin's treatment of labour absorption in an independent Palestine in their book *The Economic Case for Palestine* (Croom Helm, London, 1978), chapters 6 and 7.

10. Especially in his *Imperialism; The Highest Stage of Capitalism* (Lawrence and Wishart, London, 1948).

11. See Laurence Harris, 'Money and finance with undeveloped banking', chapter 9 of the present volume. Information is not available concerning the size of the new banks' capital and the scope of operations they are designed to undertake.

12. Professor Michel Chatelus notes in his Preface to Antoine Mansour's

book, *Palestine: une économie de résistance en Cisjordanie et à Gaza* (Editions L'Harmattan, Paris, 1983), that the author sums up the process as one of 'integration-destruction', where Israel destroys the occupied economies by integrating them into its own economy! This may sound an extreme description of the process, but the record supports it.

13. For a wide ranging study of Israel's brand of internal colonialism, see Elia T. Zureik, *The Palestinians in Israel: A Study in Internal Colonialism* (Routledge & Kegan Paul, London, 1979), especially chapters 5 and 6.

14. This literature is extensive, and impressive bibliographies can be found in many economic and sociological works. For a concise presentation of the leading 'schools' of dependency, and a comprehensive bibliography, see Magnus Blomstrom and Bjorn Hettne, *Development Theory in Transition – The Dependency Debate and Beyond: Third World Responses* (Zed Books, London, 1984). See also: Dudley Seers (ed.), *Dependency Theory: A Critical Reassessment* (Frances Pinter (Publishers) Ltd., London, 1981); Ian Roxborough, *Theories of Underdevelopment* (Macmillan, London, 1979); Aiden Foster-Carter, 'From Rostow to Gunder Frank: conflicting paradigms in the analysis of underdevelopment', *World Development*, vol.4, no. 3, March 1976; and Ibrahim Sa'd al-Din, *hawla maqulat al-taba'iya wa-al-tanmiya al-iqtisadiyya al-'arabiyya* (On the paradigm of dependency and Arab economic development), *al-mustaqbal al-'arabi*, vol. 3, no. 17 (Beirut, July 1980).

15. Of relevance here is Harold Wolpe, 'The theory of internal colonialism: The South African case' in Ivar Oxaal, Tony Barnett, and David Booth (eds), *Beyond the Sociology of Development: Economy and Society in Latin America and Africa* (Routledge and Kegan Paul, London, 1975).

16. Basically all the main features of dependence and dispossession are also to be seen in the relationship of the Arab community in the territories occupied in 1948. However, this paper is restricted to those areas occupied in 1967.

17. Estimates of the area of Palestinian land expropriated/confiscated, and tightly controlled by Israel vary, but generally exceed 50% of the total area of the occupied territories.

18. In this respect, the editor of the Israeli daily *Haaretz* wrote as early as 30 September 1951: '...Israel has been assigned by the West the role of a sort of watchdog. There is no fear that it will adopt an aggressive policy towards the Arab states if that is against the wish of America and Britain. But if the western powers ever prefer, for one reason or another, to shut their eyes, Israel can be relied upon to punish properly one or several of her neighbouring states whose lack of manners towards the West has exceeded the permitted limits.' (Quoted by Moshe Machover, 'Israel and the New Order in the Middle East', *Khamsin*, no. 6 (1978), p. 87.)

19. See, for instance, Zureik, *The Palestinians in Israel* and 'The economics of dispossession: the Palestinians', *Third World Quarterly*, vol. 5, no. 4 (1983). Several other writers have dealt with economic dispossession (water, land, work opportunities, deportations). Though the political aspects of the factor of dispossession have not been ignored by any of them, there has been insufficient integration of the political, socio-cultural and economic aspects which together constitute components of one ideology.

20. The continuity of Zionist ideology with respect to the syndrome of

dispossession, uprooting and displacement is discussed at some length in Harris, 'Money and Finance'. It is sufficient here to point to some of the landmarks in the continuous process: the First Zionist Congress at Basle in 1897; the 'Political Report' of 16 December 1918, submitted to the XIIth Zionist Congress, London, 1921, by the Executive of the Zionist Organisation; the Biltmore Programme drawn up in New York in 1942; the official statements of the Jewish Agency and the Zionist Organisation submitted in 1946 in Jerusalem to the Anglo-American Committee of Inquiry into the Palestine Problem, all the way down to the current party platforms and official statements of the supporters of 'Greater Israel' and the Likud. What is even more significant (and certainly more sinister) is the way the official Zionist line and Israel's policies and practices support, complement and sustain each other. (For documentation on the 'landmarks' mentioned above, see Robert John and Sami Hadawi, *The Palestine Diary* (The Palestine Research Centre, Beirut, 1970), vol. I, especially pp. 115 and 342; US Government, *Foreign Relations of the United States 1943: The Near East and Africa* (US Government, Washington D.C, 1964), vol. IV, pp. 776-7; Royal Institute for International Affairs, *Great Britain and Palestine 1915-1945*, pp. 139-40).

Israel Koenig resigned in 1986 after almost two decades as district commissioner for the northern district. He was notorious for a secret 1976 memorandum in which he proposed the Palestinian population of the Galilee be reduced to the status of 'hewers of wood and drawers of water'. Meir Kahane is leader of the fascist Kach movement and a member of the Israeli parliament. Yuval Neeman is a leader of Tehiya (Renaissance), an extreme right-wing party which calls for the removal of civil rights from Palestinians. Menachem Begin is the former head of the Irgun right-wing terror organisation, the right-wing Herut party and a former Israeli prime minister.

21. Ann Lesch refers to partial lists with the names of thousands of deportees in 'Israeli deportation of Palestinians from the West Bank and Gaza Strip, 1967-1978', *Journal of Palestine Studies*, Part I, no. 30, Winter 1979; Part II, no. 31, Spring 1979.

22. Adam Roberts, Boel Joergensen and Frank Newman, *Academic Freedom under Israeli Military Occupation, Report of WUS/ICJ Mission of Enquiry into Higher Education in the West Bank and Gaza* (World University Service (UK), International Commission of Jurists, London and Geneva, 1984). See also Sarah Graham-Brown, *Education, Repression & Liberation: Palestinians* (World University Service (UK), London, 1984).

23. Many scholars and researchers have dealt with the process of proletarianisation. These include among others Janet L. Abu Lughod, Elia T. Zureik, Sarah Graham-Brown, Salim Tamari, Jamil Hilal. Their contributions have appeared mainly in *MERIP Reports, Journal of Palestine Studies, Khamsin, Third World Quarterly,* in addition to chapters in collections of essays on the occupied territories.

24. The data are taken from Janet L. Abu Lughod, 'Demographic consequences of the occupation', *MERIP Reports,* no. 115 (June 1983). Her work on this subject is extensive and very thorough.

25. Herzl's prescription for the uprooting and expulsion of the 'natives' into what he called the 'transit countries' is well known. He wrote: 'If we move into a region where there are wild animals to which the Jews are not accustomed

– big snakes, etc. – I shall use the natives, prior to giving them employment in the transit countries, for the extermination of these animals ...' See Raphael Patai (ed.), *The Complete Diaries of Theodor Herzl,* translated by Harry Zohn, vol. I, p. 98.

26. Zureik, 'The economics of dispossession' quoting from *Time* (New York, 25 April 1983), p.15.

27. Quoted in David Gilmour, *Dispossessed: The Ordeal of the Palestinians* (Sphere Books Limited, London, 1980), p.94, from a statement made by Robin Maxwell-Hyslop, MP to the House of Commons in October 1973, as recorded in Parliamentary Debates (*Hansard*), Ser. 5, House of Commons, Vol. 861, Col. 502.

28. George Rowley has developed the theme in a paper entitled 'Superior-inferior relations in colonisation procedures, with special reference to Israel', forthcoming; quoted in Rowley, 'Palestinian refugees: quantitative assessment and political realities', paper for Workshop on Refugees in the Twentieth Century, Queen Elizabeth House (Oxford, August 1985), pp. 13-14.

29. A court case in Israel at the end of 1985 revealed hundreds of such instances of fraud and forgery involving very senior government officials as well as lawyers and real estate agents.

30. Moshe Machover and Mario Offenberg, 'Zionism and its scarecrows', *Khamsin,* no. 6, (1978), quote 'Arif al-'Arif's list of 385 villages destroyed by the Zionists, presented on 15 February 1973, by the Chairman of the Israeli League of Human Rights, Professor Israel Shahak.

31. The most thorough and consistently pursued effort to keep track of settlements established and areas of land expropriated/confiscated is that of the Royal Jordanian Scientific Society in Amman, supported by Crown Prince Hassan's personal interest and concern.

32. For a recent exposé of Israel's current settlement policy, see Peter Demant, 'Israeli settlement policy today', *MERIP Reports,* no. 116 (July-August 1983).

33. See Joe Stork, 'Water and Israel's occupation strategy', in *MERIP Reports,* no. 116 (July-August 1983). This article ends with a list of pertinent works on the subject. Of great relevance in this connection is the report prepared by Dante Caponera in conformity with UN General Assembly Resolution 38/14 (38th session, December 19, 1984), published as an ECOSOC Document E/1984/lll, General Assembly Document A/39/111, (New York, 29 June 1984). The report is entitled *Permanent Sovereignty over National Resources in the Occupied Territories and other Arab Territories* (excerpted in *Journal of Palestine Studies,* vol. XIV, No. 2, Winter 1985).

34. National income for 1948 projected from that of 1945, the latter as in P.J. Loftus, *National Income of Palestine, 1945* (Government of Palestine, Jerusalem, 1947). Population for 1948 projected from that for 1945, as in Government of Palestine, *A Survey of Palestine,* 3 vols. (Government of Palestine, Jerusalem, 1946), vol. 1, Table 1, p. 141. The exchange rates for all the countries covered for 1950 (except Palestine) are from United Nations, *Statistical Yearbook 1959* (United Nations, New York, 1960), Table 171, pp. 464-70.

35. National income for Transjordan for 1948 is an estimate based on a study for the years 1952-4 by the Economic Research Institute of the American University of Beirut (unpublished). The estimate for 1950 is discounted for

1948 and 1950 (the latter after the influx of some 350,000 Palestinian refugees); see Yusif A. Sayigh, *The Economics of the Arab World: Development Since 1945* (Croom Helm, London, 1978), chapter 5, Section 1, and the footnotes relating to the discussion of the national accounts and population in this section, especially footnotes 3 and 9 where the original sources are mentioned and an explanation is given of the methods whereby estimates had been made, and of their reliability.

36. National income and population data for 1953 from Government of Syria, *Statistical Abstract 1974* (Arabic), Table 31/17, pp. 868-9. Data adjusted back to 1950 on the basis of a rate of nominal growth of income of 5% per annum, and a rate of net population increase of 3.3%. The rates are collated from information in the *Abstract* referred to, chapter 17.

37. National income was first calculated by Albert Y. Badre and Associates in the unpublished study by the Economic Research Institute of the American University of Beirut for the years 1950-2. See Badre, 'Economic development in Lebanon', in Charles A. Cooper and Sidney S. Alexander (eds), *Economic Development and Population Growth in the Middle East* (Elsevier, New York, 1972). For population, I relied on the estimate of UN Economic and Social Office of Beirut (UNESOB), in 'Demographic characteristics of youth in the Arab countries of the Middle East; present situation and growth prospects, 1970-1990' in *Studies on Selected Development Problems in Various Countries of the Middle East, 1970*, which I have set at 2.75 million for end of 1974, to take into account various adjustments suggested by knowledgeable analysts. (See Sayigh, *Economics of the Arab World*, chapter 7, Section 1, for a detailed discussion of GNP and population data.) The rate of population increase used in my calculations is 2.6% per annum which is a compromise between somewhat higher and lower estimates. (The last population census was undertaken in 1932.)

38. All information on the West Bank and Gaza Strip presented here is from Central Bureau of Statistics, *Statistical Abstract of Israel*, nos. 34 (1983), 35 (1984), and 36 (1985). GNP data are from no. 36, Table XXVII/6, p. 708. The rate used for conversion from Israeli shekel to US dollar is IS 107.77 = US$ 1.00, which is the 'market rate/par or central rate' as per *International Financial Statistics* (IFS), September 1985. Life expectancy is from no. 35, Table III/29, p. 117. Calorie intake is from no. 36, Table XXVII/13, p. 715. School enrolment rates and population per hospital bed are calculated from no. 36, Tables no. XXVII/45, p. 750 and XXVII/46, p. 751 respectively. GNP per capita for Jordan and Syria, as well as life expectancy data for Jordan, Syria and Lebanon, and daily calorie intake per capita in these three countries, are from World Bank, *World Development Report 1985* (Oxford University Press, Oxford, 1985), Table 1 and 24 in Annex.

GNP data for Lebanon were derived as follows: GNP for 1979 is recorded as US$ 2,523 million in Arab Fund for Economic and Social Development, *National Accounts Country Tables* (AFESD, Kuwait, 1980). I projected this to 1983 by using the growth rate of 8.5% per annum which applied for several years preceding the start of the civil war in 1975, on the assumption that under normal conditions this rate would have continued through 1983. (See Sayigh, *Economies of the Arab World*, chapter 7, Section 1, for a discussion of growth until 1976.) Population data for 1979 come from IFS September 1980; I extrapolated to 1983 at a rate of 2.6% per annum.

Data on school enrolment rates and population per hospital bed for Jordan, Syria and Lebanon are from *UNCTAD, Handbook of International Trade and Development Statistics, 1985 Supplement* (UNCTAD, New York, 1985).

39. Sayigh, *Economies of the Arab World,* chapter 7, Section 1. The currency conversion rates are from IFS issues of May 1975 and September 1985.

40. While the Israeli pound was equal to US$ 4.00 in 1948, the drop in the shekel (which replaced the pound at the rate of one shekel to ten pounds) was so steep as a result of several devaluations that in 1983 the rate had fallen to IS 107.77 to the dollar.

41. The first researcher referred to is Richard Ward. See 'The economics of Palestine entity' in Richard Ward, Don Peretz and Evan Wilson (eds), *The Palestine State: A Rational Approach* (National University Publications, New York, 1977). The second is Michael P. Mazur, 'Economic development of Jordan' in Cooper and Alexander (eds), *Economic Development.* The GNP data come from Table 5.1, p. 214.

42. Calculated from Central Bureau of Statistics, *Statistical Abstract of Israel,* no. 36, Table no. XXVII/6, p. 708, and population data from Ibid., Table no. XXVII/1, p. 703.

43. For data and evaluation very close to those presented earlier in the paragraph, see Central Bank of Jordan, *Fourth Annual Report, 1967* (Central Bank of Jordan, Amman, 1967), pp. 5 and 6.

44. The bulk of 'net current transfers from abroad', which add up to IS 30,837.6 million (US$ 286.1 million) originates in the wages earned in Israel. See Central Bureau of Statistics, *Statistical Abstract of Israel,* no. 36, Table no. XXVII/6, p. 708.

45. This is true whether one adopts the reasoning of anti-Marxist Lord Bauer who also denies the tenets and conclusions of 'dependency', or of the Marxist (the late) Bill Warren who tried to incorporate into his Marxist framework the possibility of capitalist development in third-world countries. See P. T. Bauer, *Equality, The Third World and Economic Delusion* (Weidenfeld and Nicolson, London, 1981) and *Reality and Rhetoric: Studies in the Economics of Development* (Weidenfeld and Nicolson, London, 1984). See also Bill Warren, *Imperialism: Pioneer of Capitalism* (Verso, London, 1985), chapters 7 and 8.

13

Development from Within:
A Strategy for Survival

Ibrahim Dakkak

Development under Israeli hegemony in the occupied territories must be discussed in the context of the external and internal conflicts affecting it. Among the external conflicts are the wider Arab-Israeli conflict, inter-Arab conflicts, problems between the Arabs and the Palestinians, inter-Palestinian disputes and difficulties in the relationship between the Palestinians inside the occupied territories and those outside. The internal conflicts are partly a function of those outside, and are exacerbated by the absence of a coherent Arab-Palestinian strategy *vis-à-vis* the occupied territories with clearly prescribed objectives and methods.

The case of Jordan provides a good example of the difficulties. Jordanian development programmes call for the efficient utilisation of the resources of the East Bank of the Jordan River and the water of the Yarmouk River. Israel, for its part, is interested in the efficient use of the West Bank of the river and in harnessing water from the Yarmouk.[1] To achieve these limited objectives, Jordan and Israel tend to seek stability in the Jordan Valley and in this regard have achieved some kind of *de facto* accommodation in this particular area. In the wider Arab context, however, there are those who view this state of affairs as tantamount to normalisation.

The wider inter-regional and international conflicts cause the focus of events in the Middle East to shift continuously and to blur the sharpness of the specific conflict in Palestine. As to the Palestinians in the occupied territories, they must focus on the difficult tasks of maintaining the fabric of their society, of resisting dissipation, counteracting normalisation of relations with the occupier, fighting potential economic, social and cultural stagnation and maintaining their Arab and Palestinian identities. External interference, with accompanying constraints on normal activity, complicates these tasks. This external control also highlights the growing differences between the immediate and projected political and social objectives inside the occupied territories on the one hand, and the Arab strategy of compromise that has been snowballing in the region since the visit of Egyptian President Anwar Sadat to Israel in 1977, on the other hand.

Questions about the nature of Arab strategy regarding the occupied territories have to be raised. Is it accommodation to the Israeli *fait accompli*? Resistance to it? Or a middle course? The limitations of this paper do not allow full discussion of the various options. It should be noted, however, that none of the parties involved is satisfied with the current situation: they seek change. Agreement on the necessity of change, however, hides sharp divergences in the scenarios each party envisages for the future of the occupied territories. All would agree that the major problem is that none of the actors can outline a way out of the present quagmire satisfactory to all of them.

If the Arabs and Palestinians are forced to accept some variation of the status quo (with cosmetic improvements such as shared sovereignty as set out in the Autonomy Plan drawn up by Israeli Prime Minister Menachem Begin after the Camp David Accords or some Israeli Labour Party variation of it) then a development plan aimed at change would not be an option. The purpose of development in such an instance would be to service and sustain the static physical existence of the Palestinians in the occupied territories with the explicit, and probably exclusive, aim of reducing Palestinian emigration. In other words it would be the promotion of static *sumud*. The resistance alternative presupposes a different strategy for development, the aim of which will be to promote *sumud muqawim*.

I. *SUMUD MUQAWIM:* THE CHALLENGES

Sumud is translated in English as 'steadfastness'. The term steadfastness, however, does not convey the dynamic nature of *sumud muqawim* (resistance *sumud*) as it has developed in recent years in Palestinian society in the occupied territories.

The notion of *sumud* has had different connotations at different times and places since the start of the occupation. Its meaning alters according to the social class or interest group using it. These differences are a function of two main factors: the emergence of Palestinian specificities as vested interests established in different diasporas, and class differentiation in Palestinian communities inside and outside the occupied territories.

1. Roots of the challenge

Funds to support Palestinian steadfastness in the occupied territories come from the various Arab regimes and from Palestinians residing outside the area. The economic and developmental potential of these funds has been diverse depending on source. Nevertheless, in the first few years of occupation their purpose was seen by all as transitional and short-term.

Whilst realisation grew of the purpose, nature and duration of Israeli occupation, *sumud* funding was never seriously considered by the donors as support for fundamental economic and social development, or for any serious long-term economic programme. On the contrary, in many cases local development and resistance initiatives designed to check growing stagnation and counter Israeli measures were hampered.

Differences between the political orientation of Palestinians 'inside' and those 'outside' were a natural outgrowth of the physical dispersion of the Palestinian people following the 1948/9 and the 1967 wars. Following the passage by the Arab League of the historic resolution at its summit in Rabat in 1974 recognising the Palestine Liberation Organisation as the sole legitimate representative of the Palestinians everywhere, the PLO was forced to become an institution-alised quasi-state and began to share with the Arab regimes some of their less benign characteristics. The leadership outside appeared, at times, to produce 'standard priorities' with little regard to the needs and interests of the occupied territories as seen by the Palestinians living there. At the same time Palestinians in the occupied territories were presenting a different order of priorities, similar in general to that of the PLO but not in emphasis. These dissimilarities found expression in overt and covert mutual criticism.[2] The divergence also concerned the nature of *sumud*: the outside inclining towards 'static *sumud*',[3] while the people inside developed a less orthodox and more aggressive approach – *sumud muqawim*.

2. The Joint Committee

The two strategies met head on after the establishment of the Jordanian-Palestinian Joint Committee in 1978. 'Static *sumud*' was institutionalised by the Arab heads of state and budgeted for at the Baghdad Summit. Initially, funds from the Joint Committee flowed in to extend higher education, encourage housing projects and support the municipalities and other institutions. The immediate popular reaction was a sense of relief and euphoria.

The Joint Committee started with a budget of JD 14 million in 1979 and between then and 1983 disbursed a total of JD 125.5 million.[4] Its activities were supported by the bureaucracy left behind by Jordan in 1967 and enjoyed the credibility of the PLO in the occupied territories. However, after the PLO established its headquarters in Tunis following the 1982 war, policies and allocations of the Joint Committee tended to reflect an affirmation of 'static *sumud*' with greater weight given in its decisions to traditional Jordanian interests in the occupied territories represented largely by charitable societies, the old Jordanian educational and medical services, the Muslim *awqaf* (endowment) department, the Shari'a courts, the Jordanian agricultural and co-operative systems and the passport offices.[5]

The operational record and performance of the Joint Committee have been less than satisfactory, however. Steadfastness and resistance were replaced with a conventional philosophy of financial support. Political divisions flourished, and dependency and social polarisation increased.[6] The euphoria which followed the announcement of 1979 dissipated and disappointment became widespread as people began to take stock of Joint Committee performance.

The most heavily funded areas of the Joint Committee's operations between 1979 and 1983 were education, housing and the municipalities. Between them they consumed 58 per cent of the total budget for this period. Availability of Joint Committee grants encouraged students to enter universities. At the same time the number of unemployed graduates increased.[7] Table 13.1, on the growth and employment of graduates, is self-explanatory. The number of students asking for support from the Joint Committee increased twenty-fold in five years.

House construction had the potential, according to Abu Kishk, of providing extra jobs and solving an acute problem. Had a target of providing one room for every three persons in the occupied territories been set, he estimated that 270,000 jobs could have been created by 1990.[8] The Joint Committee did not meet this challenge. While it spent 68 per cent of the budget Abu Kishk estimated would have been required for the above goal, it achieved nothing like the same results. The Engineers Association records show that many projects started several years earlier and financed by the Joint Committee had not been completed and that others were structurally unsafe.[9] A third group of buildings fell in the luxury category while others had to be finished on a shoestring.

Table 13.1: Graduate unemployment in the occupied territories: 1980-1985

Year	Number of Students	Increase in %	Number of Graduates	Number of Unemployed	Recipients of Aid[a]
1980	5,263	-	360	36	23
1981	7,147	36	818	364	76
1982	9,873	38	1,230	-	257
1983	11,215	14	1,077	-	469
1984	13,083	14	-	2,802	-
1985	13,581	3	-	3,320	-

Note: a. Includes graduates from institutions outside the occupied territories. Aid to unemployed graduates was halted in 1985.
Sources: S. Katba, *hawla al-ta'lim al-'ali fi al-daffa al-gharbiyya wa-qit'a ghazza* (Higher education in the West Bank and the Gaza Strip) (Council for Higher Education, Jerusalem, April 1983); S. Katba and Yusuf Qassas, *Mutakharrijun jam'iat wa-ma'ahid al-daffa al-gharbiyya* (Graduates of West Bank universities and institutions) (Council for Higher Education, Jerusalem, June 1982); Ihsan Atiyah et al., *al-kharrijun al-'atilun 'an al-'amal fi al-daffa al-gharbiyya wa-qit'a ghazza* (Unemployed graduates in the West Bank and Gaza Strip) 2 Issues, 1984 and 1985 (Arab Graduates Club, Jerusalem, 1984, 1985).

The municipalities used Joint Committee funding for cosmetic changes in the towns and to bolster their bureaucracies. Hardly any important infrastructural projects were undertaken. The only exception was the expansion of the Nablus electricity project, which in any event was not wholeheartedly supported by the Joint Committee.

The United States Agency for International Development (USAID), the United Nations Relief and Works Agency (UNRWA) and the US government-funded agencies in the occupied territories were also challenging *sumud muqawim*. They are less heavily funded than the Joint Committee, but more persistent in pursuing objectives through diversified and sophisticated programmes. USAID money was provided to projects which had the approval of the occupying authority.

Meron Benvenisti observes that the American agencies' policy accepts the Israeli *fait accompli*. It is, according to him, an expression of US readiness to ride the Israeli bandwagon of pacification.[10] He described the programmes as tantamount to encouraging 'total economic and political integration (of the occupied territories) within the Israeli Commonwealth'.[11] He describes the triangular relationship nurtured since 1967 by the open bridges policy whereby Jordan, Israel and recipient Palestinians were implicitly brought into a co-ordinated network: 'The pivotal role of the PVOs (Private Voluntary

Table 13.2: Jordanian-Palestinian Joint Committee allocations for the occupied territories: 1979-83 (in thousands of Jordanian dinars[a])

Sector	1979	1980	1981	1982	1983	Total
Agriculture	1,770.0	1,110.0	4,193.0	2,481.3	1,303.6	10,857.9
Industry	10.0	30.0	2,056.0	3,984.7	593.0	6,673.7
Water	784.0	443.2	481.8	489.4	511.5	2,312.9
Electricity	1,150.0	1,730.6	802.9	1,800.8	1,214.0	6,698.3
Transportation	300.0	1,357.3	1,323.0	1,735.7	85.0	4,802.0
Housing	–	6,419.0	2,800.0	13,588.2	978.5	23,784.7
Education	1,796.5	4,007.0	6,127.3	6,038.1	8,035.0	26,003.9
Health	310.0	793.3	502.0	849.3	164.0	2,618.6
Municipalities	6,274.0	7,221.0	8,500.0	50.0	800.0	22,854.0
Social Development	1,253.8	2,226.5	3,116.8	1,958.4	1,916.6	10,512.1
Awqaf[a]	476.0	105.0	110.0	34.0	10.0	735.0
Administration & Services	39.9	150.0	150.0	200.0	300.0	839.9
Studies & Consultations	–	149.0	–	100.0	54.5	303.5
Emergencies	–	600.0	–	631.6	121.8	1,353.4
Demolished Houses	–	1,000.0	1,000.0	431.5	103.1	2,534.6
National Sponsorship	–	–	–	1,032.5	1,511.4	2,543.9
Buying Land	–	–	–	100.0	–	100.0
TOTAL	14,164.2	27,380.9	31,162.8	35,505.5	17,306.0	125,519.4

Notes: a. JD 1 = US$ 2.8 (January 1986). b. Muslim Endowment Fund.
Source: Joint Committee.

Organisations) is clear,' Benvenisti states, 'for they are the only factor maintaining contact with all other authorities and coordinating the process.'[12] He was referring to the US government (through USAID), the Jordanian Government and the Israeli authorities.[13]

Questions have also been raised about the role of UNRWA. David McDowall, writing in *Middle East International* stated that 'despite the value of the services it provides, UNRWA reinforces a state of dependence which many thinking Palestinians realise must cease if the Palestinian community is to mature both socially and politically'. He points out the irony that 'the majority of the 70 or so international staff posts are held by Americans and Britons, who come from the two countries held most responsible by many Palestinians for the disaster of 1948 and its aftermath'.[14]

Since the occupation in 1967 UNRWA has continued to cater for the needs of refugees. It has shown itself ready, however, to exert pressure on them through cuts in rations and educational and health services. The explanation given is that the budget is shrinking. Many Palestinians, however, question the motives behind the decision, and ask why the cuts coincided with the activities of the Israeli Ben Porath Committee set up in 1983 to dismantle the refugee camps in the absence of a political solution.

3. Reaction in the occupied territories

In reaction to the activities of the external funding agencies including those of the Joint Committee a conference on Development in the Service of Steadfastness was held in the West Bank in 1981/2. The preamble to the resolutions agreed to by the conference stated:

> ...the success of any plan for development to serve the purpose of *sumud* depends basically on a clear political outlook aimed at the establishment of a just and durable peace based on the recognition of Palestinian rights. Until this is achieved, reaching this solution from a Palestinian perspective requires an emphasis on building national unity on a democratic basis, taking consideration of the social, economic and political conditions of those 'inside', their daily confrontation with the occupying authority and the constellation of these conditions within the general Palestinian struggle. Palestinian decision-making is faced with many difficulties because of the dispersion of the Palestinians. Therefore the formulation of the local part of this decision, in a democratic way within the parameters of national unity, enables the sole leadership

of this people (the PLO) to formulate the general Palestinian resolution in its final and binding form.[15]

Underlying dissatisfaction with 'static *sumud*' emerged during the conference. Growing dependence imposed by the manipulation of Joint Committee funds was criticised and demands were made that it be rationalised.[16] The open bridges policy initiated by Israeli Defence Minister Moshe Dayan in 1967, also came under attack. While the conference felt it was too late to close the Damia and Allenby Bridges over the Jordan River immediately, they demanded that their use be highly restricted.

> The danger lies in that those who are developing vested interests from the open borders[17] may acquire a role in the decision making (process) under certain conditions. Normalisation of relations with the occupation may therefore become a natural demand for them. This probability prompts us to draw attention to the necessity to tackle the problem with wisdom and patience.[18]

The conference proposed the following rational guidelines for the promotion of *sumud muqawim:*

> ...*sumud* in the face of Israeli colonial occupation... requires a revision of previous methods in order to stop the ongoing deterioration engendered by the (Israeli) authorities. It requires also the provision of an acceptable standard of living for the Palestinians in order to support their ability to challenge the occupation within a clear strategic outlook. This could be done by utilising development as one of the effective means of achieving this purpose and by discouraging political relaxation under any pressure to guide *sumud* in the wrong direction.[19]

Internal conflicts impeding the process of *sumud muqawim* still have to be resolved.

II. DEVELOPMENT UNDER CONSTRAINTS

In the context of the occupied territories, any attempt arbitrarily to divorce political and social needs, neglecting the first and concentrating on the latter, is tantamount to accepting the dictates of the occupier that relations be normalised.[20] Insistence that the market economy in the occupied territories is the only way to promote *sumud*, while neglecting the political context, only leads to a dead end.

There are five points which need to be taken into consideration when assessing the potential for development under the present constraints:

(a) The basic assumption must be that the West Bank and the Gaza Strip are the future site of a Palestinian state. They are the only places where the Palestinians have maintained an uninterrupted relationship with the land and have a valid claim to sovereignty over it. Palestinian resistance to other proposals containing less than that is legitimised on the grounds of their demand for their internationally recognised rights.

(b) Social and economic development in the occupied territories is not a choice but a necessity. Israel's planned destruction of Palestinian infrastructure and denial of their right to grow must be countered by a strategy of resistance and development. If the Palestinians in the occupied territories are forced into submission and surrender by the pressure of Israeli measures, the establishment of a Palestinian state would be in jeopardy.

(c) There is growing concern that Israeli policies may fragment Palestinian society if they are not checked by *sumud muqawim*. The fear is that socio-economic differentiation between geographic areas in the West Bank and the Gaza Strip could result in sub-entities being appended separately to different centres of Israeli production.[21]

(d) *Sumud muqawim* is a development strategy which attempts, through resistance development and steadfastness, to link up with Palestinian strategies developed outside the occupied territories. The imposition of 'standard priorities' developed by the 'outside' or strategies developed by 'futuristic' studies[22] could lead to misleading conclusions.

(e) The West Bank and Gaza Strip economy is small and dependent and has survived, leaving aside the extreme dependence on remittances from abroad, mainly as an appendage of the Israeli, and to a lesser extent Jordanian, economies. Under these conditions the articulation of a development strategy for the occupied territories should logically be discussed as both an interim and a transitional solution.

A case in point is that no development can take place without a market. A study of the degree of freedom the captive local market still retains is a major necessity. The quantitative and qualitative development of the potential of the market could be considered only after a thorough analysis of local requirements as reflected in prevailing consumption patterns.

1. Strategies of development

One cannot discount the valuable experience in the field of national development in other third-world countries. Their programmes may be subject to completely different conditions, but the strategies they propose can only enrich the Palestinian experience. There is a wide variety of theoretical choices in the development literature. Some are structurally irrelevant because their analytic bases or basic assumptions are not valid in the occupied territories. Others are useful but would require a degree of indigenisation amounting to almost total reconstruction. Theoretical studies are a further source of inspiration which cannot be undervalued. A careful and conscious scrutiny of the external theoretical and practical models will facilitate the choice of components for the local strategy.

Care has to be taken with models which are not related to the international, political, social and internal specificities of the occupied territories. Current discussions have focused on two possible strategies for the occupied territories: import substitution and export-oriented development. Both have shortcomings. Capital intensive, export-oriented production would sharpen social polarisation, weaken the social cohesiveness of the occupied territories and reduce the population's ability to face external dangers. Over and above this, the Israeli authorities' control of fiscal, trade and other economic mechanisms raises major questions about the viability of such proposals. A limited version of export-oriented growth does, however, appear to have some potential at present, if Jordan's open bridges policy could be rationalised. Nevertheless, it could lead to even greater peasant differentiation and marginalisation and give Jordan greater control over the occupied territories. Both these possibilities are definitely undesirable, politically and socially.

The theory of import substitution, on the other hand, was developed as a strategy for independent and generally resourceful third-world countries and not for relatively small areas under foreign domination. In the occupied territories it has been proposed basically as a policy for industrialisation, rather than as a comprehensive development plan, and as such, its capital intensive and technological orientation would, among other things, aggravate the already serious problem of unemployment.

2. Towards an indigenous strategy

The idea of import substitution should not be dismissed altogether, however. A development strategy derived from the theory, one which encouraged local production to serve local consumption, would undoubtedly strengthen self-reliance and the strategy of *sumud muqawim*. Such a process could be developed by maximising co-ordination between the different sectors to enhance their collective and integrated performance. This would also provide the means to counteract degeneration and allow Palestinians to take initiatives. In short, it would entail building an appropriate strategy for development.

Some of the problems facing the development and implementation of such a theory are clearly evident. The human resources required are clearly available. They need, however, adaptation through education, training, guidance and rationalisation. The material resources of the occupied territories fall short of the local needs to prevent stagnation and promote development. External resources need to be invited to fill the potential deficit. Some assessment therefore should be made of the maximum 'tolerable levels of stagnation', the minimum development level necessary for steadfastness and the terms and conditions under which both these limiting conditions will be administered.

Locally controlled external funding serves the *sumud* strategy and enhances co-ordination between 'inside' and 'outside'. Such a relationship would bridge the gap between the two parties caused by difficulties of communication. An 'inside' aware of its immediate and intermediate needs, and an 'outside' conscious of its role as the provider of material and moral support would pave the way for the realisation of Palestinian national aspirations. In other words, the synchronisation of the defined 'need' of the inside and the defined role of the 'outside' to serve the national cause of all Palestinians would minimise friction on secondary issues and promote greater consensus on the major ones.

Despite the drawbacks mentioned above there are grounds for guarded optimism concerning the success of a local development plan aimed at supporting *sumud muqawim*. It means an uphill struggle, however, which will need the support of the PLO leadership outside, and even more, its full commitment and understanding. Social, cultural and economic priorities established inside the occupied territories must take precedence over conceptualisations arrived at outside. Local initiatives have never been at variance with general Palestinian strategy. There is a case, however, for arguing that external conceptualisations have failed in important instances to include the 'internal' dimension. The development of an appropriately flexible relationship between 'inside' and 'outside' to facilitate development efforts and enhance *sumud muqawim* requires recognition in the interim of two complementary yet separate strategies. It also requires deeper mutual confidence and the further democratisation of Palestinian decision making processes.

The local strategy for development has to be a process rather than a static structure, a process which develops continuously towards functionality and efficiency. There is not a standard approach, though efforts to achieve one have been started. Different groups in the occupied territories have adopted different dynamics to effect development. Some have defined *sumud* in a negative or metaphysical way.[23] Istambuli, on the other hand, has suggested that solving the problems of production and consumption and the binding of the result to *sumud* in its practical meaning is the most pressing priority. He further asserts that there is a need to establish a social system able to mobilise productive efforts to serve the basic needs of society more efficiently and distribute this effort more evenly at the same time. Recognising the link between *sumud* and development, Istambuli suggests a *sumud* society does not only produce, but also responds to the needs of consumption in terms of quantity and quality.[24] While he touches on the problems of the dependent market in the occupied territories by referring to the difficulties in disposing of surpluses in the system he proposes, he makes no suggestions for a solution.[25]

Another approach, taking as its starting point the need to develop a programme not only to arrest but to reverse the degeneration of the occupied territories, finds some use in the classical approach to development. It calls for a move away from instantaneous and emotional reactions to Israeli and other external activity and towards the development of a strategy to challenge occupation.[26] Clearer than Istambuli with respect to the market, it proposes a reduction in dependence on the external market and minimisation of its negative political effects through the control of production and its diversification to meet local consumption patterns.[27]

Although these approaches, articulated in various forums in the occupied territories, touch on a number of key issues of substance and of method, the following issues must be taken into account when conceptualising a framework for development for the occupied territories:

(a) The Palestinians are living under prolonged occupation. All areas of life have been transformed since 1967 and a socio-economic specificity has developed. These conditions, though forced on the Palestinians, could be used to promote *sumud muqawim* against the occupation.

(b) To achieve this end development should be encouraged. The alternative is stagnation and degeneration.

(c) Local efforts to research and evaluate experiences in the occupied territories and to define and redefine objectives should be continuous. Use must be made of experiences in other parts of the world when drawing up development policy, but the local experience is indispensable.

(d) A brake must be put on the growth of dependence of the occupied territories. Therefore, strategies which have the effect of increasing dependence, such as export promotion, should be carefully studied.

(e) Agriculture in particular, especially in the Jordan Valley and Gaza, requires reappraisal. A study of a mixed subsistence market agriculture with the purpose of enhancing self-reliance deserves serious attention.

(f) Indigenisation of the education system is another priority. Failure to arrest its present degeneration will encourage alienation and accelerate unemployment.

4. Authority

The question arises of what local authority will implement *sumud muqawim* and create a local development strategy? The Israeli presence, Jordanian influence, the right of the PLO to represent all Palestinians everywhere and US-funded agencies all affect the ability of local Palestinians to decide on development priorities. The most destructive influence is that of Israel, which is constantly creating new facts on the ground to substantiate its claim to sovereignty over the occupied territories.

Since 1967, Israel, with the support of important external forces, has sought to prevent the establishment of a Palestinian state. Israel has always sought to obstruct the development of national institutions in the occupied territories, has also shown preference for Jordanian supported, rather than PLO supported, institutions. The former were encouraged to expand after the landslide victory of the local national movement in the municipal elections of 1976 and were allowed to re-establish relationships with central offices in Amman after the founding of the Joint Committee in 1978. Israel's objectives were clearly to curtail PLO influence and frustrate the Palestinian national movement in the occupied territories. Israel's actions in this regard were unwittingly aided by the conflicting interests, and often outright conflict, among external interested parties which held to differing views with regard to dealing with Israel's policies and actions in the occupied areas and which entertained divergent visions with respect to the future of these areas.

5. Domestic power structure

The social structure of the occupied territories also impedes the consolidation of an effective leadership in the occupied territories to co-ordinate social and economic activities. The present social structure has ancient roots. The *mukhtar*, the traditional office of village or quarter leader, was established by the Ottoman authorities to enhance their control. It was retained first by the British and then by the Israelis. The *hamula* (clan) and family structures have outlived the socio-economic conditions which forged them and withstood the dynamics of change. Non-capitalist and modern production systems are both found in the West Bank and the Gaza Strip, coexisting in a mainly rural society dominated by patriarchal relations. Productive forces have developed irrationally, adjusting to the standards of a market-orientated society and traditional village values. Hybrid social relations are developing which lack the immunity of the old social structure and have failed to acquire the modern characteristics found in Israeli society.

The position of the *fallahin* (the peasantry), provides the most stark example of social hybridisation. Forced expropriation of land has pushed them into a coercive association with modern means of production, yet they have continued dependence on agricultural work to supplement subsistence wages. Women are abandoning their traditional status and entering modern productive areas at an unprecedented rate, pushed by impoverishment and pulled by Israeli market forces. In both cases, *fallahin* and women have become part of a modern production system, yet retain most of the values of a rural society and continue to accept the controls of the traditional structure of authority. This paradox together with external interference which supports the traditional structure have inhibited both women and *fallahin* from redefining their new social status within the framework of a Palestinian nationalist consciousness.

The money coming into the occupied territories from outside has also distorted the social structure. Funding led to a certain degree of capital formation and produced real social differentiation. Other funds have produced polarisation by buying allegiances. The absence of any fundamental economic base for the Palestinian 'nouveaux riches' makes it continuously dependent on funds from abroad, which only fosters dependency and external interference.

The traditional bourgeoisie in the occupied territories, however, displays a greater flexibility towards, and consciousness of, their preferred future. While its members look forward to an independent Palestinian market, they aspire to support the winning political option. They seek the position of brokers in any future settlement between the Israeli market and the Arab market represented by Jordan. Palestinian bureaucrats form another component of the power structure. Having served more than one authority with competence and being divorced from any productive base, the bureaucracy has developed into a career structure not responsive to the intrinsic interests of the majority of the Palestinians.

Notwithstanding this constellation of problems emanating from the authority structure and external intervention, the inability of the non-indigenous actors to co-operate among themselves in any effective way leaves substantial areas free from their control. Similarly the oscillating nature of their influence, irrespective of attempts to stabilise traditional control mechanisms within the present control system and thus force absolute dependency on the Palestinians, ironically contributes to the antithetical dynamism of the traditional structure against imposed control. The Israelis' determination to force submission on a traditional system which has a vested interest in autonomy produces reaction and resistance. The local, integrated approach to the problem of authority in the occupied territories cannot be comprehensively dealt with in this paper. However, it is imperative that higher levels of co-ordination be developed among different groups along with the adaptation of traditional authority structures to the needs of *sumud muqawim*.

III. DEVELOPMENT IN THE OCCUPIED TERRITORIES: THE NATIONAL MOVEMENT AS A SOURCE OF AUTHORITY AND PROMOTER OF DEVELOPMENT

The more sophisticated urban political elite, prompted by the challenge to the national interest of unwanted external interference, mobilised against it and endeavoured to consolidate the national identity. Different forms of leadership came into being after 1967, the most political of which were the Islamic Committee, founded in 1967, the Palestine Patriotic Front, established in 1973 and the National Guidance Committee (NGC) set up in 1978. Different forms of national movement developed, responding to the contemporary needs and conditions. The only constant since 1967 has been the challenge to the Palestinians' ability to control their fate. The NGC was the most sophisticated of the groups mentioned above, bringing together in its leadership representatives of the municipalities, professional and labour unions, students, the various political movements and several independents. The Israeli authorities were hostile to it; most forces on the 'outside' looked on it with mixed feelings tinged with apprehension. Both saw it as an unwelcome competitor. When the Israelis banned it in 1982, its detractors on the 'outside' forgot to eulogise it.

However successful these initiatives were in their respective periods, external coercion and structural difficulties rendered them inoperative under the changing conditions. The removal of the mayors from office in 1982 and the promulgation of a series of military orders restricting the freedom of educational, trade union and other urban institutions exposed their individual weakness.[28] Their inability to act collectively, their divorce from the rural areas and the encouragement of factionalism by certain external factors increased their weakness.

Israeli academic and army officer Menachem Milson, in an article in the American magazine *Commentary*,[29] expounded the need of the Israelis to eradicate the influence of the PLO in the occupied territories. He was appointed to a position in the military administration to politicise the grievances of villagers *vis-à-vis* the urban leadership in the occupied territories. To this end he established the Village Leagues and the Civil Administration.[30] Both failed, but at the same time the urban leadership was not able to withstand the thrust of the Village Leagues. The net result was ambivalence and the recognition of the need for a new start.

There are many reasons for Milson's failure, but foremost among them was *ordinary villagers'* lack of confidence in the Israelis. The experience of occupation and that of the Palestinians inside Israel both generated mistrust. Another important reason was the disjointed power structure in the rural areas which Milson attempted to mobilise against the urban leadership. Jordan, with longer experience, particularly in the West Bank, made a sharp distinction between its rule and Israel's. The latter was clearly perceived as a vehicle of uprootedness, while the former presented itself as a provider of funds, facilities and protection of land ownership.

The national movement's failure was to neglect the historic differences between town and country. Its inability to mobilise the rural population left them prey to external factors. The door was left open to the US-funded agencies and the Jordanians to promote control in rural areas. The Catholic Relief Services, the Community Development Fund and American Near East Refugees Aid (ANERA), all became active in rural areas improving the 'quality of life'.[31] The Jordanian co-operative and agricultural system wielded its influence through the *mukhtars*, the village councils and the traditional rural leadership.

It is never too late to start, however, and from the late 1970s the popular movements began activities in villages. Charitable societies, which are city based, governed by Jordanian law and federated to, and governed by the regulations of, the General Federation of Charitable Societies in Amman also reoriented their work after 1967. While in general charitable societies are confined to social work and charity, serious attempts were made by some of them to start development work. The Jerusalem federation took up development activities, taking a lead from some member societies.[32] The Arab Women's Union of Bethlehem demanded the local charitable societies move from charity work to the promotion of steadfastness as far back as 1967.[33]

The In'ash al-Usra society (Family Rejuvenation Society) is a more obvious example. From its foundation in 1965 it distinguished itself by its non-traditional approach. Its main guiding principles were developmental in nature, albeit romantic.[34] The slogan of the society, 'Building the Palestinian Family is Our Job',[35] reveals a more concrete commitment to development. Among its present objectives, which matured after many years of experience, are the encouragement of rural handicrafts, the re-establishment of productive projects and the discouragement of direct charity.[36] Its programme is clearly oriented towards the maintenance of a version of the subsistence economy to promote a higher degree of self-sufficiency and self-reliance. Its most recent project, an agricultural extension programme training village women in animal husbandry and the care of family orchards and fields, indicates its dedication to development.[37]

In the Gaza Strip a survey carried out by Alison Kelly provides a wide range of information on the social service structure of the non-profit organisations. It also gives many interesting comparisons of the nature of the leadership of those societies. Kelly observed a close association of particular societies with their principal leader, to the point where people equated the society with him or her.[38] She acknowledged that at the time, these organisations provided the only opportunity for residents of the Gaza Strip to be involved in planning their futures and establishing a Palestinian infrastructure, and observed that the occupation was the single most adverse factor facing these organisations.[39]

In the majority of cases, however, charitable societies in the occupied territories have exercised a policy of pacification through charity. They have also enhanced urban control over the rural areas. Any changes in policy have been, for the most part, cosmetic and the involvement of people from the rural areas in decision making marginal. The chairman of the Jerusalem Federation of Charitable Societies confessed that funds coming in over the bridges have favoured the towns. Activities and services, he concluded, have followed the same lines.[40]

But despite their many drawbacks in performance and objectives both social and political, the potential of the charitable societies should not be underrated. Greater work is needed to redirect their efforts towards development, co-operation and co-ordination if their usefulness is to be enhanced. This change can come through a more active and direct response to grass-roots needs and demands. These have been increasingly articulated by grass-roots, popularly based organisations now active in the occupied territories.

This being the case, why did the grass-roots associations emerge? Are they an expression of defiance to the more traditional charitable societies which proved unable to meet the challenges of a development resistance to Israeli occupation? Or do they represent only political arenas disguised as developmental groups? Both elements, political and social, are certainly part of their make-up, but basically the grass-roots movement is a development instrument with political motivation. The groups are distinguished from the charitable societies in that they are based solely on popular legitimacy, that their activities are carried out through voluntary work. They are further distinguished by being able to function in both the West Bank and the Gaza Strip as a dynamic and unifying factor between the two geographic areas.[41] They are harassed by the Israelis and are categorised by the traditional leadership as radical and unorthodox.[42]

There are grass-roots movements active in the fields of health, agriculture, land reclamation and women's activities. The first two deal with technical problems, the third is promoting the traditional principle of *'awna* (mutual help) and land reclamation, while the last is concerned with women's issues and problems.

The objectives of the grass-roots organisations are best summed up in the words of the secretary of the Higher Committee for Voluntary Work.

> We do not only build a wall or pave a road. We build a new human being...Working on the land voluntarily and extending help to the village and institutions is an exercise of the first degree. It helped in the crystallisation of a new set of ethics, dearly nurtured by the Higher Committee. Our purpose is to turn voluntary work...into a workshop and a school, both able to provide our Palestinian people with pioneering individuals abiding by national ethics, firmly anchored to the land and highly dedicated to the national cause, (proving themselves) through their sweat and labour.[43]

The rural-oriented popular organisations are the national movement's answer to its previous neglect of the villages. It is a paradox that the factionalism, which spread after 1980 like an oil slick on water, produced four distinct popular movements which imitated and duplicated each other. The ideological incompatibility between them has since been overcome in some cases.

The women's movement, for instance, has seen progress in co-operation since 1983. In contrast, competition characterises the relationships of their counterparts in other fields. There is hardly any relationship, for example, between the Voluntary Work Committees and the Youth Committees for Social Work.

The explanation in the first case lies in the common problems women face. These include the problems of detainees and prisoners, juvenile delinquency and the curfews imposed on refugee camps. The secretary of the Working Women's Committee stated that co-operation had recently taken place among the movements with different political leanings at branch level. She added that while there had been no central co-ordination of social activities, she expected relations to continue to grow.[44]

It would be wrong to conclude that there is potential confrontation between the different voluntary groups, but there is room for them to complement each other's work more effectively. Given the area of the occupied territories and setting against it their limited resources, their differences have stimulated competition rather than confrontation.

The grass-roots movements do face problems, most of them emanating from the nature of the society in the occupied territories and their relationship with the 'outside'. Other factors play a part as well. On one level, some of the groups are caught in the classic rural-urban dichotomy. They function none the less in the rural areas, but are more politically motivated than development oriented. Others, especially those working in agriculture, health and voluntary work, are more development oriented. They are interested in penetrating the traditional barrier between city and village by promoting awareness of local problems and providing solutions. The Agricultural Relief Committee, the Medical Relief Committee, the Voluntary Works Committee and the Working Women's Committee are the most pioneering in that field. Their services have been long felt in recipient villages.

Other problems faced by the developmental groups are that they are not licensed by the authorities and therefore face the constant risk of being disbanded. The National Guidance Committee, which acted openly as a popular movement and was made illegal in 1982, is a case in point. The grass-roots movements already face harassment by the authorities, as do individual members. Their continuity will be determined by their ability to bypass Israeli restrictions and to regenerate themselves. On the one hand Israeli interests and behaviour are highly unpredictable and the movements must therefore face risks beyond their control. On the other, as the leaders of the movements grow older their ability to pass the spirit of voluntarism on to the younger generation will test their control of this process of social change.

IV. CONCLUSION

Since Israeli occupation in 1967 the West Bank and Gaza Strip have acquired special social, economic and psychological characteristics which were not there before. Important though this is it has not been actually internalised in the policies of the Palestinian leadership and the Arabs outside and has therefore had little impact on their strategies *vis-à-vis* the occupied territories. Because of this, a statement of purpose on development in the occupied territories based on emerging socio-economic and political realities in these territories, and unencumbered by any external objection, is a pressing need. An indigenous development strategy related to the stated purpose should likewise be formulated.

It is equally important to divide the strategy so that it substantiates Palestinian aspirations in two interrelated stages: the maintenance of *sumud* (of Palestinians on their land), and the second stage of implementing UN resolutions on the Palestinian question. *Sumud* is a prerequisite for any just and durable solution to the conflict. This *sumud* must be *sumud muqawim*. To become effective, *sumud muqawim* has to produce alternatives to what the Israelis offer or 'static *sumud*' promises. It has to embrace a new vision of development aimed at enhancing the ability of people to withstand Israeli pressure, growing social polarisation, the commercialisation of culture and material and spiritual impoverishment.

The provision of a popular moral authority will be an uphill struggle. It should be possible to promote the moral authority of the indigenous social, political and educational institutions. The existing structure of authority in the rural area, traditional though it is, has positive characteristics which can be utilised. Any attempt to promote an integrated rural-urban moral authority should be encouraged.

The integrated concerted efforts of formal local institutions and the grass-roots movements wield an authority of immense influence. The political struggle is apt to produce different combinations of alliances, but national unity and the widest alliance possible among the formal and non-formal institutions is a necessity and a matter of the highest priority.

A formal development plan cannot be drawn up or implemented in the absence of Palestinian national sovereignty. While conditions in the occupied territories are in a state of flux, however, an order of priorities for these territories could be designed by the Palestinians 'inside'.

The concept of self-reliance is taking hold in Palestinian universities, unions, associations and movements. Over-reliance on funds from politically motivated sources outside has proved self-defeating. The price tag attached to this aid in the form of political and social dependency is greater than the Palestinians can afford. The old Arab saying, 'The people of Mecca are the best experts on its topography,' has demonstrated its relevance and validity. While cast in the role of the Meccans, the Palestinians in the occupied territories are none the less aware of the indispensable relationship with the Palestinian community outside. They have no illusions that their political aspirations can be divided from those of the Palestinian diaspora. The liberation of the one lies logically and dialectically in the emancipation of the other and vice versa. A two-tier strategy conducted in two geographic locations and under two sets of different conditions does not preclude a mutually reinforcing complementarity.

Social and economic specificities exist between 'inside' and 'outside' and there are conflicts between and within them. The Palestinian leadership should recognise the dialectical nature of these conflicts and harness them in the service of a global Palestinian strategy. Maladministration of these conflicts, whether by ignoring or suppressing them, could raise the conflicts to the level of contradictions. Such a development, if it were to materialise, would, in the long term, disrupt wider Palestinian goals and strategies. The approach outlined in this paper, in recognising the specificities of both the occupied territories and the Palestinian diaspora in the present historical context, calls for an integrative approach based on the organic, and mutually enriching relationship that binds the two sides together.

NOTES

1. See for example, *Al-Tali'a,* 5 April 1984.

2. For details see: Ibrahim Dakkak, 'Back to square one: a study in the re-emergence of the Palestinian identity 1967-1980' in Alexander Schölch (ed.), *Palestinians Over the Green Line* (Ithaca Press, London, 1983).

3. Ibid., p. 79.

4. These figures are condensed from Yusif Sayigh, *'nahwa tarshid amthal li-al-musa'ada al-iqtisadiyya al-'arabiyya li-daffa al-gharbiyya wa-qit'a ghazza'* (Towards a model of Arab economic assistance to the West Bank and the Gaza Strip) (unpublished report), pp. 36-8.

5. See for example, Jordanian Law No. 33 (1966), Law of Societies and Social Institutions, especially Article 2 (definition) and Article 7(3) and 12. Dr Amin Khatib, the chairman of the Federation of Jerusalem Muhafaza (Directorate) Charitable Societies, described the activities of his societies as covering the roles and duties of three Jordanian ministries: social development, education and health. Personal interview, 6 November 1985. See also Emile Nakhle, *The West Bank and Gaza* (The American Enterprise Institute, Washington D.C., 1979), p. 35.

6. The number of trade unions multiplied five-fold in the five years up to 1986 (there were 29 unions in 1981 and 154 in 1986). This follows the split in the Federation of Trade Unions on 29 August 1981. Each part maintained the same title. See Jiyurj Hazbun, *'na'am li-mashru' al-kutla al-ummaliyya al-taqaddumiyya'* (Yes to the proposals of the Progressive Labour Bloc) *Al-Tali'a,* 30 January 1986.

7. The Joint Committee paid 85% of the tuition fees of university students for the 1982/3 and 1983/4 scholastic years. It then abruptly stopped.

8. Bakir Abu Kishk, *al-da'iqa al-sakaniyya fi al-ard al-muhtalla* (The housing problem in the occupied territories) (Engineers Association-West Bank Branch and Birzeit University Research Centre, Jerusalem, 1980), p. 62.

9. For example see the reports of Yusuf Budeiri, 'The investigating committee on the conditions of the national co-operatives housing project, 21 March 1983' (unpublished). The Juneid 'Iskan' Co-operative in Nablus in its project, for example, provides an average of 200 square metres of land and 54 square metres of building for each individual.

10. International Labour Organisation, *Report of the Director General – Appendices* (ILO, Geneva, 1983), pp. 34-6.

11. Meron Benvenisti, *US Funded Projects in the West Bank (1977-82)*, *Palestinian Sector* (The West Bank Data Base Project, Jerusalem, 1984), pp. 2 and 4.

12. Ibid., pp. 2 and 15.

13. Ibid.

14. David McDowall, 'A case for reassessment', *Middle East International*, 19 June 1981, p. 11.

15. Arab Thought Forum, *Proceedings of the Conference on Development in the Service of Steadfastness 1981-2, Final Session* (Arab Thought Forum, Jerusalem, 1984), pp. 30-3.

16. Ibid., p. 34.

17. This includes the two open bridges across the Jordan River (Damia and Allenby), the Lebanese border and the Egyptian border which was opened after the peace treaty between Egypt and Israel was signed in 1979.

18. Arab Thought Forum, *Proceedings, Final Session*, pp. 34-5.

19. Ibid., p. 8.

20. See for example, Yusif Sayigh, 'Nahwa tarshid', p. 85.

21. A road system built up by the Israelis in the occupied territories facilitates the integration of different parts of the West Bank separately into the Israeli centres of production in the north, central region and south. It will effectively disrupt any economic fabric the West Bank still maintains. For the legal aspects of the Israeli road system in the occupied territories see Aziz Shehadeh et al., *Israeli Proposed Road Plan for the West Bank* (Law in the Service of Man, Ramallah, 1984). The economic implications of the plan may be even more significant.

22. See for example, P.G. Sadler and Bakir Abu Kishk, *Filastin: khiyarat al-tanmiya al-matruha* (Palestine: alternative development choices) (UNCTAD Geneva, October 1983); P.G. Sadler et al., *Palestine: Development of the Industrial Sector* (UNIDO, Vienna, July 1983).

23. Raja Shehadeh, *The Third Way* (Quartet Books, London, 1982); 'Abd al-Sattar Qasim, *risala fi al-sumud* (A thesis on steadfastness) (Arab Studies Society, Jerusalem, 1981).

24. Da'ud Istambuli, *Al-insan al-zira'i* (Agrarian man) (Arab Thought Forum, Jerusalem, 1981), p. 21.

25. Ibid.

26. Arab Thought Forum, *Proceedings*, Part 1, p. 4.

27. Ibid.

28. Military Order No. 854 dated 6 July 1980 and Order 825 dated 20 February 1980 greatly restrict the activities of institutions of higher education and trade unions. See for analysis Jonathan Kuttab, *Analysis of Military Order 854 and Related Orders Concerning Educational Institutions in the Occupied West Bank* (Law in the Service of Man, Ramallah, May 1981); Mursi Hajir, 'tahlil qanuni li-al-amr 1108' (Legal analysis of Order 1108) in *huquq al-'umal al-'arab fi al-daffa al-gharbiyya fi zill awamir al-'askariyya al-isra'iliyya* (Arab workers rights in the West Bank under Israeli military orders) (Lawyers Guild-Jerusalem Centre, Jerusalem, July 1984), pp. 6-9.

29. Menachem Milson, 'How to make peace with the Palestinians', *Commentary*, May 1981.

30. The Civil Administration was established in accordance with Military Order No. 947. For an analysis of that order see Jonathan Kuttab and Raja Shehadeh, *Civilian Administration in the Occupied West Bank: Analysis of*

Israeli Military Government Order No. 947 (Omar International, Jerusalem, January 1982).

31. The 'improvement in the quality of life' of the Palestinians in the occupied territories was suggested by US Secretary of State George Shulz in August 1983. Professor Stephen Cohen arranged a group of American businesspeople of Jewish and Arab origins to pursue this policy. The group met the Israeli Prime Minister Shimon Peres on 11 October 1984, but there were no noticeable benefits to the population of the occupied territories.

32. Interview with Dr Amin Khatib, 6 November 1985.

33. Rita Giacaman, *Palestinian Women and Development in the Occupied Territories* (unpublished, 1982).

34. The In'ash al-Usra Society *Annual Report 1976* outlines the following principles: (a) Light one candle and do not live in the darkness for 100 years; (b) Reorientation of material, human and mental resources in the right direction; (c) The word 'impossible' should be deleted from the vocabulary of the individual in order to liberate them from potential disadvantage.

35. Ibid., *Annual Report 1978/9*, cover page.

36. Ibid., pp. 10-11.

37. It has been described as a development project and administered by the Higher Committee for the Eradication of Illiteracy (an indigenous forum made up of representatives of Birzeit University, the Federation of Charitable Societies in the West Bank and the Gaza Charitable Societies) which was set up on 22 June 1985.

38. Alison Kelly, 'A study of social service provision by the private non-profit organisations in the Gaza Strip' (unpublished, 1984).

39. Ibid.

40. Interview with Dr Amin Khatib, 6 November 1985.

41. See for example, The Higher Committee for Voluntary Work in the West Bank and the Gaza Strip, *Voluntary Work* (The Higher Committee, Jerusalem, 1981).

42. They were refused funds by the Joint Committee, harassed by the Israeli security apparatus, Jewish settlers and also by Islamic fundamentalists.

43. Walid Arramuni, Address to the Sixth Voluntary Work Camp in Nazareth, 1980, 'Masira al-'amal al-tatawwu'i fi al-daffa al-gharbiyya wa qit'a ghazza', (Progression of Voluntary Work in the West Bank and the Gaza Strip), *Al-Katib* no. 23, December 1981, p. 21.

44. Interview with the Secretary of the Working Women's Federation in December 1985.

14

Towards a Strategy for Development: Empowerment and Entrepreneurship

Harold Dick

I. INTRODUCTION

1. Empowerment and entrepreneurship in economic development

The empowerment of the economic development process begins with people, not with capital, natural resources, skills or infrastructure. This process finds its creative, energising force in the human spirit, that fixes on an idea and then drives relentlessly to achieve an economic objective. This spirit is evident in the peasant woman from Sureif (a village in the Hebron district), who excels in producing quality needlework which will command a top price on the market and is also observable in the farm equipment manufacturer from Jenin who produces highly competitive agricultural machinery. An agricultural co-operative near Hebron displays this quality in providing competitively priced seedling and olive oil press services to its members.

The empowerment of the occupied territories economy will provide a more secure financial base, which will allow Palestinians to feed, clothe, shelter and educate themselves, and enable them to enjoy their culture and religion in a manner consistent with the priorities they have set. Economic strength (empowerment) will allow Palestinians to develop structures and systems to stand fast under occupation. Palestinians themselves must then decide how they will deal, not only with matters of social justice, but also with the distribution of income they gain from their increased economic power.

It is the contention of this paper that a strategy for economic development needs to find its roots in the entrepreneurial model which is alive and remarkably vital despite the abundant constraints. Collec-

311

tive and private entrepreneurs, the flesh and blood of an economy, do not need to be taught the merits of self-sufficiency, but demonstrate resilience and vitality by their very existence. Too often development strategies have focused on such things as training, credit, subsidies, natural resources and 'experts'. These factors are all idle and immobile without the addition of entrepreneurship. This quality or ability rests in a person, or a group of people, who are prepared to incur the risks inherent in forming and operating a business enterprise. The point is that the spirit of entrepreneurship is an essential ingredient in any economic enterprise, whether collective or private, if it is to operate successfully.

2. Constraints and competition

To gain greater control of their economic destiny Palestinians in the occupied territories must confront two massive 'abnormal constraints' which compound the normal obstacles of few natural resources, competitive markets, transportation restrictions, inadequate credit or unavailable skilled manpower. Firstly, any person or group undertaking a business initiative must contend with the disruptive, oppressive role of the occupying military authorities. This role manifests itself in economic life from the denial of a permit to open a mineral water bottling plant to the physical and mental harassment of those who desire to sell their agricultural produce in Jerusalem, Israel or Europe.

Yitzhak Rabin, Israel's minister of defence, delivered the ultimate competitive challenge to the occupied territories in February 1985 by stating: 'There will be no development (in the occupied territories), initiated by the Israeli Government, and no permits will be given for expanding agriculture or industry (there), which may compete with the state of Israel.'[1] Practice confirms that the occupying authorities reject any notion of fair competition and would suggest that they are attempting to stifle the entrepreneurial will of Palestinians with raw force.

The second constraint lies in the massive injection of remittance monies from abroad and from salaries earned in Israel, that skew expectations of Palestinians and make it difficult for a more authentic local economy to compete. These funds now provide the operating funds for the hospitals, universities, co-operatives, school systems and charitable societies. Externally generated funds have also been invested in personal consumption including houses, cars and optional consumer items. The sources of these funds are becoming increasingly insecure. They are vulnerable to cycles in the Israeli economy and are sensitive to economic and political developments in the Gulf region. Dependency and insecurity result because Palestinians are not in a strong bargaining position to ensure that these funds continue to flow.

In addition to dealing with these two constraints, any economic development strategy must start from the perspective that the market for products or services is already intensely competitive. There simply are too many opportunists earning money on good ideas. Every car repair shop, blacksmith, cabinet maker and olive wood manufacturer is competing with somebody else down the street. This internal competition is further compounded by the pressure of US$ 860 million worth of imports from Israel and Europe.[2] These imports include everything from Greek olive oil, to Israeli clothing and food products, to farm machinery from Italy. These imports are of high quality. If Palestinians are to develop the productive sectors of their economy, they will need to develop a competitively priced, quality product.

Paulo Freire has stated, 'Freedom is acquired by conquest, not by gift. It must be pursued constantly and responsibly.'[3] Economic markets and freedom to pursue them will require vitality and perseverance. Some entrepreneurs in the occupied territories, both private and collective, have dealt successfully with competition, with remittances and the military. They have demonstrated that economic freedom can be created.

3. From a defensive to an offensive strategy

For an entrepreneurial spirit to flourish economic development strategies must be offensive in nature, not defensive. Following the occupation these strategies were understandably defensive in scope. There was acute dislocation, psychological immobility and political insecurity. Economic thinking was survivalist with an emphasis on the need to stay on the land, to educate children and to earn an income, no matter where. More fundamental economic planning would occur after the occupation ended in a political solution.

This strategy presented itself in the expenditure of large amounts of capital from the Arab world, the Jordanian-Palestinian Joint Committee, the UN and voluntary agencies. These funds built roads, universities, water, sewage and electrical systems and private homes. This could only be seen as a short term strategy since these developments depended on external funding. Only the investments in the agricultural sector paid off in dramatically increased productivity of 8.6 per cent per year in constant values.[4]

A strategy of empowerment must be based upon increased productivity in the agricultural, industrial and services sectors of the occupied territories. This empowerment must be achieved within the competitive nature of interdependent economic relationships with Israel, the East Bank, Europe and the Arab world. This paper does not suggest that one can become self-sufficient. No one is self-sufficient. The issue is one of how empowered can Palestinians become within these interdependent relationships. Palestinians must gain greater control over the facets of production, marketing and finance required to fuel the economic engine of the occupied territories.

This is an experiential paper that will focus on economic strategies from the perspective of entrepreneurship and will consider the role of grants/credit, agriculture produce marketing and small business/ industrial development.[5]

II. GRANTS/CREDIT AND THE ENTREPRENEUR

1. The importance of risk in capital formation

The entrepreneur thrives on the risks inherent in mobilising capital. Nothing sharpens the acuteness of the senses and motivation more than being held accountable for the performance of capital in a business enterprise. It doesn't really matter whether the capital is private, from lending institutions or the government.

Blacksmiths, who have all their own and some borrowed capital tied up in stock and equipment, must find ways to sell their product or face the prospects of losing their capital. It is this risk that causes them to work longer hours and produce the finest quality work they can. They must then develop contacts among farmers, contractors and engineers to ensure that their services and products will be considered. The Palestinian farmer is probably the quintessential risk-taker, annually gambling a large pool of their assets on fertiliser, irrigation, trellising poles, and livestock in anticipation of a good crop and superior prices.

The manner in which capital is mobilised will frequently determine how successfully it will be used in the entrepreneurial process. The more accountable a person or group is for its capital, the more rigour and discipline will be imposed to ascertain that a prospective venture is sound in the first place and then assure no effort will be spared to make the venture profitable.

2. The potentially destructive role of grants

Grants, soft loans, loans with low interest rates and long grace periods are potentially the most destructive form of capital mobilisation, particularly if these methods continue to be used for a prolonged period. 'Easy money' has to be based on some form of philanthropy. Grants and soft loans that depend on an international donor community over an extended period finally call into question the dignity of the individuals involved and perpetuate a neo-colonial type of relationship. Grants used to stimulate economic growth perpetuate the feeling that people deserve a break. This is a state of mind that is counterproductive to the development of the entrepreneurial process.[6] Money is never free anywhere. It always costs something. A grant or service rendered free of charge should be subject to suspicion and should be questioned in terms of the motive of the grantee or its quality and relevance. Serious people appreciate straightforward, honest business relationships.[7] Grants may serve a function for a time, but when they are used indefinitely they become counterproductive to sound economic development. Three examples will serve to illustrate the point.

(i) Zbeidat

During the last ten years voluntary agency funds and funds from the East Bank were mobilised in the form of grants and zero interest loans to develop Zbeidat in the Jordan Valley. Drip irrigation was introduced, houses and roads were built, a domestic water system was installed and the village was electrified. The relative well-being of the people began to express itself in the odd television set and refrigerator. The development of the village was deemed to be observably good.

However, the long period during which 'easy money' was available to the village also created dependency. Any new initiative entailed a trip to the voluntary agencies or the East Bank to get funds for a community centre, a kindergarten or a health project. This routine became a way of life and finally had a demonstrably negative impact on the collective entrepreneurial will of the community.

Nothing was more important to the economic health of Zbeidat than a reliable water supply. The primary income generator for the village was their vegetable harvest, which depended totally on irrigation. In September 1984 the village pump broke down just before the beginning of the new planting season. The people could not or would not find the resources inside the village to replace the pump. Dependency had paralysed them. In desperation they turned to the voluntary agencies and to the East Bank for funds. It was a time of economic crisis, since the life-blood of the village was at stake. In the end the traditional pattern of dependency asserted itself with a number of agencies providing the funds for a new pump. The cycle of counting on funds from 'somewhere' perpetuated itself.

The real empowering developmental issue was whether the village would begin to collect funds during the next eight years of anticipated life of the pump in order to replace it. The lesson will probably not be learned. The will of the people to act collectively in their own economic interest has almost certainly been compromised.

(ii) A seedling nursery

In 1984 approximately 650,000 olive seedlings were sold throughout the West Bank. They were supplied by approximately 15 nurseries, both co-operative and private. The smallest nursery provided no more than 20,000 seedlings, while the largest provided about 200,000 at an average price of JD 0.030 each.

Recently a group of well-intentioned, young agriculturalists petitioned funding agencies to provide the entire initial funding for a 150,000 olive seedling nursery. In terms of their application the individuals in the collective were not required to put up any money themselves. They were not being asked via a loan mechanism to be accountable for those funds, or for the viability of the enterprise. There was no financial risk for the people involved. The grant would put them in a position dramatically to affect the production of olive seedlings on the West Bank.

Agricultural experts indicate that there is no particular shortage of olive seedlings on the West Bank. Unless the collective has some new market in mind the 20-25 per cent increase in production will drastically alter the equilibrium of supply and demand by which other producers have operated. The producer of 20,000 seedlings, who had no help with start-up costs faces potential ruin. Inevitably a price war will be started as larger producers attempt to retain their market share. Price wars are not necessarily a bad thing provided the producers have sufficient margins left to capitalise production costs for the following year. In the long run the laws of supply and demand will assert themselves and after two or three years several producers will have gone out of business and a new producer because of an 'abnormal' advantage will have been launched. As many jobs will be lost as created.

If the individuals involved in the collective had been dealing with effectively costed money, and if they had been liable for the capital in question, a much more thorough market study would have been undertaken. The research might have showed them that a grape seedling nursery with phylloxera-resistant root stock would provide a business opportunity where the use of effectively costed capital would produce a good profit.

(iii) An egg producer

In 1982 an organisation received approximately US$ 40,000 from several funding agencies to establish a 3,200 bird poultry operation to produce eggs as an income generating project for the organisation. The money was all delivered in the form of grants and capital did not need to figure in the costs of production. After some initial problems the operation began to generate income.

As the eggs from this organisation began to appear in the shops, the impact was felt by other producers in the area. It became apparent that the new producer organisation could command whatever market it wanted because of the inflexibility in pricing. After considerable consternation and frustration had developed on the part of other egg producers, they came up with a rather ingenious and logical plan. They presented a grant application to a second agency to enable them to compete in the market place with the new operation. The effect of grants on the risk-taking entrepreneurial farmers was very disruptive. The ultimate irony, however, came when it was time for the organisation to replace its chickens. Since they had not retained any capital to replace the chickens they had to re-apply for further grants. The organisation had not become empowered. It had simply become more dependent.

There is a role for development money in the fostering of the entrepreneurial spirit. Sections III and IV will give examples of how it may be employed so that it doesn't subsidise existing production gluts, but creates new opportunities.

3. The role of credit

Ultimately credit, accompanied by sound technical advice, is the method which will demonstrate the effectiveness of money mobilised in a particular venture. Not only will this method help give an authentic analysis of economic viability, but it will also ensure that the relationship between the source of the funds and the user of the funds will be unpatronising, professional and filled with respect. Credit structures must use penalties, social pressure and legal action to ensure compliance, with the agreed upon uses of the funds. The authentic private or collective entrepreneurs understand these requirements, will respect them and be motivated by them.

Every effort, therefore, should be made to direct economic development monies into credit mechanisms. This will not only develop discipline in the financial marketplace, but also create structures and organisations that have a life of their own, i.e. they will regenerate themselves, particularly if they charge market interest rates. They should be controlled by residents of the occupied territories so that loans can be given in accordance with their own priorities. An important secondary benefit will accrue from the creation of jobs and the development of the managerial skills required to administer such organisations as well as the skills required to provide advisory services.

Palestinians will need to demonstrate a high degree of flexibility to create such structures, since all financial institutions have been disallowed by the authorities and it does not appear that this policy will change. However, despite constraints a good deal of capital is being assembled on a private basis. A random survey of 276 businesses taken in 1982 indicated that all but 3 per cent of their start-up funds had been accumulated privately.[8] If this creativity in private financing could be somewhat formalised, more people would be able to participate in the entrepreneurial process by obtaining loans.

One of the most hopeful proposals lies in the recent establishment of a non-profit company, which plans, among other functions, to make credit available to farmers. Another proposition advanced by a Gaza lawyer capitalises on a novel but ancient solution. It would involve the creation of a financial company that would operate like an Islamic bank. There would be no interest and no customers, only partners. The company would simply be the co-ordinator between persons with capital and the individuals or collectives who have a business or the idea for a business.[9] These are partial solutions that represent what is possible. The expansion of the entrepreneurial process depends on the implementation of creative credit schemes.

III. AGRICULTURAL PRODUCE MARKETING AND THE ENTRE-PRENEUR

1. Importance of agricultural produce marketing

It is substantially true to say that the survival of Palestinians on their land depends to a large extent on achieving the effective and successful marketing of produce. Agricultural produce is an indigenous resource, where Palestinians can still significantly shape the production factors. There is also evidence to suggest that agricultural production can expand if markets can be found. Agriculture provides 24.8 per cent of all jobs in the occupied territories and is the largest Palestinian-controlled income generator.[10] The same entrepreneurial spirit that caused farmers to become more productive during the last ten years, must now also demonstrate itself in a search for new markets. This will involve considerable investment, acute attention to quality, sophisticated management techniques and marketing skills.

2. Constraints/opportunities in expansion

Except for Gaza citrus, there are no packaging and grading facilities in the occupied territories. One expert indicated that the fruit and vegetables of the occupied territories come to market in poor condition, not because there is something inherently wrong with the product, but because the produce has not been processed properly.[11] The Palestinian farmer is, therefore, left in a very poor bargaining position in the market. This represents an opportunity for a private entrepreneur or an entrepreneurial collective to increase the value of produce and bring additional revenue to the occupied territories.

The lack of packing and grading facilities is further negatively affected by the wooden boxes used for shipment. Presently the Jordan government allows only wooden crates to cross the bridge. There is some indication, however, that improved packaging such as styrofoam or cardboard boxes, may be allowed across the bridge in the near future. The restrictions on transport permitted to cross the bridge further adversely affects the profitability of produce being shipped to the East Bank. Only trucks registered before 1967 are allowed to cross. This has restricted transport and made it expensive. These are two regulations that must be lifted by the Jordanians before marketing to, or through, the East Bank can be substantially improved. It is hard to ascertain how much produce is sold to Israel and via Israel to other markets. However, Israel makes it very difficult to market produce from the occupied territories in Israel. They essentially do not allow any competition with their own produce. This is particularly the case with citrus. Conversely, the occupied territories are open to Israeli produce. Additionally the authorities have not allowed shipments to the European market. The highly restricted, utterly undeveloped marketing structure represents a substantial entrepreneurial challenge. If overcome it would create a significant opportunity to generate greater income and empower the agricultural sector of the occupied territories. The present marketing channels through the commission agents and exporters have demonstrated little interest in dealing with these issues. The marketing co-operatives are not really structured to undertake a marketing venture. The kind of dynamic strategy required does not exist.

3. Description of a marketing venture

Numerous discussions took place in the summer and autumn of 1984 between development personnel, farmers and representatives of co-operatives to review the possibilities for creating some marketing leverage for Palestinian farmers. It became apparent that there might be potential for marketing produce in Europe. At first the group thought a study might be useful. Then they decided that the best way to assess the market would be actually to go to Europe and simply sell the produce of the occupied territories.

A presentation package was developed, which focused on the vitality of the agricultural sector, its technological innovativeness and the quality of the produce. It also featured the sophistication, skills and education of Palestinians in the occupied territories. Business contacts were made in England, Norway and Sweden. The trip was convened under the auspices of the Jericho Marketing Co-operative. The manager was accompanied by a marketing consultant and an economic consultant. The objective of the trip was simply to bring produce importers from England, Norway and Sweden to the occupied territories at their own expense, to explore the possibilities of developing a business relationship.

The marketing delegation called on 15 different importers. The responses were virtually all favourable. The buyers were impressed with the quality of the produce and the comparative advantage offered by the sun-ripened Jordan Valley produce during the months of December to April. The only major questions were logistical and a number of people were willing to assist in solving these problems. They felt that a niche could be developed for produce from both Gaza and the West Bank. The 'natural hot house' of the Jordan Valley presented an opportunity to diversify into crops grown specifically for the Scandinavian and British palates.

The objectives of the trip were met. Three different individuals came to the West Bank and Gaza at their own expense to meet with producers. They liked the quality of the produce and felt there was a sound basis on which to attempt a business relationship. Five orders were placed for produce form the occupied territories to be shipped to Europe.

A good deal of research took place to determine the proper packaging and the route by which the produce could travel. Both the Jordanian and Israeli routes presented significant but not necessarily insurmountable obstacles. The Jordanian route was problematic from a transport and packaging perspective. The Israeli route presented military and political obstacles. Contacts in the diplomatic, legal and Israeli communities suggested that it might be possible to break through the Israeli barriers and sell directly to Europe with an occupied territories identity. Logistically the Israeli route was the preferred route.

4. Observations

The most empowering aspect of the whole venture was that the importers were interested in doing business because they liked the quality of the produce. Since they were constantly searching for a new source of supply, this presented a good profit-making opportunity. The importers were interested in Palestinians as equals in a business relationship which would be beneficial for both parties. There was little interest in doing business because Palestine was under occupation. A tangible financial motive existed to break out of the constraints. There was no paternalism in the relationship.

Empowerment in an economic enterprise comes from controlling as many facets of the production and marketing cycles as possible. It is imperative that Palestinians develop their own identities with the buyers. By working through middlemen, producers in the occupied territories are left in a vulnerable position. It also dilutes their profits. The flaw in the whole venture, that stymied any successfull follow-up, was that the prerequisite entrepreneurial will did not surface in the Palestinian community. The co-operative did not have the entrepreneurial determination or the managerial skill to undertake the difficult task. No one in the organisation had anything substantial at risk. The co-operative had no investment in the venture. The initiative would have had a better chance of success if the co-operative had shared in the cost of the marketing trip. Then, perhaps, there would have been a higher commitment on their part.

Although it represents significant risk, this opportunity needs to be pursued. Not continuing with this or similar initiatives means continuation of the status quo and Palestinians of the West Bank and Gaza Strip will be stifled in the expansion of their agricultural sector. Little will be accomplished by further studies. Entrepreneurship is required, either collective or private, which will invest in a modest packing facility and then secure the best packaging available. It will then ensure that all the value-added, i.e. the extra profits from well packaged and graded produce, will be returned to the occupied territories. These individuals will then need to employ determination and resourcefulness to obtain the required permits and to solve the logistical difficulties. This is the kind of initiative that will allow Palestinians to break out of the strangulation of their agricultural sector and indigenous Palestinian resources.

IV. INDUSTRIAL DEVELOPMENT AND THE ENTREPRENEUR

1. Constraints

Despite the decline of the industrial sector from 9 per cent of GDP in 1968 to 6.5 per cent in 1980,[12] it has demonstrated resilience under powerful internal and external constraints in the absence of a benign government. The 4,020 metal products, textile, clothing, leather, food and beverage establishments represent a solid core of entrepreneurial will that provides employment for over 16,000 people.[13] The industrial sector is in a position to provide some stimulus to the economy of the occupied territories that would empower them in the interdependent regional economic relationship.

This vitality is even more noteworthy given the structural constraints described by Van Arkadie, '... the poorest economies, lacking sovereignty, of course, have had no opportunity to use traditional policy instruments, such as tariffs or the exchange rate adjustment to serve their own economic objectives'.[14] Several development theorists speculate that in some cases this lack of formality and structure allows some businesses to exercise their entrepreneurial spirit.

The industrial sector has also survived despite the fact that remittances and foreign donor financed consumer spending has compelled domestic entrepreneurial will away from higher risk industrial ventures into mercantile and speculative strategies for capturing externally originating cash flow.[15] This has been further compounded by the fact that about 80 per cent of all private capital is spent on house construction.[16]

Mercantilism and construction are important components in the economic strength of any society. In the occupied territories they play a disproportionately large role and have caused entrepreneurs to adopt short-term, low risk strategies. Both these sectors are heavily dependent on external funding and are therefore vulnerable to a reduction in that funding.

2. Simple strategies to promote import substitution and product innovation

This paper does not envision a strategy that will radically or quickly alter the percentage of GDP that the industrial sector provides. However, it may be possible to encourage small tangible steps to reverse the trends evident since 1967 and change attitudes to industrial development that will allow latent entrepreneurial will to expand and think creatively. This may lead to business opportunities that produce products to replace some of the US$ 860 million worth of imports with occupied territories production, as well as products that can be successfully exported.

A development agency planned to encourage the introduction of a portable sprayer in the highlands of the West Bank, particularly for spraying pesticides on trees. No suitable sprayer was available from existing West Bank suppliers and the agency began to look elsewhere. Eventually a firm in Israel developed a very simple spraying unit by mounting a three horsepower gasoline engine and a suitable pump on a metal frame with handles so that it could be carried.

In this case all the value added that might have been earned by a West Bank metal or machine shop was lost. An opportunity was also lost to develop a West Bank production, distribution and service organisation which would ensure that this fine piece of technology continued to be produced and sold.

The agency could have used its financial clout not only to effect technology distribution, but also develop a business opportunity to encourage the entrepreneurial spirit. It could have provided a challenge and an incentive to a metal workshop. This incentive could have been in the form of a performance subsidy. The shop would be guaranteed a premium price for the first 30 units produced. There would have been a risk-sharing incentive where the entrepreneur would have been guaranteed a return if he developed an acceptable product. The development agency could also have provided technical design support.

An example from the garment trade will also illustrate the opportunity for creative development work. Over 400 establishments are involved in the garment trade in the occupied territories. Approximately 80 per cent provide subcontracting services to Israeli entrepreneurs. The value-added from this production which relies on relatively unskilled female labour all accrues to the Israeli economy. This clothing is generally of low quality both in material and workmanship. It is ironic that a good deal of it is sold in the occupied territories. Approximately 20 per cent or 80 other establishments provide cheap finished clothing, where the garment is sold either in Israel or the occupied territories.

Palestinian garment manufacturers only provide the cheaper clothing bought in the occupied territories. Virtually all the better quality product is imported from Israel and Europe. The ability of Palestinian garment manufacturers to capture some of this market will depend on their ability to provide fashionably designed, high quality garments.

One small garment manufacturer on the West Bank is attempting to produce high quality garments for local consumption as well as for export to Israel and the European market. This requires careful attention to detail and sophisticated design capability. The entrepreneurial will in the firm has already dealt successfully with the technical skills required to produce a top quality garment. Development money was used to provide the training and to bring workers to a high level of technical development.

However, to expand into the potentially lucrative export field the firm needed sophisticated European design capability. The kind of talented individual capable of providing design support was expensive and beyond the firm's financial capability. The firm needed venture capital to share the risk with them. The firm was able to attract two development partners who were impressed by their entrepreneurial capability. One is financing the export market. The other is funding the design capability. If the venture is profitable they will recoup their investments. Both of the development partners were interested in an organisation that had demonstrated competence and was attempting to develop productive capacity that would add to the ability of occupied territories industry to provide new skills, a competitive edge, jobs and improvements to the economy.

This section will conclude by drawing attention to an under-utilised resource that has much to offer the entrepreneurial spirit of the occupied territories. The business community, particularly the highly successful diaspora Palestinian business community, has a great deal to offer in technical knowledge, potential joint venture capital and solidarity that is good for morale. It might be worthwhile for a development agency to bring delegations of entrepreneurs to the occupied territories to view the situation, exchange ideas and discuss business opportunities. These delegations could meet with both collective and private entrepreneurs. It would be particularly useful to draw on this expertise and investment potential as different individuals and groups are presently focusing on the potential for a variety of food processing ventures in the occupied territories.

It is essential that the development of the industrial sector be supported by design and technical advice. The occupied territories do not need more, but better, more innovative metal workers, garment makers, soap manufacturers and food processors. However, this initiative can build on the entrepreneurial will in the 4,020 industrial establishments.

V. CONCLUSION

In his book Entrepreneurship for the Poor, Malcolm Harper under-scores the importance of entrepreneurial will

> It has become clear that finance, raw materials, markets and buildings are not enough; business success requires the intangible quality of entrepreneurship, which can often enable somebody to obtain the necessary resources, without external assistance, while people without this quality appear to be unable to make effective use of the most lavish forms of assistance.[17]

An economic development strategy for the occupied territories must be built on the intangible quality of entrepreneurship and root itself in people prepared to incur the risks required to achieve an economic objective.

The development of the entrepreneurship can be supported both financially and technically. This assistance must be deftly administered. Money is a particularly blunt instrument and can be detrimental to the entrepreneurial process. Authentic economic development will function through credit and joint venture schemes, accompanied by technical support. The validity of a particular initiative will be demonstrated by how the entrepreneurial spirit responds, in developing new products, in selling agricultural produce and in expanding financial services. Entrepreneurship must be broadly defined if it is to be strategically useful in the quest for a Palestinian national identity. Simply creating more wealth limits the potential power of this concept. Meaningful entrepreneurship will lead to the empowerment of the Palestinian people in the struggle for their legitimate rights and aspirations.

The development of a vibrant internal market can lead to the strengthening of links between Palestinians in the occupied territories. The successful manufacturing and marketing of products for internal consumption will promote self-awareness and lead to less dependence on imports. Company labels on products exported abroad will develop a positive international identity for Palestinians. The entrepreneurial wealth generated can provide a capital base to lessen the dependence of Palestinian institutions on external funding sources. These institutions will then have greater control over their financial resource base, and be able to implement policies based on Palestinian priorities.

If such specific entrepreneurial endeavours are viewed in the full context of the Palestinian struggle, then the fostering of entrepreneurial will can be a powerful tool that will empower Palestinians as they gain greater control of their destiny.

NOTES

1. Mohammed K. Shadid, 'Israeli policy towards economic development projects in the West Bank and Gaza' (paper presented at the second NGO meeting on the Question of Palestine, Geneva, Switzerland, 9-12 September 1985), p. 25.
2. Ibid., p. 4.
3. Paulo Freire, *Pedagogy of the Oppressed* (The Seabury Press, New York, 1970), p. 31.
4. David Kahan, *Agriculture and Water in the West Bank and Gaza* (The West Bank Data Base Project, Jerusalem, 1983), p. 77.
5. Note: the examples used in this paper will focus on the West Bank, since the writer is unfamiliar with Gaza.
6. Michael Schulz, 'The Port Sudan small scale enterprises programme', (paper presented to workshop on the Development Approach to Refugee

Assistance, organised by UNHCR and ICVA, Lusaka, Zambia, July, 1985).
7. Ibid., p. 9.
8. Kate Rouhana, 'Economic trap in the territories', *Al Fajr Palestinian Weekly*, vol. 4, no. 289 (15 November 1985) p. 8.
9. Ibid., p. 9.
10. Central Bureau of Statistics, *Statistical Abstract of Israel*, no. 35 (Central Bureau of Statistics, Jerusalem, 1985) p. 725.
11. Ian Gibson, interview conducted February 1984.
12. Meron Benvenisti, *The West Bank Data Base Project: A Survey of Israel's Policies* (The American Enterprise Institute for Public Policy Research, Washington D.C., 1984), p. 15.
13. Central Bureau of Statistics, *Statistical Abstract of Israel*, no. 35, pp. 736, 737.
14. Brian Van Arkadie, *Benefits and Burdens: A Report on the West Bank and Gaza Strip Economies Since 1967* (Carnegie Endowment for International Peace, Washington D.C., 1977), p. 45.
15. Charles Shammas, 'Light industry in the West Bank', (unpublished study), Mattin, Rammalla, West Bank, 1984, p. 10.
16. Ibid., p. 11.
17. Malcolm Harper, *Entrepreneurship for the Poor* (Print Power, London, 1984), p. 5.

15

Summary and Conclusions

George T. Abed

The presentations at the symposium elicited lengthy and serious discussions both during the structured sessions, where individual papers were delivered, and at the final, open session where all participants had the opportunity to offer their own comments and analyses. This concluding chapter seeks to highlight the main points brought out by the discussions, presented in some useful perspective, both for the record and as an aid to further consideration by others.

Indeed, the material in this volume has raised a number of theoretical and practical issues concerning economic development under repressive conditions that are worthy of further consideration and analysis. As one of the participants aptly noted, 'most of the underdeveloped societies are, in one way or another, occupied'. Scholars, students and activists in the various fields of social and economic development in the third world are invited to pursue the issues raised here in their own study and research. This applies especially to those who are engaged in the process of development in the occupied areas of Palestine. It is hoped that the presentation of this material will enrich the debate on 'development under prolonged occupation' and, more importantly, point the way to a better understanding of the issues and, ultimately, to the design of more relevant development strategies.

I. THE NATURE OF THE PROBLEM

A number of participants posed basic questions about the nature of the Palestinian economy, whether in the occupied areas or in Israel, and about the nature of the challenge this economy faced in the domain of social and economic development. Some even wondered about how to view the Palestinian economy under the British mandate. Roger Owen, in his paper, had noted the ambiguity in the literature about what sort of economy that was and provided a useful, if rather succinct, answer as he proceeded to give his highly informative analysis of what happened during the mandatory period.

But questions remained for the more historically minded participants. Was the Jewish economy in Palestine a capitalist economy interacting with an Arab economy in pre-capitalist formation? But if the Jewish economy was indeed a *capitalist* economy, as its level of development at the time may have indicated, then how did it get to that stage? As one participant noted, capital accumulation (at least according to a Marxist perspective) depended on the generation of high rates of profit, which the Jewish economy clearly did not do. The Jewish economy in Palestine depended rather on considerable capital imports (as well as technology and know-how) from Jewish communities abroad. Does this feature invalidate the hypothesis of a capitalist economy or does it merely modify it?

Another, perhaps more substantial point, raised by another participant was the policy of 'Hebrew labour' (the employment of Jewish workers to the exclusion of cheaper Arab labour) adopted and generally adhered to by the Yishuv. To the extent this was true, it would introduce more ambiguity into the hypothesis of a capitalist Jewish economy. Moreover, it is known that in the case of Jewish colonisation of Palestine, strictly economic factors were generally subordinated to ideological and strategic considerations, even in what appeared to be economic undertakings such as the purchase of land, the location of settlements, the choice of industries and of course employment and wage policies. On the other hand, as one participant noted, there were signs of emerging class distinctions in the Jewish society and even examples of strikes by Jewish labour against Jewish enterprises. One may note that these capitalistic features have become more pronounced in the modern economy of Israel in recent years.

One participant viewed the development of the Yishuv in Palestine from yet another angle – that of a settler community, which, in due course, transformed itself into an imperialist power in the shape of the contemporary Israeli state. How accurate is this paradigm of a settler community and would it be applicable to the Jewish-Arab relationship during the British mandate? Did the fact that the settler (Jewish) community lacked the political authority with which to implement a classical settler programme over the native Palestinian population invalidate this paradigm? And did the settler-native paradigm apply in what became the State of Israel after 1948? And how well does this paradigm hold up in the context of Israel's occupation and gradual settlement of all of mandatory Palestine since 1967?

Although the discussions at the symposium did not reach a consensus on these issues, the issues themselves remain central to an understanding of the dynamics of the Zionist political programme in Palestine. They are even more essential for delineating a Palestinian Arab strategy for dealing with the effects of this programme. What the discussion did make clear, however, was the primacy of the doctrine of political Zionism in every facet of the Jewish colonisation of Palestine. This doctrine, in its most elementary form, essentially viewed all of mandatory Palestine (and, according to some interpretations, certain areas beyond) as the historic land of Israel which belonged to the Jewish people and to which Jews everywhere have a right to return. All other 'non-Jewish' people living on this land would thus be viewed either as squatters to be evicted or, at best, as tenants to be merely tolerated. This became paramount in clarifying two issues that figured prominently in the discussions: the thesis advanced by Raja Khalidi which postulated a regional analytic framework for studying the Arab economy within Israel and the more central issue of 'uprootedness and dispossession' which permeated the discussions on the nature of Israel's relationship with the occupied Palestinian territories.

Khalidi's thesis, essentially a methodological proposition with deeper implications, proved, not surprisingly, somewhat controversial. Some participants doubted, if not the accuracy, then at least the usefulness of the characterisation of the Arab economy in Israel as a regional economic unit of analysis. Khalidi himself had underlined the limitations, as well as the analytical strengths, of a regional approach in his presentation to the symposium (which, though not elaborated in his contribution to this volume, is more fully developed in his book on the subject). As an alternative, it was proposed that the 'Arab minority' in Israel be viewed as a national, ethnically distinct, group whose economic interactions with the Jewish economy were kept within a narrow sphere defined by the Jewish state's own exclusions and proscriptions. The differences in viewpoint could perhaps be examined in terms of the scope of this interaction and its susceptibility to expansion. Are the limits of this interaction pre-determined and final, or would the 'Arab minority's' economy gradually overcome the 'regional' disparities and ultimately fuse with the Jewish economy and become indistinguishable from it? If not, why not?

Many among the participants thought it would not, for fundamental and immutable reasons. The 'Arab minority' will, given the nature of the State of Israel, always be excluded from exercising meaningful influence within Israel's Zionist political structure. Its economic role is therefore predestined to remain within a clearly defined, rather inconsequential sphere of activity. While recognising the value of the insights gained from the Khalidi analysis, many thought that the relationship of the Jewish majority with the Arab minority in Israel was perhaps more usefully viewed through the analytic framework of 'internal colonialism' or the 'settler-native' paradigm postulated by others.

The primacy of Zionist ideology in Israel's policies and conduct also defined the nature of the struggle over the Palestinian territories occupied since 1967. As some participants observed, Israel's historical and strategic claims in these territories were inconsistent with the hypothesis of a simple occupation made necessary by the unfortunate exigencies of war, the consequences of which could therefore be rolled back by the mere settlement of certain outstanding issues. Many emphasised the continuity of Zionist policies from the pre-1948 period through the occupation of the West Bank and Gaza. They underlined the importance of incorporating into the analysis of Israel's policies in the occupied areas the central concepts of 'uprootedness and dispossession' (not only in the physical sense, but also in the social and cultural meanings of the terms as well). This would clarify not only the nature of the political struggle in which the Palestinian people were engaged, but also the true dimensions of their struggle for social and economic development in the occupied areas as well.

Some emphasised the exploitative character of the relationship between Israel and the occupied territories. Highlighting the enormous disparity in power between the occupier and the occupied, they noted the almost unlimited capacity of the oppressor to recast the outcome of any activity undertaken by the oppressed, so as to validate the status quo and reinforce his own hold on the oppressed. In this connection, Israel's non-annexation of the occupied areas has had the beneficial effect (for Israel) of shifting virtually the entire cost of reproduction of labour to the Palestinians themselves (and, to a lesser extent, to the Arab countries and to the international community at large). Not only has Israel absolved itself of the costs of educational, health and social services needed to maintain the 100,000 Palestinian workers or more who labour in its economy, it has also devised a system of excise fees and taxes that has rendered the occupation itself an economically painless enterprise. In such a situation, one wondered, was there any significant act of development that the Palestinians could undertake (such as in the fields of education, health or economic development) that would not in the end feed into, and thus reinforce, this exploitative relationship?

Comparisons with the South African situation naturally emerged during and following a presentation (not included in this volume) on South Africa's policies toward the black population, in the context of the white regime's evolving search for solutions to the economic dilemmas posed by its own policy of apartheid. The speaker noted all the important differences between the two situations and warned against superficial comparisons. He did suggest, however, that in terms of a policy of effective separation, the Israelis had been more successful in the West Bank and Gaza than the South African whites were in the case of the Bantustans. Clearly, the demographic balance in the two places was an important factor in this outcome. For whereas the South African economy has grown more dependent on black labour and has therefore had to compromise its own restrictions on the residence and movement of blacks, an important factor in the gradual breakdown of the Bantustan system, the Israelis have succeeded in keeping Palestinian Arab labour totally separate, economically marginal, and its movement a strictly controlled commuting exercise.

II. THE CONTEXT AND THE AIMS

The symposium participants, almost without exception, appeared to subscribe to the view that genuine and lasting economic development was possible only under conditions of full sovereignty for the Palestinian people in their homeland. This to most meant the end of occupation and the exercise of the right of self-determination. It should be pointed out that not all of the participants came to the symposium with this view in mind. Rather, they appeared to have reached this conclusion as a result of discussion and debate.

If participants appeared to have reached a consensus on this fundamental conclusion, no clear convergence of views emerged on the intermediary questions of what to do in the meantime. Some of those who were engaged in development projects in the occupied areas raised the basic question of the kind of society for which a development programme was to be formulated. Wouldn't this society and its requirements for development be different before and after the

333

occupation ends? If the development process itself is not neutral, and given the long-term nature of the struggle against dispossession and occupation, how does one ensure that the development programme will escape self-bred corruption, external disruption or mere dissipation in the course of its long journey forward?

It was noted that economic development programmes would be pointless if not directed by a vision of the kind of society one is seeking to build. Hence the need to clarify and outline such a vision. Moreover, a 'purely economic' development programme, even if accompanied and reinforced by social mobilisation at the grass-roots level, still lacked the basic ingredient of a political doctrine to be derived from the 'vision of society' noted earlier. Such a doctrine, it was thought, was essential for sustaining the forward momentum of development and for consolidating its gains over the long term. For in the absence of such a programme, material progress could become meaningless and even ephemeral. Even social mobilisation itself may not be benign. Grass-roots organisations that operate without a political programme could be exploited and turned into movements of mass demagoguery, with potential for corruption and even oppression. Others, however, emphasised the 'national liberation struggle' phase of current Palestinian history and underlined the potentially divisive efforts that might arise out of an insistence on a specific, ideologically anchored political programme. In any event, there was little time for pursuing these questions and, given the diversity of views represented at the symposium, it was clear that the discussion would have been lengthy and, most probably, inconclusive.

There were also those few who disputed the need for a political programme on narrow and more pragmatic grounds. They contended that any economic activity leading to the creation of employment and increased production, regardless of the broader social or political implications, should be encouraged. The task of economic development was, according to this view, a technical one to be handled by experts; the imposition of a political context on the process would only confuse the issues and jeopardise progress. As some pointed out, however, the avoidance of a commitment to a political programme by exponents of this view, especially in the circumstances of occupation and repression, was itself a reflection of a certain political stance, whose consequences could obviously be equally grave and damaging.

This debate on the political content of development in the context of the occupied areas was echoed in a discussion of a presentation (not included in this volume) on the experience of Sarvadoya Shramadana, a non-political, grass-roots organisation that operates mainly in the rural areas of Sri Lanka. It seeks to provide the population with basic needs through self-reliance and voluntary work. Although the movement appeared to have succeeded in mobilising large sections of the rural population to address their own basic needs (with a mixture of spiritualism, organisation, and appeal to self-worth) there was, in the minds of many, something missing in the formula. As admirable as the work of Sarvadoya Shramadana may have been, its greatest instructive value was in the simplicity, consistency and pragmatism of the approach. For the politically minded Palestinian development specialist, the approach appeared somewhat remote from the highly charged Palestinian experience.

Even if one could set aside, for a moment, questions concerning the indispensability of a political programme to the development process, one could not avoid the fact that this process itself evolved within a political context. In the case of the occupied areas, this context is defined first and foremost by Israel's own objectives and policies in the areas; but it is also shaped by the larger struggle of the Palestinian people for self-determination and independence. This raises the question of the links between the development process within the occupied areas and its larger context. One is not speaking here about operational links, only about conceptual and programmatic interactions that would provide for a modicum of harmony in objectives and consistency in approach.

There was little doubt in the minds of many of the participants about the degree to which the Palestinians' broader struggle should influence the sort of development programme to be undertaken within the occupied territories. Some however lamented the small extent to which the valuable and specific development experience of the people in the occupied areas was used in the external formulation of development plans and programmes for the benefit of the occupied areas.

Some of the papers and subsequent discussion dealt for instance with the aims, strategies and impact of the development assistance programmes operated by various official and non-official bodies, foremost among them the Joint Jordanian-Palestinian Committee which, during the period from 1979 to 1985, had allocated more than US$ 400 million to the occupied areas. Other development assistance agencies, some private Palestinian charities but mainly international official and quasi-official organisations, provided smaller amounts of project-related assistance. However, with only rare exceptions, each agency brought along, and introduced into a highly charged and fragile political environment, its own development doctrine and, more importantly, its own political agenda. These different, and often contradictory, cross-currents have caused much confusion and have slowed, perhaps frustrated, the creation of a clear consensus on the outlines of an indigenous programme of development.

This situation spurred one of the participants to point out the 'permeability' of the Palestinian struggle for national development within the occupied areas, in contrast perhaps with other liberation struggles elsewhere in the third world, notably in South Africa. The ensuing discussion underlined the limits this permeability had placed on the ability of the leadership within the occupied areas to fashion an indigenous strategy of self-reliant development. The question was not how to isolate the occupied areas from these external influences, for in the circumstances this would be impossible and certainly undesirable, but how to take advantage of such influences to enrich and amplify the development effort.

III. ELEMENTS OF STRATEGY

Concerning the more specific aspects of social and economic development of the occupied areas, the discussions at the symposium underlined certain issues that emerged from among many others as deserving priority attention and suggesting identifiable programmatic themes.

Among the more recurring themes in the discussions was the notion of dispossession and dispersion of the Palestinian people. As one participant emphasised, nearly all of the problems faced by the Palestinian community in the occupied areas were solvable – perhaps not soon and maybe not easily or completely. Many of the trends cited by the speakers and the discussants, including the deterioration of social and economic conditions, were similarly reversible. What was not reversible, however, was the depopulation of Palestine. One of the key priorities of any development programme must therefore be the maintenance of a strong and vibrant Palestinian Arab community in Palestine. This echoed the call for incorporating the concept of *dynamic sumud* into the formulation and implementation of such programmes.

Related to this overriding concern for *sumud* was the recognition of the potentially debilitating impact of a prolonged occupation. Many of the participants emphasised the long-term nature of the occupation as being crucial to an understanding of its lasting effects and to the articulation of an effective counter-strategy. Such a strategy would entail giving high priority to institutional development and to social mobilisation. These would constitute the best means for consolidating the gains of development and for promoting self-sustained economic growth. Some noted the remarkable capacity of the Palestinian community under occupation to grow and regenerate itself in defiance of the constraints, pointing to the large number and extensive scope of voluntary organisations in various fields of social, economic and cultural activity. The substantial body of experience accumulated by this section of society, and the self-reliant nature of the development programmes administered by it, represented a major source of strength and resiliency for the whole of society. It should stand the Palestinian community in good stead during their lengthy struggle against the occupation, and it should constitute a more solid basis for undertaking genuine, democratically based development under conditions of full sovereignty in the future. In this regard, one participant noted, the Palestinian community in the occupied areas was probably better equipped to deal with the challenges of nation-building and modernisation than some of the other Arab or third-world societies which had grown accustomed to the patronising guardianship of their bloated government structures.

The dynamic, or perhaps more accurately the dialectic, nature of the political environment which governs the development effort in the occupied areas was also noted by some participants. Accordingly, development must not only strive to overcome the 'fixed' obstacles in the traditional social and economic structures, it must also confront the 'dynamic' drive of Israel to expropriate and colonise the land, and in various ways to disrupt and frustrate the normal processes of social and economic change. In such an environment, the development process takes on the character of a dynamic 'war game' rather than a simple duel with static obstacles. This characterisation would imply the need for pro-active and flexible strategies. Development programmes must adapt to continuously changing conditions but must also maintain a steady course towards the overall objectives – not a trivial challenge.

Another corollary of this characterisation is that development programmes may have to be constantly on the alert to address the most urgent problems, often in reaction to a policy or decision taken by the occupation authorities, rather than routinely seek opportunities for economic growth in a static environment. In this sense, the development programme may have to be highly unconventional, at least in some of its features. Marginal land may have to be farmed even at an economic loss if that helps save it from confiscation. Traditional industries may have to take priority over new, perhaps more profitable, industries if the former help preserve threatened resources or enhance economic independence at the local level.

Many of the participants tended to emphasise the non-economic aspects of development which, although relevant in any development context, were even more critical in the case at hand. One participant expressed this point of view stating that economic development in the occupied areas did not 'really come down to economics, it came down to spirit...People can have a spirit within them which is undefeatable, and that is ultimately what we are aiming for under a situation of indefinite, or certainly prolonged, occupation'.

Others who spoke to the same point underlined the importance of the human being in the process of social and economic change. Investment in human resources, whether in the form of academic or technical education or in the form of community service training or political education, becomes a critical, and largely unassailable, ingredient in this process. This point was highlighted in a presentation (not included in this volume) on the experience of the Caja Laboral Popular (CLP) in the Basque country of Spain, a burgeoning industrial co-operative which has developed into a remarkable example of self-reliant development. It was significant, one participant noted, that for nearly the first fifteen years of the CLP programme, the focus was on training and human skills development. Despite the phenomenal growth of the programme into a vast network of industrial and banking co-operative enterprises, the emphasis on the development of the human resources remained paramount. This point was also underlined in the context of the discussion of entrepreneurship in the economic development of the occupied areas. Whether viewed in the traditional context of business development or in the broader domain of social activism, it was emphasised that the central element in the process of change was the human being as an entrepreneur – his ability to cut through the veil of convention and banality and perceive opportunities, not discerned by others, for undertaking novel activities with a larger economic or social impact.

The absence of national institutional structures in the occupied areas to serve as frames of reference for the articulation of comprehensive development plans and programmes necessitated resort to a decentralised approach to development. It was noted, however, that the development effort, decentralised by necessity, has become even more fragmented under the influence of multiple interferences from the outside. Some participants underlined the need, therefore, for more effective co-ordination among the various agencies of development active in or on behalf of the occupied areas. It was noted that co-ordination in the circumstances would not be easy, not least of all because of basic differences in political orientation and objectives. One obstacle that could continue to hamper effective harmonisation of development programmes, according to some participants, was the lack of clarity about an authentically Palestinian agenda for development in the occupied areas. Only by articulating such an agenda can the Palestinian people hope to rally other development programmes around a purposeful and common strategy.

IV. PROSPECTIVES

Some of the participants tried to deal with the difficult question of what would constitute a genuine Palestinian agenda for the development of the occupied areas. As indicated earlier, many saw the need for a vision of the future which would in turn elaborate a political programme capable of giving the development process the needed context. More specifically, and given the transitory nature of current conditions in the occupied areas, how did one formulate and implement a development programme that would reinforce the latent tendencies towards liberation and self-renewal rather than confirm existing injustices and repressive relationships? In other words, what constitutes emancipatory, as distinct from accommodating, development in the context of prolonged occupation?

At the practical level, whether a development programme is emancipatory or accommodating depends in the end on how it deals with existing constraints and impositions. It may reinforce them and hence perpetuate the status quo, or it may seek to break them down and hence pave the way for liberationist development.

Redirecting the focus of development to the most fundamental tasks, many of the participants emphasised that the development process must seek to preserve the basic fabric of the Palestinian Arab society that was threatened with dismemberment and disintegration. Development plans and projects must therefore be formulated so as to promote social cohesion in the community, to encourage collective effort and to reinforce shared values and beliefs. Resources must be protected even beyond their immediate economic value because of their crucial role in safeguarding the material foundation of society. Physical and social infrastructure must be maintained and, where possible, strengthened and made more integrated.

Beyond this, the development process must seek to build on existing indigenous strengths so as to extend the frontiers that define what is possible. This would require that development programmes and projects challenge existing constraints, either by breaking them down or simply by stretching their limits. As a minimum, the development process must not have the effect of reinforcing existing constraints and impositions. Projects must be directed at negating the unequal relationships created by the occupation, at reinforcing the links between the occupied areas and the larger Arab world, and at reducing the state of dependency on the Israeli economy.

Further on, and beyond this more or less defensive strategy, the discussants touched upon the outlines of a somewhat more active approach which would seek to confront more directly the web of constraints that frustrate genuine development. This approach would require that the development process be viewed more appropriately in a dynamic context. This evoked the concept of *sumud muqawim* (active or dynamic steadfastness) as a strategy for resisting the debilitating effects of the occupation and for moving on to a development process anchored in self-reliance. Interpreting the dynamic context in its most authentic form, that of a war situation, and if one seeks emancipatory development in the face of such overwhelming odds, one might have to resort to a 'guerilla warfare' strategy of economic development. The large and dominating presence of the occupier's economy would not be confronted head on, but instead, one would search for opportunities for self-generated development at the micro, grass-roots level and, once the process took hold, build on the accumulated experience. The strategy would have to be anchored to the central role of the human being and to social organisation, rather than capital or technology.

The approach as highlighted in the course of discussion would have to be highly decentralised, but internally consistent. Development would proceed horizontally, rather than vertically. The notion of 'growth nodes' elaborated by some development economists in the context of the theory of unbalanced growth would be exploited, but as a basis for generalising the experience of growth horizontally, i.e. across economic sectors and geographic regions. The growth process under such a scheme would be balanced and synchronised, and it would seek to lift the whole socio-economic structure gradually but unrelentingly, up to a higher plateau of development.

It was emphasised that such a strategy did not necessarily tie the Palestinian economy to primitive technology nor even to small-scale production. Any technology that could be indigenised, no matter how advanced, would be admissible. Large-scale production was possible so long as it evolved out of a network of small-scale enterprises and provided that key elements of the production process were kept under local control.

Some of the participants, while fully convinced of the merits of this approach, pointed out the risks involved. These arose not only from the adversary forces that could confront and disrupt this strategy; they could also emanate from other external interests which may, with the help of ample resources and in coalition with local vested interests, act to frustrate the grass-roots approach to self-reliant development in the occupied territories, which in the final analysis would inevitably challenge any externally imposed authority.

Nonetheless, this approach could, with time and perseverance, help transform the society and economy. But by virtue of its inherent limitations it was bound to be slow, subtle and difficult. Only a long-term perspective will do. Most importantly, by transcending existing constraints and impositions, this approach would present a vision of strength, self-renewal and hope. Such an undertaking would not only help the Palestinian community survive during the period of prolonged occupation, it could also form a more enduring basis for establishing a more democratic and just society once the occupation has ended.

Selected Bibliography

Abu 'Ajamiya, Y. (1982) *Al-bibliyughrafiya al-filastiniyya 1948-1980* (Palestine bibliography 1948-1980), *Jam'iya al-mak-taba al-urdunniya,* Amman.

Abu 'Amr, Z. (1980) *Al-hijra min qit'a ghazza* (Emigration from the Gaza Strip), Al-Najah National University, Nablus.

Abu Ayyash, A. (1976) 'Israeli regional planning policy in the occupied territories', *Journal of Palestine Studies,* vol. 5, pp. 83-108.

Abu Hijlah, A. (1981) *Al-qit'a al-sina'i fi al-manatiq al-muhtalla wa-ta'thir al-ihtilal al-isra'ili 'ala awda'iha* (The industrial sector in the occupied territories and the effects on it of Israeli occupation), Bank of Jordan, Amman.

Abu Kishk, B. (1981) *Human Settlements: Problems and Social Dimensions in the West Bank and the Gaza Strip,* Birzeit University, Birzeit.

— (1981) *The Industrial and Economic Trends in the West Bank and the Gaza Strip,* UNECWA, Beirut.

— and Jaraysi, S. (1976) *Al-aradi fi al-wasat al-'arabi: ahdaf isti'maluha wa- al-mashakil allati ta'uq tatawwuraha* (Land in the Arab sector: the aims of its use and the problems facing its development), *Al-majlis al-sha'bi li-al-ina'sh al-ijtima 'i* (Popular Council for Social Rehabilitation) Nazareth.

Abu Lughod, J. (1980) *Demographic Characteristics of the Palestinian Population: Relevance for Planning Palestine Open University,* UNESCO, Paris.

Abu al-Namil, Husayn (1979) *Qit'a ghazza 1948-1967* (The Gaza Strip 1948-1967) Palestine Liberation Organisation Research Centre, Beirut.

Amiri, A. (1974) *Al-tatawwur al-zira'i wa-al-sina'i al-filastini: 1900-1970* (Palestinian agricultural and industrial development: 1900-1970) Palestine Liberation Organisation Research Centre, Beirut.

Arab Scientific Institute for Research (ASIR) (1986) *Finance in the Occupied Territories: The Financial Problems of Industrial Activities,* ASIR, Ramallah, West Bank.

Arab Thought Forum (ATF) (1984) *Proceedings of the Conference in the Service of Steadfastness 1981-2, ATF,* Jerusalem.

Arnon, Y. and Raviv, M. (1980) *From Fellah to Farmer: A Study of Change in Arab Villages,* Settlement Studies Centre, Rehovot, Israel.

Aronson, G. (1978) 'Israel's policy of military occupation', *Journal of Palestine Studies,* vol. 7, pp. 79-91.

Aruri, N. (ed.) (1983) *Occupation: Israel Over Palestine,* Association of Arab American University Graduates (AAUG), Belmont, Mass., 1983.

'Atiya, I.N. (1980) *Musadara al-aradi fi al-manatiq al-muhtalla 1967-1980* (Land confiscation in the occupied territories 1967-1980) Arab Studies Society, Jerusalem.

'Awad, M.A. (1982) *Al-jadwa al-iqtisadiyya al-zira'iya fi al-manatiq al-muhtalla* (The economic feasibility of agriculture in the occupied territories) Al-Najah National University, Rural Research Centre, Nablus.

Awartani, H. (1980) *Water Resources and Policies,* Arab Thought Forum, Jerusalem.

— (1986) *'Taqyim ijmali li-mashakil taswiq al-mantujat al- zira'iya fi al-manatiq al-muhtalla'* (Overall evaluation of the marketing problems of agricultural products from the occupied territories), *Samid al-iqtisadi,* vol. 8, no. 61, Amman.

Bahiri, S. (1987) *Industrialisation in the West Bank and Gaza,* The West Bank Data Base Project, Jerusalem.

Ben-Porath, Y. (1966) *The Arab Labour Force in Israel,* Maurice Falk Institute, Jerusalem.

Ben Shahar, H., Berglas, E. and Mundlak, Y. (1971) *Economic Structure and Development Prospects in the West Bank and the Gaza Strip,* Rand Corporation, Santa Monica, California.

Benvenisti, M. (1984) *West Bank Data Base Project: A Survey of Israel's Policies,* American Enterprise Institute, Washington D.C.

— (1986) Report 1986: *Economic, Legal, Social and Political Developments in the West Bank,* The West Bank Data Base Project, Jerusalem.

— (1987) *The West Bank: A Generation After,* The West Bank Data Base Project, Jerusalem.

— and Abu Zayad, Z. and Rubinstein, D. (1986) *West Bank Handbook: A Political Lexicon,* The West Bank Data Base Project, Jerusalem.

Bregman, A. (1975) *Economic Growth in the Administered Areas 1968-1973,* Bank of Israel, Jerusalem.

Budeiri, M.K. (1982) 'Changes in the economic structure of the West Bank and Gaza', *Labour, Capital and Society,* vol. 15, no. 2.

Bull, V.A. (1975) *The West Bank: Is it Viable?,* Lexington Books, Lexington, Mass.

Cahan, D. (1987) *Agriculture and Water Resources in the West Bank 1967-1987,* The West Bank Data Base Project, Jerusalem.

Centre for Engineering and Planning (1985) *Mashru' takhtit wa-tanzim al-qura fi al-aradi al-muhtalla: taqrir an al-wad' al-hali* (Village planning in the occupied territories: report on the current situation) Centre for Engineering and Planning, Ramallah.

Cooley, J.K. (1984) 'The war over water', *Foreign Policy,* no. 54, pp. 3-26.

Coone, T. (1980) *An Aerial Photographic Analysis for Agricultural Development Planning in the West Bank,* Aston University, London.

Czamanski, D. (1984) *Employment Potential of University Graduates in the Arab Localities in Israel,* Technion Centre for Research of City and Region, Haifa.

Davis, U. (1983) *Comparative Study of Land, Labour and Citizenship Control in Israel and South Africa,* United Nations International Conference on the Question of Palestine, Paris.

Demant, P. (1983) 'Israel's settlement policy today', *MERIP Reports,* vol. 13, pp. 3-13, 29.

Dether, A. (1987) *How Expensive Are West Bank Settlements?* The West Bank Data Base Project, Jerusalem.

Farjoun, E. (1979) 'Palestinian workers in Israel – a reserve army of labour', *Khamsin,* no. 7.

Frisch, H. (1983) *Stagnation and Frontier: Arab and Jewish Industry in the*

West Bank, The West Bank Data Base Project, Jerusalem.

Gharaibeh, F.A. (1985) *The Economies of the West Bank and the Gaza Strip*, Westview Press, Boulder.

Ghayth, H. (1985) *Al-bibliyughrafiya al-filastiniyya fi al-watan* (Palestine – local bibliography) Arab Studies Society, Jerusalem.

Government of Israel, Central Bureau of Statistics (1949-1987) *Statistical Abstract of Israel* nos. 1-38, Central Bureau of Statistics, Jerusalem.

— Central Bureau of Statistics (1967-1986) *Administered Territories Statistical Abstract/Judaea, Samaria and Gaza District Statistics Quarterly*, Central Bureau of Statistics, Jerusalem.

— Central Bureau of Statistics (1979) *National Accounts for Judaea, Samaria, the Gaza Strip and Sinai for the Decade 1968-1977*, Central Bureau of Statistics, Jerusalem.

— Economic Planning Authority (1967) *Israel: Economic Survey of the West Bank*, Central Bureau of Statistics, Jerusalem.

— Ministry of Defence (1983) *Judaea, Samaria and the Gaza District: A Sixteen Year Survey*, Ministry of Defence, Tel Aviv.

Graham-Brown, S. (1984) *Education, Repression and Liberation: the Palestinians*, World University Service, London.

Granott, A. (1976) *Land Policy in Palestine*, Hyperion Press, Westport, Conn.

Gross, N. (1982) *The Economic Policy of the Mandatory Government in Palestine*, Maurice Falk Institute, Jerusalem.

Hadawi, S. (1957) *Land Ownership in Palestine*, Palestine Refugee Office, New York.

— (1970) *Village Statistics 1945: A Classification of Land and Area Ownership in Palestine with Explanatory Notes*, Palestine Liberation Organisation Research Centre, Beirut.

Al-Haj, M. (1986) *Social Change and Family Processes: Arab Communities in Israel*, Westview Press, Boulder.

Halabi, U., Turner, A. and Benvenisti, M. (1985) *Land Alienation in the West Bank: A Legal Spatial Analysis*, The West Bank Data Base Project, Jerusalem.

Harris, W.W. (1980) *Taking Root: Israeli Settlement in the West Bank, the Golan and Gaza-Sinai 1967-1980*, Research Studies Press, New York.

Hashemite Kingdom of Jordan, Ministry of Planning (1986) *Mashru' khitta al-tanmiya al-iqtisadiyya wa al-ijtima'iyya fi al-ard al-muhtalla 1986-1990* (Plan for the social and economic development of the occupied territories, 1986-1990), Ministry of Planning, Amman.

— (1986) *Plan for the Economic and Social Development of the Occupied Territories, 1986-1990: English Summary*, Ministry of Planning, Amman.

Heller, M. (1983) *A Palestinian State: The Implications for Israel*, Harvard University Press, Cambridge, Mass. and London.

Hilal, Jamil (1974) *Al-daffa al-gharbiyya: al-tarkib al-ijtima'i wa-al-iqtisadi 1948-1974*, (The West Bank: social and economic structure 1948-1974), Palestine Research Center, Beirut.

Himadeh, S. (ed.) (1938) *Economic Organisation of Palestine*, Syracuse University Press, New York, 1938.

Hlaileh, S. (1986) *Ta'thir siyasat al-intidab al-baritani wa-al-istitan al-*

sahyuni 'ala milkiyat al-ard fi filastin, 1929-39 (The impact of British Mandate policy and Zionist settlement on land ownership in Palestine 1929-39) Birzeit University, Birzeit.

Hobman, J.B. (1946) *Palestine's Economic Future*, London.

Hochstein, A. (1983) *Metropolitan Links Between Israel and the West Bank*, The West Bank Data Base Project, Jerusalem.

Institute of Palestine Studies, (1972-81) *The Arabs Under Israeli Occupation: 1972-1981*, nos. 1-12 (2 vols. each for 1975 and 1976) Institute of Palestine Studies, Beirut.

International Centre for Peace in the Middle East (1984) *Peaceful Separation or Enforced Unity: Consequences for Israel and the West Bank/Gaza Area*, International Centre for Peace in the Middle East, Tel Aviv.

Jiryis, S. (1976) *The Arabs in Israel*, Monthly Review Press, New York.

Joint Jordanian-Palestinian Committee for the Steadfastness of the Palestinian People in the Occupied Palestinian Territories (1985) *Financial and Banking Situation in the West Bank and the Gaza Strip*, Royal Scientific Society, Amman.

Jundi, I.R. (1986) *Al-sina'a fi filastin ibban al-intidab al-baritani* (Industry in Palestine during the British Mandate) Dar al-Karmil, Amman.

— (1986) *Siyasat al-intidab al-baritani al-iqtisadiyya fi filastin, 1922-1939* (British Mandate economic policy in Palestine, 1922-1939) Dar al-Karmil, Amman.

Kan'ana, Sharif and al-Madani, R. (1985) *Al-istitan wa musadara al-aradi fi qit'a ghazza: 1967-1984* (Settlement and land confiscation in the Gaza Strip: 1967-1984) Birzeit University Research and Documentation Centre, Birzeit.

Kassim, A. (ed.) (1984-5) *The Palestine Yearbook of International Law*, nos. 1 and 2, Al-Shaybani Society of International Law, Nicosia.

Kazi, U. and H. Jabr (1984) *Survey of the Manufacturing Industry in the West Bank and the Gaza Strip: Final Report*, UNIDO, Vienna.

Khalidi, R. (1988) *The Arab Economy in Israel*, Croom Helm, London.

Khalidi, W. (ed.) (1971) *From Haven to Conquest: Readings in Zionism and the Palestine Problem Until 1948*, Institute for Palestine Studies, Beirut.

Khouja, M.W. and Sadler, P.G. (1981) *Review of the Economic Conditions of the Palestinian People in the Occupied Palestinian Territories*, UNCTAD, Geneva.

Khulusi, Muhammad 'Ali (1967) *Al-tanmiya al-iqtisadiya fi qit'a ghazza: 1948-1967* (The Economic Development of Gaza: 1948-1967) United Commercial Printhouse, Cairo.

Khuri, R.S. (1980) 'Israel's imperial economics', *Journal of Palestine Studies*, vol. 9, pp. 71-8.

Kossaifi, G. (1985) 'Forced migration of the Palestinians from the West Bank and the Gaza Strip', *Population Bulletin of UN ESCWA*, no. 27, Baghdad.

Kubursi, A. (1981) *Economic Consequences of the Camp David Agreements*, Institute for Palestine Studies, Beirut.

Kushner, D. (ed.) (1986) *Palestine in the Late Ottoman Period: Political, Social and Economic Transformation*, Yad Itzhak Ben Zvi, Jerusalem, 1986.

Lehn, W. and U. Davis (1988) *The Jewish National Fund*, Routledge and

Kegan Paul, London.

Lesch, A.M. (1985) 'Gaza: forgotten corner of Palestine', *Journal of Palestine Studies*, vol. 15, pp. 43-62.

Loftus, P.J. (1948) *National Income for Palestine, 1945*, Government of Palestine, Jerusalem.

Lustick, I. (1980) *Arabs in the Jewish State: A Study in the Effective Control of a National Minority*, University of Texas Press, Austin.

Makhoul, N. (1982) 'Changes in the employment structure of Arabs in Israel', *Journal of Palestine Studies*, vol. 11, pp. 77-102.

Mansour, A. (1983) *Palestine: Une économie de résistance en Cisjordanie et à Gaza*, Editions l'Harmattan, Paris.

Meron, R. (1983) *Economic Development in Judaea, Samaria and the Gaza District: Economic Growth and Structural Change 1970-1980*, Bank of Israel, Jerusalem.

Metzger, J., Orth, M. and Sterzing, C. (1983) *This Land Is Our Land: the West Bank Under Israeli Occupation*, Zed Press, London.

Migdal, J.S. (ed.) (1980) *Palestinian Society and Politics*, Princeton University Press, Princeton, 1980.

Miller, Y.N. (1985) *Government and Society in Rural Palestine, 1920-1948*, University of Texas Press, Austin.

Al-Najah National University, Rural Research Centre, (1981-1985) *Statistical Abstract for the West Bank and the Gaza Strip, 1981-1985* (nos. 1-5), Al-Najah National University, Nablus.

Nakhleh, E. (1979) *The West Bank and Gaza: Towards the Making of a Palestinian State*, American Enterprise Institute, Washington D.C.

— (ed.) (1980) *The Palestinian Agenda for the West Bank and Gaza*, Institute for Public Policy Research, Washington D.C., 1980.

Nakhleh, K. (1982) *The Two Galilees*, Association of Arab American University Graduates, Belmont, Mass.

— and Zureik, E. (eds) (1980) *The Sociology of the Palestinians*, St Martin's Press, New York, 1980.

Nathan, R.R., Gass, O. and Creamer, D. (1946) *Palestine: Problem and Promise*, American Council of Public Affairs/American Palestine Institute, New York.

Owen, R. (ed.) (1982) *Studies in the Economic and Social History of Palestine in the Nineteenth and Twentieth Centuries*, MacMillan, London, 1982.

Palestine Government (1946) *A Survey of Palestine: Prepared in December 1945 and January 1946 for the Information of the Anglo-American Committee of Inquiry* (3 vols.), Government of Palestine, Jerusalem.

Palestine Liberation Organisation, Palestine National Fund, Central Bureau of Statistics (1979-1982) *Palestine Statistical Abstract*, nos. 1-4, Palestine Liberation Organisation, Damascus.

Pollock, A. (1986) 'Aspects of selected strategies for rural development', *Birzeit Research Review*, no. 3, Birzeit, pp. 28-53.

Roy, S. (1986) *Gaza Survey*, The West Bank Data Base Project, Jerusalem.

Ruedy, J. and Abu Lughod, J. (n.d.) *The Dynamics of Land Alienation in Palestine*, Association of Arab American University Graduates Information Paper, no. 5, Belmont, Mass.

Sa'ad, A. (1985) *Al-tatawwur al-iqtisadi fi filastin* (Economic development in Palestine) Dar al-Ittihad wa al-Nashr, Haifa.

Sabatello, E. (1983) *Populations of the Administered Territories: Some Demographic Trends and Implications*, The West Bank Data Base Project, Jerusalem.

Sadler, P.G. and Abu Kishk, B. (1983) *Palestine: Options for Development: A Report*, UNCTAD, Geneva.

Saket, B. (1982) *Al-qit'a al-sina'i fi al-daffa al-gharbiyya wa- qit'a ghazza* (The industrial sector in the West Bank and the Gaza Strip) Royal Scientific Society, Amman.

Saleh, H. A. (1987) 'Al-intaj al-zira'i fi qit'a ghazza' (Agricultural production in the Gaza Strip) *Samid al-iqtisadi*, vol. 9, no. 65, Amman, pp.32-59.

Schölch, A. (ed.) (1983) *Palestinians Over the Green Line: Studies on the Relations Between Palestinians on Both Sides of the 1949 Armistice Line*, Ithaca Press, London, 1983.

Shehadeh, O. (1986) 'Economic impediments to development in the occupied territories', *Birzeit Research Review*, no. 3, pp. 63-4.

Shehadeh, R. (1980) *The West Bank and the Rule of Law*, International Commission of Jurists, Geneva.

— (1985) *Occupier's law: Israel and the West Bank*, Institute for Palestine Studies, Washington D.C.

Smooha, S. (1984) *Social Research on Arabs in Israel 1977-1982: A Bibliography*, University of Haifa, Haifa.

Stein, K.W. (1984) *The Land Question in Palestine 1917-1939*, University of North Carolina Press, Chapel Hill, North Carolina.

Szereszewski, R. (1968) *Essays on the Structure of the Jewish Economy in Palestine and Israel*, Maurice Falk Institute, Jerusalem.

Tamari, S. (1983) 'The dislocation and reconstitution of a peasantry: the social economy of agrarian Palestine in the central highlands of the Jordan Valley, 1960-1980', unpublished Ph.D. thesis, University of Manchester.

— and R. Giacaman, (1980) *Zbeidat: the Social Impact of Drip Irrigation on a Palestinian Peasant Community in the Jordan Valley*, Birzeit University, Birzeit.

Tuma, E.H. and Darin-Drabkin, H. (1978) *The Economic Case for Palestine*, Croom Helm, London.

Union of Professional Associations (1986) *Al-takhtit wa al-tanzim: al-ghayat wa-al-ahdaf wa-al-ab'ad li mashru' al-tanzim al-iqlimi* (Town planning and organisation: the aims, purposes and dimensions of the regional planning project) Union of Professional Associations, Jerusalem.

United Nations, Commission for Trade and Development (1985) *Review of the Economic Conditions of the Palestinian People in the Occupied Palestinian Territories*, UNCTAD, Geneva.

— Economic Commission for West Asia (1983) *Final Report of the Economic and Social Situation and Potential of the Palestinian Arab People in the Region of West Asia*, ECWA, Baghdad.

— General Assembly, Committee on the Exercise of the Inalienable Rights of the Palestinian People (1980) *Acquisition of Land in Palestine*, United Nations, New York.

— Committee on the Exercise of the Inalienable Rights of the Palestinian People (1982) *Israeli Settlements in Gaza and the West Bank (Including Jerusalem)*, United Nations, New York.

— Committee on the Exercise of the Inalienable Rights of the Palestinian People (1982) *Social, Economic and Political Institutions in the West Bank and the Gaza Strip,* United Nations, New York.

— International Labour Organisation (1974-1986) *Reports to the Director General on the Situation of Workers in the Occupied Territories, 1974, 1976-1982 and 1985-1986,* nos. 1-10, ILO, Geneva.

United States, Congress, Joint Economic Committee (1980) *The Political Economy of the Middle East 1973-1978,* Government Printing Office, Washington D.C.

— Library of Congress, Foreign Affairs and National Defense Division (1980) *The West Bank-Gaza Economy: Problems and Prospects* (Report Prepared for the Subcommittee on Europe and the Middle East of the Committee on Foreign Affairs), Government Printing Office, Washington D.C.

— Congress, Senate, Committee on the Judiciary, Subcommittee on Immigration and Naturalisation (1977) *The Colonisation of the West Bank Territories by Israel,* 95th Congress, 1st Session, Government Printing Office, Washington D.C.

Van Arkadie, B. (1977) *Benefits and Burdens: A Report on the West Bank and Gaza Strip Economies Since 1967,* Carnegie Endowment for International Peace, Washington D.C.

Ward, R., Peretz, D. and Wilson, E. (eds) (1977) *The Palestine State: A Rational Approach,* National University Publications, New York, 1977.

Zakai, D. (1986) *Economic Development in Judaea, Samaria and the Gaza District, 1983-4,* Bank of Israel, Jerusalem.

Zureik, E. (1979) *The Palestinians in Israel: A Study in Internal Colonialism,* Routledge and Kegan Paul, London.

Index